THE WOULD-BE AUTHOR

Purdue Studies in Romance Literatures

Editorial Board

Íñigo Sánchez Llama, Series Editor
Brett Bowles
Elena Coda
Paul B. Dixon

Patricia Hart
Gwen Kirkpatrick
Allen G. Wood

Howard Mancing, Consulting Editor
Floyd Merrell, Consulting Editor
Susan Y. Clawson, Production Editor

Associate Editors

French
Jeanette Beer
Paul Benhamou
Willard Bohn
Gerard J. Brault
Thomas Broden
Mary Ann Caws
Glyn P. Norton
Allan H. Pasco
Gerald Prince
Roseann Runte
Ursula Tidd

Italian
Fiora A. Bassanese
Peter Carravetta
Benjamin Lawton
Franco Masciandaro
Anthony Julian Tamburri

Luso-Brazilian
Fred M. Clark
Marta Peixoto
Ricardo da Silveira Lobo Sternberg

Spanish and Spanish American
Maryellen Bieder
Catherine Connor
Ivy A. Corfis
Frederick A. de Armas
Edward Friedman
Charles Ganelin
David T. Gies
Roberto González Echevarría
David K. Herzberger
Emily Hicks
Djelal Kadir
Amy Kaminsky
Lucille Kerr
Howard Mancing
Floyd Merrell
Alberto Moreiras
Randolph D. Pope
Francisco Ruiz Ramón
Elżbieta Skłodowska
Marcia Stephenson
Mario Valdés
Howard Young

 volume 63

THE WOULD-BE AUTHOR

Molière

and the Comedy

of Print

Michael Call

Purdue University Press
West Lafayette, Indiana

Copyright ©2015 by Purdue University. All rights reserved.

∞ The paper used in this book meets the minimum requirements of American National Standard for Information Sciences—Permanence of Paper for Printed Library Materials, ANSI Z39.48-1992.

Printed in the United States of America
Template for interior design by Anita Noble;
template for cover by Heidi Branham.
Cover photo: *Trissotin Reading His Sonnet*, from *Les Femmes Savantes*, by Molière (1622–73) 1846 (oil on canvas). Leslie, Charles Robert (1794–1859) / Victoria & Albert Museum, London, UK / The Bridgeman Art Library.

Library of Congress Cataloging-in-Publication Data

Call, Michael, 1976–
 The would-be author : Molière and the Comedy of Print / Michael Call.
  p. cm. — (Purdue studies in Romance literatures ; v. 63)
 Includes bibliographical references and index.
 ISBN 978-1-55753-708-9 (pbk. : alk. paper) — ISBN 978-61249-385-5 (epdf) — ISBN 978-1-61249-386-2 (epub) 1. Molière, 1662-1673—Criticism and interpretation. 2. Publishers and publishing in literature. 3. Authors in literature. I. Title.
 PQ1860.C35 2015
 842'.4—dc23   2014040751

Contents

vii **Acknowledgments**
  1 **Introduction**
     The Death of the Author
 27 **Chapter One**
     Molière's Writers
 65 **Chapter Two**
     The Early Plays and the Pirates Who Loved Them
103 **Chapter Three**
     Comedic Authorship and Its Discontents
141 **Chapter Four**
     "Je veux qu'on me distingue"
175 **Chapter Five**
     The School for Publishers
207 **Chapter Six**
     Collaboration's Pyrrhic Triumph
229 **Afterword**
     The Death of the Actor
249 **Notes**
277 **Bibliography**
287 **Index**

Acknowledgments

It is a great pleasure to reflect on all those who have helped to bring this project to completion. My sincerest thanks to Julia Prest, an inspiring teacher-scholar, unsparing in her time, careful and insightful in her critiques. I wish also to express my gratitude to Eva Guggemos, Vincent Giroud, Robert Babcock, and the Beinecke Rare Book and Manuscript Library for their generosity and assistance in introducing me to the wonders of the Pforzheimer Molière collection; and to Annie Parent-Charon and Élisabeth Parinet of the École des Chartes, and Joël Huthwohl of the Bibliothèque de la Comédie-Française, for their warm encouragement of this project. To Françoise Jaouën goes my appreciation for a great and generous teacher.

The Yale French Department was unwavering in its support, and my colleagues in the Department of Comparative Arts and Letters at Brigham Young University, as well as Dean John Rosenberg, provided encouragement and a wonderful work environment. I greatly appreciate the feedback and support from many members of SE17 and NASSCFL, in particular Francis Assaf, Larry Norman, Faith Beasley, James Gaines, Stephen Fleck, and Perry Gethner. Susan Clawson at Purdue Studies in Romance Literatures has served as a sure and patient guide in the sometimes bewildering process of transforming the manuscript into the finished book, illustrating in exemplary fashion Roger Chartier's axiom that "les auteurs n'écrivent pas des livres: non, ils écrivent des textes que d'autres transforment en objets imprimés." To the *paroisse* of Pontault-Combault, my thanks for a year of hospitality and one cherished *soirée Molière*. To Huguette Richard, "J'étais étranger, et vous m'avez recueilli"—we will never forget.

An early version of Chapter 4 appeared in *Romanic Review* 104.1–2 (Jan.–Mar. 2013): 65–82 as "Alceste at the Print Shop: *Le Misanthrope*'s Response to Molière's 1666 *Œuvres*." Likewise, a section of Chapter 5 was published as "The Author's Farce: Printing Theft in *Les Fourberies de Scapin*," in *Origines: Actes du 39ᵉ congrès annuel de la North American Society for Seventeenth-Century French Literature* (Tübingen: Gunter Narr, 2009). I appreciate their permission in allowing me to reprint and expand that material here.

Finally, my deepest expressions of appreciation and gratitude are to my parents, Michael and Connie, with love and

Acknowledgments

admiration; to my children, Adam, Samuel, Matthias, Elizabeth, Madeleine, and Benjamin, who provided both purpose and perspective; and to my wife, Becky, my constant partner through all.

Introduction

The Death of the Author

> Il est mort, ce Grand Homme, mais il est mort trop tost pour luy, trop tost pour les siens, trop tost pour ses camarades, trop tost pour les grands divertissemens de son Prince, trop tost pour les libraires, musiciens, danceurs et peintres, et trop tost enfin pour toute la terre. Il est mort, et nous vivons; cependant il vivra après nous, il vivra toûjours, et nous mourrons; c'est le destin des Grands Hommes.
> —Jean Donneau de Visé
> *Conversation dans une ruelle de Paris sur Molière défunt*

This study at its most essential is about finding the answer, or more realistically a plausible answer, to a single question: What did Molière think about publication? The possible implications are more significant than they might at first appear, since the need to keep in mind the material methods of production is particularly acute in Molière's case. He left no written manuscripts of his theater, no journal, and no written correspondence. While such documents are typically scarce for French writers of the seventeenth century, the lack in Molière's case is total: his entire handwritten production consists of a few signatures on legal documents.[1] The vital corollary to this lack of handwritten material is that Molière's theater owes its existence and its survival entirely to the medium of print, and specifically to the seventeenth-century editions published during or shortly after the author's lifetime. Elucidating the precise nature of the relationship between Molière and the printed books that constitute his artistic legacy is of central importance to any consideration of Molière's theater.

Understandably, this complex relationship has been the subject of considerable critical disagreement. In 1999, Larry Norman

Introduction

observed, "As an author, Molière's reputation has always been oddly precarious. Few literary figures have found themselves so thoroughly canonized and yet so sharply challenged in their very function as author" (26). Debates about the nature of Molière's dramaturgical production have often hinged on whether or not their author conceived them primarily to be read or to be seen. Describing Molière as a *grand auteur* or as an *homme de théâtre* implies critical judgments concerning appropriate methodology and interpretation. A crucial indicator of the changing fortunes and assessment of Molière's theater from the posthumous 1682 edition of the playwright's complete works to its 2010 Bibliothèque de la Pléiade descendent is the degree to which Molière can be deemed responsible for the printed texts that have conserved— while possibly deforming—the plays that bear his name.

The simplest answer to this vexed question would be to look at Molière's most direct statement on the matter: his note to the reader contained in the printed edition of *L'Amour médecin* (1666): "Il n'est pas nécessaire de vous avertir qu'il y a beaucoup de choses qui dépendent de l'action; On sait bien que les Comédies ne sont faites que pour être jouées, et je ne conseille de lire celle-ci qu'aux personnes qui ont des yeux pour découvrir dans la lecture tout le jeu du Théâtre" (*Œuvres complètes* 1: 603).[2] Molière the actor and the director here warns the reader against the mistake of conflating the text and the play. The act of printing has in fact removed all the play (*jeu*) from the living work: the letter killeth. Only through an extraordinary act of reading—represented here as a multimedia reimagining—can the missing *supplément* be restored, and the work, truncated through the printing process, be made whole again. The reader must in effect restage the play for herself, conjuring up the "Airs, et les Symphonies de l'incomparable Monsieur Lully," the elegant setting of Versailles, where the work premiered, and the witty banter of the actors, an act that apparently not all readers are capable of performing. For those without the imaginative resources to take the play from printed page to mental stage, Molière implicitly recommends reading something that is "fait pour être lu."

Molière's warning does appear, though, as the preface to a printed book; comedies may be made for performance, but there must be some justification for printing them as well. Furthermore, if we turn the page of the original edition, we notice that this printed warning is followed immediately by the royal privilege, authorizing the printing and sale of this particular volume and issued to Molière himself, indicating that the playwright (and not a *libraire*, that is, a bookseller) took the trouble and expense to obtain the legal rights to a future printed version—royal privileges of this kind conferred no protection or additional control over the performance.[3] Publication was intentional, and Molière arranged for the edition to be printed and sold by the Parisian *libraires* Trabouillet, Girard, and Legras. In other words, Molière may well state his reluctance to see the play printed, but he is an active agent (indeed, the prime mover) in the play's publication.

For that matter, is the reader confronted here with a clever variety of paralipsis, a rhetorical trope dear to seventeenth-century paratexts (although usually more prominent in the dedicatory epistle)? By mentioning the omission of "les Airs, et les Symphonies," the "beauté des Voix," and the "adresse de Danseurs," Molière does more than draw attention to the reductive quality of print: he underscores the glorious trappings that accompanied the work's premiere "chez le Roi" (1:603). Whether or not one could conjure up these stage elements while reading, the work's links to royal entertainment—not so subtly emphasized by the preface's handwringing over the published edition's deficiency—serve as an advertisement to prospective buyers. Far from culling unimaginative dullards from the ranks of prospective customers, the note *au lecteur* reminds the reader that the printed edition gives them access of a sort to a privileged entertainment space. Like the published account of Louis XIV's 1664 grand fête *Les Plaisirs de l'Île enchantée* (in which Molière's *La Princesse d'Élide* appeared for the first time), the edition bills itself as an early modern version of celebrity entertainment, giving the reader a glimpse into the fabulous life of the young and wealthy.

Does it matter as well that Molière's often-cited admonition regarding printed theater comes at the beginning of a *comédie-ballet*? The *grandes comédies* carry no such warning. Their Alexandrine couplets, perhaps punctuated occasionally by a spare *didascalie*, allow the reader to appreciate in their fullness lines only partially heard or understood in a Palais-Royal performance. Or even lines omitted: as the 1682 edition of his theater makes clear, even Molière himself did not perform every line of a Molière play, and reading consequently can involve a different sort of *supplément*,

Introduction

restoring the play's dialogue to its full parameters. The faulty sightlines of an awkwardly designed theater, the rambunctious noise of a *parterre* without seats (and in 1666 with only a makeshift roof), and the obnoxious presence of aristocrats seated on the stage (the kind that Molière mocked in *Les Fâcheux*) are all mercifully removed by the printed edition, allowing the play to exist in a form not contingent upon actors' health or an audience's patience. The author-director's cut can play out uninterrupted in a quiet *cabinet* as the reader savors a play whose language is among its chief concerns. A *comédie-ballet* may indeed look spare on the page, stripped of the dances, music, and costuming that formed such an essential part to its aesthetic. *Le Misanthrope* might well be a different matter. Can we entertain the notion of a Molière whose take on publication differed according to the individual play to be printed?

A brief look at the publication record of Molière's works would appear to demonstrate that genre did play a significant part in the playwright's attitude toward publishing. Eight plays remained unpublished during Molière's lifetime. One of these—*Le Malade imaginaire*—must be omitted from the list, as the author died during the initial performance run. There is little doubt that Molière would have printed the play had he lived. Molière consciously decided not to print the other seven plays: *Dom Garcie de Navarre, L'Impromptu de Versailles, Dom Juan, Mélicerte, Pastorale comique, Les Amants magnifiques,* and *La Comtesse d'Escarbagnas*. The first was a theatrical failure; the third was a scandal. In both of these cases, any author worried about his reputation could have justifiably decided to let the play slip into oblivion. The remaining five plays all share a common characteristic: they were court productions, and often executed in haste (and the *Impromptu* even stages this haste). Molière may well have held notions regarding what sort of play could or should be printed, and which ones were not deemed sufficiently literary or finished to make, as he termed it in the preface to *Les Précieuses ridicules*, the leap from the theater to the booksellers' stands at the Palais de Justice. Such a statement does not at all imply that Molière—a pioneer in incorporating additional spectacular elements into his theater—estimated these works as inferior, but that he may have considered that they were less apt to print.

Does it matter that Molière's statement about plays being meant to be played is made in 1666? Or, in other words, can we assume that Molière's attitude regarding printing stays constant throughout his career? Molière's participation with theater incontrovertibly begins with acting, first with the failed Parisian experiment of the *Illustre Théâtre* from 1643 to 1646, and then touring the provinces with Charles Dufresne's itinerant company. But at some point in the trajectory that led Molière, now the leader of Dufresne's former troupe, back to Paris in 1658, the actor began producing scripts, and not just performing them. As Roger Duchêne has noted, over the course of their subsequent Parisian career, Molière's troupe increasingly specialized in Molière plays: the earliest years show the troupe performing plays by a variety of different authors, but the preponderance of Molière's own productions becomes ever greater, until the *Troupe du Roi* is performing plays by their leader almost exclusively.[4] This increasing literary output is duly noted by Molière's peers, such as when Jean Chapelain recommends him in 1663 for a royal pension, describing him as an "excellent poète comique." Molière remains committed to the troupe and to his acting vocation to the very end of his life—in fact, it arguably kills him.[5] But increasingly throughout the 1660s there are milestones that mark the parallel evolution of an authorial career.

The most important evidence for this comes from the printed plays themselves. Molière's publishing practice undergoes substantial changes from his first editions to his last. We might legitimately speak of a reluctance to publish in 1660, the year that *Les Précieuses ridicules*, his first printed play, was issued. By 1671, such a label would be inconceivable. That year sees Molière take the initiative in obtaining a general privilege to print all his plays, force the registration from the resistant *Communauté des libraires*, personally arrange the publication of three plays, and use print as a way of appropriating for himself the collaborative *tragédie-ballet* of *Psyché*. Faced with an informed and active author, creatively using publication as a way of establishing ownership and increasing profit, booksellers and rivals may well have wished for the return of the author *malgré lui* of 1660 or, for that matter, 1666.

Questions of genre, rhetoric, and Molière's own authorial evolution make it hazardous to turn any single statement from the playwright into a general axiom on publishing. Given his triple theatrical involvement as actor, director, and playwright, Molière surely felt deeply the transformation that a play underwent in its transition from stage to page (and vice versa). Just as certainly, however, he himself initiated that transformation in the majority of cases. If the elements of staging that accompanied the plays in performance did indeed confer upon them, as he described it regarding *L'Amour médecin*, "des grâces, dont [ces sortes d'ouvrages] ont toutes les peines du monde à se passer" (1:603), it was the playwright who was the ultimate cause for this "passage."

But given the playwright's own statements on the matter, critics can hardly be faulted for taking Molière at his word, particularly since the resurgent twentieth-century image of Molière as a "man of the theater" correlated well with a reluctance to publish and a wariness of print's reductive effects. In fact, we might say that in one sense Molière the author died young—not Jean-Baptiste Poquelin, whose sudden death after the fourth performance of *Le Malade imaginaire* led to the "quatre grosses liaces" of epitaphs, sonnets, elegies, and panegyrics that Donneau de Visé mentions in his funeral oration (23), but the image of Molière as a *grand auteur*, promised immortality by Donneau de Visé. If Despois and Mesnard's late nineteenth-century edition of Molière's complete works had placed the writer in the pantheon of "les grands écrivains de France," the critics of the mid-twentieth century drew attention to the fact that Molière's plays stemmed from a theatrical, and not necessarily a literary, impetus. In 1949, W.G. Moore published *Molière: A New Criticism* in which he stated: "Perhaps the most obvious thing to say about Molière is just that he was an actor. It was as such that he was first, and chiefly, known to his contemporaries. It was for acting rather than for reading that he composed his plays" (27). In 1954, René Bray published *Molière, homme de théâtre*, in which the French critic similarly stressed that Molière's plays were not written as literature, but to be performed. Bray infamously entitled his second chapter "Molière pense-t-il?" and later added:

> Celui qui veut rencontrer Molière ne doit pas le chercher là où il chercherait Racine ou Boileau. Il ne doit pas le transformer en moraliste, bien moins en philosophe, c'est-à-dire lui imputer des soucis altérant la création dramatique. Il ne doit pas non plus voir en lui l'écrivain, attaché à une perfection du verbe qui lui est étrangère ou désireux d'exprimer sa nature au plus près, de délivrer l'authenticité de son message spirituel. Molière est un comédien: il vit pour le théâtre. (42)

The Death of the Author

For Bray, as for Moore, the image of Molière as an author—that is, as an individual primarily concerned with generating texts through which to expound a morality, philosophy, or even a pure aesthetics—is primarily a deformation of an individual whose works were generated in and for the theatrical milieu in which he was a vigorous participant. As Bray argues, "Molière n'a de réalité que sur les planches de son théâtre" (43).[6]

This theoretical transformation of Molière to an *homme de théâtre* meant that the notion of an authorial Molière—in the sense of a dominating consciousness—was already long dead by the time that Roland Barthes proclaimed *la mort de l'auteur* in 1968. To Barthes's query regarding the authorial voice ("Qui parle ainsi?") and his claims of writing as the sign of authorial absence, scholars like Bray could respond that the search for Molière's voice had already been declared impossible. Flaubert's unitary "Madame Bovary, c'est moi" had become a theatrical polyvocality that could claim that Molière is "successivement Arnolphe et Agnès, il est Alceste et Philinte et il est Célimène, il est Don Juan et Sganarelle, Orgon et Tartuffe, Harpagon, Philaminte, Argan" (Bray 32).

Fragmenting Molière across the divergent spectrum of his theatrical characters might appear to be the ideal way to move beyond the questions driving the sort of "l'homme et l'œuvre" criticism that Michel Foucault criticized in his landmark "Qu'est-ce qu'un auteur" in 1969: "On n'entendrait plus les questions si longtemps ressassées: 'Qui a réellement parlé? Est-ce bien lui et nul autre? Avec quelle authenticité, ou quelle originalité? Et qu'a-t-il exprimé du plus profond de lui-même dans son discours?'" (95). If Molière is driven by issues of performance, constrained by the need to make a living in Paris and at the court, obligated to write his works for a pre-existing set of troupe members, with their own limited abilities, then we might well doubt that these contingencies could lead to any overriding philosophy or expression of the self.

Any philosophy other than the lack of one, that is. For if the theatrical Molière of Moore and Bray can be said to express any single theme, it is precisely the lack of consistency or coherence in the plays, or perhaps the refusal to create or impose such a coherence. In his excellent studies of Molière's monomaniacal central characters (most often played by the author himself), Larry Riggs argues that the central tenet of Molière's major plays is the resistance of hegemony or absolutism. As characters like Arnolphe, Alceste, or Orgon seek to impose a rigid structure on their surroundings, justified by pseudo-rational philosophies, their ultimate defeat—the demonstrative and disastrous failure of their mental worldviews to obtain in reality—shows an almost postmodern resistance to these sorts of master narratives.[7] Furthermore, the failures of Molière's protagonists become emblematic of the author's own awareness of his inability to control or contain the possible meanings of his own work. The work escapes the author, even as the author, himself a participant in the action, strives in vain to exert his control upon it.[8]

Drawing on the main characters from *L'École des femmes*, Max Vernet, in his insightful *Molière: Côté jardin, côté cour*, similarly describes Molière as a sort of anti-author, that is, one aware of the ideological implications of Barthes's "Auteur-Dieu" and who rejects them. For Vernet, the key to understanding Molière lies precisely in recognizing the danger of author-centered interpretation:

> Nous ... conviendrons que Molière n'est que ce nom sur la couverture d'un dossier, que le code qui permette, dans cette vaste mémoire qu'est la littérature, d'accéder à un ensemble de textes. Je dirais plus: en faire un *auteur*, en faire le responsable de ce *corpus* que nous connaissons si bien, c'est faire la première et irréparable erreur d'interprétation, et c'est ce dont il s'agira ici sous la figure d'Arnolphe qui se voulait maître et possesseur d'Agnès, comme vous pourriez dire la nature. (21)

The work's polyvalence is recognized and respected not only by the critic, but by the prescient seventeenth-century author himself. As Vernet continues: "En contrepartie, tout ce que demande Molière, c'est que le critique (la critique) ne se croie pas non plus maître et possesseur du texte qu'il interprète" (21). Upon the failures of Arnolphe to impose his will upon Agnès, or perhaps we should say upon Agnès's successful resistance, Vernet establishes the portrait of an author who recognizes and respects the ultimate alterity of the work. *L'École des femmes* becomes a school for critics, a sort of parable in which a particularly clumsy act of presumptive interpretation is staged and satirized.

To find a more legitimate metaphor for theatrical interpretation, Vernet turns to *Amphitryon* and its themes of doubling. The struggle between Amphitryon and a disguised Jupiter over

The Death of the Author

the same woman—Amphitryon's wife, Alcmène—and over the right to the name and identity of "Amphitryon" becomes for Vernet an apt description of the theatrical project, including the struggle between the text (the work's stable characteristics) and the performance (the infinite possibilities of variation). Just as a confused Alcmène, when pressed by Jupiter to hate the husband and accept the lover, refuses to distinguish between the two roles ostensibly joined in the same person, so any self-reflexive approach to Molière's theater must embrace a view of the work that includes both its fundamental identity and its potential mutability. Vernet writes, "Si Alcmène la sage a raison, pourtant, le mari et l'amant, le texte comme puissance de représentation et la représentation qui l'actualise, sont tous deux nécessaires" (114). Alcmène's wisdom is by extension Molière's as well—the actor-author sees a privileging of either text or performance as contradictory, since the two are merely different sides of the same theatrical coin. Interpretive excesses in either extreme come from having conserved "la catégorie de sujet, et son corollaire l'auteur," locking the critic into one of two modes: "la répétition" or "la transgression" (114). An imagined "spirit of the author" becomes either the guarantor of a staging's (or an edition's) legitimacy, or a norm to be violated. For Vernet, as for Riggs, such a dichotomy is antithetical to the very theater that it purports to preserve or reinvent.

Molière consequently becomes in some senses a "proto-postmodern" whose plays stage the defeat of the subject's unitary identity. With the traditional notion of authorship taken as a particular instance of subjectivity, Molière therefore anticipates the notion's critical death by committing a sort of authorial disappearing act, substantiated by the playwright's alleged opposition to publication. Print eliminates the theatrical voice, the dialogic nature of the play, and the contingency of performance. Its fixity and uniformity also make it an ideal vehicle for authority and power.[9] It follows, then, that the resistance to an overweening Logos evident in the plays' plots should correspond to their decidedly forward-looking author's hesitation regarding publication, or in the words of Abby Zanger, his "suspicion of the precision of the printed page" (170). Considering the disjunction between performance and print, Vernet states: "Ce que nous avons donc devant nous est un autre genre littéraire: c'est la-pièce-imprimée, domaine de l'*Auteur*, ce que Molière se défend d'être chaque fois qu'il le peut" (40).[10]

Introduction

Bray had similarly seen in Molière's disinterest in correcting his printed editions the evidence of his focus on performance. According to Bray, Molière had little time or interest in overseeing his plays through to their definitive printed state, consecrating his efforts instead to the world of performance:

> Molière ne prit jamais la peine de donner une véritable édition de ses œuvres. Il livrait à l'éditeur une copie de la pièce qu'il venait de présenter sur les planches et il semble bien que dès lors il abandonnait le texte à l'ouvrier. On a des raisons de croire qu'il ne corrigeait pas les épreuves: la diversité de l'orthographe, celle de la ponctuation, celle de la disposition des actes et des scènes, ou de la présentation des personnages induisent à penser qu'il se désintéressait de l'imprimé, peut-être par manque de loisirs, assurément aussi parce qu'il ne pouvait y voir une matière digne de son attention. (38)

Bray is correct in the details, even if the conclusions that he draws from them are overstated. There is little if any evidence of Molière frequenting the print shop, correcting proofs, or editing his plays for later editions. Significant textual variants are rare, and there are even few "bad quartos" to allow us glimpses into alternative states of the plays.[11]

But a disinterest in correcting proofs does not necessarily correlate to a disavowal of authorship in the early modern period. Seventeenth-century France experienced sweeping changes in literary commerce, regulation, and professionalization, as the work of scholars like Henri-Jean Martin, Roger Chartier, and Alain Viala has demonstrated. If, as Viala has claimed, the seventeenth century is the historical moment when it first becomes possible to earn a living as a literary professional, this is not to suggest that these newborn professional writers were able to experience complete creative autonomy, living off of book sales. This first French *champ littéraire* was instead characterized by the need to cobble together a variety of revenue sources (labeled by Viala the "multiple alliance" [*Naissance* 184]), including pensions, *charges* or ecclesiastical *bénéfices*, and gifts from patrons. Payments from *libraires*, while an important new factor in the writer's career strategy, were in almost all cases not sufficient to free the writer from the need to find additional means of support.[12]

Complicating the matter, the new professionalism and economic incentives associated with publication contrasted strongly with older notions of authorship as disinterested art. The result was the well-known stigma attached to printing or to the mercenary poet.[13] Authors from the nobility such as La Rochefoucauld and Madame de La Fayette published anonymously, distancing themselves as much as possible from the printing process; writers like La Bruyère and Boileau had their works printed, but cited higher artistic motives for doing so, such as the desire to provide the public with a correct copy of their works. La Bruyère even famously gave the payment he would have received for his *Caractères* to his *libraire*'s daughter for her dowry. Attempting to accommodate both sides of the debate—maintaining the reputation of a literary artist while profiting from the new commercial opportunities available—required careful rhetorical positioning. Even for writers fully participating in a commercial logic of publication, it was considered good form to express reluctance or disdain of publication. Corneille, for example, writes in the preface to the first edition of his collected works (1644):

> C'est contre mon inclination que mes libraires vous font ce présent, et j'aurais été plus aise de la suppression entière de la plus grande partie de ces poèmes, que d'en voir renouveler la mémoire par ce recueil. Ce n'est pas qu'ils n'aient tous eu des succès assez heureux pour ne me repentir point de les avoir faits; mais il y a une si notable différence d'eux à ceux qui les ont suivis, que je ne puis voir cette inégalité sans quelque sorte de confusion. Et certes, j'aurais laissé périr entièrement ceux-ci, si je n'eusse reconnu que le bruit qu'ont fait les derniers obligeait déjà quelques curieux à la recherche des autres, et pourrait être cause qu'un imprimeur, faisant sans mon aveu ce que je ne voulais pas consentir, ajouterait mille fautes aux miennes. (2:187)

Corneille's protests to the reader contrast sharply with his practice: as early as the *querelle du Cid* Corneille had been labeled as over-eager to rush his play into print.[14] Furthermore, Corneille's constant re-editing of his plays, as well as his careful supervision of their printing, testifies to a deep—and even, for the time period, an exceptional—interest in publication. Corneille may well have attributed the printing of his works to his *libraires* and even, in the preface to *Mélite*, stated, "Publier [une pièce], c'est l'avilir" (Peters 206, 409), but it is evident the extent that printing contributed to Corneille's authorial ethos: he was the first living French author to be honored with an in-folio edition of his complete works (Martin, *Livre* 2:634).

Standard early modern practice was to sell a manuscript to a *libraire* and then let the professionals of the trade turn this text into the printed book, a procedure that Roger Chartier has succinctly described by the formula: "Les auteurs n'écrivent pas des livres: non, ils écrivent des textes que d'autres transforment en objets imprimés" ("Le Monde comme représentation" 1513). The very nature of the printing process made it difficult for an author to control: because the forms containing the type were often not kept in place longer than the time required to print the sheets, any reading of proofs or correction of errors by the author would typically have necessitated the author's presence in the print shop as the pages were being produced.[15] Heavy involvement in the printing process—an attitude typical of modern authorship—was the exception, not the rule. In *Publishing Drama in Early Modern Europe,* Chartier cites a passage from Furetière, "L'exactitude de cet Auteur va jusques là qu'il prend soin des points et des virgules," noting that the example "implicitly referred back to a common lack of interest on the part of authors concerning punctuation" (17). Intense participation in the printing process could in this time period even be read as degrading to an author's status, rendering them mere employees of the publisher (Dobranski 115). In other words, a seventeenth-century author's antipathy toward the mechanical reproduction of his or her work does not necessarily imply a disinterest in authorship. In fact, as Geoffrey Turnovsky has argued, such a stance could be constitutive of a claim to legitimate authorship.[16] Many of the alleged proofs of Molière's indifference toward print could alternatively be interpreted as signs of his authorial ambitions.

Beyond the various modes of early modern authorship's relation to publishing, there is also the important matter of Molière's own extensive interactions with *libraires*. Molière may not have corrected proofs, but legal documents and the paratexts of Molière's own plays show a high level of involvement in other aspects of the publication process, in particular obtaining and protecting the legal ownership to the plays. In this respect, the pioneering work of C.E.J. Caldicott has contributed greatly to an increased appreciation for Molière's investment in his theater's literary fortunes. In *La Carrière de Molière,* Caldicott drew much-needed attention to Molière's lengthy struggles with Parisian *libraires*, a clash that began with Molière's first published play and continued even after the author's death. Rather than a Molière who abjures responsibility for his plays, Caldicott asserts that Molière's authorial sensibility was indeed so developed that it potentially damaged his relationships with both the king and his *libraires* (138).[17]

Certain claims of Caldicott's study require additional support or revision, but the overarching conclusion has not been sufficiently emphasized, nor the resultant paradox sufficiently explored. Molière's most active engagement with authorship is found in precisely the area where it is least expected, an interest in ownership and in what Julie Stone Peters has called print's "individuating" tendency—the fiction of a single author, suppressing the more dynamic and complicated genesis of theatrical productions (137–38). Such a stance seems antithetical, particularly given Molière's theatrical commitment. As Vernet reminds us, "Il reste que chez Molière, et suivant une longue habitude des troupes de théâtre, imprimer une pièce est en perdre le contrôle, et ne se fait d'abord que lorsqu'on estime qu'elle a fait son temps sur scène" (40). Printing did indeed represent a loss of control for the theatrical troupe, as it marked the moment after which any actors could perform the work, without remuneration to the troupe that originally commissioned and paid for the play; however, in a crucial distinction, early modern publication constitutes a statement of ownership on the part of the author. Publication, then, marks not the disappearance of control, but the change of control from the communal troupe to the solitary author. And Molière, as a member of a theatrical troupe, did not hesitate to make this transition, repeatedly substituting individual (authorial) possession for group ownership.

Critics who have detected in the plays a celebration of theatricality and a wariness of text's control are certainly correct: the major plays offer a de-centered, dialogical worldview in which the protagonist fails to impose his supremacy; however, the supporting corollary—that Molière hesitated to print—is demonstrably untrue in the majority of cases. Molière may or may not be an artist who thinks (in the narrow sense that Bray gave the term), but he is certainly an artist who publishes. The printed plays contain ample evidence of a Molière actively at work in reducing his plays to text, and in asserting his authorship and ownership. In other

Introduction

words, in Molière's case there is a conflict between what H.L. Hix has termed the "creative author"—the historical Molière—and the "created author"—the Molière that readers construct by asking what kind of person could have written the text (39).[18] Disagreements regarding Molière's opinion of publication may be due to the fact that critics are discussing different Molières.

The 2010 Bibliothèque de la Pléiade edition of Molière's complete works has made this paradox more apparent. The principal editors, Georges Forestier and Claude Bourqui, responded to the increased interest in Molière's publication practices generated most notably by Caldicott (who also served on the edition's editorial team) by including significant bibliographical material for each play. Furthermore, they took the controversial steps of establishing the text based on the first printed editions and arranging the plays by publication order. While these measures would argue for a more literary view of Molière, attempting to recapture any possibly authentic involvement by the playwright in the publication process, the edition does so without questioning the nature of this involvement or its diachronic evolution. Even more significantly, the edition fails to consider the portrait of the author that is crafted within the plays themselves (and by extension through performance), and thus serves to heighten the bifurcation between the decentered and theatrical logic of the plays and the critical apparatus's desire to resurrect a controlling and solitary authorial subjectivity.

By contrast, Molière seems well aware of authorship's contingency, as evidenced by the preface to his first printed play, *Les Précieuses ridicules* (1660). While theorists such as Barthes describe writing as the author's death, the space in which subjectivity disappears, Molière employs language that suggests that entry into print is a birth, exclaiming, "qu'un Auteur est neuf, la première fois qu'on l'imprime" and adding, "[O]n me met au jour, sans me donner le loisir de me reconnaître" (1:4). Printing constitutes a creation, an originary moment for both book and, significantly, author. The preface creates a fusion between writing and writer, the author a personification of his book: "[O]n ne me laisse pas le temps de respirer, et Monsieur de Luynes veut m'aller relier de ce pas" (1:5). In essence, Molière places himself, a new author, *inside* the book, coterminous with it, or even a product of it. Well aware of the nebulous distinction between author and character,

The Death of the Author

Molière uses the preface to show in a wry manner the artificial way in which authorship's authority is constructed and provides for the reader a compelling and pleasing authorial persona. Molière the author is as acutely aware of audience expectations (and is as eager to please) as Molière the actor and director, immediately cognizant of an audience's pleasure or boredom. And, as Molière indicates, this authorial character is a *product* of the book, not its cause.[19]

A curious statement made by Georges Couton shows the extent to which the authorial character that Molière constructed came to have a certain consistency. In his commentary on *Dom Garcie de Navarre*, Couton writes about this failed *comédie héroïque*: "[Molière] n'est pas résigné encore à n'être pas Corneille, ou Quinault, pas encore résigné à être Molière" (Molière, *Œuvres complètes* [1971] 1:340). Couton's commentary presents the strange image of an author resisting his own destiny, or his true identity, seeking to cast himself in a different manner (Molière as author of "serious" plays) only to find himself unable to do so, trapped by some essentializing force that obligates him to a predefined Molièreness. Subtly, the fact that Couton can describe Molière becoming Molière without falling into a complete tautology (although he arguably comes close) demonstrates the distinction between the historical and the authorial figure: Molière the author is a role with certain defined characteristics, a part that Jean-Baptiste Poquelin learns how to play. Couton's statement constitutes an awkward *ex post facto* recognition of this, but does so in a way that suggests that the limiting factor is Molière's own self. *Dom Garcie de Navarre* is somehow an unnatural attempt that runs counter to Molière's identity.

Such a position tends to overlook the fact that Molière very well could have continued to write tragedies and tragicomedies for the rest of his life if he wished: the unknown variable is whether or not the Parisian public would have paid to see them. In this sense, the factors inviting Molière to become "Molière" are not merely the characteristics of some native genius of the playwright, but the community of theatergoers and fellow professionals who negotiate the value of Molière's dramatic production. While his individual artistic freedom is relatively unfettered, if he wishes to succeed, Molière must learn to play and win the complex artistic game of Parisian theater, a *champ* (to use Pierre Bourdieu's notion) with its own particular conventions and codes. Molière's failure in the specific case of *Dom Garcie* can be attributed to his unfamiliarity with this new world, a misstep quickly overcome as his career from *L'École des maris* to *L'École des femmes* indicates. Such a series of theatrical triumphs represents an author acquiring a feel for his world, the *habitus* that Bourdieu describes as "cette sorte de sens pratique de ce qui est à faire dans une situation donnée—ce que l'on appelle, en sport, le sens du jeu, art d'*anticiper* l'avenir du jeu qui est inscrit en pointillé dans l'état présent du jeu" (*Raisons pratiques* 45).

Bourdieu's use of *jeu* takes on additional significance in the theatrical *champ* of Molière, where parts are played as well as games. "Molière becoming Molière" represents not only an evolution in response to external pressures—economic, critical, censorial—but also the fashioning of an *alter ego*, an authorial persona that is played to the audience as much as Arnolphe or Alceste. Among the various authorial subject positions made available by a changing *champ littéraire*, Molière does not have absolute freedom, but instead enjoys a certain limited space in which to maneuver. From this perspective, Molière does not resign himself to the expression of his own true self, but instead invents "Molière" as a calculated response to what the theatrical "game" allows him. His popular success illustrates to what extent he has anticipated the future state of this game, and his own savvy moves will in turn alter the Parisian literary playing field. We might usefully invoke here Stephen Greenblatt's notion of improvisation, described as "the ability both to capitalize on the unforeseen and to transform given materials into one's own scenario" (227). Commenting on an act of treachery in which Spanish sailors tricked natives onto their ships by claiming to have come from the natives' paradise and promising to take them there, Greenblatt notes the "Europeans' ability again and again to insinuate themselves into the preexisting political, religious, even psychic structures of the natives and to turn those structures to their advantage" (227). It is telling that Greenblatt chooses a theatrical term for such maneuvering, combining as it does psychological acumen with a chameleon-esque ability to forge a new but convincing (*vraisemblable*) alternate self. Such self-fashioning dexterity has its limits, of course—it is dependent, as noted above, on the possibilities that the audience affords the performer, or as Greenblatt writes of his English Renaissance authors: "If there remained traces of free choice, the choice was among possibilities whose range was strictly delineated by the social and ideological system in force" (256).

At first glance, it would appear that one of these initial limiting factors was Molière's continued theatrical commitment. Despite the improving social status of the actor in the seventeenth century, Molière's chosen profession brought with it a very real literary and moral stigma that his enemies would not cease to exploit.[20] Even some of Molière's friends and admirers shared the general bias. The *Bolaeana* notes that Molière "n'avait rien contre lui que sa profession," and recounts that Boileau urged Molière to give up acting entirely and devote himself to writing: "Contentez-vous de composer, et laissez l'action théâtrale à quelqu'un de vos camarades: cela vous fera plus d'honneur dans le public, qui regardera vos acteurs comme vos gagistes; et vos acteurs d'ailleurs, qui ne sont pas des plus souples avec vous, sentiront mieux votre supériorité" (Boileau, *Œuvres complètes* [1873], ed. Fournier 453). When Molière responds that "[I]l y a un honneur pour moi à ne point quitter," Boileau comments to himself:

> Plaisant point d'honneur ... à se noircir tous les jours le visage pour se faire une moustache de Sganarelle, et à dévourer son dos à toutes les bastonnades de la comédie! Quoi! cet homme, le premier de son temps pour l'esprit et pour les sentiments d'un vrai philosophe, cet ingénieux censeur de toutes les folies humaines, en avait une plus extraordinaire que celles dont il se moquait tous les jours! (453)

Boileau's comments underscore how, for Molière's contemporaries, the *folie* of acting was incompatible with the moral authority that the author was supposed to embody.

Molière's authorial ethos was compromised by more than the social taboo associated with his theatrical profession, though. The triad of hallmarks that Marilyn Randall identifies as the historical traits of authorship—authority, authenticity, and originality—is challenged by theater's fundamental polyvocality.[21] A playwright's discourse is fragmented and displaced, and the resulting ambiguity shatters the traditional relationship between author and text (author guaranteeing the authority of the text; text transparently delivering the authentic, and authoritative, author). As Pierre Corneille writes in the dedicatory epistle to *La Place Royale* (1634):

Introduction

> Un Poète n'est jamais garant des fantaisies qu'il donne à ses Acteurs; et si les dames trouvent ici quelques discours qui les blessent, je les supplie de se souvenir que j'appelle extravagant celui dont ils partent, et que par d'autres Poèmes j'ai assez relevé leur gloire, et soutenu leur pouvoir pour effacer les mauvaises idées que celui-ci leur pourra faire concevoir de mon esprit. (1:470)

The demands of characterization lead the author to write against his own opinions; with no character ostensibly identified as the author's spokesperson, it becomes necessary for the reader or spectator to deduce and piece together the authentic authorial voice from the polyvocal theatrical performance. Corneille's disclaimer points to the difficulty that some audience members experienced in separating author from character; with the author as the source of the character's discourse, there was a strong tendency to create an equivalency between the two. Corneille feels it necessary to underline the ironic distance between himself and his character ("j'appelle extravagant celui dont ils partent"), refusing to assume the character's "fantaisies" and alleging other, more authentic, works ("d'autres poèmes") to confirm his true opinions.

If Corneille's audience was tempted to equate character with author, Molière's dual status as author and actor only reinforced this propensity, and the resulting confusion is apparent in the contemporary writings of Molière's friends and foes alike. At the première of *Le Misanthrope* (1666), Donneau de Visé took great pleasure during the famous scene of Oronte's sonnet in observing the frustration of the audience's expectations: "J'en vis même, à la première Représentation de cette Pièce, qui se firent jouer pendant qu'on Représentait cette Scène; car ils crièrent que le Sonnet était bon, avant que le Misanthrope en fît la Critique, et demeurèrent ensuite tout confus" (Molière 1:638). However, those siding with Alceste in condemning Oronte's fashionable salon verse (bolstered by the fact that the author was playing the role) soon have their own expectations reversed when Alceste in turn becomes a figure of ridicule by proposing an antiquated and absurd popular song as an alternative to Oronte's sonnet. With part of the audience predisposed to accept the sonnet as good and another awaiting a castigation of salon culture similar to *Les Précieuses ridicules*, Molière frustrates both expectations, presenting both a ridiculous poet and a ridiculous critic (one of whom is played in person by the playwright). Confronted with this sort of complexity, the audience can be forgiven a certain hesitation in deciding where the author is in all of this. Perhaps the best solution is in the end suggested by Donneau de Visé: the real comedy may very well be the audience's (or even the reader's) confusion in the face of the author's magisterial game of hide-and-seek.

However, such confusion could easily be turned to Molière's disadvantage, and it often was by his literary opponents. It is a commonplace among the pamphleteers and minor authors who fueled the quarrels that surrounded Molière's work to identify the author with the actor, that is, to attribute to Molière himself the characteristics of the roles that he depicted on stage. Gustave Michaut, in his early twentieth-century biography and retrospective of Molière criticism, astutely pointed out how frequently such figures as Arnolphe and Agnès were mapped onto the biographies of Molière and his wife, Armande Béjart.[22] In similar fashion, Molière's seventeenth-century critics readily identified him with other ridiculous figures and ideas presented in the plays: the imposter valet-poet (Mascarille) or the cowardly, jealous husband (Sganarelle). Even more dangerously, Molière's enemies were able to play off this ambiguity in order to attribute to the playwright compromising opinions and philosophies. In this manner, the maxims of Arnolphe, Tartuffe, and Dom Juan were all interpreted as the author's, forcing Molière on occasion to respond by underlining the disjunction between author, actor, and character.[23]

Molière's plays were thus easily subjected to egregious, and often deliberate, misreadings of authorial intention. For example, Robinet, in his *Panégyrique de L'École des femmes* (1663), presents two young women, Célante and Bélise, worried that their suitors have become corrupted by the patriarchal maxims of *L'École des femmes*. The women's hatred of Molière, fully evident in the resulting conversation, stems from their belief that Arnolphe's maxims recommending a near-total imprisonment of the wife reflect accurately the position of the playwright and the moral of the play. It is important to note that Célante and Bélise are not worried that their suitors have misread or misunderstood the play's intended meaning, fearing instead the play's "contagion." The suitors, for their part, similarly do not invoke any disparity between the playwright's opinion and that of Arnolphe. On the contrary, when one of them defends Molière, it is precisely by asserting the morality and utility of Arnolphe's maxims.[24] Robinet's surprise for the reader is that Molière's avowed defenders at the end of the play abandon their position, stating that they had defended the playwright merely for the sake of making conversation and that they abhorred Arnolphe's maxims (Mongrédien, *La Querelle* 1:239–41). However, the ending is doubly surprising for the careful reader of Molière, attentive to how Arnolphe's ridiculous behavior and ultimate punishment belie the principles that he sets out early in the play. That *L'École des femmes* could be (and was) passed off as a manifesto against the liberty of women speaks to the difficulty for Molière's contemporaries in placing ironic distance between written or spoken words and the playwright's intentions.[25]

Such ambiguities and ironies, however, could also be turned to Molière's advantage and allowed the playwright some sly metatheatrical effects: Alceste/Molière's angry dismissal of Philinte's comparison of him to the Sganarelle/Molière of *L'École des maris*; *L'Impromptu de Versailles*'s "Molière" (the actor playing at times a ridiculous marquis and at times supposedly himself); or Argan/Molière's famous (self-)curse in *Le Malade imaginaire*.[26] Such baroque moments of doubling demonstrate the degree to which Molière was aware of the incongruity of his two roles, as the play's source but also as a singular participant in the drama. In fact, Molière's adroit and playful references to his split creative roles of actor and author hearken back to the terms' Latin roots in *actor* and *auctor*. Yves Delègue's useful disambiguation of the fraught word that he labels "l'a(u)(c)t(h)eur" points out that the French Middle Ages used both *auctor* and *actor* to express the sense of "auteur," but did so in order to create a distinction between different sorts of authors: the *actor* was a contemporary author of a work, while the term *auctor* (linked to the Latin *auctoritas*) became associated with notions of authority, dignity, and causation (15, 18–19). While an *actor* was still technically an author, it was a subject-position of literary humility—as Delègue writes, the *actor* "est celui qui s'éclipse pour laisser parler les autres" (20), a well-placed witness who records the actions and words of others and who stitches the narrative together, but who hesitates to speak in his or her own name or make authoritative pronouncements (the domain of the *auctores*). While *acteur* had long lost this literary sense by Molière's day, the medieval *actor/auctor* split is deeply suggestive in the playwright's case. While remaining the hidden architect of all that is said and done in the play, Molière nevertheless consistently casts himself as a participant, a singular agent overwhelmed by the actions and agency of the other characters. More significantly, while Molière often rhetorically casts himself as an *actor*, the passive and almost accidental transmitter, his dealings with publishers situate him as the work's origin, its *auctor*.

I would argue that it is precisely Molière's experience as an *homme de théâtre* that makes such authorial dexterity possible. Far from relegating his literary career to the theatrical wings, Molière's deep engagement with performance sensitizes him to the possible ways in which authorship may be "played." Molière the author thus places a Gordian knot before the critic: writing in a genre whose effect depends on distortion and misrepresentation, Molière, even when ostensibly addressing the reader directly, is always playing a double game, creating disjunctions and ironies between words and actions, intentions and realities, or stated beliefs and actual behavior. Molière may well have expressed reluctance to print, but the author of *Tartuffe* is no stranger to the utility of insincerity. This is not to suggest that Molière was an authorial hypocrite, "impie en librairie," but merely to repeat a subtle warning that is evident from every title page of Molière's theater: the author of the plays is an actor. Effacing his original name under a stage name as early as 1644 (Duchêne 68), Molière's stage name becomes his pen name—he is, in effect, writing through his theatrical mask. Molière's authorship essentially becomes one of his many roles.[27]

To study Molière the author does not imply proposing a single dominating consciousness entirely responsible for the Molière corpus, a sole origin whose intentionality evacuates the work of all ambiguity. Rather, the aim of the present study is to examine how Molière and his contemporaries, conscious of authorship's connotations and utility, constructed, negotiated, and debated the image of Molière the author. Instead of making of Molière an author, as Vernet has warned, my objective is to show how Molière sought to make *himself* into an author and lay claim to "ce *corpus* que nous connaissons si bien" (21). If Molière became "ce nom sur la couverture d'un dossier," it was not through the playwright's passivity—the creation of Molière the author, through the writing and printing of Molière's theater, was deliberate and difficult. Not that Molière or his contemporaries were always fully aware of the consequences or implications of their actions and rhetorical stances. As Gregory Brown writes:

> To speak of an individual's actions as "strategic" is to suggest that it is indeed a willful and intentional attempt to achieve an end. It should not be taken to imply, however, that the individual is acting instrumentally, or is even fully conscious of the context for or consequences of their action. Rather, it is to suggest an instinctive attempt to produce an effect based on an always imperfect understanding of the situation…. (27)

In fact, the polemics that accompanied Molière's career testify to the unintended consequences generated by the playwright, publishers, and critics in the elaboration of Molière's authorial image.

While I try to trace Molière's navigation of the changing nature of authorship and its social, legal, and literary implications, I do not mean to suggest that Molière is a modern author, or to privilege ways in which he anticipates future developments in authorial subjectivity. Defining authorship in light of its later iterations obscures the particular characteristics of its possible formulations in the early modern period. As Brown notes, early modern writers often constitute "case studies of cognitive dissonance" (G. Brown 11). Attributing to Molière current opinions regarding print and author's rights risks creating a critical blind spot, cloaking the likelihood that Molière's approach to authorship is incongruous to modern (and even early modern) eyes. If the seventeenth century did indeed see a substantial rearrangement in how authors interacted with the printing industry, the legal system, and the public, many of these innovations evolved alongside or within more archaic institutions.[28] The changes in the literary field of seventeenth-century France created new possibilities, but they did not prohibit Molière and his contemporaries from drawing on both old and new behaviors, creating heteroclite and highly individual career paths and authorial strategies. Rhetorically, legally, and economically, Molière consistently fought to maintain and extend the rights to his plays, and did so in a remarkably effective way. That he did so in ways unlike or antithetical to modern ideas about authorial practice or intellectual property rights does not make of him a non-author—measuring the seventeenth-century playwright against the standard of twenty-first century authorship is looking for Molière the author in all the wrong places. The real value of Molière's literary career is found in the way that it serves as an important "cas particulier du possible" (to borrow Bourdieu's phrase) (*Raisons pratique*s 16), illustrating the early modern writer's capacity to combine practices and stances that seem incompatible when measured against a teleological narrative of authorship.

Any attempt to account for the complex and fractured authorial persona (both *actor* and *auctor*) that Molière forges from the possible subject-positions afforded him must deal with both the plays themselves and the external evidence of Molière's interactions with *libraires*, authors, and the legal machinery governing publication. My study consequently begins with a synchronic examination of writers and writing in Molière's theater, attempting to situate Molière's most direct staging of his own creative activities in *L'Impromptu de Versailles* within the context of his longstanding theatrical exploration of the Parisian literary world. The chapters that follow constitute a diachronic investigation into Molière's literary career, tracing the parallel evolution of the playwright's authorial persona as defined rhetorically and empirically. In Chapter 2, I discuss the publication histories of Molière's first three published plays—*Les Précieuses ridicules* (premiered 1659; published 1660), *Sganarelle* (1660), and *L'École des maris* (1661)—to outline the playwright's early defining efforts to navigate the Parisian *champ littéraire* while struggling with rogue *libraires* and plagiarists. Chapter 3 examines the *querelle* de *L'École des femmes*, the most protracted literary and theatrical attempt to characterize Molière's authorship, albeit one that demonstrates the ways in which Molière troubled and divided his contemporaries, or even deliberately antagonized them. Chapter 4 explores a crucial turning point in Molière's publishing career—the 1666 rift with his original *libraires*—and traces the author's consequential changing views on reception and ownership in *Le Misanthrope*. With a look at the final plays published in Molière's lifetime, Chapter 5 illustrates the drastically different approach to publishing that emerges in the aftermath of 1666, as Molière's canny exploitation of the book trade leads to a highly individual printing strategy and significant conflicts with the publishers' guild. The singular case of *Psyché*, Molière's most successful production and his most dramatic demonstration of possessive authorship, constitutes the subject matter for Chapter 6. I conclude by examining the case of the 1682 *Œuvres de Monsieur de Molière*, the posthumous collection

Introduction

of Molière's plays that, in attempting to invoke a coherent and authoritative portrait of the author, admirably reproduces instead the inherent tensions and challenges. These moments that I have chosen to privilege are periods of flux for Molière's reputation and are symptomatic of the ambiguity surrounding the concept of authorship. Whether in the ways he adapts and reinvents both the comedic tradition and the works of his contemporaries, or in his subtle manipulation of the legal machinery governing the printing trade, Molière provides an important touchstone for the seventeenth-century debates over originality, imitation, plagiarism, and intellectual property. Molière's literary career demonstrates the individualistic nature of early modern authorship, continually renegotiated between writer, *libraire*, patron, and the reading public. The texts that emerge from these debates bear witness to the competing and emerging literary mentalities defining the author at this historical moment, and Molière, as a writer, is situated on several major ideological fault lines. The solutions, compromises, and paradoxes—and, perhaps, the very debate itself—apparent in the texts and career of France's most celebrated comic playwright help to trace the birth of one particular writer in this era of the *naissance de l'écrivain* and by extension elucidate the possibilities and limits of authorship in the French seventeenth century.

Let us return for a moment to *L'Amour médecin*. While the printed volume begins with a warning against reading plays, the work's conclusion serves as a kind of counterweight to this advice in its reappraisal of writing and the theatrical *jeu*. Convinced by the sham doctor Clitandre (in reality his daughter's suitor) that his daughter's illness is a sort of gamomania, an obsession with marriage that needs humoring, Sganarelle is persuaded to sign a purportedly fake marriage contract—in actuality a real notarized document marrying the two young lovers. To the nonplussed father, the servant Lisette explains, "[V]ous avez cru faire un jeu, qui demeure une vérité" (1:632). Writing's utility, as this scene demonstrates, comes from its permanence, its ability to remain—and in turn its ability to confer this durability. While never an adequate substitution for performance, print can provide a fitting denouement for the *jeu*, in this sense both for the manic comic business on stage and for the work of art itself. After the play's initial performance run, Simeon Piget, *syndic* of the guild of *libraires, imprimeurs*, and *relieurs*, records on 4 January 1666:

"Ledit jour nous a esté presenté un privilege du Roy par le Sr Jean Bapt. Poquelin de Moliere, comedien du Palais-Royal, d'un livre intitulé *L'Amour medecin*" (Thuasne 22–26). Molière's trip to the guild offices that day does not make him any less the *comédien*; it shows instead a willingness—despite his awareness of the resultant changes—to let the play of the theater extend into a new venue, moving from stage to page. To elucidate the evolving and elusive nature of that engagement will be the object of the chapters that follow.

Chapter One

Molière's Writers

Insufferable pedants, polished courtiers, hopeless amateurs, and aspiring social climbers, writers populate and animate Molière's theatrical performance space as well as the pages of the printed text, producing letters, poems, ballads, and even projected volumes of Roman history in madrigal form. Through their activities, they both stage the act of writing and demonstrate the extent to which authorship itself constitutes a delicate literary and social performance. In the process, they provide invaluable context for situating Molière's own authorial practices, since the playwright's portrayals of authorship in its myriad seventeenth-century forms constitute implied stances that together construct a portrait of the author *en creux*. In addition, they serve as useful points of reference for evaluating Molière's own performance as "Molière," demonstrating how the author chose to define himself within seventeenth-century France's emergent literary field.

Almost every Molière play contains either writers or discussions of writing.[1] This is not to claim that most of the plays present writing or writers as their central subject matter—although Molière's works do include examples such as *Les Précieuses ridicules, Les Femmes savantes,* or the polemical plays *La Critique de L'École des femmes* and *L'Impromptu de Versailles* that fit this description—but rather that the majority of the plays incorporate writing or written documents as important props, plot devices, or thematic elements. At times, these documents exist only as verbal references, such as the incriminating papers that Orgon entrusts to Tartuffe that form a frequent topic of discussion in the play's final act, but which are never seen on stage or read. At other moments, the documents are present on stage, but their contents are not fully made known to the audience, as is the case with Célimène's letter in the fourth act of *Le Misanthrope* or Clitandre's letter to Angélique in *George*

Dandin—in both instances, the paper is a theatrical prop and its contents are discussed and analyzed, but the text is omitted. Frequently, however, the reading of a written composition forms an important part of the theatrical action, and the content of such documents as the *Maximes du mariage* in *L'École des femmes* or the loan details in *L'Avare* performs important functions of characterization and plot.

A special case should be made for the legal documents in Molière's theater. Other than personal correspondence, the single most prevalent and persistent example of writing in the plays is the marriage contract, the drafting or signing of which appears in *L'École des maris*, *L'École des femmes*, *L'Amour médecin*, and *Les Femmes savantes*, while four other plays (*Le Dépit amoureux*, *L'Avare*, *Monsieur de Pourceaugnac*, and *Le Bourgeois gentilhomme*) make significant references to it. When the contract is not merely performing a banal official gesture recognizing the comedy's ending, it is usually part of the traditional comic topos that involves the tricking of the *barbon* and the unification of the happy couple—*L'École des maris* and *L'Amour médecin* contain important examples of the contract's use as a ruse. The contents of the contracts in *L'École des femmes* and *Les Femmes savantes*, however, are explored in greater detail. In the first, the drafting of the contract's terms allows for a farcical *dialogue de sourds* in which Arnolphe's soliloquy regarding his standing with Agnès is transmuted by the notary into acceptable contractual terms. In the second, the style of the contract is called into question by the *femmes savantes*, who wish to extend their linguistic domination even into the heavily regulated and formulaic world of legal documents. Philaminte asks the notary, "Vous ne sauriez changer votre style sauvage, / Et nous faire un Contrat qui soit en beau langage?" (2:617). Upon the notary's refusal, Bélise asks that the dates and monetary amounts could at least employ archaic units of money and time (*mines, talents, ides, calendes*). Of course, the wrangling over the stylistic wording of the contract is only a precursor to the more serious struggles between Philaminte and her husband, Chrysale, over one of the document's miniscule but more significant possible variants: the name of the groom.

The marriage contracts and other official papers (e.g., depositions, edicts, *sommations*) that appear in Molière's plays represent writing at its least creative or original—although an exception might be made for the chicaneries of Harpagon's loan articles, the shady notary's rendition of Argan's *testament,* or Nérine's *faux contrat* alluded to in *Monsieur de Pourceaugnac.*[2] However, their prominent appearance in Molière's theater serves to reinforce a certain view of textuality, equating the written word with power and control. Larry Riggs reminds us, "Standardized language and print facilitate both long-distance projection and long-term storage of messages," adding, "They also make the messages appear more authoritative" (*Plurality* 87). Consequently, Riggs has noted that "[m]ost of Molière's *ridicules* identify their ambitions with books and hasten to institutionalize their preferences in the form of binding legal documents" (89). In part, this is because, as Walter Ong has pointed out in discussing the difference between orality and literacy, "[w]riting establishes what has been called 'context-free' language," that is, "discourse which cannot be directly questioned or contested as oral speech can be because written discourse has been detached from its author" (77). Abby Zanger's analysis of Molière's attitude toward print—particularly as it contrasts with the dynamics of performance—has similarly drawn attention to the playwright's awareness (or should we say wariness?) of "the precision of the printed page" (170).[3] The plays' legal documents consequently bring to the forefront the image of writing as an activity that structures, organizes, and controls.

Writers, even the humblest notary, accordingly are producers of authority, albeit an authority that is frequently undermined, as Riggs notes. This is readily apparent in the practice of Molière's characters to cite ancient authors, whose *auctoritas* commands deference and respect, at least from the more simple-minded.[4] Additionally, those characters without extensive literacy have a tendency to equate writing with logic, persuasion, and conceptual sophistication. In *Dom Juan,* for example, Sganarelle will respond to his master's defense of *libertinage,* "Vertu de ma vie, comme vous débitez; il semble que vous ayez appris par cœur cela, et vous parlez tout comme un Livre" (2:853). When summoned to comment on Dom Juan's argumentation, the servant responds, "Ma foi, j'ai à dire, et je ne sais que dire, car vous tournez les choses d'une manière qu'il semble que vous ayez raison, et cependant il est vrai que vous ne l'avez pas; j'avais les plus belles pensées du monde, et vos discours m'ont brouillé tout cela: laissez faire, une autre fois je mettrai mes raisonnements par écrit, pour disputer avec vous" (2:853–54). Sganarelle's theory of writing is here doubly on display. Dom Juan's oral statements have for Sganarelle the effect of writing, which apparently for him equates to an ability to convey a point of view with authority and convincing power. Furthermore, by noting that his own counterarguments will need to be written down, Sganarelle makes writing the site of complexity and authority. Other illiterate or semi-literate characters in Molière's theater will express similar opinions. The peasant Lucas in *Le Médecin malgré lui*, awed by Sganarelle's macaronic Latin, will state of the "doctor" to his master Géronte: "Quand il s'y boute, il parle tout fin drait, comme s'il lisait dans un Livre" (1:744). As Riggs comments, "Many of Molière's characters can be said to speak like books, and most of them explicitly associate authority with text" (*Modernity* 12).

Not only text, but literacy in general: "book learning" allows Molière's characters—and the *ridicules* above all—a sense of mastery over language itself. The ability to analyze and comment about language or style, that is, to create a meta-language, frequently occurs in the plays linked to an effort to control, as the case of the *femmes savantes* clearly shows. Moreover, a little literacy can go a (deceptively) long way. No sooner does Monsieur Jourdain learn that "[t]out ce qui n'est point prose, est Vers; et tout ce qui n'est point Vers, est Prose" (2:283) than he proceeds to use (or rather abuse) his new-found capacity for linguistic abstraction to demonstrate his intellectual superiority over his wife:

> Monsieur Jourdain: Par exemple, savez-vous, vous, ce que c'est que vous dites à cette heure ?
> Madame Jourdain: Oui, je sais que ce que je dis est fort bien dit, et que vous devriez songer à vivre d'autre sorte.
> Monsieur Jourdain: Je ne parle pas de cela. Je vous demande ce que c'est que les paroles que vous dites ici ?
> Madame Jourdain: Ce sont des paroles bien sensées, et votre conduite ne l'est guère.
> Monsieur Jourdain: Je ne parle pas de cela, vous dis-je. Je vous demande; Ce que je parle avec vous, Ce que je vous dis à cette heure, qu'est-ce que c'est?
> Madame Jourdain: Des Chansons. (2:291)

To Monsieur Jourdain's abstract (and ridiculous) questions regarding the nature of language, his wife responds with a view of language that remains practical and situational. In this respect, the couple's dialogue recalls the conclusions drawn by A.R. Luria in his fieldwork with the largely illiterate population of Uzbekistan in the early twentieth century. As summarized by Ong, Luria discovered that individuals of a primarily oral background thought "not in categorical terms ... but in terms of practical situations" (51), and that they assessed intelligence "not as extrapolated from contrived textbook quizzes but as situated in operational contexts" (55). To Madame Jourdain, her husband's question makes little sense: he continues to ask about the words that she has said, while demonstrating no awareness of having heard them. Her sound advice about the need to find a suitable match for their daughter has fallen on deaf ears. His response is indeed nonsense, *chansons*, and it potentially raises doubts about Monsieur Jourdain's sanity—why would he need to have explained to him what his wife and he have just said? The demonstration to Nicole about how to pronounce the letter *u* likewise shows the gap between the spontaneous and instrumental use of language, and its useless abstraction. However, these *fariboles*, in the words of Madame Jourdain, serve as the basis for Monsieur Jourdain's sense of intellectual superiority, as he exclaims to the two women: "Vous parlez toutes deux comme des Bêtes, et j'ai honte de votre ignorance" (2:291).

The link between power and writing (and more precisely print) is exemplified in a passage from *Les Amants magnifiques* in which the principal characters discuss the merits of astrology. With the princess Ériphile undecided on a choice of husband, the astrologer Anaxarque suggests settling the matter through the means of his horoscopes and predictions. The two suitors, Iphicrate and Timoclès, express enthusiasm for the idea, arguing in favor of astrology's ability to foretell accurately the future. As Iphicrate states, "La vérité de l'Astrologie est une chose incontestable, et il n'y a personne qui puisse disputer contre la certitude de ses prédictions" (2:980). While Ériphile's mother, Aristione, is sympathetic to astrology, her daughter is more skeptical, joined in her opinion by the *plaisant de cour* Clitidas and the general Sostrate, Ériphile's true love interest. To convince the doubters, Timoclès points to recorded incidents of successful astrological predictions: "Peut-on contester sur cette matière les incidents célèbres, dont les Histoires nous font foi?" (2:981). The link to print is made explicit by Clitidas, who responds, "Il faut n'avoir pas le sens commun. Le moyen de contester ce qui est moulé" (2:981). Print is the guarantor of the *histoires*' truth content, presumably constituting an epistemological sieve that only lets pass items of unquestioned (and henceforth unquestionable) credibility. The astrological forecast thus assumes some of the characteristics—precision, immutability, accuracy—of the cast (*moulé*) type that records and preserves it.

But the play consistently undermines this idea. In the first place, the futility of resisting "ce qui est moulé" is announced by the court buffoon, an implacable enemy of Anaxarque, and whose statement must be taken ironically. The disbelief of Ériphile, Sostrate, and Clitidas is demonstrably justified when it is revealed that Anaxarque's predictions are the product of self-interest rather than a dispassionate reading of the stars, and the two princely suitors' defense of astrology is likewise shown to stem not from *histoires*, but from their connivance with the astrologer.[5] Likewise, the failures of Molière's other *ridicules*—those who "speak like books" and who try to muster the authority of writing and texts in order to shore up their own—attest to the complicated and embattled nature of textuality in Molière's theater. If it frequently appears with its connotations of precision, power, and authority, those who trust in what is *moulé* typically find that its pretensions are as much a sham as the purported abilities of the astrologer. The metatheatricality of *Les Amants magnifiques* on a larger scale plays a role in demystifying the spectator, revealing the inner workings of the *comédie-ballet*'s effects, and celebrating those who resist them: Venus's appearance owes more to theatrical machines than miracles, and the magnificent spectacles produced by the princes fail to win the princess's heart. It is Sostrate, absent from the spectacles, who eventually wins the princess's heart and hand. Molière's plays as a whole could be said to effectuate a similar demystification for writing, showing the inner motivations, the deceptions, the rules of the rhetorical game that allow writing (and writers) to enjoy prestige and power over others. In fact, we might note that it is Molière himself who played the part of Clitidas. The suspicion that Zanger attributes to Molière in this sense could be equated with a warning, and the plays' victorious protagonists are those who are not duped. Sganarelle of *Le Médecin malgré lui* may speak like a book, but it is a book that mixes up the location of vital organs ("du côté gauche, où est le Foie, au côté Droit, où est le cœur" [1:752]); while this might fool the gullible Géronte, no amount of appeals to Aristotle or Hippocrates can conceal the sham from the alert reader or spectator.

Of the actual examples of writing present within the plays, that is, written compositions that are read or recited, many likewise serve to undermine the authority of their authors. Bernard Magné's analysis of "métapoèmes" in Molière's theater finds eight examples: Mascarille's impromptu in *Les Précieuses ridicules;* Oronte's sonnet and Alceste's *vieille chanson* from *Le Misanthrope;* the Vicomte's sonnet and the two "épigrammes" from Monsieur Tibaudier in *La Comtesse d'Escarbagnas;* and Trissotin's two poems in *Les Femmes savantes* (109). For these "textes dans le texte," the proportion of ridiculous compositions is remarkable: while all of the works are presented by their authors in good faith, in seven out of the eight instances (the Vicomte's sonnet serving as the lone exception) the literary work in question is comically inept and provokes the audience's laughter. The texts by Mascarille and Monsieur Tibaudier are the most straight-forward examples, exaggerated doggerel whose poor literary quality is never in doubt. Oronte's sonnet and Trissotin's poems, however, require a little more comedic framing—in these three instances the poems could (and did) pass as commendable in certain circles. Donneau de Visé, in his *Lettre écrite sur la comédie du Misanthrope* that accompanied the first edition of Molière's play, noted about Oronte's poem: "Le Sonnet n'est point méchant, selon la manière d'écrire d'aujourd'hui: et ceux qui cherchent ce que l'on appelle Pointes ou Chutes, plutôt que le bon Sens, le trouveront, sans doute, bon" (1:638). Trissotin's two poems are taken verbatim from the Abbé Cotin's works, and had circulated in salons before being published in 1659 and 1663, respectively (Mongrédien, *Recueil* 106, 165–66). In both of these cases, the theatrical context for the poems (either Alceste's critique—and the subsequent petty quarrel that erupts—or the *femmes savantes*' exuberant praise) orients the audience's opinion, encouraging a view of the poems (and their authors) as presumptuous and affected.

Poetry, the loftiest of the seventeenth-century literary arts, fares the worst in Molière's theater, almost invariably dismantling the authority or persona that the writer seeks to establish through it. It is not the only example of self-destructive writing within the plays, however, and illustrations that serve a similar comic end abound in a wide variety of different genres.[6] Among the *épistoliers*, letters composed or read in the plays point out Monsieur Jourdain's imbecility, Célimène's duplicity, and Monsieur Tibaudier's love of horrid puns.[7] Éraste and Lucile, the quarreling lovers from *Le*

Dépit amoureux, return each other's correspondence in a huff, the saccharine *billets doux* forming an amusing contrast with their present behavior.[8] The pompous tone of Caritidès's *placet* to the king in *Les Fâcheux*, requesting that the pedant be appointed "Contrôleur, Intendant, Correcteur, Réviseur, et Restaurateur général" (1:183) of all the nation's inscriptions and shop signs immediately persuades the audience to the contrary, and Moron's attempt at a tender song in *La Princesse d'Élide* (no doubt hindered by its comic delivery) hardly merits the *vivat* with which Moron congratulates his own performance. Monsieur Fleurant the apothecary's "fort civiles" bills in *Le Malade imaginaire*, documenting "un petit Clystère insinuatif, préparatif, et rémollient, pour amollir, humecter, et rafraîchir les entrailles de Monsieur" (2:641), invite mockery of the language of the medical establishment and those, like Argan, who admire it. And perhaps no character in Molière's theater subverts his own attempts at authority faster through the presentation of a text than Arnolphe, whose archconservative *Maximes du mariage*, designed to monopolize all domestic power "du côté de la barbe," immediately align the audience against him.

This is not to suggest that all the examples of writing included in the plays reflect poorly upon those who wrote them. In addition to the Vicomte's sonnet, listed above, Isabelle and Agnès, the two persecuted girls of the *Écoles*, each write a letter that is celebrated for its ingenuity.[9] Several other letters, parts of successful ruses, do credit to their writers if not for their fairly anodyne style, at least for their utility: we might cite here Ariste's two letters at the end of *Les Femmes savantes* that reveal Trissotin's greed, the letter written by Adraste's friend in *Le Sicilien* that gets him admittance into Dom Pèdre's house, or even Done Elvire's innocent letters that chasten the boundless jealousy of the eponymous character of *Dom Garcie de Navarre*.[10] To this list could be added some of the other cultural productions written by Molière's characters: *La Critique de L'École des femmes* is presumably the result of the *mémoire* of the group's conversation written by Dorante, and in spite of the marquis's statements to the contrary, the *chevalier* does indeed come off looking well; in addition, the songs of Tircis and the satyr in *La Princesse d'Élide* and the various performances in *Le Bourgeois gentilhomme* appear to be presented without irony or satirical aim.[11] The final, and most important, example to add to this list would be the excerpt of Molière's own projected "comédie des comédiens" presented as part of *L'Impromptu de Versailles*.

While irony could be said to dominate the majority of the texts presented in Molière's plays, it is irony of a second degree—that is, the characters themselves are generally unaware of the unappealing authorial persona that their text is creating. Rare indeed are those characters who misrepresent themselves in writing, that is, who write in such a way as to create a deliberate tension between their character and the implied author generated by their text: the letters in *Les Femmes savantes*, *Le Sicilien*, and *L'Étourdi* mentioned above, with the significant addition of Célimène and her correspondence, comprise the entire total of disingenuous or duplicitous texts quoted in the plays.[12] In other words, the "texts within a text" in Molière's theater may well be bad—in fact, most of them are, or are intended to be perceived as such—but they are sincere, often painfully so. Writing, even more than speaking, becomes the linguistic locus in which, as the philosopher Pancrace from *Le Mariage forcé* claims, "la parole est *animi index, et speculum*. C'est le Truchement du Cœur; c'est l'Image de l'Âme. C'est un Miroir qui nous représente naïvement les Secrets les plus *Arcanes de nos Individus*" (1:969). Pancrace is more right than he knows. Within the plays, writing is indeed a faithful vehicle for the individual's thoughts and a reliable benchmark for evaluating character, but most often the result is a mirror image—that is, the exact reversal of the writer's perceived reality.

If texts in the plays often serve as a means of characterization, it is due to Molière 's intense interest in those who produce them. References to writers and the literary world of the mid-seventeenth century will span Molière's career, from the authorial pretensions of the Marquis de Mascarille in *Les Précieuses ridicules* to Trissotin and Vadius's *combat de prose et de vers* in *Les Femmes savantes*. While talking with the professional writer Lysidas, Dorante in *La Critique de L'École des femmes* will identify authors as worthy company for Molière's traditional satirical targets:

> [E]t si l'on joue quelques Marquis, je trouve qu'il y a bien plus de quoi jouer les Auteurs, et que ce serait une chose plaisante à mettre sur le Théâtre, que leurs grimaces savantes, et leurs raffinements ridicules; leur vicieuse coutume d'assassiner les gens de leurs ouvrages; leur friandise de louanges; leurs ménagements de pensées; leur trafic de réputation; et leurs ligues

offensives et défensives; aussi bien que leurs guerres d'esprit, et leurs combats de Prose, et de Vers. (1:506)

Of course, the project is already well underway, as Lysidas's *mauvaise foi* and pedantic pettifoggery are on ample display. The cross-section of France's first *champ littéraire* that will parade across Molière's stage will explore writers' various social conditions, motives, institutions, language, and comportment, in the aggregate every bit as thoroughly as the playwright's portrayal of the petty nobility or the medical profession.[13] As Molière's authors seek distinction and legitimation within the literary world and wider society, they also provide a portrait of authorship in the seventeenth century comparable in its insight and value to Flaubert's description two centuries later, used by Pierre Bourdieu in his analysis of "the rules" governing the creation, circulation, and evaluation of literary works (and reputations).[14]

Like the doctors or the marquis, Molière's writers inhabit a distinctive and specialized social space, one of the "highly differentiated social worlds" (labeled "$champ_2$," by William Earle in his discussion of Bourdieu) within the larger social sphere (or "$champ_1$"). It is precisely for this reason that authorship's dynamics can become such a ready source of amusement to outsiders: the practices, constraints, and language of a particular $champ_2$, while at once normal (in both senses of the word) and invested with meaning for its participants, appear to the bemused inhabitants of the wider social sphere as arcane and, consequently, ridiculous. When Lysidas, the professional poet of *La Critique de L'École des femmes*, objects to "la Protase, l'Épitase, et la Péripétie," Dorante retorts, "Ne paraissez point si savant, de grâce; humanisez votre discours, et parlez pour être entendu" (1:508). While thoroughly familiar with the terms himself, Dorante points out Lysidas's inability to move from the language of *messieurs les auteurs* to that of polite company. Lysidas can only peevishly respond, "Ce sont termes de l'art dont il est permis de se servir" (1:508).

While we might laugh at the different sense of value that, for example, leads Vadius to argue that Trissotin is unworthy of Henriette's hand because of "tous les endroits qu'il a pillés" from Horace, Vergil, Terence, and Catullus (2:607), it is important to bear in mind that such transgressions will have real consequences in the $champ_2$ within which Vadius and Trissotin are operating. In this sense, they are similar to the courtiers surrounding Louis XIV, of whom Bourdieu has written:

> Le capital symbolique qui fait qu'on s'incline devant Louis XIV, qu'on lui fait la cour ... qu'il peut déclasser, dégrader, consacrer, etc., n'existe que dans la mesure où toutes les petites différences, les marques de distinction subtiles dans l'étiquette et les rangs, dans les pratiques et dans le vêtement, qui font la vie de cour, sont perçues par des gens qui connaissent et reconnaissent pratiquement (ils l'ont incorporé) un principe de différenciation qui leur permet de reconnaître toutes ces différences et de leur accorder valeur, qui sont prêts, en un mot, à mourir pour une affaire de bonnets. (*Raisons pratiques* 161)

Substituting "sonnets" for "bonnets," Molière's *Le Misanthrope* stages just such a confrontation, as Alceste's refusal to praise Oronte's poem threatens to descend into physical violence, requiring the intervention of the *maréchaux*. And while the audience is certainly invited to laugh at the incongruity between the risibly small initial stakes of the conflict and its ultimate consequences, it bears mentioning that Molière himself was no stranger to such escalating imbroglios: if the *querelle de L'École des femmes* began as an exchange of satirical plays, it culminated in personal attacks of a very serious and direct nature, including Montfleury's denunciation to the king of Molière's purported incest (Duchêne 253).

While the collective authorial portrait that Molière's theater fabricates is fictional, and frequently satirical, it is important to bear in mind that the notion of the literary field—or of the literary market—is itself largely conceptual, rhetorically elaborated and reified by early modern writers in their search for distinction and legitimation, as Geoffroy Turnovsky reminds us. Criticizing the "overriding focus on 'objective' circumstances," Turnovsky notes, "But the 'literary market' is a qualitatively different type of configuration, which finds its conceptual coherence not in the economic reality of the book trade but in the convergence of the book trade's 'objectivity' with the evolving expectations of those who aspire to a literary identity" (6). While these "objective" factors—such as the development, organization, and regulations of the Parisian book trade, or the fluctuations of patronage and other sources of income—certainly shape the literary landscape of Molière's era, equally important are the ways in which writers seek to define

Chapter One

themselves and their activities. Molière's author-dense theatrical representations, and in particular the correlative self-portrait that the playwright constructs through them, play a significant role in defining writers and writing within and for Viala's inaugural generation of *écrivains*.

But depicting the seventeenth-century author involves a moving target. In Tristan L'Hermite's autobiographical *Le Page disgracié* (1643), the author recounts an exchange with a young officer in love with the daughter of a washerwoman and who has composed a comically infantile ode that he presents to the page to read. When Tristan admits that he is unable to make any sense of the handwriting, the officer volunteers to read him the poem, and the narrative specifies that he "en était l'auteur et l'écrivain tout ensemble" (50). Tristan's text here splits writing into two components, each of which is attributed to an agent: the composition of the poem, product of the *auteur*; and the physical writing of the words on the page, done by the *écrivain*. The *auteur* is the work's intellectual source and cause, and his work is in the realm of ideas. Tristan links the term *écrivain* to the production of the physical vehicle for the text; it is implied that the *écrivain* could just as readily transcribe any *auteur*'s work onto the page.

However, the officer who fuses the two activities together, becoming both *auteur* and *écrivain* inseparably, is a prescient image for the second half of the seventeenth century, in which the activities that Tristan rhetorically separates will become ever more convoluted as the new figure of the writer is increasingly concerned with both the intellectual conception of a work and the means of its dissemination. Authorial self-fashioning in this emergent era of the birth of the writer (to invoke Viala's phrase) involves strategic choices that position oneself in relation to a complex network of patrons, other writers, and a variously defined public. A large array of options (or authorial subject-positions) is available to the seventeenth century's newborn writer, many of which collapse traditional boundaries, such as the ones cited by Tristan.[15] Within this historical context, Molière's plays and career become doubly important: first of all, they provide fictive representations of writing's new conceptual space, the new literary "field"; secondly, Molière's own rhetorical construction of his authorship within the plays themselves creates a persona (only possibly correlating to his actual authorial practices) that situates the playwright in relation to the new Parisian literary topography.

The seventeenth-century dictionaries of Furetière and Richelet bear witness to this definitional shift in words such as *écrivain* and *auteur*. A study of the word *auteur* reveals a term very much in flux, metonymically incorporating some of the very difficulties encountered in the concept it seeks to describe. Antoine Furetière, in his 1690 *Dictionnaire universel*, states, in his first definition of *auteur*: "L'*Auteur* est celuy qui n'a pas pris son ouvrage d'un autre; c'est luy qui l'a produit, qui l'a mis au jour" (V2v). Notable in Furetière's definition is the notion of the author as the singular agent in the entire creative process. Richelet's *auteur* emphasizes the notion of temporal primacy: "Le premier qui a inventé quelque chose, qui a dit quelque chose, qui est cause de quelque chose qui s'est fait" (1:56). For both Furetière and Richelet, authorship has something of the divine. Furetière states of *auteur*, "On le dit par excellence de la premiere Cause qui est Dieu. L'*Auteur* de toute la nature, le Souverain *Auteur* du monde" (V2v), and Richelet writes, "Dieu est l'auteur de notre felicité" (1:56). Such examples reinforce Marilyn Randall's observation that authority, authenticity, and originality "form the historical constants of authorship" (28). An *auteur* is a single and original cause, and his or her ethos is a guarantor of truth: Richelet and Furetière both include the expression *nommer son auteur*, meaning to cite an authority to prove one's proposition.

While *auteur* could be employed in abstract—and even metaphysical—ways, Furetière, writing about the literary use of *auteur*, proceeds to add a very specific and physical qualification: "Se dit de tous ceux qui ont mis en lumière quelque livre. Maintenant on ne le dit que de ceux qui en ont fait imprimer" (Peters 209, 410). Richelet similarly defines the term as "celui qui a composé quelque Livre imprimé" (1:56). Both of these definitions attest to the importance of print as the benchmark by which authorship was evaluated—in fact, Furetière's definition even underlines the novelty of this criterion. As Chartier remarks, "Pour 's'ériger en auteur,' écrire ne suffit pas; il faut plus, faire circuler ses œuvres dans le public par le moyen de l'imprimé" (*L'Ordre* 50). By very definition, the seventeenth-century author is thus a locus of struggle between competing aesthetic ideologies, the lofty authority of the singular creator and the writer newly characterized by his or her relationship with the printing industry.

Conversely, the definition of *écrivain* moves from the prosaic and concrete to the abstract. The first two definitions for *écrivain* in Furetière's dictionary concern the mechanical act of writing—the first defines the term simply as "Qui escrit," providing as an example of usage that "les Sergents font d'ordinaire de meschans *escrivains*, on ne peut lire leur escriture," while the second definition points to the organized *métier* of scribe: "se dit plus particulierement de celuy qui est receu Maistre en l'art d'escrire" (Bbbbb1v). Only then does Furetière arrive at the sense that has become the most prominent: "se dit aussi de ceux qui ont composé des Livres, des Ouvrages." Richelet similarly begins with the profession, "Maître à écrire," before defining the term as an "auteur qui a fait imprimer quelque ouvrage considérable" (1:266). The reversal is complete—not only is the *écrivain* an *auteur*, but an exceptional one, combining publication with esteem. What Richelet and Furetière demonstrate above all is the confluence of the two terms, whose different trajectories along the axes of the abstract and the concrete meet in a new synonymity. Like Tristan's officer, the new seventeenth-century writer must be "l'auteur et l'écrivain tout ensemble," conscious of the ways in which rhetoric and publication intersect in the production and reception of his work and his authorial image.

Molière's plays depict authorial types in several stages of this evolution. In the first place (and the least adapted to these new conditions) are the pedants and philosophers, such as Métaphraste from *Le Dépit amoureux*, Caritidès from *Les Fâcheux,* Pancrace and Marphurius from *Le Mariage forcé*, *Le Bourgeois gentilhomme*'s *maître de philosophie*, and the doctors from *L'Amour médecin* and *Le Malade imaginaire*.[16] The link between this group and writing is clearly expressed by Pancrace when, in his anger at a colleague's malapropism (*la forme d'un chapeau* instead of *la figure d'un chapeau*), he exclaims, "Je crèverais plutôt que d'avouer ce que tu dis; et je soutiendrai mon opinion jusqu'à la dernière goutte de mon Encre" (1:946). Pancrace is a creature of paper and ink; his writing is coterminous with his life, and he dialogues much more readily with texts than with people, as his inability to listen to Sganarelle illustrates. Pancrace and his ilk owe much to the *dottore* of the *commedia dell'arte* and the widespread traditional comic criticism of the overly erudite. Living in a world of Aristotle and Seneca, this group has few social aspirations outside of a general recognition of their knowledge: as Pancrace emphatically states to Sganarelle, he will prove to him "en toute rencontre, par raisons démonstratives et convaincantes, et par Arguments *in Barbara*" that Sganarelle is an idiot and that Pancrace is an "Homme savant, savantissime *per omnes modos et casus*" (1:970).

In fact, the very erudition possessed by this group makes them socially awkward, unable to integrate into polite society, as Bernard Magne points out in his discussion of these characters' use of *métalangage*: "En tant que discours scientifique, le discours métalinguistique ne saurait trouver place dans la société des 'honnêtes gens'" (108). A prime example is Thomas Diafoirus's courting of Angélique in *Le Malade imaginaire*: Thomas presents his intended fiancée with a medical thesis "comme un hommage que je lui dois des prémices de mon esprit" and then invites her to see a dissection (2:676). Toinette draws the ironic comparison: "Il y en a qui donnent la Comédie à leurs Maîtresses; mais donner une Dissection est quelque chose de plus galant" (2:676). When Angélique proves resistant to the marriage, Thomas tries to convince her in the language and style of an academic debate, citing Classical justifications for the use of force in concluding marriages. Angélique's response—"Les Anciens, Monsieur, sont les Anciens, et nous sommes les gens de maintenant" (2:683)—condemns Thomas and his associates to irrelevance, out of touch with the contemporary world that they inhabit. Angélique's *nous* does not include the likes of Thomas Diafoirus. Along similar lines, Magne cites the emblematic ending of *La Jalousie du Barbouillé*, in which the *docteur* leaves without participating in the concluding celebratory feast, bidding the company farewell in Latin ("bonsoir, *latine bona nox*" [2:1087]), a fitting salutation that encapsulates the pedant's linguistic and social exclusion (108).

A second authorial group consists of the amateur writers, individuals who lack the professional training of the pedants and who are not seeking to make a living from their productions, but see in literature a path to cultural capital. Unlike the first group, these authors are generally highly social—indeed, their writings usually target specific audiences, and their writing attempts to enhance their reputation within this coterie or, even more narrowly, with the individual recipient of their efforts. Prominent examples include Mascarille from *Les Précieuses ridicules*, *La Princesse d'Élide*'s Tircis, Éraste from *Les Fâcheux*, *Le Misanthrope*'s Oronte, and the Vicomte and Monsieur Tibaudier from *La Comtesse d'Escarbagnas*.[17] To this list could be added as well Célimène from *Le Misanthrope* and Clitandre from *George Dandin*, letterwriters whose correspondence transcends mere communication through their attention to style and wit. As evidenced by this list, most of these writers come from *le beau monde*, or aspire to mingle with such elevated social company. La Grange makes this connection explicit in the opening scene of *Les Précieuses ridicules* when he states: "J'ai un certain valet nommé Mascarille, qui passe au sentiment de beaucoup de gens pour une manière de bel esprit, car il n'y a rien à meilleur marché que le bel esprit maintenant. C'est un extravagant, qui s'est mis dans la tête de vouloir faire l'homme de condition. Il se pique ordinairement de galanterie, et de vers, et dédaigne les autres valets jusqu'à les appeler brutaux" (1:8). In his parodic imitation of salon life, Mascarille demonstrates the utility (or even the necessity) of writing for gaining a reputation as a *bel esprit*. With its ability to project an image of the author, writing becomes an important component of social posturing or social distinction: when Angélique reads Clitandre's letter in *George Dandin*, she exclaims, "Ah Claudine que ce billet s'explique d'une façon galante! que dans tous leurs discours, et dans toutes leurs actions les gens de Cour ont un air agréable, et qu'est-ce que c'est auprès d'eux que nos gens de Province?" (1:993–94). The sophisticated courtier, even in his letters, needs to distinguish himself from his provincial imitators. As Nicolas Faret counsels would-be social climbers in *L'Honeste Homme* (1640): "Outre les Sciences & l'Histoire, il est tellement necessaire de se former un stile à bien escrire, soit de matieres serieuses, soit de compliments, soit d'amour, ou de tant d'autres suiets dont les occasions naissent tous les iours dans la Cour, que ceux qui n'ont pas cette facilité ne peuvent iamais esperer de grands emplois, ou les ayant n'en doivent attendre que de malheureux succez" (52).[18]

Molière's upper-class amateurs also demonstrate the complex causality of seventeenth-century authorship. While certain of these individuals, like Oronte, are the actual authors of the works that they exhibit in society, others remove themselves from the details, in rhetorical terms taking responsibility for the *inventio* while having others—such as those whom Georges Couton labeled "les ouvriers spécialisés de la mise en vers" (Couton, *Richelieu et le théâtre* 24)—create the finished product. In *Le Bourgeois gentilhomme*, Dorante persuades Dorimène to stay despite her unpleasant encounter with Madame Jourdain by promising some after-dinner entertainment in which he has had a hand: "Outre cela, nous avons ici, Madame, un Ballet qui nous revient, que nous ne devons pas laisser perdre, et il faut bien voir si mon idée pourra réussir" (2:328–29). Dorante has provided the *idée* for the concluding ballet, leaving the details to be worked out by the specialists, but this rhetorical position places Dorante as the ultimate cause of the work, recalling Furetière's and Richelet's definition of *auteur*. The ballet ultimately will be not a verdict on the work of the *maître de musique* or the *maître à danser*, but instead a test of Dorante's originary concept.

Likewise, in *Les Amants magnifiques*, when Aristione asks Timoclès about his efforts in courting her daughter, the prince states, "[J]'ai fait chanter ma passion aux voix les plus touchantes, et l'ai fait exprimer en Vers aux plumes les plus délicates" (2:957). The impressive spectacles that form the comedy-ballet's *intermèdes*, like Dorante's ballet, become ways in which the princes express themselves through the craft of others. "Authors" of the original ideas or emotions, these individuals continue to appropriate for themselves the active role in the productions that result ("j'ai fait exprimer," "mon idée").[19] One final significant example of this authorial variant at work is *La Critique de L'École des femmes*, the idea for which is purportedly supplied to Molière by Dorante in a *mémoire* that recounts the group's conversation. Molière, the *ouvrier spécialisé*, presumably then adapts the work from page to stage.[20]

The final group of authors—and the ones most often given the title—are the professionals, the *gens de lettres* determined to make a career out of writing. Easily outnumbered by the amateurs, they are relatively few: Lysidas in *La Critique de L'École des femmes* and *L'Impromptu de Versailles*, and Trissotin and Vadius in *Les Femmes savantes*. Distinguishing these individuals from the older model of philosopher-pedants is their social facility. These are the aspiring authors described by Alain Viala and Geoffroy Turnovsky who, not coming from privileged backgrounds, are anxious to *faire carrière* by mingling with polite society and forging for themselves an image as witty conversationalists and arbiters of taste. In a sense, this group seeks to combine the erudition of the first group with

Chapter One

the *honnête* ideal of the second, tempering or adapting their humanist education (not always successfully) to the new social milieu of the literary salon. Molière draws attention to this hybridity when he instructs du Croisy in *L'Impromptu de Versailles*: "Vous faites le Poète, vous, et vous devez vous remplir de ce personnage, marquer cet air Pédant qui se conserve parmi le commerce du beau monde" (2:828). The social pretensions of this group oblige them to a difficult balancing act, eschewing the tangible material rewards of authorship, while at the same time using publication to propagate this image. As Turnovsky writes, such feigned disinterest becomes vital for these authors' claims to the social equality of salon attendees, since it "allows the writer, through self-denigration and modesty to lay strong direct claims to the credibility of the *honnête homme*" (57).

The careful rhetorical posing required of authors is readily apparent in Molière's representation of the fraught relationship between authors of all kinds and the publishing industry. The problem is most acute for the amateurs, writers for whom a serious involvement with printing would jeopardize their stance as disinterested dilettantes, "gens de qualité" who can do everything "sans avoir jamais rien appris," in the words of Mascarille (1:19). However, the lure of fame beyond the salons that they frequent tempts these writers to publish their works in more concrete forms than private readings. A prominent example is Oronte: his works have often been recited at the gatherings that Célimène hosts, as evidenced by her letter to Clitandre in which she describes Oronte as "l'Homme à la Veste, qui s'est jeté dans le bel Esprit, et veut être Auteur malgré tout le Monde," adding that "sa Prose me fatigue autant que ses Vers" (1:721); however, despite the circumscribed nature of his original audience—and the sonnet that he recites to Alceste refers directly to his relationship with Célimène—it appears as if Oronte has higher aspirations, indicating to Alceste that he wants to know regarding his sonnet "s'il est bon qu'au Public je l'expose" (1:659). Alceste's response shows clearly that he understands this public exposition in terms of printing, not salon recitation:

> Si l'on peut pardonner l'essor d'un mauvais Livre,
> Ce n'est qu'aux Malheureux, qui composent pour vivre.
> Croyez-moi, résistez à vos tentations,
> Dérobez au Public, ces Occupations;

> Et n'allez point quitter, de quoi que l'on vous somme,
> Le nom que, dans la Cour, vous avez d'honnête Homme,
> Pour prendre, de la main d'un avide Imprimeur,
> Celui de ridicule, et misérable Auteur. (1:663)

Alceste's recommendations to Oronte (jaundiced by his own rivalry with the aspiring poet) establish a strict difference between those to whom printing is permitted—the professionals, those "Malheureux, qui composent pour vivre"—and those who should abstain, namely, the *honnêtes hommes*. Such a view corresponds well with the era's most famous denunciation of printing, Boileau's strict warning to would-be writers in his *Art poétique* (1674):

> Travaillez pour la gloire, et qu'un sordide gain
> Ne soit jamais l'objet d'un illustre Ecrivain.
> Je sçai qu'un noble Esprit peut, sans honte et sans crime,
> Tirer de son travail un tribut legitime:
> Mais je ne puis souffrir ces Auteurs renommez,
> Qui dégoûtez de gloire, et d'argent affammez,
> Mettent leur Apollon aux gages d'un Libraire,
> Et font d'un Art divin un métier mercenaire.
> (*Œuvres complètes* [1966], ed. Escal 183)

While these two statements share an aversion to the book trade and its members (*libraire* or *imprimeur*), the change in audience is significant, although ultimately complementary—Alceste is recommending to an *honnête homme* that he should shun publication in order to avoid becoming an author; Boileau is recommending that authors limit their contact with the book trade in order that they might pass as *honnêtes hommes*. By imitating the detachment of the nobility with regards to the business of writing, Boileau's ideal writer hopes to demonstrate his aptness for polite society, drawing him into the network of patronage that Boileau envisions as the writer's more dignified means of subsistence.[21]

But Molière shrewdly skewers this pretense of disinterest, particularly as it manifests itself in attitudes toward writing or print. In *La Comtesse d'Escarbagnas*, the Vicomte—amateur poet and playwright—recites a gallant poem to Julie, who responds, "[J]e serais bien aise que vous me donniez ces Vers par écrit" (2:1022). The Vicomte protests, "[I]l est permis d'être parfois assez fou pour faire des Vers, mais non pour vouloir qu'ils soient vus" (2:1022). To the Vicomte's continued resistance, Julie replies, "C'est en vain que vous vous retranchez sur une fausse modestie," and later adds, "[V]ous avez beau dire, je vois avec tout cela que vous mourez d'envie de me les donner, et je vous embarrasserais si je faisais semblant de ne m'en pas soucier" (2:1022). The Vicomte's statements are nothing more than a rhetorical pose, *de rigueur* for a nobleman interested in literature, and Julie, perceptive enough to see through the act, obliges him by making the request, her solicitation allowing him to circumnavigate the apparent presumption of presenting his works in written form. Such an excuse is also employed by Mascarille when he mentions the printing of his madrigal history of Rome, stating to Cathos and Magdelon: "Cela est au-dessous de ma condition; mais je le fais seulement pour donner à gagner aux Libraires, qui me persécutent" (1:18). Julie's comments, however, as well as Mascarille's own ridiculous behavior, demonstrate just how much this reticence is merely "fausse modestie," a pretense belied by the true desires and actions of would-be authors.[22]

While the amateur writers must deploy the most careful rhetoric in articulating their relationship with the printing industry, Molière's professionals also tread lightly, particularly since their admission into polite society often involves at least a tacit eschewal of such activities. It is significant that in Trissotin and Vadius's conversation, references to publication appear only once the social niceties are abandoned and the two authors come to verbal blows. Trissotin's first poem is introduced by the author as "un Sonnet, qui chez une Princesse / A passé pour avoir quelque délicatesse" (2:574), placing the poem within the context of a salon recitation. Likewise, when Trissotin introduces Vadius, he describes him as one of the *beaux esprits*, thereby stressing the author's sociability. Vadius himself, although he roundly condemns "l'indigne empressement de lire leurs ouvrages" that is the "défaut des Auteurs" (2:587), nevertheless immediately proposes to read to the company a *ballade* of his own composition. He later also remarks to Trissotin that he heard the latter's sonnet "dans une Compagnie" (2:589).

In short, Trissotin and Vadius, as long as they are maintaining a polite façade, accentuate their social contacts and the salon setting of their productions. However, when the two turn to insults, the more material elements of the literary market make an appearance, as Trissotin states to Vadius, "Souviens-toi de ton Livre, et de son peu de bruit," and Vadius retorts, "Et toi, de ton Libraire à l'Hôpital réduit" (2:591). The fortunes of publication, including book sales, become measures by which to evaluate each other's authorial success, a point reinforced when both agree to settle their literary duel "seul à seul chez Barbin" (2:592). The shop of the *libraire*, while humorously invoked as a convenient site for their combat, becomes also the true arbiter of such a contest: only through the tangible success of their works as demonstrated in the world of *librairie* can the two authors judge who is the victor. Like the lowly "sens et matière" that the *femmes savantes* try in vain to suppress, authorship's connection to the physical world of print inevitably surfaces.

Of all the authors in Molière's corpus, the playwright himself shares the most in common with the professionals—after all, they are fellow playwrights and poets, committed to the *métier*, and engaged in similar efforts at social and literary legitimation. What is surprising, then, is the vehemence with which Molière dismantles the pretensions and posturing of these individuals. The denouement of *Les Femmes savantes* will reveal Trissotin's baser drives, demonstrating that his reputed material disinterest served only to cloak his greed. Furthermore, the polite compliments that Trissotin and Vadius pay, demonstrating deference and admiration for each other's works, degenerate into farcical insults. Similarly, although Lysidas in *La Critique de L'École des femmes* initially refuses to attack Molière's play, stating, "Je n'ai rien à dire là-dessus; et vous savez qu'entre nous autres Auteurs, nous devons parler des Ouvrages les uns des autres, avec beaucoup de circonspection" (1:501), such fine sentiments quickly vanish as Lysidas becomes the work's principal critic. Even before Tartuffe, the professional writer is an emblem of hypocrisy, a manipulator of words whose ultimate goals are far more earthly than the Parnassian glory (or the esteem of his peers) that he cites to justify his actions. Literature turns out to be a lot like lying, as illustrated by Henriette's exchange with Trissotin in *Les Femmes savantes*. When the poet begins to employ the language of poetic gallantry, Henriette objects: "Eh Monsieur, laissons là ce galimatias. / Vous avez tant d'Iris, de Philis, d'Amarantes, / Que partout dans vos Vers vous peignez si charmantes, / Et pour qui vous jurez tant d'amoureuse ardeur …" (2:612). Trissotin responds, "C'est mon esprit qui parle, et ce n'est pas mon cœur. / D'elles on me voit amoureux qu'en Poète; / Mais j'aime tout de bon l'adorable Henriette" (2:612). By Trissotin's

Chapter One

own confession, poetry is an exercise in fiction even when addressed to real people, the creation of a false persona that allows one to speak without engaging the true self. However, Trissotin's declaration of love to Henriette is as fictional as his poetry, as the play's ending will reveal. The author consequently is a dangerous person: a forger of new identities, a cynically calculating rhetorician whose craft involves the precise estimation of the effect on an audience of language designed to pass as authentic.

The professional authors in Molière's theater are the writers who most closely adhere to what Alain Viala called the "stratégie de la réussite." In his examination of seventeenth-century French writers, Viala distinguishes between two different career approaches, the "stratégie de la réussite" and the "stratégie du succès" (184). Of the first, Viala writes:

> La première, la plus fréquente, s'inscrit dans le cadre des normes définies par la structure du champ. Elle se fonde sur des acquis successifs et cumulés de positions dans les secteurs institutionnalisés. Ce principe de progrès dans la hiérarchie au moyen de gains lents, prudents, mais stables, justifie qu'on la désigne comme une "stratégie de la réussite," au sens où l'on parle de réussite sociale pour l'accès à une position influente et solide. (184)

In their social visits, Trissotin, Vadius, and Lysidas are trying to accumulate cultural capital (as Bourdieu would label it), striving for the distinction that can be conferred upon them by *le beau monde*. In addition, they rely on a support network of their fellow writers, looking to them for confirmations of their status. Lysidas's initial critique of *L'École des femmes* is that Molière's play "n'est pas approuvée par les Connaisseurs" (1:501). Lysidas's similar statements questioning the judgment of the court (1:505) and mentioning that "ceux qui possèdent Aristote et Horace voient d'abord ... que cette comédie pèche contre toutes les règles de l'art" (1:506) show his efforts to ground all literary distinction within the narrow social sphere of practitioners, rather than allowing for popular approval to confer such status upon writers. In response to Dorante's axiom that "la grande règle de toutes les règles" is to please, Lysidas sulks, "Enfin, Monsieur, toute votre raison, c'est que *L'École des femmes* a plu; et vous ne vous souciez point qu'elle ne soit pas dans les règles" (2:508). Likewise when Lysidas surfaces again in

L'Impromptu de Versailles, he cites the approval of his peers as the proof of his works' quality: "Il est vrai que j'ai l'avantage de ne me point faire d'ennemis, et que tous mes ouvrages ont l'approbation des savants" (2:838). Lysidas's career strategy, true to Viala's description of the professional trajectory of individuals like Jean Chapelain, is to create connections within his social *champ* and mobilize peer approval into popular success. When he arrives at Uranie's house in *La Critique de L'École des femmes*, he has just given a reading of his new play to another company (and will read the play here as well after all have dined). He adds that "[t]ous ceux qui étaient là, doivent venir à sa première représentation, et m'ont promis de faire leur devoir comme il faut" (1:500). Mascarille in *Les Précieuses ridicules* is more forthcoming regarding the *devoir* to which Lysidas alludes:

> Mais je vous demande d'applaudir, comme il faut, quand nous serons là. Car je me suis engagé de faire valoir la Pièce, et l'Auteur m'en est venu prier encore ce matin. C'est la coutume ici, qu'à nous autres gens de condition, les Auteurs viennent lire leurs Pièces nouvelles, pour nous engager à les trouver belles, et leur donner de la réputation, et je vous laisse à penser, si quand nous disons quelque chose le Parterre ose nous contredire. Pour moi, j'y suis fort exact; et quand j'ai promis à quelque Poète, je crie toujours, voilà qui est beau, devant que les chandelles soient allumées. (1:20)

For authors participating in a *stratégie de la réussite*, the network of support created by academies, salons, and peers is not an alternative to popular success—it is designed to highjack opinion, manipulating the larger public (the *parterre*, as Mascarille mentions) through the ardent backing of the author's allies. Instead of an open forum where the audience acts as an impartial jury, the theater instead becomes the locus of a struggle between partisans whose opinions are decided before the play even begins.[23]

Contrasting with the conservative and ladder-climbing strategy of *réussite* is the authorial strategy of success, of which Viala writes, "La seconde, plus rare, se fonde sur une production destinée en priorité au public élargi, à la conquête de succès, plus éphémères, mais plus spectaculaires" (184). The archetype for this approach is Pierre Corneille, who defended his 1637 tragicomedy *Le Cid* against those who claimed that it violated Classical rules by declaring the pre-eminence of public opinion over the narrower approval of specialists. Writers pursuing this career path leverage the opinion of the *parterre* into authorial legitimation. But public acclaim alone does not suffice—Viala notes that writers pursuing a *stratégie du succès* cannot afford to ignore the powerful institutions of the *champ littéraire*, which still must serve as the foundation for any lasting success: "[T]émoignant d'une plus grande mobilité au sein de l'espace littéraire, elle [la stratégie du succès] repose sur la reconversion de ces profits de renommée publique en signes de reconnaissance et légitimation décernés par les institutions" (184). Corneille's later career is an excellent illustration of this principle: Corneille's membership in the Académie Française (the group responsible for the most notorious criticism of *Le Cid*), his magisterial editions of his complete works, and his theoretical writings allowed him to convert one form of capital into another and ensured the aging playwright continued influence and relevance even after his popularity began to wane.

However, as Mascarille had pointed out, authors relying on peer approval also sought to convert this into a broader form of popularity. In other words, these opposing strategies are really two sides of the same coin, each ultimately aiming at an authorial legitimacy confirmed by both the institutions of the narrower *champ littéraire* and the public at large. Success in one arena is employed to force recognition from the other. Given that, as Viala mentions, the actual careers of seventeenth-century writers show evidence of switching between these approaches, depending on their circumstances, it would appear that the two strategies, despite their "objective" reality, exist in their purest forms as rhetorical stances. Lysidas, for example, trumpets the "approbation des savants" in order to avoid mentioning the lack of success his plays currently enjoy with the wider public—he has certainly not abandoned the possibility of popular success, but falls back upon his strong suits: the theatrical rules that demonstrate that his plays are "toujours bien écrites" and the institutional approval that he receives from his "Confrères" (2:838). If his play were to be performed to great acclaim, a convenient shift in the value to accord to the public's judgment would undoubtedly occur in his argumentation.

Viala's *stratégie du succès* implies a deliberate authorial self-alienation, since writers pursuing this path define themselves in opposition to the collective, their dissimilarity both reinforcing and reinforced by popular appeal. In all of Molière's theater, there is only one writer who takes this stance: Molière himself, staged in *L'Impromptu de Versailles* and played by the author. In this carefully controlled representation of himself and his activities, Molière emphasizes his outsider status. When Lysidas announces the pending debut performance of *Le Portrait du peintre*, the attack on Molière to be staged by the Hôtel de Bourgogne, he states that the play is a collective project:

> Comme tous les Auteurs, et tous les Comédiens regardent Molière comme leur plus grand ennemi, nous nous sommes tous unis pour le desservir; chacun de nous a donné un coup de pinceau à son portrait, mais nous nous sommes bien gardés d'y mettre nos noms; il lui aurait été trop glorieux de succomber aux yeux du monde, sous les efforts de tout le Parnasse. (2:836–37)

Such a statement obviously distorts the reality of Molière's position in the Parisian theatrical and literary worlds. While the Hôtel de Bourgogne clearly aligned itself against the playwright, the actors of the other two major Parisian theaters—the Marais theater and the Italians—never targeted Molière. The Italians shared a theater with Molière's troupe for most of the playwright's Parisian career: from 1658 to 1659 at the *théâtre du Petit-Bourbon* (the Italians will depart for Italy in July) and at the Palais-Royal from January 1662 (date of the Italians' return to Paris) to Molière's death in 1673. One of the members of the Marais troupe, Chevalier, wrote a play—*Les Amours de Calotin*—relatively friendly toward Molière's work. As for the writers, Molière's isolation may be more true—Scott mentions that he "chose to remain on the periphery of literary Paris" (207)—but even in the embattled moments like the *querelle de L'École des femmes*, Molière was not alone: writers like Boileau rallied to Molière's cause precisely because of the literary dispute.[24] Molière's statement (in the character of a ridiculous marquis) that "les Comédiens et les Auteurs, depuis le cèdre jusqu'à l'hysope, sont diablement animés contre lui" (2:838) certainly exaggerates the situation, but it does so deliberately in order to depict Molière as isolated from the *confrérie* of authors, an outsider whose only concern is to please the public and the "Augustes personnes, à qui particulièrement je m'efforce de plaire," as he asserts (2:840).

Chapter One

Molière often adopts an outside perspective in order to mock the eccentricities of smaller and distinctive social worlds (Earle's *champs₂*): recurrent targets like the petty nobility or doctors testify to this interest in the characteristic language and comportment of the inhabitants of these spaces, in which distinction or success are measured in ways invisible or ridiculous to non-participants. However, Molière is not a marquis or a doctor. The situation is much more charged when Molière applies this same treatment to writers and playwrights, as it sends a clear signal that he is a dissenter, a nonconformist who aligns himself with the larger social sphere in ridiculing the authorial world, as his repeated use of the collective and lightly pejorative *messieurs les auteurs* or *messieurs les poètes* demonstrates.[25] Whatever the actual truth may be regarding Molière's interactions with other writers, he chooses to portray himself as a literary maverick who challenges the legitimacy of the "highly differentiated social world" of the *champ littéraire*.

But *L'Impromptu de Versailles* goes beyond merely defining Molière's authorship in opposition to other writers. A supposedly candid portrait of the author, albeit a portrait that shows a harried man busily trying to prepare a new play for the king while he and his troupe deal with the emotional fallout of the *querelle* in which the success of *L'École des femmes* has embroiled them, the play constitutes Molière's authorial *apologia*, the moment when Molière stages himself, his troupe, and his theatrical activities. Of course, the candid and unfiltered portrait that the play supposedly offers needs to be taken with a grain of salt. This is, after all, a representation, and a painstakingly constructed one—Molière's opponents, recognizing its artifice and drawing attention to the piece's deliberately calculated air of negligence, will label it a "three-year impromptu," in reference to the time that it allegedly took Molière to compose it.[26] While the actors answer to their own names, they are nevertheless playing roles (and we might bear in mind as well that many of these proper names are pseudonyms in the first place).

Molière's discussion with Mademoiselle du Parc about the role in which she has been cast subtly alerts the spectator or reader to the *Impromptu*'s game of mirrors: when the actress alleges, "[J]e m'acquitterai fort mal de mon personnage, et je ne sais pas pourquoi vous m'avez donné ce rôle de façonnière," Molière reminds her of her success playing a similar role in *La Critique de L'École des femmes*, before ironically adding, "[E]t vous le jouerez mieux que vous ne pensez" (2:827). To Mademoiselle du Parc's continued protests that "il n'y a point de personne au monde qui soit moins façonnière que moi," Molière responds, "Cela est vrai, et c'est en quoi vous faites mieux voir que vous êtes excellente Comédienne de bien représenter un personnage, qui est si contraire à votre humeur" (2:828). The humor lies in the actress's blindness to her own character traits, as Molière persuades her that the role is designed to highlight her acting abilities, while in reality she is being typecast. But the "reality" here is an illusion—as Molière finely intimates, it is the actress's prior role of Climène, the affected prude of *La Critique de L'École des femmes*, equally resistant to acknowledging her own social posturing, that has led to the popular association between Mademoiselle du Parc and *préciosité*. The *Impromptu* purportedly reveals to a delighted audience that the actress's performance as Climène was in fact no act, inviting the spectators to collapse the distinction between the two of them.[27] For more careful observers, though, the secret is not that Climène corresponds to a real-life Mademoiselle du Parc, but that *L'Impromptu*'s "Mademoiselle du Parc" is as much a fictive *personnage* as the character in *La Critique*.[28]

This in turn highlights the more significant fact that "Molière" is equally fictive, an act of self-fashioning constructed with full consciousness of the spectator's gaze.[29] One spectator in particular: the play turns the king's unseen arrival into the denouement, but it is the king's presence that dictates both the play's existence and the representation that it gives of Molière's authorial activities. When Molière's fellow actors express that he should beg to be excused from the king's command, the playwright contends that "nous ne devons jamais nous regarder dans ce qu'ils [les rois] désirent de nous, nous ne sommes que pour leur plaire; et lorsqu'ils nous ordonnent quelque chose, c'est à nous à profiter vite de l'envie où ils sont" (2:823). Such pious platitudes are the sign of an author who knows that he is being watched.

While *L'Impromptu de Versailles* is not an unmediated magic window into the secret workings of the Palais-Royal, its artificiality makes it instead a valuable document for how Molière chose to portray himself and his work. Perhaps the most surprising aspect of this is how forthcoming the play is regarding the material rewards available to modern successful playwrights. In contrast to Molière's other staged professionals, who seek to hide their appetite for popular success and money, *L'Impromptu de Versailles* flaunts it. Mademoiselle Molière's ironic criticism of Molière's plays underscores their enormous success, describing that "tout Paris" goes to see them and wondering why he cannot be more like Monsieur Lysidas, whose plays may not have "ce grand concours du monde," but that on the other hand enjoy the esteem of his authorial peers (2:838). When Monsieur Lysidas responds that his works are sanctioned by the "savants" (2:838), Mademoiselle Molière responds, "Vous faites bien d'être content de vous, cela vaut mieux que tous les applaudissements du public, et que tout l'argent qu'on saurait gagner aux pièces de Molière. Que vous importe qu'il vienne du monde à vos Comédies, pourvu qu'elles soient approuvées par Messieurs vos Confrères?" (2:838).

It is difficult to imagine a more direct reference to, as Boileau would term it, the "sordide gain" that a playwright could make, and Mademoiselle Molière's statement runs directly counter to the notion that seventeenth-century writers constructed their authorial identities in opposition to the market. In addition, the statement is being made in the most aristocratic setting possible, in the middle of a command performance for the king. That Molière would do so (and equally importantly that he would continue to enjoy the patronage of the king after doing so) speaks to the flexibility of authorial subject-positions in the period. While Molière deliberately reveals his rather bourgeois motivations, such a stance must not have been seen as unbecoming, given that the author was working in the very materialist (and disreputable) world of the (comic) theater.[30] Molière's own reduction of authorship to entertainment ("nous ne sommes que pour leur plaire") presented no claim to moral or social authority—popularity and remuneration undoubtedly seemed the only rewards that someone in Molière's position could expect. The presumptions of Lysidas, who apparently aspires to something more, are laughable, if not disingenuous, and *L'Impromptu de Versailles* claims that the attacks on Molière are motivated not by disinterested authors and actors worried about maintaining theatrical and theoretical purity, but by those who are not as successful as Molière.[31] As Molière stridently announces to his cast members, who recommend that he continue the literary and theatrical quarrel with these opponents, the best possible response to his adversaries is another popular play, particularly since their attacks have as a secondary motive an attempt to make him waste the time that he could otherwise put to more productive use.[32] In other words, not only does Molière emphasize the material rewards that he is receiving as a playwright, but he insists that only such tangible marks of success matter—those who disagree do so out of strategic necessity.

Mademoiselle Molière's irony suggests that "applaudissements" and money are superior benefits to the approval of authorial "confrères," but how significant were Molière's earnings? Turnovsky warns against an excessive reliance on numbers in evaluating the careers of early modern authors, particularly given the difficulties in translating these figures into equivalent modern amounts or estimating buying power.[33] The relative scarcity of reliable data for seventeenth-century writers is a further deterrent. In Molière's case, though, attempts at numerically calculating Molière's earnings as an author have a clear frame of reference: his earnings as an actor, readily known through the *registre* maintained by La Grange, in addition to the surviving account books kept by members of the troupe (La Thorillière for 1663–65; Hubert for 1672–73). Jean-Louis Loiselet's *De quoi vivait Molière?* estimates Molière's total authorial earnings from 1659 to 1673 at 68,000 *livres* (111). This reflects, of course, a number of different revenue sources. The most difficult to calculate is the money that Molière would have received from *libraires* for the publication of his plays. Not much reliable information in Molière's particular case is available, but Alain Viala calculates the typical rate for theater plays to be two hundred to three hundred *livres* (108). One source indicates that Molière received ten times that amount for *Tartuffe*, but this payment appears to have been exceptional (and a bad business deal for the *libraire*).[34] Molière published twenty-two plays over a period of thirteen years (1660 to 1672); if we were to assume that on average he received payments on the upper end of Viala's estimate (the later plays once his reputation was established balancing out the smaller payments he undoubtedly received in the early part of his publication career), that still would indicate that he received somewhere in the order of 6600 *livres* as payment for his publications, or around 500 *livres* annually.[35] To place that number in context, the numbers from La Grange's *registre* place the average annual actor's part from 1659 to 1673 at 3690 *livres*, 2848 of that from public representations alone, with the remainder coming

Chapter One

from *gratifications* for command performances. An actor receiving a full share of the troupe's proceeds during Molière's Parisian career would have received 51,670 *livres* (Duchêne 750). In other words, Molière's earnings from his publications most likely were only between ten to fifteen percent of what he earned as an actor.

However, payments from *libraires* represent only a fraction of Molière's authorial earnings. If, as Viala has claimed, the seventeenth century is the historical moment when it first became possible in France to earn a living as a literary professional, it is not due entirely to profits from publishing, which formed an important but insufficient part of a professional writer's revenue. Instead, as noted above, a writer's total income stems from a variety of sources, including pensions, revenue associated with *charges* or ecclesiastical *bénéfices*, and gifts from patrons. The same is true for Molière—in addition to payments from his *libraires*, the supplemental income that Molière received for his writing must also take into account the annual royal pension of a thousand *livres* that the playwright began to collect in 1663 as a *bel esprit*, upon the recommendation of Jean Chapelain in his *Mémoire sur quelques gens de lettres vivant en 1662* to Colbert, as well as occasional acts of royal largesse directed specifically to Molière, most likely in recognition of having authored the work being performed (Duchêne 323–25).[36]

More significant are the payments from the troupe that Molière received in recognition of his literary efforts. For Molière's earlier Parisian plays, the troupe paid the playwright periodic lump sums: a thousand *livres* for *Les Précieuses ridicules*, paid in two installments; 1500 *livres* for *Sganarelle*, in three installments; 550 *livres* for the theatrical failure *Dom Garcie de Navarre*; and a hundred *louis d'or* (or 1000 *livres*) for *Les Fâcheux*.[37] These amounts are roughly in line with the sums paid to other playwrights who furnished works for the troupe: Gilbert will receive 550 *livres* from the troupe in May 1660 for his *Vraie et Fausse Précieuse* (1:1039), while Pierre Corneille will receive two thousand *livres* each for *Attila* in 1667 and *Tite et Bérénice* in 1671 (1:1083, 2:1126). For Molière's plays beyond *Les Fâcheux*, however, we have little evidence regarding how much the playwright received from the troupe, due most likely to a change in how the payments were determined. Regarding the financial arrangements between actors and authors, Chappuzeau writes, "La plus ordinaire condition &

le plus iuste de costé & d'autre est de faire entrer l'Autheur pour deux parts dans toutes les representations de sa piece iusques à un certain temps" (85–86).³⁸ This was certainly the bargain that the troupe struck with the novice playwright Racine when in 1664 they premiered his first play, *La Thébaïde*. La Grange notes in his *registre* that two parts were given to the author, and La Thorillière later records in his account book that on 31 August 1664 the troupe paid Racine 348 *livres*, "a quoy ont monté les deuz parts dHauteur de la Thebayde" (Schwartz 1066).³⁹

None of the troupe's surviving records is particularly informative regarding the author's shares that Molière received—while La Grange indicates the total ticket receipts for a given performance and the amount of each share, he does not indicate the *frais* that were deducted from the total nor the number of shares; while the *registres* of La Thorillière and Hubert document the expenses, they are equally vague regarding the number of shares. While one might anticipate that this calculation should remain fairly constant, Sylvie Chevalley's analysis of Hubert's *registre* shows that this is not at all the case. Relying on the mathematical calculations on the back of fifty-eight of the daily accounts, Chevalley records that over a period during which the membership of the troupe remained constant (thirteen actors, of which two had half-shares) the number of shares into which a given night's proceeds were divided varied wildly, from 11 ½ to 16 (178).⁴⁰

These calculations do show, however, that the troupe left very little money on the table, essentially distributing each night's profit immediately and entirely—Chevalley remarks, "Il est évident que la troupe fonctionnait sans capital" (149).⁴¹ This observation, coupled with the more precise expenditure details left by La Thorillière and Hubert, can lead to some broad conclusions. Running the numbers from La Thorillière's record of the opening run of *L'Impromptu de Versailles* in 1663, for example, shows that a simple division into the standard number of actors' parts (at the time fourteen) would have left an average of eighty *livres* undistributed; a division into sixteen shares, allowing Molière two author's shares, brings the totals much more in line (an average surplus of just eight *livres*). When *L'Impromptu*'s run ends and the troupe resumes performing older material, such as the performance of *Le Dépit amoureux* on 6 January 1664, a division by sixteen would create a significant deficit (34 *livres*), while a division by fourteen—eliminating any author's shares—would return us to our familiar margins (a slight excess of eleven *livres*). In short, it would appear safe to assume that after *Les Fâcheux,* Molière on the whole began to be paid shares of the opening run, as opposed to receiving a set sum from the troupe for his works.

Undoubtedly the various fortunes of Molière's early plays and the correlative difficulty in estimating a fair author's fee might well have provoked this change, leading the troupe and the playwright to look for a more equitable way to evaluate and recompense Molière's contributions. After all, the theatrical failure *Dom Garcie de Navarre* had earned the playwright 550 *livres*, although the individual actor's part had come to only a little more than 107 *livres*.[42] Conversely, the triumphant first performance run of *Les Fâcheux* brought each actor over 1400 *livres*; an arrangement like that described by Chappuzeau would have brought Molière almost three times the sum actually paid him by the troupe. While it unfortunately remains an argument from silence, the disappearance of authorial payments to Molière in La Grange's *registre* after *Les Fâcheux* most likely means that the troupe reached an arrangement with the playwright similar to that offered later to Racine, in which the author's payment was in direct correlation to the financial fortunes of the play.[43]

Such ambiguities account for the widely divergent estimates of Molière's total authorial earnings over his career: Loiselet mentions scholarly estimates from 57,000 *livres* to 200,000 *livres* before settling on the figure of 68,000 *livres* (112). If Loiselet's assumptions are correct (and his figures on payments from *libraires* seem a bit low), then Molière's authorial earnings at least equaled and most likely exceeded his income from his actor's share. As Loiselet writes, "Ces 68.000 £ représentaient une somme considérable; il faut en effet songer que les camarades de Molière purent mener une vie très aisée avec seulement les deux tiers de cette somme" (112). Factored over the course of his Parisian career, Molière's authorial income, stemming from three sources (book sales; pensions and *gratifications*; payments from the troupe), would have provided a majority of his income, particularly after 1663.

Loiselet notes, "Comme auteur, [Molière] gagnait donc plus que comme acteur, de même que sa renommée d'auteur l'a finalement emporté sur ses succès d'acteur" (112). However, parsing out his income in this manner ignores the symbiosis of Molière's dual careers. Molière's ability to write hits ensured a steady flow of spectators to the Petit-Bourbon and later to the Palais-Royal. Furthermore, his acting abilities (acknowledged even by his enemies) made financial successes out of plays whose literary merits were slender. The result was that Molière became a very wealthy man, undoubtedly surpassing even the economic rewards he would have enjoyed if he had pursued the family business and become a *tapissier*. There was no irony in Mademoiselle Molière's statement about "tout l'argent qu'on saurait gagner aux pièces de Molière" concerning the very real financial rewards that the actor and playwright received from his theatrical career.

While Molière's insistence on defining theatrical success in terms of popularity and money are surprising to the degree that it runs counter to the image of noble disinterest that many of his contemporaries tried to convey, equally surprising (though for different reasons) is his representation of theatrical composition. Scholars since Bray have insisted on the dynamic and dialogical roots of Molière's plays, undoubtedly the products of theatrical "workshopping" in which the members of the troupe brought their own contributions and corrections to the playwright's original draft both before and during the course of a performance run.[44] Zanger writes, commenting on the preface to *Les Fâcheux*, "What Molière is showing, I believe, is that theater is not a phenomenon ruled by one authority—the lonely actor can do nothing to pull together chaos, nor can his failure mean the failure of the play. Theater is not the precisely controlled product of one mind; it is precipitated, coagulated out of many elements" (181). To a certain degree, *L'Impromptu de Versailles* demonstrates this collaborative and collective nature of theater, as the various troupe members resist Molière's efforts to rehearse his new play and eventually refuse to act—in fact, Molière's wife tells her husband, "[V]ous deviez faire une Comédie où vous auriez joué tout seul" (2:824). However, despite whatever actual compositional conditions may have prevailed in Molière's troupe, the way that theatrical authorship is portrayed in *L'Impromptu de Versailles* is strikingly absolutist, with the playwright clearly in charge, assigning roles, words, and delivery to the other actors. Molière is the author as source, and the actors become consequentially the (imperfect) receptacles for a text that is given to them by a higher authority. Their only responsibility is to transmit the original word in a form that is as uncorrupted as possible, exemplified by the fact that Molière not only communicates to the actors the words they are to say, but how they are to say them.[45]

More importantly, Molière draws a very clear contrast between his activity and theirs, responding to their anxieties by exclaiming, "Vous voilà tous bien malades d'avoir un méchant rôle à jouer, et que feriez-vous donc si vous étiez en ma place?" (2:822). The specificity of this "place" is defined in the resulting exchange: when Mademoiselle Béjart replies, "Qui vous! vous n'êtes pas à plaindre, car ayant fait la Pièce vous n'avez pas peur d'y manquer" (2:822)—situating Molière among the actors and remarking that he already knows his lines—Molière points instead to his role as author, distinguishing himself from the rest of the troupe, stating, "Et n'ai-je à craindre que le manquement de mémoire? ne comptez-vous pour rien l'inquiétude d'un succès qui ne regarde que moi seul?" (2:822). The collective enterprise has here become remarkably singular, as Molière claims to be running the only real risk, his authorial reputation riding on the outcome of the play. Of course, if the play's failure due to the incompetence of the actors will be attributed to the playwright, it is implied as well that the lone individual would also enjoy the credit for the play's success. Authorship is at the root of this distinction, as Molière's reply makes clear, moving from the individual responsibility of the actor ("le manquement de mémoire") to the larger liability of the playwright, reinforced a few lines later when Molière adds, "Est-il Auteur qui ne doive trembler, lorsqu'il en vient à cette épreuve?" (2:822). While Molière's celebration of theater's polyvocality might be discerned in his theater as a whole, it is significant that in *L'Impromptu de Versailles*, his most direct representation of theatrical authorship, Molière does indeed portray theater as ruled by a single controlling authority, unable at times to submit everything to his will, but who will bear the ultimate responsibility.

This is in part because Molière's theater, following the French theatrical tradition, remains on solidly textual grounds. While numerous studies have pointed out the significant and extensive influence of the Italian *commedia dell'arte* on Molière's acting style and plots, Molière's troupe never adopted the improvisational approach of their transalpine colleagues with whom they shared a theater for most of Molière's career.[46] Or, more cautiously, we might state that the more literary approach is at least the image that Molière would like to convey. In *L'Impromptu de Versailles*, the actors' sense of their role remains emphatically text-based, as the exchange between the principal actresses illustrates:

> Mademoiselle du Parc: Pour moi je vous déclare que je ne me souviens pas d'un mot de mon Personnage.
> Mademoiselle de Brie: Je sais bien qu'il me faudra souffler le mien, d'un bout à l'autre.
> Mademoiselle Béjart: Et moi je me prépare fort à tenir mon rôle à la main. (2:822)

Rôle here is both abstract and concrete, as the actress needs the literal piece of paper in hand in order to know her part. When Molière suggests that, given that the play is in prose and that they already know the general outlines of plot and character, the actors could "suppléer," inventing and improvising in the moment, Mademoiselle Béjart responds, "Je suis votre Servante, la Prose est pis encore que les Vers" (2:823). Her rejection, echoed at the end of the play by the chorus of actresses refusing to perform when the king arrives, emphasizes not only the importance of word-for-word memorization of the part, but also the more elevated literary status of French theater—as Mademoiselle Béjart insists, she is more accustomed to reciting theater in verse.

But Madeleine's response also constitutes a refusal to become a creative agent, at least on the order of the script. If *L'Impromptu de Versailles* is meant to show us the preparation of a new play, it does so in a way that is remarkably author-driven. In Samuel Chappuzeau's *Théâtre françois*, the description of a new play's reception emphasizes the discernment, critical judgment, and editorial capacities of the actors. As Chappuzeau writes:

> [O]n s'assemble ou au Theâtre, ou en autre lieu, & l'Autheur sans prelude ny reflexions (ce que les Comediens ne veulent point) lit sa piece avec le plus d'emphase qu'il peut; car il n'y a pas icy tant de danger de jetter de la poudre aux yeux des Iuges, & il ne s'agit ny de mort, ny de procez. Ioint qu'il seroit difficile de tromper en cela les Comediens, qui entendent mieux cette matiere que le Poëte. A la fin de chaque Acte, tandis que le Lecteur prend haleine, les Comediens disent ce qu'ils ont remarqué de fâcheux, ou trop de longueur, ou un couplet languissant, ou une passion mal touchée, ou quelques vers rudes, ou enfin quelque chose de trop libre, si c'est du Comique. Quand toute

> la piece est leüe, ils en jugent mieux, ils examinent si l'intrigue
> est belle & bien suivie, & le denoûment heureux. ... (80–82)

While *L'Impromptu* stages a precipitated and unfinished instance of the process, the play nevertheless underlines Molière's control—there is little to none of the dialogue or exchange that Chappuzeau describes. Perhaps the nearest equivalent is Mademoiselle Béjart's interruption of the rehearsal to say to Molière, "[S]i j'avais été en votre place, j'aurais poussé les choses autrement" (2:839), followed shortly by Mademoiselle de Brie's statement, "Ma foi, j'aurais joué ce petit Monsieur l'Auteur, qui se mêle d'écrire contre des gens qui ne songent pas à lui" (2:840–41). Both of these suggestions are immediately dismissed by Molière, and there is no indication that the other actors could or will follow up on their own ideas.

But if *L'Impromptu de Versailles* portrays the theatrical process as author-driven, it appears to highlight the failure of this model. Despite his superior position, Molière is unable to enforce his commands or make the actors behave in the ways that he would like. Remarkably, *L'Impromptu de Versailles* consequently places Molière in the same situation as most of his other writers—a would-be authoritarian, trying to enforce his control through texts and whose efforts are ultimately frustrated. The candid portrait seems to be one of authorial failure, the interruptions and unrelated tangents leaving an embarrassed Molière apologizing to the king. Like Arnolphe, Sganarelle, or Alceste, at the end of the play Molière is standing in the midst of a theatrical situation that has bested him, careening out of his control. Despite the differences that he has alleged between him and *messieurs les auteurs*, the end result seems to be the same. We might almost expect a final Arnolphian "Oh!" as the author, bereft of all authority and having failed to impose his scripted will onto others, retreats into solitude.

But such a reading ignores the fact that *L'Impromptu de Versailles* is constructing the authorial image of two Molières, not one. The play does indeed stage the failure of what we might call Molière$_1$, the character on stage (or the *actor*, to borrow the medieval sense of the term, that is, the interior author unable to intercede in the work). But the production itself—supposedly spontaneous and unscripted—is generated by another authorial Molière, Molière$_2$, the authoritative *auctor* whose careful planning is fully evident in the play's witty and deceptive denial of its own artifice. The disorder is all feigned, the failure to mount an adequate response to the attacks of Molière's enemies contradicted by the play's adept mockery. To the extent that it accomplishes precisely what it claims to be omitting, the play is one long theatrical exercise in preterition. Like Molière's prologue to *Les Fâcheux*, which it imitates, the seeming disarray in *L'Impromptu de Versailles* is a model of *sprezzatura*, an air of charming negligence hiding its careful and deliberate crafting.[47] Since even the presumed objections of the actors are scripted, the reign of the author is total, not the author on the stage, but the author behind the scenes, who deliberately and triumphantly represents his own failure. As the playwright stands before the king, scraping and apologizing, in actuality two models of absolutism are brought face to face. That both are ultimately theatrical and fictive does not change the significance of the intended representation. Molière's counterfeit unpreparedness asserts all the more forcefully that the author really has everything in hand, like the young king who had just adopted the year before the image of the sun as his *devise*, persuaded by those who claimed to see him "gouverner avec assez de facilité et sans être embarrassé de rien" (Louis XIV, *Mémoires* 172).

The ordered chaos of *L'Impromptu de Versailles*—a display of the studied naturalness so prized by the era—has important implications for Molière's other works in which the defeat of authority (and writing) is staged. The irony of such reverses is that they are always scripted. Clitidas, to recall the example of *Les Amants magnifiques*, may mock those who blindly defer to what is printed, and yet he himself exists only as the product of writing. Moreover, the mocking of astrology or the inevitability of *histoires* becomes doubly ironic within the context of the printed text, where *ce qui est moulé* does in fact become incontestable. If Anaxarque's reading of the stars is inexact, unable to read the teleology of the story in which he himself is a character, the reader suffers from no such blindness. Unlike astrology, whose falsity is demonstrated by the princess Ériphile's observation that, following Anaxarque's premises, "il faut donc qu'on trouve écrit dans le Ciel, non seulement ce qui doit arriver, mais aussi ce qui ne doit pas arriver" (2:980), the play's printed text contains only what must inevitably take place.

To this extent, Molière's writing works in opposition to the writing and writers that he stages, and not only because Molière defines his own professional comportment in sarcastic counterpoint to *messieurs les auteurs*. In the majority of cases Molière's writers self-assuredly present texts designed to increase their authority but that ultimately betray them, revealing an unflattering image of their writers as *ridicules*. If the texts of Molière's writers are mirrors in which their own flaws unwittingly appear, Molière's texts, by incorporating these flaws, point to a self-aware author who transcends them. The critique of writing is a game that the writer has already co-opted. If the individual authors (or the *actores*) of Molière's theater fare poorly, the overarching authority of writing is guaranteed by the *auctor*, who even while staging his own defeat remains in charge, as the spectacular "failure" of *L'Impromptu de Versailles* demonstrates. For Molière, theater is certainly performance, but it is a performance that he wants to insist is rooted in textuality and authorial control.

That such control is impossible—and probably at odds with Molière's own actual dramaturgical praxis—merely serves as an important but subtle reminder: "Molière," the implied author forged by the plays and their representations of writers and writing, is as much a fictional character as the "Molière" presented on stage in *L'Impromptu de Versailles*. A seventeenth-century author, in the end, is not so much born as negotiated—rhetorically and concretely—through often-acrimonious relations in a world of new and dizzying possibilities. As Molière himself wrote, making people laugh was "une étrange entreprise" (1:505). To a similar degree, comedic authorship for the playwright was a constant work in progress, and the following chapters will trace the changing ways in which Molière played his authorial role. In this sense, "Molière"—the stage name that became a pen name—represents nothing less than Jean-Baptiste Poquelin's greatest and longest-running creation, an invented character carefully elaborated over time as the real-world author navigated the changing world of the Parisian *champ littéraire*.

Chapter Two

The Early Plays and the Pirates Who Loved Them

> Il est vrai, pour me consoler, que j'ai du moins cette ressemblance avec Shakespeare et Molière, que ceux qui les ont attaqués étaient si obscurs, qu'aucune mémoire n'a conservé leur nom.
> —Alexandre Dumas
> "Comment je devins auteur dramatique"

Molière returned to Paris in 1658 after thirteen years performing in the provinces. The years that followed saw an extraordinary rise in the success and fortunes of the actor, author, and director. A mere six years after Molière's return, a character resentful of the playwright's success will lament in Philippe de La Croix's *La Guerre comique*:

> De La Rancune: C'est le diable qui l'emporte, l'ignorant qu'il est, les poètes et les comédiens ont éte de grands sots de le laisser prendre racine à Paris, au lieu de former une bonne cabale la première fois qu'il montra son nez, au lieu de publier que sa troupe était détestable et de la décrier fortement. (Molière, *Œuvres complètes* [1971] 1:1141)

Cléone, another participant in the staged discussion, confirms that in the few short years following his arrival, Molière has acquired a certain immunity to criticism—the attacks of his rivals are at base merely parasitic: "Il n'y a plus que lui qui enrichisse les comédiens, et quand on a fait *Le Portrait du peintre*, on n'avait pas dessein de diminuer sa réputation, elle est trop bien établie, on cherchait seulement le moyen de gagner de l'argent à la faveur de son nom" (1:1142). While the other theatrical interlocutors do not always agree with Cléone and De La Rancune, La Croix's characters are unanimous in acknowledging that Molière's theatrical successes have given him a degree of invulnerability: his opponents may criticize him for their own profit, but they are now powerless to make their accusations stick because of Molière's standing with the general public.

The following two chapters examine Molière's ultimately successful attempts to establish his authorial reputation despite the efforts of rival authors and actors, as well as unscrupulous *libraires*. While De La Rancune's comments are spoken in the context of the *querelle de L'École des femmes*, discussed in Chapter 3, they draw particular attention to the vulnerability of new arrivals on the Parisian literary scene, as Molière would have been in 1658. De La Rancune's description of Molière's early years and his regret for "une bonne cabale" falsely intimate that the rivals of Molière did little to impede his success. This chapter's study of Molière's first three printed plays—*Les Précieuses ridicules* (premiered in 1659; printed in 1660), *Sganarelle* (1660), and *L'École des maris* (1661)—reveals instead that Molière had to assert his authorial rights vigorously in the face of numerous attempts by *libraires* and rival authors looking to take advantage of his newcomer status to appropriate his works for their own gain. If by the time of *L'École des femmes* Molière had become untouchable, it is only as the result of the protracted struggles fought during this early period of his Parisian career, struggles that proved vital to the shaping of Molière's authorial persona and to the nature of his later interactions with the publishing industry.

Piracy and Plagiarism

The key figure in the attempts to profit unethically from Molière's theater was a Parisian *libraire* named Jean Ribou, about whom little is known prior to his interactions with Molière. Aiding Ribou were several minor authors—Baudeau de Somaize, the sieur de Neuf-Villenaine, F. Doneau—whose identities and professional trajectories have been the subject of much speculation and debate with little clear consensus on the subject.[1] Their attempts to profit from Molière's plays took two forms: outright attempts to publish and sell Molière's plays themselves (a practice, similar in some respects to modern examples of copyright infringement, referred to as piracy for the purposes of this study), and efforts to take the language and ideas of the plays and produce closely derivative works attributed to another author (here loosely labeled plagiarism).[2]

Piracy and plagiarism correspond roughly to the main returns that an author of Molière's generation could expect from a successful literary publication: money and reputation. Books, and particularly the novels, poetry, and theatrical works that comprised the category of *nouveautés*, were becoming an increasingly valuable commodity, and an entire industry (especially prominent in the provinces and the Netherlands) was rapidly developing of *libraires* who made a living printing books for which they had not purchased the rights nor paid the authors. At times, these pirate editions were simple reproductions of published Parisian editions, closely mimicking the layout and typeset of their model.[3] On other occasions rogue printers succeeded in procuring an unpublished manuscript and brought out editions for which the authors received no payment and which could even be potentially embarrassing or incriminating.[4]

Book piracy represented the failures of the administrative structure that had come to be the chief regulatory method for the printing industry, the royal privilege system. At its origin, the royal privilege was far removed from modern concepts of copyright or *droit d'auteur*. A special dispensation of the king administered through the officers of the *Chancellerie*, a royal privilege granted to either author or bookseller a special monopoly for the sale of a particular title and, by so doing, helped to assure a return on the financial investment necessary to print the book. The privilege was often given as a favor for services rendered or as a reward for works considered beneficial to the public, much the way that early patents were used to reward useful innovations (Armstrong 1). This changed in 1566, when Charles IX decreed in the Edict of Moulins that no new book could be printed without a royal privilege. The Edict of Moulins transformed what had formerly been a voluntary request for the king's favor into an obligatory and, more importantly, regulatory part of the printing process during a time when the printing press had become a favorite weapon of feuding religious factions. Receiving a privilege was contingent upon review and censorship by royal officers, which allowed for stricter control over what had proved over the course of the sixteenth century to be an industry apt to spreading unorthodox and, from the monarchy's point of view, seditious ideas.

Chapter Two

Thus from 1566 onward, the privilege system had acquired a dual function: to grant whoever had paid the printing costs a period in which to recoup their investment and to ensure that published materials were not, to use a contemporary phrase, "composez contre l'Estat, contre la Religion et les bonnes mœurs" (Thuasne 54). This second function gained importance under Cardinal Richelieu and into the reign of Louis XIV, with additional measures taken to further control the printing and sale of new books. Most significantly, in 1649 laws were passed requiring that all privileges be registered with the *Communauté des libraires* in order to be valid (Pottinger 216).

The author was by no means obliged to participate in this process, as a privilege could be requested by either the author or the prospective publisher of a manuscript. By the mid-seventeenth century, the proportions were roughly even (Schapira 125). Where the author requested the privilege, it was almost always immediately transferred to one or more *libraires* for a set sum of money, determined in a private transaction. The sale of the privilege represented the end of an author's legal control over the text; while an author could be involved in proofreading the printed copies, the transfer of the book's privilege meant that the *libraire* became the sole proprietor and, under the terms of most seventeenth-century contracts between author and publisher, was the only one to profit or lose from the book's sales.

With the eventual rights to the book ending up exclusively in the hands of booksellers, the privilege system worked largely in the favor of *libraires*, rather than authors, whose rights, commoditized by the privilege, were completely transferred upon the sale of the privilege and manuscript. In fact, the ability for authors to be completely absent from the process of obtaining a privilege could lead to ambiguities and fraud: in cases where a publisher submitted an author's manuscript to the censors and requested a privilege, royal officers at the *Chancellerie* would have had little way of knowing whether the publisher's manuscript was legally obtained or not, due to the private nature of all transactions between authors and publishers. It is important to note, though, that even if the privilege system itself did not always grant to authors direct control over their manuscripts, the larger legal system did: French courts as early as 1504 had ruled against publishers who printed manuscripts against the will of their authors, ordering that the author in such cases be given the printed books or be fairly compensated (Cynthia Brown 19).[5]

By the mid-seventeenth century, the privilege system was a strange hybrid. Although it had become heavily bureaucratized, administered by the officers of the *Chancellerie*, and an integral part of the publication process, it was not synonymous with modern conceptions of copyright or personal property. The title page of every legally published new book reminded the reader that printing was literally a privilege, not a right, and that this privilege did not exist independent of the special grace that only the sovereign could bestow. With the multiplication of printed books, and the attendant multiplication of royal permissions to print, the privilege system constituted to an ever greater extent a strange paradox, a tenuous marriage between official standardized procedure and personalized exception.

While the privilege system certainly had its flaws, the most notable of which was its underlying refusal to accord any sort of statutory right of authors to their texts, its normalizing effect did much to control unauthorized printing. This was of course limited to the realm of royal jurisdiction: as a purely national (and more particularly Parisian) system, officers of the *Chancellerie* could do little about the Dutch printing of French editions, for example, and had to content themselves with controlling their sale in France. Although the counterfeiting of French books in the provinces or abroad was at times widespread, the privilege system nevertheless created a useful distinction between "good" and "bad" editions by specifying a proper legal avenue for publication. Since texts (and not just books as objects) had owners, theft became both possible and prosecutable.

For another, and far older, literary crime, such clear-cut legal distinctions were noticeably lacking. Of plagiarism, Georges Maurevert has pessimistically written, "[R]ien jamais ne guérira les écrivains du plagiat; aussi vieux que la littérature, il ne finira qu'avec elle" (319). If book piracy, as the violation of *privilège* or copyright, can only occur when a society has commoditized the abstract "text" of a particular work, plagiarism, or the unauthorized use of a work's ideas or expressions, has indeed been a constant companion of literary creation.[6]

In its seventeenth-century form, however, the idea of plagiarism presents certain difficulties, the chief of which is its existence in

Chapter Two

an era that actively encouraged literary imitation and had only the most rudimentary legal specifications of intellectual property or authors' rights. Georges Forestier, commenting on the accusations of plagiarism brought against Molière, has written, "Ce qui surprend, ce n'est pas l'existence du fait, c'est qu'il ait été dénoncé" (70), adding that Molière's enemies "se disqualifiaient eux-mêmes en reprochant à Molière un principe esthétique qui était celui de tout un siècle" (70).[7]

It should be noted, though, that imitation had its limits. Not all models were considered equally available for appropriation, and it is not surprising that an era so familiar with literary imitation would seek to distinguish between various forms—legitimate and illegitimate—of borrowing. La Mothe Le Vayer sought to make explicit such distinctions when he wrote, "Prendre des anciens et faire son profit de ce qu'ils ont écrit, c'est comme pirater au delà de la ligne; mais voler ceux de son siècle, en s'appropriant leurs pensées et leurs productions, c'est tirer la laine aux coins des rues, c'est ôter les manteaux sur le pont Neuf" (Randall 292). The seizure of property was morally relative: a French privateer attacking Spanish ships was ostensibly not committing the same act as a thief operating in central Paris. Similarly, distance—whether spatial, temporal, or linguistic—allowed authors to portray their borrowings as a useful service for the common good, either metaphorically plundering an enemy or rescuing and rehabilitating texts which might otherwise be lost.[8] In François de Callières's *Histoire poëtique de la guerre nouvellement déclarée entre les Anciens et les Modernes* (1688), for example, Plautus and Terence express their gratitude to Molière for refamiliarizing French audiences with their works, eliding the fact that Molière had never identified them as sources for his plays (143–46). Such borrowings, straddling the border between translation and adaptation, could be considered legitimate forms of imitation, whether they were acknowledged or not. As Pierre Perrault wrote:

> Que si un traducteur se sent plus capable que l'Auteur même de traiter son sujet, je trouve fort bon qu'il fasse comme a fait Scarron pour ses *Nouvelles espagnoles*, ou Molière pour les comédies d'*Amphitryon*, de l'*Avare*, du *Médecin malgré lui* & autres. Ces deux illustres Auteurs se sont contentez de prendre seulement les sujets de ces nouvelles & de ces comédies lesquels ils ont traités à leur manière qui est toute différente de celle de

> leurs premiers auteurs, laissant à juger à qui le voudra faire s'ils y ont bien ou mal réussi, ce qui est une émulation non seulement honnête & louable & qui n'offense personne, mais qui donne du plaisir & du contentement par la diversité de la narration & du style; & c'est en ce sens & cette façon, que des Traductions se peuvent appeler d'autres originaux. ... (Yilmaz 174)

In this passage, Perrault not only excuses Molière and Scarron, but even elevates them to the status of models to be imitated. Not everyone, however, agreed with Perrault on where to draw the line between legitimate imitation and plagiarism. The identical compositional process advocated by Perrault could still expose an author to accusations of theft, as demonstrated by the arguments brought against Corneille during the 1637 *querelle du Cid*. More surprisingly, even the open acknowledgement of a literary source could fail to excuse an author's literary borrowings, as will be seen below in the case of Doneau and *La Cocue imaginaire* (1660). Considering the number of authors accused of plagiarism, and the variety of authorial methods condemned in such attacks, it is tempting to conclude that the seventeenth century is the era *par excellence* for Marilyn Randall's aphorism that "plagiarism is in the eye of the beholder" (vii).

While it may indeed seem surprising to see the number and scope of such accusations in an era before the codification of authors' rights, it is precisely this legal lacuna that explains their presence and proliferation. Without a legal definition of the phenomenon, and with little or no possible legal repercussions for the accuser or the accused, accusations of plagiarism for Molière and his contemporaries were ubiquitous. Such accusations, however, remained largely an internal affair of the Republic of Letters, adjudicated only by fellow authors and the reading public. In this sense, such attacks targeted only an author's reputation, and it is thus not surprising at all to see jealous rivals take aim at spectacularly successful works such as *Le Cid* and *L'École des femmes*, not because they were the authors robbed, but in an attempt to undermine the works' claim to novelty and dampen the public's enthusiasm. Plagiarism, according to the broad definition espoused by Molière's contemporaries, thus became one more way in which authorial reputation was measured and negotiated.

While plagiarism and book piracy are distinct in their methods and aims—one focusing on what might be called the properly literary, the other acting in the realm of property or commodities—they are linked in concrete ways, as payment for manuscripts was tied to authorial reputation.[9] There nevertheless remains an important difference: while book piracy aims strictly for profit, plagiarism (while potentially lucrative as well) has the additional goal of setting up the plagiarist as author, and the numerous condemnations of the practice by Molière and his contemporaries underline that plagiarism is an attempt to "se donner de la réputation à peu de frais," in the words of a spectator who, according to Grimarest, found that Molière was borrowing too closely from his sources (16–17).

Les Précieuses ridicules: An Author Is Born

Issues of plagiarism and piracy marked Molière's publishing career from the very outset: in fact, Molière's entry into the world of print in 1660 was precipitated by an attempt to publish and sell *Les Précieuses ridicules* without the author's consent. The perpetrator was the Parisian *libraire* Jean Ribou, who acquired a copy of Molière's popular play through unknown means, and proceeded to ask for and obtain a royal privilege granting him the rights to the play's publication and sale.[10]

In some respects, Jean Ribou's projected edition of *Les Précieuses ridicules* seems just one more occurrence of book piracy—after all, as discussed above, printing a stolen manuscript was not legal, but neither was it unusual. However, in other regards Ribou's attempt to steal Molière's play was distinct from conventional book piracy. In the first place, Ribou applied for a privilege and received permission to print Molière's play. While pirate editions occasionally included a privilege, this was most often either a copy of the original to which the publishers did not have the rights, or a purely fictitious one. Such privileges were included to give an air of legitimacy to the edition, although, as Henri-Jean Martin has remarked, there is a certain irony in such publishers including in their pirate editions the very text that spells out the punishment for the book's theft (*Livre* 2:755).

Ribou's privilege, though, was not fabricated or falsified, obtained, as it was, from the proper authorities and duly registered with the *Communauté des libraires*. In effect, Ribou sought out and obtained the permission of all the officers in a position to legitimate his printing, with the sole exception of the author. Ribou's purpose, it can thus be assumed, was not so much an outright attempt to steal the play, publishing it without any sort of permission, as it was an effort to produce an edition that bordered on legitimacy, contingent upon the author's apathy or unwillingness to assert his rights aggressively. The explicit permission of the author, the first step toward publication, was both institutionally unnecessary from the point of view of the privilege system, and the most difficult element to verify. Physical possession of a manuscript was beyond doubt, as was that manuscript's approval or rejection by royal censors; ascertaining the author's approval, on the other hand, could only take the form of legal investigations into the contract (or lack thereof) between author and *libraire*.

Ribou's edition was in many ways a calculated crime. Although obtaining and registering a privilege would have sharply increased the visibility of his publication attempt, thus increasing the chances of getting caught, this very participation could also serve as his legal defense. The *Chancellerie* and the *Communauté des libraires* were both charged with policing the book trade in the capital, which made it significantly more dangerous for Parisian *libraires* to engage in the sorts of wholesale book piracy that occurred regularly in the provinces. Ribou's shop was located on the Quai des Augustins, far from the fashionable center of the *nouveautés* trade near the Palais de Justice, which suggests that his economic situation did not permit him to compete effectively against the more established *libraires*. Ribou may have thus attempted to produce his semilegitimate edition on a calculated wager that Molière, as a vulnerable new author, would have neither the means nor the knowledge to find out about, prevent, and punish a stolen edition of his play.

Ribou obtained his privilege from the *Chancellerie* on 12 January 1660 and registered it with the *Communauté des libraires* on 18 January 1660. Ribou's edition, however, was stifled before it could appear, as Molière learned of the scheme in time to block Ribou's edition and rush into print his own version printed by Guillaume de Luyne. De Luyne obtained a new privilege for the *Les Précieuses ridicules* with Molière's permission on 19 January 1660 and had it registered on 20 January 1660, thereby annulling Ribou's privilege (Thuasne 7). No copies of Ribou's edition are known to exist, making it doubtful that he actually carried through with the printing. In a sense, this supports the hypothesis that Ribou was not interested in outright piracy—as soon as his privilege was annulled, which would have made his edition clearly illegal, he abandoned the project, backing down in the face of an author who had not proved sufficiently complacent.

Molière demonstrated a clear degree of assertiveness in rapidly blocking Ribou's edition and producing his own, but the preface that he included to *Les Précieuses ridicules* seems to contradict this by portraying the author as passive and reluctant, even loftily removed from the world of printing and profits. This preface allowed Molière his first opportunity to appear before the reading public as an author, but the opening sentence emphasizes instead his unwillingness to do so: "C'est une chose étrange, qu'on imprime les Gens, malgré eux" (Molière 1:3). Molière insists that he was content with his work's theatrical success and had no desire to see it move "du Théâtre de Bourbon, dans la Galerie du Palais" (1:3). He cites the events surrounding Ribou's edition as the reason for his change of opinion:

> Cependant je n'ai pu l'éviter, et je suis tombé dans la disgrâce de voir une copie dérobée de ma pièce, entre les mains des Libraires, accompagnée d'un Privilège obtenu par surprise. J'ai eu beau crier, ô temps! ô mœurs! on m'a fait voir une nécessité pour moi d'être imprimé, ou d'avoir un procès, et le dernier mal est encore pire, que le premier. Il faut donc se laisser aller à la destinée, et consentir à une chose, qu'on ne laisserait pas de faire sans moi. (1:3–4)

By insisting that his play is only being published as a preventative measure against Ribou's pirate edition, Molière neatly avoids the stigma associated with print in the early modern period. Molière also makes a clear, and traditional, distinction between his play as performance and as text. As performance, the play is demonstrably good, according to its favorable popular reception. However, the passage from performance to print supposedly troubles the playwright: "comme une grande partie des graces, qu'on y a trouvées, dépendent de l'action, et du ton de voix, il m'importait, qu'on ne les dépouillât pas de ces ornements" (1:3).

It is difficult to ascertain to what extent Molière is sincere in his stated reluctance to publish. On the one hand, this sort of coy positioning on the part of an author was typical of an era when tensions were strong between the older authorial (and aristocratic) stance that discouraged the professionalization of literature and the emerging generation of writers eager to take advantage of their new economic possibilities. The reluctance to publish, coming as it does in the preface to a printed work, is particularly untrustworthy, and even at times deliberately ironic. Molière may very well be insisting that he wants no part of the sordid world of *libraires* and literary profits while secretly rejoicing that Ribou's attempted piracy afforded him such an ideal chance to publish.

On the other hand, there are other factors that could support a reading of Molière's preface as at least partially sincere. Publishing meant making certain literary claims that performance did not, and an author attentive to literary reputation would have been discriminating in what she or he chose to publish. It was a critical commonplace to point out the disparity between a play's performance and its reception in the *cabinet* of the reader, a comparison that rarely worked in favor of the printed text.[11] The difference in reception would be greater for genres such as farce, whose success depended heavily on performance and *lazzi*, than for "serious" literary comedies following Renaissance and Classical models. In its discussion of the now-lost Molière farce *Le Docteur amoureux*, the preface to the 1682 *Œuvres de Monsieur de Molière* posthumously attributes to the playwright an editorial sensibility most likely shared by many of his contemporaries, stating, "Cette Comédie qui ne contenait qu'un Acte, et quelques autres de cette nature, n'ont point été imprimées: [Molière] les avait faites sur quelques idées plaisantes sans y avoir mis la dernière main; et il trouva à propos de les supprimer, lorsqu'il se fut proposé pour but dans toutes ses pièces d'obliger les hommes à se corriger de leurs défauts" (1:1101).

The preface's statement on Molière's publishing practices merits a closer look, even as it needs to be taken with a healthy degree of skepticism. The notion of Molière striving in "toutes ses pièces" to correct faults is hagiographic, a vice in which the preface does not hesitate to indulge itself. Furthermore, Molière could not have possibly reserved for publication only those works with significant moral heft. After all, while it is unsure what vices a play such as *Les Fourberies de Scapin* (1671) could have possibly purged in its spectator, Molière did not hesitate to publish it. Molière certainly did not suppress the performance of farces, and even incorporated elements of farce into his *grandes comédies*—rival authors during the *querelle de L'École des femmes* would incessantly point to these "baser" elements in the play. But if Molière did indeed pen short farces like the two that have been attributed to him retrospectively—*La Jalousie du Barbouillé* and *Le Médecin volant*—they do not appear among his printed editions, evidence that the degree of Molière's hesitation to print might be directly linked to issues of genre.

In the preface's statement, genre intersects with morality, attributing to "high" comedy a moral utility that is lacking in the early farces. Even more interesting is the way in which this moral utility is tied to print, and not performance. When the preface speaks of the farces' suppression, it specifically means that Molière omitted them from the published repertoire, not from performance. Whether or not the sentiments expressed in this passage were shared by Molière himself, explicit in the language of the text is the idea that "s'ériger en auteur" still retained some of the Latin connotations of *auctor* and *auctoritas*: that is, the idea that to be an author was to be an authoritative figure communicating indisputable moral truth (Randall 32–36). Publishing a book (which, as Furetière stated, had become a defining requirement of authorship) constituted a claim to a certain status both for its author and for its content. To be an author of (published) farces therefore was something of a contradiction, and indicated a ridiculous presumption.

Evidence that Molière was fully cognizant of these and other conventions surrounding writing and publication is readily to be found within *Les Précieuses ridicules* itself. The play includes literary practices among its central concerns, from Cathos and Magdelon's novel reading to Mascarille's *impromptu*. A key component to Mascarille's self-construction as a "bel esprit" is his literary flair—as his master La Grange puts it, "Il se pique ordinairement de galanterie, et de vers" (1:8). Mascarille claims to have written "deux cents Chansons, autant de Sonnets, quatre cents Epigrammes, et plus de mille Madrigaux, sans compter les Énigmes et les Portraits" (1:17), in addition to his project to "mettre en Madrigaux toute l'Histoire Romaine" (1:18). Upon hearing of this latest work, Magdelon requests a copy "si vous le faites imprimer." Mascarille responds, "Je vous en promets à chacune un, et des mieux reliés. Cela est au-dessous de ma condition; mais je le fais seulement pour donner à gagner aux Libraires qui me persécutent." When Magdelon exclaims, "Je m'imagine que le plaisir est grand de se voir imprimé," Mascarille responds with a curt and haughty "sans doute" (1:18). The play's closing lines, the general imprecation uttered by Gorgibus, attribute to literature and reading the motivation behind the entire plot of the play: "Et vous, qui êtes cause de leur folie, sottes billevesées, pernicieux amusements des esprits oisifs, Romans, Vers, Chansons, Sonnets, et Sonnettes, puissiez-vous être à tous les Diables" (1:30).

Molière might well have hesitated to launch his career as a published author with a play like *Les Précieuses ridicules*, not only tending so closely to farce, but also treating as one of its principal satirical targets presumptive authorship and the desire to print. If he was interested in becoming a published author, he had options other than *Les Précieuses ridicules*. By 1660, Molière's production was not limited to farces, and while touring in the provinces he had penned two five-act plays, *L'Étourdi* and *Le Dépit amoureux*. Both of these plays followed respected and traditional Italian models and were moderately successful, and yet both remained unpublished until 1663. This would suggest that Molière did indeed feel an initial reluctance in bringing his work to the press, aside from considerations of genre. While there is no way to ascertain the exact reasons behind this hesitation, it may also have something to do with a concern that printing would lead to a loss of control over the plays. Publishing a play meant that it could be performed legally by any other troupe; while this possibility would have carried little real consequences for Molière later in his career (Who would have paid to see a Molière play performed by anyone else?), during the beginning years in Paris, before his reputation was firmly established, Molière may well have feared to lose the unique elements of his troupe's repertoire.[12]

While Molière had many reasons not to publish *Les Précieuses ridicules* at this particular moment, it is nonetheless difficult to imagine him as completely disinterested in the advantages that publication afforded both for authorial reputation and income. It is also difficult to take seriously Molière's reluctance to publish because of the comedic effects that his preface derives from it—being published "malgré lui" allows him to mock his fellow authors even as he joins their ranks. While the first half of Molière's preface is dedicated to crafting the persona of the reluctant author, the

Chapter Two

second half continues to emphasize the "un-authorial" nature of this publication by listing all the elements that a typical preface should include and which this one will not.

Molière states that if he had been given more time, he could have taken "toutes les précautions, que Messieurs les Auteurs, à présent mes confrères, ont coutume de prendre en semblables occasions" (1:4). The first of these usual "précautions" that Molière is satirizing and that his publication will ostentatiously not include, is a flowery dedicatory epistle designed to coax money out of a "grand Seigneur" chosen against his will. The second element missing, *faute de temps*, is a scholarly preface, and in a taunt at his colleagues' often cheaply acquired erudition, Molière adds, "et je ne manque point de Livres, qui m'auraient fourni tout ce qu'on peut dire de savant sur la Tragédie, et la Comédie, l'Etymologie de toutes deux, leur origine, leur définition et le reste" (1:4). And lastly, Molière mocks the laudatory verses and poems that habitually appeared in printed theatrical editions, claiming that he has friends who would have praised him in French, Latin, and even Greek, adding that "l'on n'ignore pas qu'une louange en Grec, est d'une merveilleuse efficace à la tête d'un Livre" (1:4).

While all of these elements lampooned by Molière are fairly typical of seventeenth-century editions, it is remarkable how many of them, in all of their excesses, find their prototypical examples in the published works of a single playwright: Pierre Corneille. With the publication of *Cinna* (1643), Corneille raised the dedicatory epistle to infamous new heights of flattery and thinly veiled avarice when he compared the *financier* M. de Montoron to the emperor Augustus:

> Je dirai seulement un mot de ce que vous avez particulièrement de commun avec Auguste. C'est que cette générosité qui compose la meilleure partie de votre âme, et règne sur l'autre, et qu'à juste titre on peut nommer l'âme de votre âme, puisqu'elle en fait mouvoir toutes les puissances, c'est, dis-je, que cette générosité, à l'exemple de ce grand Empereur prend plaisir à s'étendre sur les gens de lettres en un temps où beaucoup pensent avoir trop récompensé leurs travaux quand ils les ont honorés d'une louange stérile. (Corneille 1:906, qtd. also in Lough 39)

Nothing "stérile" about Montoron's praise: Corneille's dedication apparently earned the playwright the healthy sum of two hundred *pistoles*, in addition to the enmity of his fellow authors.[13] Corneille's plays can also serve as standard reference points for the other practices mocked by Molière. Corneille's *La Veuve* (1634) included no fewer than twenty-five verse tributes at the beginning of the printed edition, contributed by authors including Scudéry, Mairet, and Rotrou. Furthermore, the landmark 1660 edition of Corneille's plays, printed in-octavo, included the famous *Discours*, theoretical treatises on the nature of the theater, and the *examens* of each play.

It would be dangerous, though, to narrow Molière's satire to a critique of Corneille. Corneille represented the most successful playwright of the period—any satire of authors' "précautions" would certainly take into account his personal authorial practices. However, the practices mocked in the preface to *Les Précieuses ridicules* were widespread. Molière purports to be satirizing a collectivity ("Messieurs les Auteurs"), and it is in this opposition to the group, not to the single individual of Corneille, that he portrays himself as the author "malgré lui."

And, ironically, it is in this very opposition to the group that Corneille's authorial example becomes most detectable in the preface to *Les Précieuses ridicules*. Molière claims that the only reason that his edition does not include many of the typical elements of a seventeenth-century paratext is that he was not given time to prepare them, but his satirizing of each of these elements ultimately suggests instead a quite different interpretation. Within the rhetorical logic of this anti-preface, the real reason Molière's play does not need the usual "précautions" is two-fold. First of all, playing the part of the reluctant author to the hilt, he only publishes against his will and is therefore unconcerned with obsequiously soliciting the reading public. Secondly, in a brash Cornelian way, his very success in the theater makes him a sort of "über-author," with no need to inflate artificially the interest in his work, as his lesser colleagues, "Messieurs les Auteurs," must do. This move, equating success in the theater with liberation from standard authorial practice, places Molière squarely in the wake of the author of *Le Cid* who, a generation earlier, had established himself as the paragon of the French theater according to these same criteria.[14] Little wonder that one of Molière's rivals, Baudeau de Somaize, wrote in response: "Depuis que la modestie et l'insolence sont deux contraires, on ne les a jamais veuës mieux unies qu'a fait dans sa Preface l'Autheur pretendu des Pretieuses ridicules" (Mongrédien, *Comédies* 36).

Baudeau de Somaize, *Préciosité*, and Plagiarism

In order to diffuse any resentment directed toward him on the part of offended Parisian *précieuses*, Molière had reminded readers in his preface that "les plus excellentes choses sont sujettes à être copiées par de mauvais Singes, qui méritent d'être bernés, que ces vicieuses imitations de ce qu'il y a de plus parfait, ont été de tout temps, la matière de la Comédie ..." (1:4). While applying specifically to the relationship between Cathos and Magdelon and their Parisian models, the statement is also strangely appropriate to Molière's play itself and to the literary texts that it spawned, "vicieuses imitations" that used *Les Précieuses ridicules* as the subject matter for comedy and satire. Jean Ribou's pirate edition actually represented only half of the *libraire*'s attempt to profit from *Les Précieuses ridicules*. The privilege that Ribou received on 12 January 1660 covered not one, but two works: Molière's *Précieuses ridicules* and a new play by Baudeau de Somaize entitled *Les Véritables Précieuses*.

Somaize's play is an obvious effort to profit from the vogue created by *Les Précieuses ridicules*, and it borrows from its predecessor a good deal of its language and plot: after some initial dialogues among two *précieuses* and their servants designed to highlight certain expressions unique to *préciosité* (Somaize provides translations in the margins), a reputed baron and poet arrive at the home, discuss current events (including the success of *Les Précieuses ridicules*), and then give readings of their latest works, which the *précieuses* admire. The inopportune arrival of a neighbor reveals that the baron and poet are actually *farceurs* trying to drum up support for their latest plays and the imposters take their leave.

Les Véritables Précieuses owes much to Molière's play, but it is difficult to say by modern standards whether Somaize's imitation amounts to plagiarism or if the resemblance is a deliberate attempt to satirize *Les Précieuses ridicules*. The substitution of *farceurs* for valets is an important one: the baron (La Force, or, in his theatrical name, Gilles le Niais) insists in the final scene that if the ladies accept the social visits of Mascarille (Molière), then they have no real grounds on which to evict him. If we are to read *Les Véritables*

Précieuses generously, it could be maintained that Somaize uses the success of *Les Précieuses ridicules* as a metaphor for Molière's own social posturing, comparing the author Molière's deceptive success with the Parisian *beau monde* with Mascarille's, and attempting through *Les Véritables Précieuses* to foist upon Molière himself the sort of humiliating reversal that constitutes the denouement of *Les Précieuses ridicules*.

The reader of *Les Véritables Précieuses* cannot help but notice that Somaize's play devotes a good deal of attention to a critique of Molière and his plays. Most of these attacks seek to undermine Molière's claim to originality by naming various sources for the *Les Précieuses ridicules*. Somaize's poet, when asked to give his opinion of Molière's play, responds that it is a simple imitation of the play written by the Abbé de Pure for the Italian troupe: "Premierement il faut que vous sçachiez qu'elle [la pièce] est plus agée de trois ans que l'on ne pense, et que dès ce temps-là les Comediens Italiens y gagnerent dix mil escus" (Mongrédien, *Comédies* 52). When the baron disingenuously objects that Molière claims to have not imitated anyone, the poet exclaims:

> Ah! que dites-vous là, c'est la mesme chose, ce sont deux valets tout de mesme qui se deguisent pour plaire à deux femmes, et que leurs Maistres battent à la fin: Il y a seulement cette petite difference, que dans la premiere les valets le font à l'inceu de leurs Maistres, et que dans la derniere, ce sont eux qui leur font faire. (52–53)

Georges Couton has compiled the information available about the Abbé de Pure's Italian play in order to see if Somaize's comparison is justified (Molière, *Œuvres complètes* [1971] 1:250–53). His conclusion, that the Italian play was a highly individualized effort to prevent a poor marriage between a well-placed young woman and a poet, suggests that Somaize's poet is overstating his case. Many of the salient features of Molière's play, in particular the satire of *précieux* language, are absent from the descriptions given of Pure's work.[15]

However, while this may excuse Molière in modern eyes, it is important to note that Somaize's accusation of plagiarism concerns only elements of the plot: two valets disguise themselves to trick two young women and are then beaten by their masters. This single-minded insistence on plot resemblance may explain

Chapter Two

an important element of Somaize's own play: when the baron, poet, and their valet are exposed as *farceurs*, they boldly reply to the bourgeois visitor who threatens to force them out: "Nous craignons peu vos menaces, et nous sommes tous trois bien resolus de nous defendre si l'on nous attaque" (Mongrédien, *Comédies* 61). Although the imposters leave the home, Somaize takes great pains to insist that they do so without the humiliation of being physically expelled, a deliberate contrast to both the ending of Molière's play and that of Pure's Italian play as described by Somaize's poet. The *farceurs*' defiance seems calculated on the part of the author to excuse himself of having produced a third "identical" play. It passes without saying, however, that in Somaize's satire of *précieux* language and manners, his play is only original in its addition of new phrases; in its method and theme, it is entirely derivative.

For a work that bases itself so closely on Molière's, it is surprising to see such acerbic accusations of plagiarism. In addition to the poet's comments, Somaize himself in the preface to *Les Véritables Précieuses* is remarkably aggressive:

> il [Molière] fait plus de Critique[r], il s'erige en Juge, et condamne à la berne les Singes, sans voir qu'il prononce un Arrest contre luy en le pronançant contre eux, puis qu'il est certain qu'il est Singe en tout ce qu'il fait, et que non seulement il a copié les Pretieuses de Monsieur l'abbé de Pure, joüées par les Italiens, mais encore qu'il a imité par une singerie, dont il est seul capable, le Medecin volant, et plusieurs autres pieces des mesmes Italiens qu'il n'imite seulement en ce qu'ils ont joüé sur leur theatre, mais encor en leurs postures, contrefaisant sans cesse sur le sien et Trivelin et Scaramouche, mais qu'atendre d'un homme qui tire toute sa gloire des Memoires G[u]illot-Gorgeu, qu'il a acheptez de sa veuve, et dont il s'adopte tous les Ouvrages? (Mongrédien, *Comédies* 36)

Reconciling this strident preface with the imitative work that follows presents clear challenges, especially if Somaize is refused the sort of egoistic blindness that would allow him to behold the proverbial mote in Molière's eye without considering the beam in his own. Somaize's imitation of Molière is deliberate, as is his denunciation of just such imitation in the prologue and in the text of his play.

But the accusations of plagiarism constitute only part of Somaize's wider attack on Molière. A close look at the dialogue of Somaize's play reveals what at times seems an attempt to dismantle term by term the self-portrait that Molière had drawn in the preface to *Les Précieuses ridicules*. Whereas Molière had referred flatteringly to the performance aspects of his play, Somaize's baron, in discussing the failure of Magnon's *Zénobie*, states of Molière's troupe: "les Comediens ne joüoient rien qui vaille, et qu'ils ne sont bons à rien qu'à joüer la farce" (Mongrédien, *Comédies* 55). Molière had spoken of the popularity of his play; Somaize attributes Molière's successes to cheap seats and fawning publicity campaigns. The poet states that Molière has been giving readings of his *Dom Garcie* in several circles, and adds, "Il est vray que je n'aurois pas pensé qu'il eust brigué comme il fait; mais je sçay de bonne part qu'il a tiré des Limbes son Despit amoureux à force de coups de chappeau et d'offrir des loges à deux pistolles" (53). Molière's private readings here serve not only as an object of ridicule but as the base of the entire plot: *Les Véritables Précieuses* fictionally portrays an attempt by *farceurs* to create support for their "gentrified" farces by giving readings of their works *à la Molière* in the homes of the gullible bourgeoisie. After the true identities of the *farceurs* are revealed, the poet states of the baron: "et comme il sçavoit que le succez des Pieces ne dependoit pas tant de leur bonté que de la brigue de leurs Autheurs, il a trouvé moyen de m'introduire dans les Compagnies, et il y a desja plus de deux cens personnes qui sont infatuez de mes Pieces" (60). Molière's popular success here becomes in effect the product of the same sort of obsequiousness multiplied many times over.

A comment by one of Somaize's *précieuses* reveals much of the play's satirical positioning with regards to Molière's play. After the poet discusses Molière's private readings, Iscarie responds, "Ce que vous nous dites est furieusement incroyable; car il me souvient bien que dans ses Precieuses, il improuve ceux qui lisent leurs pieces avant qu'on les represente, et par la vous me diriez qu'il s'est tourné luy-mesme en ridicule" (53). Iscarie is referring to the moment in *Les Précieuses ridicules* when Mascarille tells Cathos and Magdelon: "C'est la coutume ici, qu'à nous autres gens de condition, les Auteurs viennent lire leurs Pièces nouvelles, pour nous engager à les trouver belles, et leur donner de la réputation" (1:20). By insisting that Molière the author imitates the practices approved by Mascarille the character, Somaize effectively collapses the distance between the two, taking the satirical traits of

Chapter Two

Mascarille the imposter as an accurate representation of Molière the author. The whole thrust of Somaize's play is to convince the reader that Molière *is* Mascarille: a *farceur* introducing himself into polite society under the pretenses of authorship and taking advantage of his hosts' poor taste. To this end, Somaize's use of Molière's stage name, Mascarille, to refer to the author in *Les Véritables Précieuses* serves as a neat synecdoche for Somaize's larger project of fusing (and confusing) the two.

While it is indeed possible to read *Les Véritables Précieuses* as a satirical send-up of its better-known predecessor, thus justifying the resemblances in language and plot, Somaize's later career shows a dogged determination to exploit *préciosité* for his own profit: his subsequent works would include *Le Procès des Prétieuses* (1660), as well as, published on the same day, the *Grand Dictionnaire des Prétieuses ou la clef de la langue des ruelles* and a verse adaptation of Molière's *Précieuses ridicules* (1660). Apparent in this list is Somaize's desire to go beyond merely attacking Molière's play and supplant him in the satirical field that Molière had opened up. Somaize's jealous rivalry, since the author is both indebted to Molière for creating a vogue for *préciosité* but resentful of his success, places him in an awkward combination of imitation and denigration, producing works that both base themselves on, and attempt to debase the quality of, Molière's original.

Nowhere is this awkward posturing more apparent than in Somaize's verse adaptation of *Les Précieuses ridicules*. Somaize initially confesses in his preface that the reader may find it odd for him to have undertaken this project considering the treatment he had given "Mascarille" in *Les Véritables Précieuses*, and then repeats his accusations that Molière had stolen his material from the Italian *comediens*, who in turn received it from the Abbé de Pure. Somaize then admits that *Les Précieuses ridicules* "ont esté trop generalement receues et approuvées pour ne pas avouer que j'y ay pris plaisir," adding mean-spiritedly, "et qu'elles n'ont rien perdu en françois de ce qui les fist suivre en italien" (Mongrédien, *Comédies* 32). Somaize insists that he has added to the play's charms by placing it in verse, qualifying his statement, though, by stating that "ce n'est en bien des endroits que de la prose rimée, qu'on y trouvera plusieurs vers sans repos et dont la cadence est fort rude" (33). The reason for this is "la difficulté qu'il y a de mettre en vers mot à mot une prose aussi bizare que celle que j'ay eue à tourner, que je pense facilement faire voir que tout le plaisant des Pretieuses consistoit presque en des mots aussi contraires à la douceur des vers que necessaires aux agremens de cette comedie" (33).

Why does Somaize both imitate and deprecate Molière's play? As noted earlier, Somaize's imitation of Molière goes beyond mere satire to a clear indication of asserting himself as the chief author of *préciosité*. To this end, Somaize's attacks on *Les Précieuses ridicules* most often take the form of an accusation of plagiarism, as if eliminating Molière's claims to originality opens up the field for his own. That Somaize is uneasy about his artistic dependence on Molière's play is evident from the vehemence with which he accuses Molière of copying from sources: Guillot-Gorju's farces, the Italians, the Abbé de Pure. By portraying Molière's artistic production as illegitimate, Somaize justifies his own appropriation of it, a sort of vigilante justice that, in a parallel movement, steals back material in the name of Molière's sources, which then serves to establish Somaize's own authorial identity. Not that Somaize intended to share: as Georges Mongrédien has pointed out, Somaize's *Grand Dictionnaire des Prétieuses* included in the privilege a provision forbidding anyone to "se servir des mots contenus en iceluy sans le consentement dudit exposant ou ceux qui auroient droict de luy, à peine de quize cens livres d'amende" (*Comédies* 16). By identifying sources for Molière's work and undermining the playwright's claim to authorship, Somaize was not intending to make of *préciosité* a comic topos, free for anyone to exploit. His pretensions of authorship, here synonymous with ownership, were every bit as great as his model's.

However, as with Ribou's pirate edition, Somaize's attempts to appropriate Molière's material met with a strong assertion of proprietary rights, this time from the publishers who had purchased the privilege to *Les Précieuses ridicules*. At the end of his preface to the verse edition of *Les Précieuses ridicules*, Somaize adds:

> Il faut que les procez plaisent merveilleusement aux libraires du Palais, puisqu'à peine le *Dictionnaire des Pretieuses* est en vente et cette comedie achevée d'imprimer, que de Luynes, Sercy, et Barbin, malgré le privilege que Monseigneur le Chancelier m'en a donné avec toute la connoissance possible, ne laissent pas de faire signifier une opposition à mon libraire: comme si jusques icy les versions avoient esté defendues et qu'il ne fust pas permis de mettre le *Pater noster* françois en vers. (34)

Chapter Two

Somaize's example of the *Pater noster* is designed to show that since the most sacred of texts can be versified, by extension more secular ones can be as well. But Somaize, of course, is situating the debate over "versions" on the wrong axis: the distinction is not between sacred and secular, but rather between public and private. *Les Précieuses ridicules* had an owner, or three to be precise: in a typical move for the small-scale purveyors of *nouveautés*, De Luyne had shared the *privilège*, and by extension the printing expenses, with two other publishers, Charles de Sercy and Claude Barbin.

Sganarelle, or the Return of Ribou

Somaize's *libraire* for his versified *Précieuses ridicules* was once again Jean Ribou, and Ribou's complicity in the project apparently earned him some time in prison (Thuasne 53).[16] Ribou's interest in Molière's plays was not limited, though, to the *préciosité* vogue. *Sganarelle ou Le Cocu imaginaire* debuted on 28 May 1660 and a mere three days later, Molière obtained a privilege, suggesting that he may have made the request before performance began (Guibert, *Molière* 1:38). This haste to procure a privilege did not, however, mean that the author intended to rush *Sganarelle* into print. On the contrary, Molière's privilege went unused for several months.[17] Molière must have considered the privilege a sufficient preventative measure against those who would have printed the play "malgré lui," but once again he underestimated Jean Ribou. As with *Les Précieuses ridicules*, Molière's play was subject to an attack on the twin fronts of plagiarism and piracy: on 25 July 1660, Jean Ribou obtained a privilege for a work entitled *La Cocue imaginaire*, written by an F. Doneau, and the following day, 26 July 1660, an author by the name of the Sieur de Neuf-Villenaine obtained a privilege from the *Chancellerie* for Molière's *Sganarelle ou Le Cocu imaginaire* and transferred the rights of the play to Ribou.[18]

Although Ribou's approach in this instance seems remarkably similar to his earlier attempt to steal *Les Précieuses ridicules*, the unauthorized printings of *Sganarelle* in fact employed a very different strategy. Whereas Somaize had turned Mascarille's ironic posturing against the playwright, making it serve as an expression of Molière's own career, Ribou and the authors working with him took as their model for the "authentic" Molière not Mascarille, but the authorial persona from the preface of *Les Précieuses ridicules*. Furthermore, rather than disputing Molière's description of himself, they accepted it at face value. Like Somaize, they thus collapsed the difference between Molière and a representation, but did so not in the name of satire, but of flattery.

On 12 August 1660 Ribou completed the printing of Neuf-Villenaine's edition of *Sganarelle*. Although the text of the play was Molière's, Neuf-Villenaine had added prose descriptions, or *arguments*, at the beginning of each scene that summarized the plot and gave indications of how the scene had been acted by Molière and his troupe. Much more interesting than the *arguments*, though, is the dedicatory epistle, for the Sieur de Neuf-Villenaine, in a surprising gesture, dedicated the stolen version of *Sganarelle* to none other than Molière himself. In his letter, Neuf-Villenaine explains the circumstances that supposedly led to this edition's publication. An ardent fan of Molière, Neuf-Villenaine attended five or six performances of *Sganarelle*. Then, at a social gathering where people were discussing Molière's work, Neuf-Villenaine thought that he would cite a few lines from the play to illustrate the genius of his favorite playwright. To his amazement, he discovered that he knew almost every line. One more trip to the theater allowed him to fill in the gaps. Upon the request of a friend, Neuf-Villenaine wrote out the text, including summaries of each scene, only to have his trust betrayed and see several incorrect copies of the manuscript circulating around town. Suspecting the worst, namely, that a rapacious publisher would obtain a copy of the manuscript and print a sloppy pirate version, Neuf-Villenaine decided that the only solution was for him to take his impeccable version—albeit pirated as well—directly to a (rapacious) publisher, Jean Ribou.

Neuf-Villenaine's letter is remarkable for its brazen hypocrisy, not only due to Neuf-Villenaine's improbable account of how he procured a copy of Molière's play, but also in the justification of his decision to bring the play out in print.[19] Regardless of how Neuf-Villenaine acquired the text to *Sganarelle*, there is the simple fact that it would have been much more logical, and ethical, to warn Molière of the ensuing pirate publications than for Neuf-Villenaine preemptively to steal the play himself. Furthermore, he suggests that his own prose descriptions of each scene invest him as fully as the author in the success and correctness of the printed version ("comme il y alloit de vostre gloire & *de la mienne*" [Molière, *Sganarelle* a2r]; italics added). The moment of highest irony, however, is undoubtedly Neuf-Villenaine's paraphrase of Molière's preface to *Les Précieuses ridicules* ("ces Messieurs, qui impriment les gens malgré qu'ils en ayent" [Molière, *Sganarelle* a2r]) even as he arranges to print his pirate version with the same publisher who had prompted the comment in the first place.

This textual echo is evidence of a deeper relationship between the two texts, and a closer look shows that Neuf-Villenaine has crafted his letter to correspond in almost every particular to Molière's self-portrait of the artist. Molière in his preface to *Les Précieuses ridicules* had talked about the popular success of his play; Neuf-Villenaine describes himself as one of those avid enthusiasts. Molière had expressed great reluctance to publish his play, a reluctance only dispelled by the threat of the purloined manuscript about to be printed by Ribou. Neuf-Villenaine tells his own story of a stolen manuscript, on the verge of being printed, and like Molière, stoically resigns himself with great effort to the evils of publication: "[J]'ay pourtant combattu long-temps avant que de la donner; mais enfin i'ay veu que c'estoit une necessité que nous fussions imprimé" (Molière, *Sganarelle* a2r–a2v). Molière had portrayed himself as disinterested in the sordid financial rewards of printing, and Neuf-Villenaine, of course, also nicely elides any reference to the financial benefits that he might be receiving for printing Molière's play, merely adding that his publication could not possibly hurt Molière or his troupe, since the play has already been performed fifty times.[20]

From the perspective of the preface to *Les Précieuses ridicules*, Neuf-Villenaine gives Molière in his letter everything he could want: inordinate praise of his theatrical success, a convenient excuse for publication, and a correct version of the text. In many respects, Neuf-Villenaine (and by extension Jean Ribou) is calling Molière's bluff, seeing if he will conform to his authorial image of disinterest in profits and "précautions" and allow an accurate edition of his play to be printed and sold that gives him all of the glory, and none of the money.

Molière, however, did not stay in character. Roughly two weeks after Ribou began selling his pirate edition, Molière obtained a court order prohibiting the sale and authorizing a search of Ribou's shop. Contradicting his stated position on the relative evils of printing and lawsuits, Molière began lengthy legal proceedings against Ribou that, as far as the court documents reveal, resulted in a settlement allowing Ribou to continue to sell the edition, but requiring him to pay Molière roughly 1800 *livres* (Jurgens and Maxfield-Miller 349).

At the same time that Neuf-Villenaine's edition was being sold, Ribou printed F. Doneau's *Les Amours d'Alcippe et de Céphise ou La Cocue imaginaire*. Similar to the pirate edition of *Sganarelle*, Doneau's play is preceded by a preface that is highly flattering of Molière and his previous plays, and also represents his critics in an unfriendly light. Of *Les Précieuses ridicules*, Doneau writes:

> [E]lle a passé pour l'ouvrage le plus charmant, et le plus delicat qui ait jamais paru au Theatre. L'on est venu à Paris de vingt lieües à la ronde, afin d'en avoir le divertissement; il n'estoit [fils] de bonne mere, qui, lorsque l'on la joüoit, ne s'empressast pour la voir des premiers, et ceux qui font profession de galanterie, et qui n'avoient pas veu representer les Pretieuses, d'abord qu'elles commencerent à faire parler d'elles, n'ozoient l'avouër sans rougir. (6–7)

Even more importantly, though, Doneau suggests that the popularity of the play forced even Molière's opponents to acknowledge its merits:

> Cette piece enfin a tant fait du bruit, que les ennemis mesmes de Monsieur Molier, ont esté contraints de publier ses loüanges; mais non pas sans faire connoistre par leurs discours, qu'ils ne le faisoient que de peur de passer pour ridicules. Les uns disoient que veritablement, la piece estoit belle, mais que le jeu faisoit une grande partie de sa beauté. Les autres adjoustoient que la recontre du temps où l'on parloit fort des Pretieuses, aidoit à la faire reussir, et qu'indubitablement ses pieces n'auroient pas toujours de pareils succez, quand le temps ne les favoriseroit pas. (7)

Doneau's description of Molière's enemies and their jealous reaction to his popularity presents many of the arguments that Somaize had already used: the importance of the performance to the play's success and prior works that had created the vogue of *préciosité*. Doneau could be suspected of a certain duplicity, claiming to praise Molière while listing in detail the attacks of his enemies, were it not for Doneau's depiction of Molière's critics as hypocrites afraid of ridicule. Later in his preface Doneau will satirically wonder if Molière's critics will continue to accuse him "d'avoir de l'esprit, et de sçavoir choisir ce qui plaist" (8). In any case, Doneau's praise for *Sganarelle* is unsparing: "Jamais on ne vit de sujet mieux conduit, jamais rien de si bien fondé que la jalousie de Sganarelle, et jamais rien de si spirituel que ses vers" (9).

Doneau's excessive praise for Molière's play, as with Neuf-Villenaine, serves as the excuse for a literary project. In Neuf-Villenaine's case, it produced the verbatim transcription to convince a friend of the play's merits. For Doneau, the project will be a literary corollary to the original: "presque tout Paris a souhaitté de voir ce qu'une femme pourroit dire, à qui il arriveroit la mesme chose qu'à Sganarelle, et si elle auroit autant de sujet de se plaindre, quand son mary luy manque de foy, que luy quand elle luy est infidelle" (9). Nothing easier to do: as Molière's play deals with the symmetrical couples Célie/Lélie and Sganarelle/wife, all Doneau has to do is take the exact plot already established by Molière and reverse the roles of the men and women. As he states in his preface, his play serves "de regard au Cocu imaginaire, puisque dans l'une, on verra les plaintes d'un homme qui croit que sa femme luy manque de foy, et dans l'autre celles d'une femme qui croit avoir un mary infidelle" (9). The specific nature of the project presumably excuses Doneau from suspicions of plagiarism. He writes:

> J'aurois bien fait un autre sujet que celuy de Monsieur de Molier, pour faire eclatter les plaintes de la femme; mais ils n'auroient pas eu tous les deux les mesmes sujets de faire eclatter leur jalousie, il y auroit eu du plus ou du moins; c'est pourquoy il a fallu, afin que le divertissement fust plus agreable, qu'ils raisonnassent tous deux sur les mesmes incidens; tellement que j'ay esté contraint de me servir du mesme sujet. C'est ce qui fait que vous n'y trouverez rien de changé, sinon que tous les hommes de l'un, sont changez en femmes dans l'autre. (9–10)

The problem with this, as Doneau himself admits, is that this symmetrical role reversal, easily effectuated on the literary level, runs into social conventions that detract from the intended comic effect: "ce qui passe pour galanterie chez l'un, passe pour crime chez l'autre, outre qu'il n'y a pas le mot pour rire du costé de la femme, son front estant trop delicat pour porter des cornes, ce qui rend le plaisant difficile à trouver" (10).

A more striking contrast to Somaize could hardly be found. Doneau combines excessive praise of his model and an open acknowledgement of his artistic debt with an explicit admission that the copy is inferior to the original. If Somaize's denunciation of Molière's reputed plagiarisms formed an essential part of an overall strategy to construct his own authorship, Doneau's approach (as well as that of Neuf-Villenaine) is a deliberate self-effacement behind the figure of Molière. Any authorial pretension on the part of these two writers is further undermined by the careful way in which they delimit their projects as strictly personal. Neuf-Villenaine writes for a friend; Doneau's play is dedicated in intimate terms to a "Mademoiselle Henriette." While Doneau's dedicatory epistle occasionally strays into the genre's typical bombast, it contains other elements that point to the highly individual nature of the dedication:

> Advoüez la verité: n'est-il pas vray que ce nom vous embarrasse? et qu'après l'avoir leu, vous vous estes arrestée tout court, pour songer quelle peut estre cette Henriette? Mais n'y resvez pas davantage, et si vous avez eu quelque soupçon que ce fust vous, demeurez dans cette pensée, et ne vous amusez point à repasser dans vostre esprit toutes les Henriettes que vous connoissez, puisque je ne pretends parler qu'à vous. Mais d'où vient que vous faites encore une pause, après que j'ay esclairay vostre trouble? Ah! j'en devine facilement le sujet! Vous estes surprises sans doute, et vous ne vous attendiez pas qu'une personne à qui le sang vous lie, vous dediast un Livre. ... Mais vous devez sçavoir, que quand une fois on a pris de l'amitié pour eux, l'amitié jointe au sang a beaucoup plus de chaleur, et devient si puissante, qu'il n'est rien qu'elle ne nous fist entreprendre pour leur en donner des preuves. (3–4)

The addressees of Neuf-Villenaine and Doneau serve to qualify the two plays as unique personal projects, devoid of the aspirations to universality or reputation that are the hallmarks of authorial production. To write for an audience of one is not strictly to be an author; only the gesture of publication, with its inherent sense of addressing the public, constitutes a claim to authorship.[21] By openly rejecting any assertion of originality and couching themselves as personal projects, Neuf-Villenaine's *Sganarelle* and Doneau's *Cocue imaginaire* at least rhetorically disavow any such pretensions. This is belied by the very fact that both plays were

Chapter Two

published, implying that Neuf-Villenaine and Doneau intended to receive from their works benefits other than (in Doneau's case) the undying gratitude of Mademoiselle Henriette. Both Neuf-Villenaine and Doneau took out privileges for their works and sold those privileges to Jean Ribou. For his part, Neuf-Villenaine received 220 *livres* (Jurgens and Maxfield-Miller 350). While Neuf-Villenaine and Doneau rhetorically refused the quality of author, it is apparent that they were not disinterested in being owners of the texts that they had produced, and it is precisely this split that they propose in turn to Molière.[22] In clear distinction from Somaize, Doneau and Neuf-Villenaine loudly proclaim Molière's authorship, reserving to him the attendant reputation and honors, at the same time that they reap the immediate material benefits.

Molière's reaction to Doneau's play is difficult to ascertain. Paul Lacroix, in a preface to a nineteenth-century reprint of *La Cocue imaginaire*, notes the lack of any surviving copies of the first print run and suggests that Molière must have taken legal action: "l'on est forcé de supposer que Molière l'avait fait saisir et mettre au pilon, en accusant de plagiat l'auteur" (in Doneau ix). That a first edition was indeed printed is evidenced by contemporary documents (*Le Songe du resveur*; see below), but Couton confirms Lacroix's bibliographical research by stating that no copies of the first edition survive (Molière, *Œuvres complètes* [1971] 1:292). Duchêne, on the other hand, provides a description of the first few pages of the initial edition: "La première édition de cette pièce [*Les Amours d'Alcippe et de Céphise*] porte un achevé d'imprimer du 14 août. On y voit en page intérieure le titre déclaré dans le privilège, mais agrémenté d'un sous-titre: *ou La Cocue imaginaire*. C'est ce sous-titre qui figure seul sur la couverture" (253).[23] The rarity of this first edition and its calculated attempt in the title and layout to ape Molière's play support the possibility that legal action was taken. This raises the question, though, of who would have undertaken the action and in what name: if *La Cocue imaginaire* was indeed printed in August 1660, it would have appeared during the time that Molière and Ribou were disputing the ownership to *Sganarelle*, and ownership of this play was bound up inherently with the right to challenge Doneau's work. The court decision of 16 November 1660 in favor of Molière seems to have left the ownership of *Sganarelle* in some sort of legal limbo: by virtue of being ordered to pay Molière (or give him the copies), did Ribou become the legal owner of *Sganarelle*'s privilege? The short-term answer appears to be negative, as a 1662 edition of the play lists Molière as the recipient of the privilege and a transfer of the rights to Guillaume de Luyne and Estienne Loyson (Guibert, *Molière* 1:45). However, a 1666 edition, published by Ribou, features the original privilege with Neuf-Villenaine listed as the recipient (Guibert, *Molière* 1:49–50). This is further complicated by Claude Barbin and Gabriel Quinet registering a privilege with the *Communauté des libraires* on 27 October 1662 for four Molière plays including *Le Cocu imaginaire* (Thuasne 13).

The question of the legal rights to *Sganarelle* is by no means incidental to a discussion of *La Cocue imaginaire*, as it was the owner of a play, and not necessarily its author, that stood to lose from what would amount today to copyright infringement. In this regard, it is useful to compare the legal difficulties that surrounded *Les Précieuses ridicules* and *Sganarelle*. In the first case, it was Molière's *libraires*, and not the author, that consistently took the active role of asserting the rights to the play. Molière's preface (partly for comic effect) casts his *libraire* (the legal owner of the play) as the one hurrying his play into print to combat Ribou's pirate edition: "M. de Luynes veut m'aller relier de ce pas" (1:264). Legal action against Somaize's verse translation was taken by Molière's publishers, and not by Molière himself. Interestingly enough, Estienne Loyson, a frequent business partner of De Luyne and Barbin, the original publishers of *Les Précieuses ridicules*, brought out a second edition of the verse translation in 1661 (Mongrédien, *Comédies* 15). As an associate of the holders of the privilege, Loyson must have felt authorized to print the formerly contested work, a good demonstration that the legal challenges disappear when the rights to the original and the derivative work are in the same hands.[24] If Molière had harbored any objections to the reissuing of Somaize's verse edition, he would have had no legal grounds for lodging a complaint—in the strictest sense, *Les Précieuses ridicules* no longer belonged to him.

A similar situation may have arisen with respects to *Sganarelle* and *La Cocue imaginaire*. With the legal settlement leaving in question the owner of *Sganarelle*, it may have been difficult to determine whose rights were being infringed upon with the publication of *La Cocue imaginaire*. In the event that he retained rights to *Sganarelle*, Ribou may have been in the unlikely position of stealing from himself.

The examples of *Sganarelle* and *La Cocue imaginaire* bring into clear focus the distinction to be made between authors and owners at this time period. While the author was the owner of an unpublished manuscript, these rights associated with possession of the manuscript were alienable, that is, they could be bought and sold, as the privilege system amply demonstrates. The potential, and indeed, common split between authors and owners, the latter being primarily *libraires*, theoretically allows for forms of piracy and appropriation that harm only booksellers while leaving authors unscathed, and it seems to be this position that Neuf-Villenaine and Doneau adopt: their publications may indeed be benign with regards to Molière, as they insist in their prefaces, but they could hardly argue the same with respect to Molière's publishers.[25] If, as Neuf-Villenaine insists, the text of *Sganarelle* is correct, then the only complaint that Molière the author (as opposed to Molière the owner) might proffer is the specific printed form in which his play was made to appear.[26]

However, it is not on these properly "authorial" grounds that Molière seeks redress: his suit against Ribou establishes quite clearly that Molière will consider himself satisfied with either the unauthorized copies of the play or their monetary equivalent of 30 *sols* apiece (Jurgens and Maxfield-Miller 348). Nowhere is there mention of the *arguments*, and the only real change to the text of Ribou's edition that Molière seems to insist on is the substitution of his name for Neuf-Villenaine's in the privilege (Guibert, *Molière* 1:39). If Ribou and his associates switched tactics in their appropriations of *Sganarelle*, Molière correspondingly switched his defense: where he had previously presented himself as the "auteur malgré lui," interested more in theatrical reputation than printing and money, he shows in his suit against Ribou a dogged determination to claim the play as his property, a property directly convertible into a cash equivalent. That Molière chose to force the honoring of his rights in a situation where he had only money to lose shows how invested he had become in what Joseph Loewenstein calls "possessive authorship" (82).

L'École des maris: Possession and Publication

The rights that Molière had asserted and defended against Ribou in court would find a new manifestation with the publication of *L'École des maris* in 1661. As with *Les Précieuses ridicules*, Molière uses the paratext of his play to construct an authorial persona, but this time, the persona is strikingly different. Instead of Molière's mocking reference to flowery epistles and "grands seigneurs," the 1661 edition of *L'École des maris* included a dedication to Monsieur, the duc d'Orléans, patron of Molière's troupe and brother of Louis XIV. In his letter, Molière presents his play by stating that he had an obligation to dedicate to Monsieur "le premier Ouvrage que je mets de moi-même au jour" (1:85), a pointed reference to Ribou's attempts on *Les Précieuses ridicules* and *Sganarelle*. After insisting on the poor match between Monsieur's noble standing and the comedy, Molière states, "[T]out ce que j'ai prétendu dans cette Épître, c'est de justifier mon action à toute la France, et d'avoir cette gloire de vous dire à vous-même, Monseigneur, avec toute la soumission possible que je suis, De Votre Altesse Royale, Le très humble, très obéissant et très fidèle serviteur, J.-B. P. Molière" (1:85–86).

Molière had additional reasons for wishing to publicize his relationship with Monsieur that are made more explicit in the unusual privilege that accompanies the play. The rigid form of the standard seventeenth-century book privilege makes any departures particularly significant, and Molière's privilege contains two such instances. In the first place, it is printed in its entirety: while privileges could legally be printed either in full or abbreviated form, the extra cost, both in time and paper, incurred by printing the full text meant that the majority—around eighty percent—were printed as excerpts of the complete legal document (Lévy-Lelouch 144). The decision to print the full text of the privilege in the case of *L'École des maris* is explained by a second departure from the norm—the privilege contains a special section describing the attempts to steal *Les Précieuses ridicules* and *Sganarelle*, and expressly condemning Jean Ribou by name:

> Nostre amé *Iean Baptiste Pocquelin de Moliers, Comedien de la Troupe de nostre tres-cher & tres-amé Frere unique le Duc d'Orleans*, Nous a fait exposer qu'il auroit depuis peu composé

> pour nostre divertissement une Piece de Theatre en trois Actes, intitulée *L'Escole des Maris*, qu'il desireroit faire imprimer; mais parce qu'il seroit arrivé qu'en ayant cy-devant composé quelques autres, aucunes d'icelles auroient esté prises & transcrites par des particuliers qui les auroient fait imprimer, vendre & debiter en vertu des Lettres de Privileges qu'ils auroient surprises en nostre grande Chancellerie à son preiudice & dommage; pour raison dequoy il y auroit eu Instance en nostre Conseil, iugée à l'encontre d'un nommé Ribou, Libraire, Imprimeur, en faveur de l'Exposant, lequel craignant que celle-cy ne luy soit pareillement prise, & que par ce moyen il ne soit privé du fruict qu'il en pourroit retirer, Nous auroit requis luy accorder nos Lettres, avec les deffences sur ce necessaires. (Molière, *L'Escole des maris*)

Like most privileges, this document is designed to deter unlawful publication and theft of the play. It is perhaps significant that the privilege is so precise in specifying Molière's position and his troupe's links to royal authority, as an added disincentive to would-be pirates, much like the dedicatory epistle. However, the paragraph detailing Jean Ribou's misdeeds, published in every copy of *L'École des maris*, transforms the privilege from a legal document prohibiting future acts of piracy into a public censuring of past crimes. The privilege and the dedicatory epistle thus serve a double function: they claim a heightened professional visibility for Molière and his works by emphasizing his connections with royal power, and they increase Jean Ribou's visibility, advertising his misdeeds in order to prevent future occurrences. Molière bases the security of his intellectual property on a double foundation of royal authority and publicity. In this sense, Molière's privilege is surprisingly transparent, an important demonstration that the property rights that the privilege system appeared to guarantee in a systematic way were in actuality highly individual and relative, dependant upon the recipient's notoriety and personal connections. It is a lesson that Molière will remember.

Of his dedicatory epistle to Monsieur, Molière writes:

> Tout le monde trouvera cet assemblage étrange; et quelques-uns pourront bien dire, pour en exprimer l'inégalité, que c'est poser une couronne de perles et de diamants, sur une statue de terre, et faire entrer par des Portiques magnifiques, et des Arcs triomphaux superbes dans une méchante Cabane. (1:85)

Molière's comment suggests that he was well aware of the extra attention that he was paying to the paratext of his edition; he similarly wanted no reader to ignore the "Arcs triomphaux superbes" marking the boundaries of what he was claiming as his exclusive property. In another reversal of his authorial construction in the preface to *Les Précieuses ridicules*, Molière literally surrounded his play with the authorial "précautions" that he had once mocked: the text of the play is preceded by the dedicatory epistle and followed by the privilege (Guibert, *Molière* 1:61).

The distinction that Molière makes between the text and the paratext ("Arcs triomphaux superbes" / "méchante Cabane") concerns the majesty of Monsieur and the lowly nature of the literary production that Molière is offering to him, and the contrast draws on the self-deprecation typical of dedicatory epistles. However, the contrast between text and paratext, particularly in the 1661 edition, could just as well be thematic: whereas the play emphasizes the vanity of Sganarelle's jealous efforts to control Isabelle, the dedicatory epistle and royal privilege represent a corresponding intention on the part of Molière to limit his text's diffusion and appropriation. Sganarelle's brother Ariste famously proclaims in the play that "les soins défiants, les verrous, et les grilles, / Ne font pas la vertu des femmes, ni des filles" (1:94), but Molière has taken great pains to construct around his play the legal equivalent of these very constraints. Discussing the text's resistance to univocal critical determination, Vernet has written, using the characters from *L'École des femmes* as illustrations, "Comme Agnès, avec la même obstination douce, l'œuvre résiste et revient à son lieu propre. Nous n'avons pas, sur elle, tous les droits" (21). In the case of Molière's first two printed plays, it would seem that this "lieu propre" to which Molière's plays inevitably drifted was a sort of public domain effectuated by pirate *libraires* and plagiarists. For his third play, Molière takes no chances, and in his paratext publicly claims over it "tous les droits."

The contrast between text and paratext makes for some moments of high irony. In *L'École des maris*, Sganarelle shows a ridiculous interest in legal documents, in particular the king's edict against excessive expense in dress. After exulting "Ô trois et quatre fois béni soit cet Édit," Sganarelle proclaims he has obtained a copy and that Isabelle's reading of the edict will be "le divertissement de notre après-soupée" (1:114). If the reading of legal documents is in the play the object of satire, one has to wonder about Molière's insistence on including the complete text of his royal privilege for the delectation of his readers. In this and other respects, the text and the paratext seem to be at odds, one advertising the precautions the owner has taken to safeguard his property, and the other suggesting the futility of all such precautions.

A solution to this seeming paradox can be found by reexamining the way in which Molière characterizes *L'École des maris* in his dedicatory epistle: "le premier Ouvrage que je mets de moi-même au jour" (1:85). The phrase itself contains a revealing ambiguity: what is Molière insisting is "de moi-même?" The "ouvrage?" Or the "mise au jour" of the "ouvrage?"[27] The edition of *L'École des maris* certainly asserts Molière as the play's origin and owner (in short, its author): the volume begins with the title page, which states, "*L'Escole des maris, comédie, de I.B.P. Molière*," the first title page of a Molière edition to include the author's name; the volume concludes with the first privilege that Molière took out in his own name. In Molière's "de moi-même," any notion of the collaborative nature of theater, or the primacy of performance over print, is elided. That this assertion of sole authorship is perhaps false—and Grimarest notes that *L'École des maris* was in particular accused of being simply a reworking of Terence (16–17)—is, or becomes, irrelevant.

However, Molière is more probably emphasizing that it is the "mise au jour" that is "de moi-même," and this latter interpretation presents the suggestive idea of a work of neutral (and perhaps composite) origins claimed for a single individual by the very act of publication.[28] While publication (and dedication) presupposes a particular relationship between an individual and a text, one that implies causality or creation, it is difficult to say whether it merely assumes or actively establishes this relationship. For this historical moment when literary production was so closely tied to imitation, and for a genre built upon particular instantiations of universal types and themes, authorship constituted as much the act of making public as the act of original writing (to the extent that this can even exist). By bringing *L'École des maris* "au jour," Molière becomes its de facto author, regardless of the details of its composition, and it is in this manner that the question of origin ("ouvrage de moi-même") is effectively rendered immaterial by the second assertion ("mise au jour de moi-même").

The efficacy of this claim to authorship (and ownership), divorced as it is from more straight-forward links between author and text, is determined by personal notoriety. Randall has noted that "authorship, that is, mastery over one's discourse, can be seen as a matter of converting public property into private by means of properly assimilating it and marking it with one's transforming individuality" (68). However, the key to successfully claiming as private what ostensibly belongs to everyone is not always the degree of artistic transformation that has occurred in the text. Formalistic considerations aside, authors of a certain status can literally and literarily "prendre leur bien où ils le trouvent," to paraphrase Molière's apocryphal statement, an idea that Randall summarizes in the suggestive maxim that "[g]reat authors don't plagiarize" (26)—in this case, not because they do not engage in the practice, but because their very individuality (established reputation, popularity) is itself transforming, regardless of what changes they actually make to the text.[29]

It is in this regard that the act of publishing *L'École des maris* assumes its full significance. To paraphrase Randall's statement about plagiarism, authorship (that is, control over a text) is also in the eye of the reader, or in this case, the multiplicity of readers. As Martial wrote, "mutare dominum non potest liber notus" (Randall 62).[30] Publishing *L'École des maris* is as much an authorial "précaution" as the dedicatory epistle and the privilege that accompany the text. Or even more so: if the law in and of itself were sufficient protection for Molière's play, there would be no need to publish the privilege in its entirety. Although the elements mocked by Molière in his preface to *Les Précieuses ridicules* are now present, they are still subordinate to, or gain their efficacy from, the supreme theatrical good, which Dorante will expound in *La Critique de L'École des femmes*: "Je voudrais bien savoir si la grande règle de toutes les règles n'est pas de plaire; et si une pièce de Théâtre qui a attrapé son but n'a pas suivi un bon chemin" (in Molière 1:507). Far from controlling his play by removing it from public circulation (a Sganarelle-esque approach to property), Molière is cementing his authorial control over the play through publication. The very act of allowing his work to circulate is what will guarantee its return to him. Ariste could not have agreed more.

Chapter Two

Author and Owner

With the publication of *L'École des maris*, Molière successfully established himself as a committed participant in the publication process and in the patronage system, challenging the image that he had constructed of himself in the preface of his first publication, *Les Précieuses ridicules*, as a non-author at the whim of contending *libraires*. But the particular nature of Molière's authorship evident in these early struggles should give pause to those eager to see in the playwright a pioneering authorial sensibility that anticipates the codification and protection of authors' rights in the eighteenth and nineteenth centuries.[31] At least in the early part of his career, it is not clear whether Molière's notion of authors' rights extended in any significant way beyond the right to choose the time of publication and the right to profit from his text. These are the rights that he defends in court, leaving aside considerations (including actual alterations of his text, in the case of Neuf-Villenaine's *arguments*) that others may have considered to be of paramount significance. All Molière seems to insist upon is the opportunity to follow the standard practice of seventeenth-century publication: a sale of his rights to a *libraire*. While certain elements of this will shift as Molière's career progresses, the emphasis on ownership and the right to profit from his work will remain the foundations upon which Molière's concept of authorship rests.

That Molière did not exhibit a particular attention to what could be labeled literary concerns (e.g., the establishment of a correct printed text or the reading of printer's proofs) should not be read as insouciance or a disregard for establishing his authorship. The early modern period permitted a wide variety of attitudes regarding an author's role in the printing process, and it is of far greater interest to examine how Molière's particular stance would have been interpreted by his contemporaries than to note anachronistically how Molière does or does not match the characteristics of modern authorship.

In this respect, a key text is an anonymous pamphlet entitled *Le Songe du resveur*, which appeared in 1660 and illustrates Molière's successful ascension to the rank of established author during the years following his return to Paris. The pamphlet is a response to Baudeau de Somaize's *La Pompe funèbre de M. Scarron*, a satire of all the major comedic playwrights that had attacked Molière as "un bouffon trop serieux" (*Songe* viii). *Le Songe du resveur* presents a fictional dream in which the author sees Apollo receiving the Muses' reports on the current disorder in the French Parnassus caused by Somaize. While *Le Songe du resveur* names more literary victims than Molière, and more perpetrators than Somaize (it includes satires of Ribou, Neuf-Villenaine, and Doneau), in the end it is around these two figures that the fiction revolves, and the dream concludes with Somaize humbly apologizing to Molière before Apollo and being "berné" in fanciful fulfillment of the punishment affixed in Molière's preface to *Les Précieuses ridicules*: "les plus excellentes choses sont sujettes à être copiées par de mauvais Singes, qui méritent d'être bernés" (1).

Even more importantly, *Le Songe du resveur* posits a clear distinction between two classes of authors: the established playwrights whom Baudeau de Somaize has attacked, and the swarm of lesser authors, described in terms of *gueux* or "beggars" (8), who live off of the first group by copying and stealing from their works.[32] While Somaize had accused Molière of belonging to this second group, the writer of the *Songe* places Molière in the company of writers such as La Mothe Le Vayer, Quinault, Boisrobert, Pierre and Thomas Corneille, and Furetière. These are Molière's peers and competitors: for Somaize, there is nothing but contempt for a "pauvre misérable" who is "fort indigne" of Molière's, or anyone else's, "courroux" (24). Molière is becoming untouchable; De La Rancune's lament can already be seen on the horizon.

Le Songe du resveur provides important evidence of Molière's establishment as a major author in the eyes of his contemporaries and according to seventeenth-century criteria. This development owed much to Molière's own conscious efforts, from the Ribou trial, during which Molière aggressively refused Neuf-Villenaine's gambit of authorship divested of ownership, to the paratext of *L'École des maris*, which provides further confirmation of a Molière determined to assert his rights over the texts that bear his name. Furthermore, Molière's increasing reliance on publication and popularity to secure his property indicates a growing awareness on his part of the utility of authorship, namely, that an author's name, in addition to permitting "d'accéder à un certain nombre de textes" (Vernet 21), could protect those texts and stake a claim to the words and ideas that they contained.

The silence that reigned among Molière's former antagonists following the publication of *L'École des maris* is strong evidence

Chapter Two

of the playwright's success in this regard. Molière would still be subject to both piracy and plagiarism in the provinces and abroad, and he would also have to resist attacks on his authorship from jealous rivals, as the following chapter on the *querelle de L'École des femmes* demonstrates.[33] However, in the Parisian literary world, Molière would never again be subjected to the sorts of whole-scale textual appropriation that Ribou, Somaize, Neuf-Villenaine, and Doneau had attempted. The publication of the first three plays traces a trajectory that finds its accomplishment in the paratext of *L'École des maris*: the newly arrived actor had become an author. The moniker "Molière," long a stage name, had now become a pen name as well.

Chapter Three

Comedic Authorship and Its Discontents

If Molière the author was invented in the sequence of plays culminating with *L'École des maris* (1661), Molière's second school, *L'École des femmes* (first performed in December 1662; published in March 1663) and the quarrel that it generated marked an important new step in the playwright's artistic trajectory. While the debates over Molière's authorship continued to revolve around similar poles (originality and imitation, literary worth and popular success), the participants and the stakes increased substantially. Molière's previous adversaries were Jean Ribou and the relatively obscure writers working with him; the *querelle de L'École des femmes* opposed the playwright to the Hôtel de Bourgogne, the premier troupe in Paris, as well as a wide variety of authors, many of them destined for significant literary careers.[1] In addition, while the earlier plays may have cemented Molière's position as a successful author in the Parisian *champ littéraire*, *L'École des femmes*—and the reaction that it provoked—established his comedic dominance.

The sites of the struggle changed as well. The earlier skirmishes, confined almost entirely to the arena of publication, took place behind the scenes, or literally in the margins—the paratexts—of the printed editions. With the polemical sequels to *L'École des femmes*, quarrels and controversies moved to center stage, becoming the very subject matter of theater. The result is that Molière, responding to his adversaries, came as close as he ever did to elaborating an actual poetics, discussing questions of genre, dramatic composition, and reception. The exchange of barbed theatrical productions, both staged and printed, shows that far from remaining exclusively a man of the theater, Molière eagerly exploited the new legal, rhetorical, and social status afforded by authorship in surprising and paradoxical ways. Playing rivals and audiences against each other, Molière the actor-author constructed an image

Chapter Three

of himself that challenged existing notions of comedic authorship. In so doing, he not only exposed the ideological tensions present in the early modern conception of authorship, but also illustrated the unusual possibilities and freedoms that this very ambiguity afforded.

In one sense, it is not surprising that the quarrel surrounding *L'École des femmes* should involve more significant stakes than Molière's earlier difficulties. The play itself represents a considerable shift in its treatment of literature, writing, and identity. In *Les Précieuses ridicules*, Mascarille had openly mocked certain conventions of the Parisian literary scene, but the critique was limited and superficial, a caricature of circumstantial details. *L'École des femmes*, by contrast, focuses on larger questions regarding writing's power to control. In part, this is highlighted by the play's own stylistic characteristics: a five-act play written in alexandrine verses, *L'École des femmes* casts itself in the tradition of high literary comedy, or what the participants in the quarrel will call *la belle comédie*. It is not the sort of work that allegedly could have been stolen from *farceurs*, as Baudeau de Somaize had claimed about *Les Précieuses ridicules*. In other words, it is a comedy that demands to be taken seriously.

But beyond its own literary styling, *L'École des femmes* also contains a thematic analysis of writing and authorship, since the fundamental conflict that sets Arnolphe and Agnès in opposition takes literary form at important junctures in the play. Like *L'École des maris*, the plot in *L'École des femmes* grapples with the problem of authority, expressed once again in the efforts of an older man (in this instance, Arnolphe) to force a young woman (Agnès) to marry him. But authority in *L'École des femmes* is linked explicitly with its etymological cousin, authorship. Significantly, Arnolphe and Agnès are both authors, or at least they are both closely associated with texts: Arnolphe with the *Maximes du mariage* that form the keystone to his domestic curriculum; and Agnès with the charming letter that she dexterously manages to send to Horace. These literary productions constitute key moments in the plot, and they will also become virulent points of contention among the play's later supporters and critics.

Arnolphe represents the most advanced stage of this attempted fusion between power and writing. In its most abstract sense, authorship is Arnolphe's highest goal: his new name, Monsieur de La Souche, reflects an unfettered desire to become a source, reminiscent of Furetière and Richelet's definitions of the author as a single and original cause.[2] Arnolphe's ultimate intended creation is Agnès, whom he has found and groomed from a young age to be his naïve and entirely subservient wife, incapable of thoughts or actions that deviate from his own all-powerful will. As Arnolphe boasts in Act 3, drawing on a related artistic image: "Ainsi que je voudrai, je tournerai cette âme. / Comme un morceau de cire entre mes mains elle est, / Et je lui puis donner la forme qui me plaît" (1:438).

Arnolphe sees in writing the vehicle by which to transform Agnès into the ideal spouse, and his reliance on text to bolster his authority appears prominently in the character's iconography. The printed edition of *L'École des femmes* was the first Molière play to contain an engraved frontispiece, and the artist (François Chauveau, one of the era's premier engravers) depicts the scene where Arnolphe is instructing Agnès in her domestic duties—Arnolphe's attempted "school" for his future wife. As Arnolphe's right hand gestures toward his forehead (the cuckoldry-portending "Là, regardez-moi là" [1:433]), his left hand holds a small book, the "écrit" that contains the maxims of marriage and that, as Arnolphe explains to Agnès, "vous enseignera l'office de la femme" (1:435). Chauveau revisited his earlier work when he was commissioned to engrave the frontispieces for the two volumes of Molière's 1666 *Œuvres*, the second of which depicts Thalie, the muse of comedy, placing laurel leaves on the heads of Agnès and Arnolphe. As in the earlier engraving, Arnolphe clasps in his hand his precious book of *maximes* (Guibert, *Molière* 2:565).[3]

As Arnolphe presents the book of maxims to Agnès in the play, he remarks, "J'en ignore l'Auteur: mais c'est quelque bonne âme" (1:435), a statement that is at best ironic and at worst another of Arnolphe's deceptions. On one level, the authorship of the *maximes* is not at all in doubt—Molière wrote them, and with Molière himself playing the part of Arnolphe, the character's ignorance of the *maximes*' provenance is comic. Even more amusing is Arnolphe's reference to the author as a "bonne âme," an unlikely portrayal of Molière as a pious versifier of patriarchal bromides. Arnolphe's comments are an early example of the common metatheatrical joke in Molière's theater in which characters will demonstrate a humorous lack of awareness or even active resentment toward Molière the author.[4] While Arnolpe's statements are certainly meant at least partially to operate on this level, there is a second and more troubling irony potentially at work: in addition to the *maximes*' real or eventual author, they may very likely have a diagetic author in the person of Arnolphe himself. The *maximes* adhere so closely to Arnolphe's own philosophy and respond in so calculated a fashion to the observations he has made regarding the dangers of cuckoldry that he likely wrote them, making his statement of ignorance particularly duplicitous.

Hypothetical attributions aside, what is certain is that Arnolphe is trying to efface the author from the text—either he honestly does not know and makes no effort to find out, or he is deliberately withholding that information (and given his continued pattern of deception, the latter seems the more probable). Such a strategy might seem counter-intuitive, since dropping (in the sense of citing) an author's name is a much more common way of legitimating a text than literally dropping (or omitting) the author.[5] But Arnolphe's elision here is designed to move the *maximes* from identifiable and contingent utterances to the realm of the universal. Were he (or an authorial proxy) to relay these ideas directly to Agnès, it would situate them temporally and dialogically. Arnolphe instead relies on the distancation of writing to lend to the maxims the "vatic" or "oracular" quality that Walter Ong attributes to writing (78). As Ong states:

> Like the oracle or the prophet, the book relays an utterance from a source, the one who really "said" or wrote the book. The author might be challenged if only he or she could be reached, but the author cannot be reached in any book. There is no way directly to refute a text. After absolutely total and devastating refutation, it says exactly the same thing as before. ... A text stating what the whole world knows is false will state falsehood forever, so long as the text exists. (78)[6]

Arnolphe's maxims of marriage contain no contextualization, introduction, or apology. They merely state in lapidary terms the complete subjection of an ideal wife to her husband, and acquire their force from their very anonymity. The comparison to religious authoritative texts (whose human authors are secondary to the divine Word that manifests itself through them) is made explicit by Arnolphe's introductory comments that Agnès should learn these maxims by heart just as "une Novice / Par cœur dans le Couvent doit savoir son office" (1:435). And parallel to the medieval humility with respect to the written (sacred) word, Arnolphe disavows direct authorship and offers instead to comment or gloss the central text: "Je vous expliquerai ces choses comme il faut" (1:437).

In the event that Arnolphe did in fact write the maxims, maintaining the pretense of anonymity might seem like a needless doubling of author and commentator. As such, though, it recalls the similar name (and title) game in which Arnolphe is already engaged. The same Arnophe that has "debaptized" himself and, by his own authority given himself the new name of Monsieur de La Souche—and tried to force the recognition of this change by the rest of his society—erases his own authorial name to pretend instead to the authority of divine authorship.[7] In other words, Arnolphe the author might be pursuing in his writing much the same strategy that the socially aspiring bourgeois adopts. In both cases, "Arnolphe" is eliminated in order to forge a new and more powerful alter ego, one who can be a source (or "souche") of progeny and authoritative texts, a double paternity that is the expected outcome of Arnolphe's school. As if to reinforce the connection between hierarchies both textual and sexual, Arnolphe's instruction, designed to make Agnès the unerring mother of his children, begins with a phrase rich in printing imagery: "[J]usqu'au moindre mot imprimez-le-vous bien" (1:433).

Of course, Arnolphe is more unequivocally the author of another literary project within the play. From the very first scene, the audience learns that Arnolphe takes particular delight in discovering the misfortunes of the town's cuckolds ("Enfin ce sont partout des sujets de Satire, / Et comme Spectateur, ne puis-je pas en rire?" [1:400]), but when Arnolphe encounters Horace the audience learns that Arnolphe preserves these stories in writing. Upon hearing that Horace has embarked upon an amorous adventure, Arnolphe remarks in an aside: "Bon, voici de nouveau quelque conte gaillard, / Et ce sera de quoi mettre sur mes tablettes" (1:414). It is presumably from these *tablettes* that Arnolphe has deduced his particular foolproof method for avoiding cuckoldry, keeping a meticulous record of "les tours rusés, et les subtiles trames, / Dont, pour nous en planter, savent user les Femmes" (1:401). Arnolphe is therefore an author of stories exactly like the one in which he is presently living. Like the maxims, Arnolphe's *tablettes* are intended to be a tool of control, asserting his superiority over others by chronicling their shame and ridicule. The play therefore becomes Arnolphe the author's worst nightmare: a story that escapes his domination and turns him into the object of ridicule, instead of the laughing outside observer. Arnolphe's *tablettes* flattered him into thinking he was a "Spectateur" (1:400); what he did not realize is that he was actually one of the characters in the drama.

Given Arnolphe's view of writing as synonymous with control and authority, it follows that he has a deep anxiety regarding female literacy. In speaking with Chrysalde, he casts aspersions on any woman who "de Prose, et de Vers, ferait de doux écrits," and alleges that he wants a wife who does not even know "ce que c'est qu'une Rime" (1:402). He will later add that Agnès was taught to write "contre mon dessein" (1:443) and the seventh of the *maximes du mariage* will specifically forbid all writing:

> Dans ses meubles, dût-elle en avoir de l'ennui
> Il ne faut écritoire, encre, papier ni plumes.
> Le mari doit, dans les bonnes coutumes,
> Écrire tout ce qui s'écrit chez lui. (1:437)

Agnès's quest for independence thus necessarily goes by way of authorship, not only in the abstract sense of acquiring agency, but also in the very real action of writing. When Arnolphe obliges her to chase away Horace by throwing a rock, Agnès adroitly attaches a love letter to it, transforming the erstwhile missile into a romantic missive that escapes her guardian's jealous supervision. Agnès's letter is a response not only to Horace's advances, but also to Arnolphe's use of writing to enforce his control, a deliberate challenge to male authority as expressed and enforced through the written word.

Agnès's letter is meant to be read with the *maximes du mariage* in mind. The most prominent examples of writing in the play, both texts appear in Act 3 in close proximity. In addition, both are the only stylistic departures from the alexandrine lines that are employed in the rest of the play: Arnolphe's maxims are *vers libres*, mixing syllable counts and rhyme structures, while Agnès's letter is prose. The juxtaposition of these two moments of writing and their stylistic difference from the rest of the text are further dramatized by the typography of the printed text of the play edition. Arnophe's maxims are introduced by a font and layout typical of a title page and the maxims themselves appear in italics—Molière's readers have Arnolphe's book placed literally before their eyes. Agnès's letter is similarly set in italics, begins with a large capital, and incorporates a larger font size and different margins. Aurally and visually, the written texts stand out, interruptions of the regular rhyming couplets that carry along the play's dialogue. Even the notary's turgid contract advice in Act 4 is shoehorned comically into the conventional poetic structure—only the two opposed texts of the play's central characters break the form.

The extraordinary attention paid to these texts helps to highlight their differences, since Agnès's letter is not only an attempt to thwart Arnolphe's dominance, but also a rebuttal of his views on authorship and writing. The maxims that Arnolphe advocates are couched as anonymous and authoritarian, inviting exegesis but not dialogue or response. Agnès's letter, on the other hand, is intensely author-focused, meaningful precisely because of the ways in which it reflects the character of the individual who wrote it. As Horace exclaims to Arnolphe:

> Mais il faut qu'en ami je vous montre la lettre.
> Tout ce que son cœur sent, sa main a su l'y mettre:
> Mais en termes touchants, et tous pleins de bonté,
> De tendresse innocente, et d'ingénuité,
> De la manière enfin que la pure nature
> Exprime de l'amour la première blessure. (1:443)

Agnès certainly does not suffer from writer's block—the feelings of her heart and the writing of her hand are identical, at least according to Horace. Nor does it appear as if Agnès is aware of writing's potential disjunction of subjectivity, thereby creating a distance between her and "Agnès the writer," a split that Arnolphe might be exploiting in his maxims (and that Célimène will elevate to an art form in *Le Misanthrope*). Agnès is the quintessential author whose ideas and thoughts flow without constraint or refraction into her written words, thus connecting her to the image of the genius—her writing stems not from study and imitation, but from her own *ingenium*, and Horace connects her unstudied writing style to the innocence of her character (*naturel*): "Avez-vous jamais vu, d'expression plus douce, / Malgré les soins maudits d'un injuste pouvoir, / Un plus beau naturel peut-il se faire voir?" (1:444).

Stated otherwise, Agnès's *caractère* (her innate personality) transmits itself perceptibly through her written style, that is, through the written *caractères* that she fixes on paper. Her written language bears her unique stamp (the etymological root of *character*); Agnès, the ingenious *ingénue*, in essence "prints" herself on paper in the letter that she throws to Horace, and Horace is able to discern by the style of her writing the nature of her soul. Her unadulterated style, the naïveté of her phrasing, her *naturel*—these symbolize for Horace Agnès's untainted innocence and continued resistance to the domination (stylistic and otherwise) of her guardian. Agnès thus exemplifies the early modern period's myth of writing as an effect produced by a single cause, and capable of preserving and manifesting that cause—Julie Stone Peters has noted the era's enduring fascination with "the idea of a single, unitary author, an authoritative genius whose intentions—linguistic or dramatic—the printed text could represent in unadulterated form" (142–43).

The connection between Agnès's character and her writing style is something of a commonplace in Molière's theater. For good or ill, Molière's characters often reveal themselves through what they write—beyond the obvious antecedent in Isabelle's letter in *L'École des maris*, a brief list would include Oronte's sonnet in *Le Misanthrope*, Monsieur Tibaudier's letter in *La Comtesse d'Escarbagnas*, or even Harpagon's lending contract in *L'Avare*. The connection's most extreme form is found in *Les Femmes savantes*, in which a reading of Trissotin's poetry purportedly allows Clitandre to identify the pedant when he first sees him.[8] Beyond these overtly authored texts, other pieces appreciated or recommended by characters also serve to characterize them: Monsieur Jourdain's "mouton" song and Alceste's "vieille chanson" present two prominent examples.

Arnolphe's *maximes* certainly belong on this list as well. Regardless of who actually wrote them, the implied author that the work constructs through theme and style is nearly identical to Arnolphe: solidly bourgeois, patriarchal, old-fashioned, tedious, and preachy. If the form and content of Agnès's letter portray her as resistant to constraints, unaffected, and genuine, Arnolphe's preferred text conveys a characteristic attention to control and structure. *Vers libres* notwithstanding, the *maximes*' poetic form serves to close them off, self-contained axioms whose ending rhyme signals a parallel end to discussion. As Arnolphe states after Agnès finishes reading the initial *maxime*, "Je vous expliquerai ce que cela veut dire: / Mais pour l'heure présente il ne faut rien que lire" (1:436).

Agnès's prose, unpredictable and informal, begs a response both in its conversational style and its content: "Dites-moi franchement ce qui en est" (1:444).

At the center of his play, then, Molière sets in opposition two writers and two writing aesthetics. More importantly, the triumph of Agnès's letter over Arnolphe's versified rules serves, in its larger context, synecdochally to celebrate Molière's self-proclaimed "natural" aesthetic, referenced in both of Molière's theatrical commentaries on *L'École des femmes*: in *La Critique de L'École des femmes*, Dorante will insist that comedy's role is to "peindre d'après Nature" (1:505); in *L'Impromptu de Versailles*, Molière will contrast the Hôtel de Bourgogne's stilted delivery with an example of his own actor reciting "[l]e plus naturellement qu'il lui aurait été possible" (2:825).[9] The denouement of *L'École des femmes* represents not only comedy's traditional victory of youth and love, but also a celebration of the values—self-expression, freedom from strictures, novelty, and spontaneity—that are the social and literary hallmarks of Agnès's letter and the play itself.

L'École des femmes and the Comic Quarrel

Agnès's letter had invited a rapid and frank answer, but some of the Horaces in the audience were only too happy to respond by throwing back their own "grès de taille non petite" (1:441)— the play's image of writing attached to a rock is strangely prescient, given the reception of *L'École des femmes*, which for the next two years resembled nothing better at times than an exchange of personal attacks with accompanying texts. The play debuted on 26 December 1662 and by January 1663, Boileau, writing to the author whom he had not yet met, observes in his *Stances à M. Molière*: "En vain mille jaloux Esprits, / Moliere, osent avec mépris / Censurer ton plus bel Ouvrage. ..." (*Œuvres complètes* [1966], ed. Escal 246). In his preface to the printed edition (1663), Molière notes that he had already begun thinking of a response to his critics "après les deux ou trois premières représentations de ma Pièce" (1:396), and Loret confirms in a note about the 13 January 1663 performance of the play that "en plusieurs lieux on [la] fronde" (Mongrédien, *Recueil* 1:170).

The resulting controversy produced the most concentrated discussion and criticism of Molière the author in his lifetime, rendered all the more important because of his own contributions to the debate.[10] The surviving literature of the *querelle de L'École des femmes* counts nine plays—including Molière's own *Critique de L'École des femmes* (1663) and *L'Impromptu de Versailles* (1663)—as well as two other prose works by Donneau de Visé.[11]

It is apparent that Molière had touched a nerve, and the first text of the *querelle*, Donneau de Visé's *Nouvelles nouvelles* (an *achevé d'imprimer* of 9 February 1663) gives a good indication of the aspects of Molière's play that troubled the sensibilities of his contemporaries. Taking Donneau de Visé's attacks as evidence of what he (and by extension other writers involved in the "fronde" against the play) saw as potentially threatening in *L'École des femmes* reveals two important characteristics: the play's popularity and its potential generic status. Donneau de Visé's brief account is mostly (but not entirely) critical, but it represents a singularly important step in Molière's authorial trajectory, since it provides for the first time a biography of the playwright—or, as it terms it, "un abrégé de l'abrégé de sa vie" (in Molière [1971] 1:1017), an undertaking justified because, as one of the characters states sardonically, "il [Molière] est grand auteur, et grand comédien, lorsqu'il joue ses pièces" (1:1017).[12] As grudging as it might be, Donneau de Visé's text reflects the public's rising interest in the playwright behind the plays.

To this effect, Donneau de Visé traces Molière's career along two parallel tracks. The first depicts Molière's increasing success as a result of progressive pandering to his audience's tastes: "Notre auteur ayant derechef connu ce qu'ils aimaient, vit bien qu'il fallait qu'il s'accommodât au temps; ce qu'il a si bien fait depuis, qu'il en a mérité toutes les louanges que l'on a jamais données aux plus grands auteurs" (in Molière [1971] 1:1019). To a certain degree, this criticism echoes the earlier allegations made by Baudeau de Somaize that Molière's *Précieuses ridicules* succeeded because of the connivance between the author and audience created before the performance by the playwright's visits.[13] Donneau de Visé extends this by arguing that Molière's plays were improved by the suggestions that he received: "… et jamais homme n'a su si bien faire son profit des conseils d'autrui" (1:1019).

The second progression traced by Donneau de Visé concerns Molière's push toward literary respectability, as measured against the standards of seventeenth-century genres. Donneau de Visé thus pays singular attention in his account to the literary trappings of each play, and in particular to the number of acts. His Molière, after writing a few farces, "voulut faire une pièce en cinq actes [*L'Étourdi*]" (1:1018); of *L'École des maris*, Donneau de Visé writes: "Les vers en sont moins bons que ceux du *Cocu imaginaire*, mais le sujet en est tout à fait bien conduit, et si cette pièce avait eu cinq actes, elle pourrait tenir rang dans la postérité après *Le Menteur* et *Les Visionnaires*" (1:1020). The number of acts equates to making certain literary claims, and Donneau de Visé is here noting Molière's increasing authorial ambition and literary apprenticeship: beginning with farces and early five-act experiments, Molière is slowly working up to writing *grandes comédies*. Of *L'École des femmes*, Donneau de Visé notes succinctly, "Cette pièce a cinq actes" (1:1021).

This in turn helps to explain the timing and the intensity of the *querelle*: while many of Molière's previous plays had enjoyed popular success, none, with the exception of the unfortunate *Dom Garcie de Navarre* (1661), had included the kind of textual signifiers that indicated to contemporaries that the play was to be taken seriously from a literary perspective.[14] What was particularly troubling for Molière's critics, and what is admirably underscored in Donneau de Visé's description of Molière's career, is how *L'École des femmes*, the *grande comédie*, did not represent a break in Molière's writing, but grew out of the earlier, more farcical works. In other words, Molière was not working steadily toward a rejection of the early plays as he approached *grande comédie*, but was instead effectuating an innovative reformulation of *grande comédie*, one that would fuse elements from disparate literary registers. Taking elements of farce, as well as the representation and satirizing of contemporary society that he had developed in *Les Précieuses ridicules* and *Les Fâcheux*, and combining it with the trappings of highly literary comedy (five acts of alexandrine verse; traditional ending consisting of a marriage and *reconnaissances*), *L'École des femmes* represented a clear challenge to other authors of comedy, for it had the potential to reshape the genre and fundamentally alter the criteria of success. Its very popularity obligated Molière's colleagues, like Corneille's popularity thirty years previously during the *querelle du Cid*, either to lay out in a convincing manner the reasons why, as Scudéry had written, 'l'estime qu'on en fait est injuste" (Gasté 73), or else to imitate Molière. Molière's deliberate self-marginalization with respect to the literary mainstream, coupled with his success, threatened to create a completely new aesthetic (as well as a social fad) to which other authors would need to conform.

The specific literary criticisms and defense of Molière revolve around four principal themes: the question of popularity versus artistic worth; accusations of plagiarism; discussions of genre and theatrical rules; and the disjunction between performance and print. Through these four topics, however, what is really at stake in the *querelle de L'École des femmes* is Molière's claim to literary authorship, and by extension the criteria by which comic authorship in general should be evaluated. The *Nouvelles nouvelles* makes this point explicit in its treatment of the term *auteur*, at times ironizing it ("Ce fameux auteur" [1:1093]) and at times deliberately avoiding it: "Notre auteur, ou pour ne pas répéter ce mot si souvent, le héros de ce petit récit ..." (1:1019). Through their critiques of Molière's play, the playwright's friends and foes were also arguing in the *querelle* whether writing *L'École des femmes* had in fact made of Molière a legitimate author.

Prior to a closer examination of the texts of the *querelle*, two general observations need to be made. The first concerns the status of the participants involved: the earlier *querelle du Cid* had included interventions by the premier playwrights and critics of the day (e.g., Mairet, Scudéry, Guez de Balzac, Chapelain); the *querelle de L'École des femmes*, in sharp contrast, was waged under the names of young authors with little established reputation. Molière claimed that, particularly in the case of Boursault, other more prominent writers were really at work: in the *Impromptu de Versailles* (1663), Du Croisy, portraying an author hostile to Molière, states that the literary attacks against the playwright are collaborative in nature, but in order to "rendre sa défaite plus ignominieuse," the authors have chosen to attribute the play to "un Auteur sans réputation" (Molière [2010] 2:837).

Georges Couton notes that the Abbé d'Aubignac, embroiled in a violent dispute with Pierre Corneille, accused Corneille of motivating the cabal against Molière, but also adds: "Que le vieux poète ait vu avec quelque plaisir la cabale contre Molière, il se peut: c'est humain. Qu'il en ait été l'organisateur, c'est une affirmation toute gratuite de l'abbé d'Aubignac" (Molière, *Œuvres complètes* [1971] 1:1012). Whether established poets like Corneille were secretly involved in the *querelle*, while quite possible, is difficult to ascertain. However, if the identified participants in the *querelle* were of little reputation at the time, many of them were not without talent and were ultimately successful in their authorial careers (e.g., Donneau de Visé, Montfleury, Robinet). Many also enjoyed the support of powerful institutions such as the troupe of the Hôtel de Bourgogne.

The second point to note is the element of professional jealousy and animosity that underlies the polemical literature of the *querelle*. As Molière states of his opponents in the *Impromptu de Versailles*, "Le plus grand mal que je leur aie fait, c'est que j'ai eu le bonheur de plaire un peu plus qu'ils n'auraient voulu" (Molière [2010] 2:840). Molière's enemies produced no work of reasoned criticism comparable to the *Sentiments de l'Académie sur Le Cid*, and at times even stooped to the basest of personal attacks. This being said, their very *parti pris* can be turned to critical advantage: determined to destroy Molière's reputation, writers like Boursault and Donneau de Visé paint an admirable portrait of the values and practices that qualify the ideal seventeenth-century author precisely through the attributes that they deny to Molière. Even though they often exhibit questionable motives, the attacks of Molière's enemies strive to appeal to generally accepted criteria in order to sway the reader, and in this sense they provide valuable insight into both the rhetorical construction of authorship in the mid-seventeenth century and the ways in which Molière challenged or overturned these conventions.

"Les rieurs ont été pour elle"

It is evident that the greatest problem that Molière's rivals had with the playwright was his popular success. This success was in no way incidental to Molière's defense of his plays; on the contrary, his authorial strategy, following very much the same early trajectory as Corneille, explicitly opposed popular success to the kind of legitimation that would come from peer approval. In the *Impromptu de Versailles*, Molière openly mocks writers who evaluate the fortunes of their works by the approval of "Messieurs vos Confrères," rather than the reaction of the larger public (2:838). The mention of authorial "confrères" recalls the anti-authorial preface to *Les Précieuses ridicules*—even though Molière had adopted the same publication practices as his fellow authors, he was still dedicated to portraying himself rhetorically on the authorial margins, out of favor with the *doctes*.

For the playwright, the opinion of the public is thus the pivot on which hangs the writer's rise or fall, and this opinion is also the key weapon in forcing the recognition of success from an alienated literary establishment. Molière did not hesitate to make the point explicit when he has Uranie state in *La Critique de L'École des femmes*: "[J]e connais son humeur: il [Molière] ne se soucie pas qu'on fronde ses pièces, pourvu qu'il y vienne du monde" (1:512). Evident here is the logic of Viala's *stratégie du succès*, and the texts of Molière's enemies bear witness to the anxiety that Molière's success has created. Donneau de Visé's character Clorante in the *Nouvelles nouvelles* replies bitterly to an inquiry about Molière and his new play:

> Tout ce que je vous puis dire, me répondit-il froidement, et avec un souris dédaigneux, c'est qu'il a réussi, et que vous n'ignorez pas, que
> *Quand on a réussi, on est justifié,*
> Quelque mal que l'on ait fait, et quelque mal que l'on continue de faire. ... (in Molière [1971] 1:1015)

The idea that success, and particularly laughter, the guarantor of comic success, hides a multitude of artistic sins is a point that Donneau de Visé often revisits. In *La Vengeance des marquis*, Ariste exclaims, "Il faut laisser présentement ce qui est bon, pour se servir de ce qui est risible, et abandonner les raisons; puisqu'il suffit de faire rire pour gagner sa cause" (in Molière [1971] 1:1096). Joined with this point is the notion that success renders honest criticism impossible, as it places the critic in a compromising situation. As a character in the *Nouvelles nouvelles* remarks: "[J]'aurais mauvaise grâce de ne vous pas dire du bien de ces ouvrages, puisque tout le monde en dit, et je ne puis sans hasarder ma réputation, vous en dire du mal, quand même je dirais la vérité, ni m'opposer au torrent des applaudissements qu'il reçoit tous les jours" (1:1015–16). The poet Aristide in *Zélinde* similarly points out the impossibility of attacking a writer approved by the (ignorant) public, by replying to requests that he criticize Molière, "Pourquoi voulez-vous que j'aille ruiner ma réputation, en attaquant un homme que tous les Turlupins de France assurent que l'on ne pourra jamais imiter" (1:1041–42).

Philippe de La Croix's *La Guerre comique* contains a particularly striking example of how Molière's popularity helps deflect criticisms. The character Alcipe exclaims that Molière "n'imite pas seulement les Italiens, il copie aussi les Français," to which Cléone, Molière's defender, replies, "Il est vrai qu'il les copie, mais tout le monde en rit" (1:1142). Cléone's response, elegant in its simplicity, makes no attempt to defend Molière from the charges of plagiarism, and instead points out that no matter what Molière's particular artistic practices may be, the public approves or excuses them by laughing at them. The stark fact is that as long as people are laughing at Molière's plays, no one, apart from Molière's rivals, will really care how they were written.

In dramaturgical terms, Molière's *stratégie du succès* implies privileging the audience's pleasure over the rules established by literary theoreticians, a Cornelian position espoused by Dorante in Molière's *Critique de L'École des femmes* in his dispute with the poet Lysidas. When Lysidas presumes to judge the play according to the standards purportedly deduced from Horace and Aristote, Dorante replies that the rules are merely "quelques observations aisées que le bon sens a faites sur ce qui peut ôter le plaisir que l'on prend à ces sortes de Poèmes," adding that anyone with the same good sense could figure them out without any help from the Classics (Molière [2010] 1:507). Dorante therefore concludes: "Je voudrais bien savoir si la grande règle de toutes les règles n'est pas de plaire; et si une pièce de Théâtre qui a attrapé son but n'a pas suivi un bon chemin" (1:507).

By interpreting the theatrical rules as practical guidelines, or means to an end, Molière uses his audience's approval as leverage to argue that it is irrelevant to inquire whether *L'École des femmes* does or does not adhere to them. In essence, he displaces their use from evaluative standards to dramaturgical aids—while his rivals are using the rules to judge the finished theatrical product, Molière is insisting that the rules should be used instead to help playwrights predict audience reaction, avoiding what might take away from an audience's pleasure. Molière's argument similarly displaces the time at which the theatrical rules are pertinent: helpful to consult during the composition of a play in order to assure its success, the rules become extraneous once the audience's judgment has been given. As Molière states in the *Impromptu de Versailles*: "[L]orsqu'on attaque une pièce qui a eu du succès, n'est-ce pas attaquer plutôt le jugement de ceux qui l'ont approuvée, que l'art de celui qui l'a faite?" (2:840). The end result thus retroactively justifies the means, even if the means were unorthodox.

Confronted with Molière's popularity and the immunity that this afforded the embattled playwright, Molière's opponents adopted a number of different tactics to explain away this success or turn it against Molière. In Donneau de Visé's *Zélinde*, the eponymous character attributes Molière's reputation mostly to luck: "S'il a du mérite, ce n'est pas pour ce qui regarde la comédie, et il ne doit tous ces grands succès qu'à son bonheur" (in Molière [1971] 1:1046). Not luck alone, however—Zélinde, repeating Donneau de Visé's charge in the *Nouvelles nouvelles*, adds that Molière's success also comes from an obsequious accommodation of the audience's bad taste: "Et n'est-ce pas enfin être heureux que d'avoir rencontré un siècle, où l'on ne se plaît qu'à entendre des satires?" (1:1046)

But Donneau de Visé figured that Molière's audience really could only appreciate so much satire. The characters in *Zélinde* may attribute Molière's success to the predilections of the public, but in his *Lettre sur les affaires du théâtre* Donneau de Visé tries to use Molière's penchant for derision as a way to alienate certain prominent members of Molière's audience, attempting to implicate the nobility in the ridiculous portraits that the playwright had staged. Noting that Molière's comedy only spares "l'auguste personne du roi" from mockery, Donneau de Visé writes that Molière "ne s'aperçoit pas que cet incomparable monarque est toujours accompagné des gens qu'il veut rendre ridicules," and that these members of the nobility whom the playwright satirizes are integral to the king's glory and honor: "que ce sont eux qui forment sa cour; que c'est avec eux qu'il se divertit; que c'est avec eux qu'il s'entretient et que c'est avec eux qu'il donne de la terreur à ses ennemis" (in Molière [1971] 1:1109–10). Expressing shock at this audacity, Donneau de Visé concludes: "[C]'est pourquoi Élomire devrait plutôt travailler à nous faire voir qu'ils sont tous des héros, puisque le prince est toujours au milieu d'eux, et qu'il en est comme le chef, que de nous en faire voir des portraits ridicules" (1:1109–10). Donneau de Visé's obsequious attempt to drive a wedge between Molière and the nobility, and even the king, points to the obvious advantages that Molière was deriving from his popularity among these privileged spectators.[15]

However, in addition to equating audience approval with poor literary quality or seeking to cast Molière's comedies as personal attacks, Donneau de Visé proposes a third, more direct, method for rival authors to upset Molière's privileged position. Popularity is a double-edged sword, and Molière's rapid rise to fame, like Corneille's before him, opens up the possibility for others to follow in his wake and even overturn him through a change of public opinion. It is precisely this strategy that Zélinde recommends to the poet Aristide. After Aristide exclaims, "La réputation d'Élomire n'est déjà que trop bien établie; je n'ai garde de travailler pour l'affermir davantage, et je suis assuré que plus on le critiquera, plus on le fera réussir" (1:1041), Zélinde replies, "Quoi, vous êtes encore dans cette pensée? Faites rire comme lui, et vous réussirez. Ils ne prennent son parti que parce qu'il les divertit: renchérissez sur la satire, accommodez-vous au goût du siècle, et vous verrez si l'on ne dira pas que vous aurez autant de mérite qu'Élomire" (1:1042). Zélinde's suggestion astutely points out the inherent weakness in Molière's authorial strategy: since Molière's success is based on popular approval (and not the approval of the *doctes*), the fickle nature of taste places Molière at risk for a fall that would erase his previous gains.

In his discussion of the *stratégie du succès*, Alain Viala confirms Donneau de Visé's observation, noting the importance for authors pursuing such a strategy to convert popular success into more durable and lasting forms: *charges*, pensions, Academy seats. At this early stage in his career, Molière was particularly vulnerable to such reversals of popular fortune and as a result was highly dependent on public opinion. While Molière reveled in the contrast that he could draw with "messieurs les auteurs," his independence came at a certain price, particularly since he was working in a genre at a distinct disadvantage in the literary hierarchy. As a result, Molière's career bears the marks of an accentuated attention to popular trends and public opinion. The extreme form of this idea is René Bray's suggestion of a playwright devoid of any properly literary motivations who works only to remain in tune with his audience's tastes: "Le public est complice de l'auteur et l'auteur doit veiller à ne jamais rompre l'accord" (Bray 31).[16] Regardless of Molière's artistic intentions, it is clear that, as Roger Duchêne has aptly pointed out, Molière's financial prosperity was underwritten by the receipts at the Palais-Royal.[17] However, neither Donneau de

Visé nor Bray takes into account the extent to which the relationship between playwright and audience is dynamic and reciprocal: Molière may indeed be shaping his theater to match the tastes of his audience, but his theater is also actively shaping those tastes—the worry that is lurking behind all of Molière's adversaries' criticisms of the era's "mauvais goût."

It was this careful harmony between artistic production and reception that permitted Molière to state of *L'École des femmes* in his preface to the printed play: "Bien des gens ont frondé d'abord cette Comédie: mais les rieurs ont été pour elle" (Molière [2010] 1:396). Donneau de Visé's passage from *Zélinde* had pointed out the risk of such a defense: if the *rieurs* were presently for Molière, they could potentially be appropriated to a different cause, and with Molière's authorial strategy so explicitly and tenuously linked to this popular approval, a new fashionable playwright could prove the undoing of Molière's authorial pretensions. However, the eventual triumph of *rieurs* over *frondeurs* not only signaled the justification of Molière's *grande comédie*, but, as will be seen below, allowed the author to convert success in the *querelle* into gains in other important areas.

The Jay in Borrowed Feathers

Baudeau de Somaize was only the first in a long succession of Molière source-hunters, and accusations of plagiarism were frequent in the *querelle de L'École des femmes*. These accusations served a double function: in addition to denying Molière's novelty—in effect, eliminating the difference that he prided himself on—they sought to neutralize his popularity, the motor of his artistic success. The allegations were not limited to the specific case of *L'École des femmes*, either: in his *Nouvelles nouvelles* and *Zélinde*, Donneau de Visé identified sources for *L'Étourdi*, *Les Précieuses ridicules*, *Le Cocu imaginaire*, *L'École des maris*, and *Les Fâcheux* (in Molière [1971] 1:1021, 1038).

As for *L'École des femmes* itself, the *querelle* produced an abundance of alleged literary sources, some of which were themselves in turn labeled derivative. As he did with so many other topics in the quarrel, Donneau de Visé was the first to raise the issue, writing in the *Nouvelles nouvelles* that the play has no fewer than four literary antecedents: "Le sujet de ces deux pièces [*L'École des maris* and *L'École des femmes*] n'est point de son invention, il est tiré de divers endroits, à savoir de Boccace, des contes de Douville, de *La Précaution inutile* de Scarron; et ce qu'il y a de plus beau dans la dernière, est tiré d'un livre intitulé *Les Nuits facétieuses du seigneur Straparole*" (1:1021).

However, it is curious that, for Donneau de Visé and others, such borrowing could equate to authorial misconduct. Noting that "there were no laws at the time against plagiarism," Larry Norman has written that accusations like those made against Molière pose a serious paradox: "Even if the classical age, as Foucault argued, is the period in which the author function asserted itself as a powerful organizing force in literary mentalities, and even if it was the period in which individual 'invention' determined the author's status, it still must be admitted that the aesthetics of imitation granted a great deal of leeway for recycling the texts of others" (30). Similarly, Claude Bourqui, in his examination of Molière's sources, hesitates to state whether Molière's intertextual practices exceeded respectable norms for the time period, citing the lack of a comprehensive study into such textual borrowing, but adding that the majority of the era's comedies included some sort of adaptation.[18]

The question remains why in the context of such widespread comedic adaptations Molière's adversaries would consider it damaging to Molière's reputation to accuse the playwright of an extremely common authorial practice. Part of the answer may lie in Molière's notable silence on the issue: Molière, either in his prefaces or in his meta-theatrical works like the *Critique* or the *Impromptu*, never admitted to having used a source text in the composition of his theater (Bourqui, *Sources* 18). While *La Critique de L'École des femmes*, Molière's exercise in procatalepsis—although it provokes at least as much as it diffuses arguments to come—addresses most major issues raised by the playwright's opponents (e.g., the violation of the theatrical rules, the questions of *vraisemblance*), the lack of any discussion of the numerous accusations of plagiarism, already made public with the appearance of the *Nouvelles nouvelles*, is a glaring omission.

Molière's silence on the issue is ambiguous—whereas contemporary playwrights such as Dorimon or Hauteroche loudly trumpeted either their originality or the source of their adaptation, Molière merely ignores the issue.[19] To his adversaries, this silence gives the impression that Molière is trying to pass off his borrowings surreptitiously as his own, willfully suppressing the debt that he owes to other authors. This presumed artistic and creative isolation prompts his enemies to seek to inscribe his plays within a literary genealogy.[20]

However, Donneau de Visé goes further: in addition to providing the reader with a list of literary sources for Molière's plays, he advances the rather curious notion that Molière's material is given to him by ardent admirers who wish to see themselves and their acquaintances portrayed on stage: "Notre auteur, après avoir fait ces deux pièces [*Sganarelle* and *L'École des maris*], reçut des mémoires en telle confusion, que, de ceux qui lui restaient, et de ceux qu'il recevait tous les jours, il en aurait eu de quoi travailler toute sa vie" (Molière [1971] 1:1020). Of this phenomenon, Norman has written: "It seems that the indictment is leveled in order to add some zest to these rather banal charges of literary theft" (30). Norman finds in the accusations that Molière's plays were "rhapsodies," that is, texts loosely constructed by combining previously written pieces, a provocative insight into the dynamics of social satire and the relationship between Molière and his public. Conversely, while Donneau de Visé's charge might be convincing in a case like *Les Fâcheux*, where the plot is relatively undeveloped and the interest lies in a series of character sketches, it is uncertain how it would be relevant to a play like *L'École des femmes*.

Donneau de Visé's attacks further suggest that the "aesthetics of imitation" (Norman 30) may not apply equally to the different theatrical genres. Working from source material (and even previous plays) was not a cause of reproach for authors of tragedy—on the contrary, authors like Corneille and Racine often listed and occasionally included in the paratext of their printed editions the sources that they had used in the composition of their plays.[21] Molière, however, is being held to a different standard, and Donneau de Visé's apocryphal story of Molière's *mémoires* emphasizes the primacy of invention in the ideal conception of the comic playwright. Negating the originality of the play's subject (whether through identifying published sources or through the *mémoires* authored by others) negates the authority of the author—there is no conceptual room in Donneau de Visé's account for the creative labor involved in adapting these disparate materials into a cohesive whole.

Molière's defenders argued instead in favor of a more equitable evaluation of authorial work. Philippe de La Croix has Philinte, a character in *La Guerre comique,* acknowledge Molière's use of sources, but reject the idea that such borrowing removed any creative effort: "Je crois que *La Précaution inutile* et les *Histoires de Straparole* lui ont fourni quelque chose de son sujet, qu'il lit les Italiens et les Espagnols, qu'il en tire quelque idée dans l'occasion; mais le bon usage qu'il fait de ces choses le rend encore plus louable" (in Molière [1971] 1:1139). In addition to this positive view of adaptation, Philinte astutely points out the generic double standard that critics were applying, adding, "Je voudrais bien savoir par quelle raison un auteur comique n'a pas la liberté de se servir des lectures qu'il fait, et pourquoi les poètes tragiques prennent des sujets entiers, traduisent des centaines de vers dans une pièce, et se parent des plus beaux endroits des anciens" (1:1139; also qtd. in Norman 31). A "pareille inégalité," as Philinte labels it, is indeed surprising, particularly since the genre's two Classical models—the Roman playwrights Plautus and Terence—openly acknowledged that writing comedy for them consisted largely in the reworking of pre-existing material.[22]

Molière himself ironized his enemies' bad faith in accusing him of plagiarism in works that were often closely based on his own. In the *Impromptu de Versailles,* Brécourt, speaking of Boursault's *Portrait du peintre,* states that "tout ce qu'il y a d'agréable, sont effectivement les idées qui ont été prises de Molière" (Molière [2010] 2:839). While speaking of his plays later in the *Impromptu,* Molière invites his enemies, "Qu'ils s'en saisissent après nous, qu'ils les retournent comme un habit pour les mettre sur leur Théâtre, et tâchent à profiter de quelque agrément qu'on y trouve, et d'un peu de bonheur que j'ai, j'y consens" (2:841). The metaphor of turning clothes inside-out is an apt criticism of the facile dramaturgical procedures at the base of *Le Portrait du peintre* (which borrows characters, plot, and dialogue from *La Critique de L'École des femmes*) and other works in the *querelle.* Similarly to Baudeau de Somaize and his *Véritables Précieuses,* Molière's adversaries apparently did not mind availing themselves of the same adaptational techniques that they condemned in Molière's work.

The *locus classicus* repeatedly invoked in the quarrel to discuss plagiarism and the identification of sources is Aesop's fable of the jay in peacock's feathers, and which Horace had used to refer to literary theft.[23] Molière's adversaries find the fable's retributive (or redistributive) ending particularly appealing. Donneau de Visé, for example, has Zélinde fantasize about a similar day of reckoning when Molière's victims—authors, actors, even books—return to claim what is theirs:

> Si vous vouliez, tout de bon, jouer Élomire, il faudrait dépeindre un homme qui eût dans son habillement quelque chose d'Arlequin, de Scaramouche, du Docteur, et de Trivelin, que Scaramouche lui vînt redemander ses démarches, sa barbe, et ses grimaces; et que les autres lui vinssent, en même temps, demander ce qu'il prend d'eux dans son jeu, et dans ses habits. Après cela il les faudrait faire revenir tous, demander ensemble ce qu'il a pris dans leurs comédies. Dans une autre scène, l'on pourrait faire venir tous les auteurs, et tous les vieux bouquins, où il a pris ce qu'il y a de plus beau dans ses pièces. L'on pourrait ensuite faire paraître tous les gens de qualité qui lui ont donné des mémoires, et tous ceux qu'il a copiés. (Molière [1971] 1:1040)

Zélinde's interlocutors conclude that such a scene of "entière restitution" would result in a Molière naked as Aesop's jaybird (1:1040).

Donneau de Visé's revenge fantasy, however, could only remain that: where *Zélinde* and the fable ignore important historical realities is in positing that there is a fundamental difference between metaphorical jays and peacocks, and a surefire way of identifying the rightful owner of literary feathers. A more accurate fable would point out that a jay who was charismatic enough could quite easily pass off feathers not entirely his own.[24] Popularity interferes with literary property and introduces an element of inequality among the community of writers, at least partly in the sense that those authors outside of the public's consciousness have little way of defending their works from being appropriated by more successful authors. As authors' reputations grow, texts become inextricably linked to their name, regardless at times of their original source.[25]

The lesson that Molière had learned through the publication of his early plays—namely, that popularity could prevent literary theft—here finds a corollary: popularity can excuse borrowing. Keeping prudently silent on the issue of sources and adhering to the principles of the *stratégie du succès*, Molière once again deferred judgment to the public. His approach is shrewd, since, as Julie Stone Peters has noted, originality, imitation, and intellectual property in the early modern context interface in significant ways with audience approval: "Dramatic writing is a continual process of literary inheritance, from play to play and to new play in turn, in which everyone borrows, and attribution depends, in the end, not only on origins but on merit, for one remembers (and in the theatre re-members) only what is most 'worth remembring'" (219).

However, even in the polemical world of the *querelle*, there is room for a more nuanced discussion of intertextuality that does not reduce it to theft versus originality, or a triumph of popularity. Robinet's *Panégyrique de L'École des femmes* takes a characteristically ambiguous approach to Molière's borrowings: while the play as a whole is cast as an attack on Molière, many of the arguments and responses that Molière's supposed defender advances appear reasonable and accurate. Lidamon, a Molière critic, alleges that *L'École des femmes* "n'est qu'un mélange des larcins que l'auteur a faits de tous côtés, jusqu'à son *Preschez et patrocinez jusqu'à la Pentecôte*, qu'il a pris dans le Rabelais, ainsi que dans Don-Quixot le modèle des préceptes d'Agnès" (Molière [1971] 1:1079). Comparing Molière first to "un bassin qui reçoit ses eaux d'ailleurs," Lidamon then echoes Zélinde by turning to the familiar image of the bird in borrowed feathers: "Je tais encore que son jeu et ses habits ne sont non plus que des imitations de divers comiques, lesquels le laisseraient aussi nu que la corneille d'Horace, s'ils lui redemandaient chacun, ce qu'il leur a pris" (1:1079). Crysolite, summoned to be Molière's advocate, asks in response to Lidamon's attacks: "Dans quels poèmes, même des plus beaux, ne vous ferai-je point voir quantité de très méchants vers, et un nombre infini de larcins, si la plupart ne sont que des imitations et des traductions?" (1:1082). In addition to recognizing adaptation's ubiquity, Crysolite also establishes various types of borrowing, remarking about the quotation from Rabelais, "[V]ous savez bien que c'est une réponse de Panurge à Pantagruel, qu'il a mise exprès dans la bouche d'Arnolphe, à cause qu'elle venait à propos" (1:1082). Crysolite's defense of Molière consists of two elements: in the first place, a generalization of the plagiarism attack to include all authors, and secondly, a recognition that not all examples of intertextuality constitute plagiarism. Crysolite's first point seems a remarkably cogent acknowledgment of the period's aesthetic paradox that demanded that an author be both imitative and original, and if it actually does little to excuse Molière from Lidamon's charges (to which he is, in effect, pleading guilty), it does point out the fundamental bad faith in accusing Molière of a practice in which all authors are engaged.[26]

Crysolite's second point, however, goes much further in bringing nuance to an area where Molière's enemies remained staunchly Manichean. Crysolite, alone among the numerous fictional characters created during the *querelle*, advances the idea that not all borrowing is equal, and that some can be put to legitimate artistic purposes. If Molière's characters cite a passage from Rabelais, that in and of itself does not constitute plagiarism, particularly if the author is establishing an explicit connection with the prior text. In this specific case, recognizing the citation from Rabelais provides an additional dimension to the characterization of Arnolphe and Chrysalde: by mapping onto their discussion the model of Panurge and Pantagruel, Molière gives ironic indications as to who holds the ridiculous role and serves to further undermine Arnolphe's moral authority. If such a careful reading is rare in the polemical texts of the *querelle*, it nevertheless demonstrates a capacity for appreciating and evaluating moments of intertextuality—a more complex reception of the text worthy of the ambiguities and complexities inherent in the era's approach to imitation and originality.

Farce and the Death of *La Belle Comédie*

Molière's opponents saw in the playwright's rise not only the triumph of an individual, but a shift in taste that threatened to effectuate longstanding changes in the wider Parisian theatrical world. In Robinet's *La Panégyrique de L'École des femmes*, for example, the two women leading the criticism against Molière explain their motives in terms of the negative impact that Molière's comedy is having on other theatrical genres. Célante exclaims:

> Je ne veux point déguiser mes sentiments: j'aime la belle comédie, et je ne saurais souffrir qu'à cause qu'il [Molière] n'a pas une troupe propre à la jouer sur son théâtre et qu'il est lui-même le plus détestable comédien qu'on ait jamais vu, il la détruise par des rhapsodies qui font que chacun déserte son parti, et qui obligent jusques à l'unique et incomparable troupe royale de la bannir honteusement de sa pompeuse scène, pour y représenter des bagatelles et des farces qui n'auraient été bonnes

> en un autre temps qu'à divertir la lie du peuple dans les carrefours et les autres places publiques: tâchant ainsi d'éviter le titre d'ancienne, qu'on lui donne au Louvre, à cause que ses grands poèmes ne sont plus à la mode, c'est-à-dire de la qualité de ceux de Zoïle [Molière]. (Molière [1971] 1:1073)

Célante claims that Molière is effectuating a striking change for low comedy in both performance space (from the *carrefours* and *places publiques* to respectable playhouses) and audience (from the *lie du peuple* to the denizens of the Louvre). Molière's novelty (and also his threat) lies in this displacement of traditional boundaries: the former associations of genre, audience, and location are no longer valid. Molière's innovation is causing a reorganization within genre and within the physical space of the theater.

Célante is not the only participant in the *querelle* to worry that Molière's reformulation of *grande comédie* will lead to the death of more traditional, and serious, works. In La Croix's *La Guerre comique*, the tragic playwright Alcidor gives voice to the economic worries of Molière's rivals, asking, "Les auteurs n'ont-ils pas intérêt [d'étouffer Molière]? S'ils n'ont pas le talent de réussir dans le comique comme lui, et s'il est cause qu'on méprise les pièces sérieuses, que deviendront-ils?" (Molière [1971] 1:1138).[27] One of his interlocutors responds, "Ils le regarderont faire. Ma foi, les grands hommes ne travaillent à présent que pour la gloire. Il n'y a plus d'argent pour eux" (1:1138).

The theatrical contrast between the new comedy and serious theater is quickly reduced in one of the *querelle*'s commonplaces to a literary duel between two representative authors: Molière and Pierre Corneille. About Molière's *turlupinade* paraphrased from the *Impromptu de Versailles* ("Marquis, à tes canons fais prendre médecine; / Pourquoi, marquis? pourquoi? c'est qu'ils se portent mal"), Montfleury's marquis, a ridiculously ardent Molière supporter, enthusiastically exclaims in the *Impromptu de l'Hôtel de Condé*: "Morbleu! je lirais l'un et l'autre Corneille, / Que je n'y verrais pas une chose pareille" (Molière [1971] 1:1122). La Croix's De La Rancune remarks: "On aurait peine à souffrir qu'on représentât *Le Cid* deux fois par an, et l'on irait voir son *Cocu imaginaire* s'il le jouait tous les jours" (Molière [1971] 1:1142). In Chevalier's *Les Amours de Calotin*, the baron, critical of Molière, reproaches his friend the marquis for his enthusiastic appréciation of Molière's comedies: "Hors Molière, pour vous il n'est point de salut, / Tous les autres autheurs vous sont insupportables, / Les Corneilles auprès sont autheurs detestables" (11). Two of Robinet's characters, Palamède and Lidamon, draw a particularly insulting image of the contrast between Corneille and the new comedic playwrights, of whom Molière is the model. Palamède remarks, "Il me vient sur cela une plaisante idée; je m'imagine voir le grand Ariste [Corneille], au milieu de tous les petits avortons du Parnasse qui nous donnent ces niaiseries, comme un géant investi par des pygmées, et de nains qui lui veulent faire la guerre" (Molière [1971] 1: 1073). Lidamon responds to this analogy by stating, "[C]e ne lui est pas une petite mortification de voir son grand cothurne effacé par le ridicule escarpin de ces demis ou quarts d'auteurs engendrés de la corruption du siècle" (1:1073–74). Palamède and Lidamon link genre to literary stature, and their imagined theatrical battle makes midgets of comic authors like Molière.

Donneau de Visé will repeat (and accentuate) the comparison between Molière and Corneille in his *Lettre sur les affaires du théâtre*: "Il est aisé de connaître par toutes ces choses, qu'il y a au Parnasse mille places de vuides entre le divin Corneille et le comique Élomire, et que l'on ne les peut comparer en rien: puisque pour ses ouvrages, le premier est plus qu'un dieu, et le second est auprès de lui moins qu'un homme" (Molière [1971] 1:1112). As in Robinet's play, the comic author here is portrayed as a degenerate whose profession is a derogation of his own humanity, in some respects transposing the Church's continued condemnation of acting into the realm of the author. To write comedies is to fall from literary grace.

Despite the hyperbolic insistence by Molière's enemies of the immense distance between Molière and Corneille, the omnipresence of the comparison suggests a deep-seated worry on their part that Parisian theater audiences were not quite as convinced. Donneau de Visé might well assert that "il est plus glorieux de se faire admirer par des ouvrages solides que de faire rire par des grimaces, des turlupinades, de grandes perruques, et de grands canons" (Molière [1971] 1:1112), but Molière appeared to be garnering plenty of renown as well. While the omnipresent comparison to Corneille clearly demonstrates the generic prejudices against which Molière was forced to work, these comparisons nevertheless also show how far he had come in an astonishingly short period of time to being himself the figure of the new comedy and the central challenger to Corneille's theatrical crown.[28]

By extolling the virtues of Corneille, Molière's adversaries were also responding to the assertions that Molière had made regarding the respective difficulties, and by extension, the literary status, of comedy and tragedy. Molière's *Critique de L'École des femmes* had advanced the suggestion that writing comedy, and thus painting realistic portraits, was more challenging than writing a tragedy, where the characters could remain safely abstract. Uranie had established an equality between the two genres, opining that "l'une n'est pas moins difficile à faire que l'autre" (Molière [2010] 1:504). Dorante goes a step further, however, claiming: "Car enfin, je trouve qu'il est bien plus aisé de se guinder sur de grands sentiments, de braver en Vers la Fortune, accuser les Destins, et dire des injures aux Dieux, que d'entrer comme il faut dans le ridicule des hommes, et de rendre agréablement sur le Théâtre des défauts de tout le monde" (1:504–05). The statement suggests a theoretical rehabilitation of comedy and a questioning of its traditional lowly position in the hierarchy of genres.

Molière's adversaries did not fail to point out how this apology for comedy worked in the author's personal interests. Donneau de Visé in particular linked Molière's defense of comedy to the author's failure to produce a successful play in a more respected genre, writing that Molière was avenging the "mauvais succès de son *Dom Garcie*" (Molière [1971] 1:1110). Referring explicitly to Molière's justification of comedy, albeit taking considerable license in the rewording, Donneau de Visé continues, "Voyons présentement si ce qu'il a dit est véritable: si les pièces comiques doivent étouffer les sérieuses, et si les bouffons méritent plus de gloire que les grands hommes" (1:1110). Claiming that "une pièce sérieuse réussit pour son mérite, et sa bonté seule nous oblige à lui rendre justice," Donneau de Visé attributes the success of a comedy to very different motives:

> [L]'on va souvent voir en foule une pièce comique, encore que l'on la trouve méchante, et l'on va plutôt aux ouvrages qui sont de la nature de ceux d'Élomire, pour les gens que l'on y croit voir jouer, que pour la judicieuse conduite de la pièce, car l'on sait bien qu'il ne s'en pique pas. Si l'on court à tous les ouvrages comiques, c'est pour ce que l'on y trouve toujours quelque

> chose qui fait rire, et que ce qui en est méchant, et même hors de la vraisemblance, est quelquefois ce qui divertit le plus. (1:1110–11)

The questions of "judicieuse conduite" and "vraisemblance" signal that Donneau de Visé is measuring *L'École des femmes* against the theatrical rules of serious theater. Such a standard is not unwarranted: Dorante in *La Critique de L'École des femmes* had not only claimed that composing a comedy required more skill than a tragedy, but had also stated that Molière's play did not violate any of the Classical rules, even asserting (although never proving), "[J]e ferais voir aisément que peut-être, n'avons-nous point de pièce au Théâtre plus régulière que celle-là" (Molière [2010] 1:508).[29]

Molière's adversaries responded by attacking *L'École des femmes* principally on the issue of *vraisemblance*, a topic all the more pertinent since "peindre d'après nature" served as the basis for Molière's argument that writing comedy is more demanding than tragedy. Certain seemingly trivial details consequently receive inordinate critical attention in the texts of the quarrel: Arnolphe's willingness to lend money to Horace; Horace's repeated imprudence in relating his adventures to a man who obviously does not appreciate them; the dinner invitation that Arnolphe extends to Chrysalde; or the fact that all the action takes place in the street. In an example that typifies the kinds of objections raised to the play, characters in La Croix's *La Guerre comique* condemn Arnolphe's scene with the notary, in which Arnolphe's spoken musings about Agnès's love for Horace are comically misinterpreted by the notary to refer to specifications to be made in the marriage contract. When Philinte asks, "Cette scène pèche-t-elle contre la vraisemblance?" Alcidor responds, "Pouvez-vous souffrir qu'Arnolphe réponde si à propos à ce notaire qu'il n'écoute pas! qu'il lui donne occasion de parler de toutes les clauses d'un contrat de mariage? Et ce discours qu'Arnolphe fait en lui-même doit-il être entendu de ce notaire?" (Molière [1971] 1:1137). The humor of the scene makes no difference—the dialogue's *invraisemblance* is all that matters in the eyes of the fastidious critic.

In addition to violations of *vraisemblance*, Molière's adversaries address the equally serious question of *bienséance*. Molière's infamous scene of the *le*, to cite the most significant example, became a lively subject of debate during the *querelle*, figuring prominently in the writings of Donneau de Visé, Boursault, Robinet, La Croix, and Molière himself.[30] However, if it is easy to see why the *le* scene would have troubled seventeenth-century sensibilities, it is not at all difficult to find equally suggestive or blatantly indecent scenes in other theatrical productions of the period, some of them from the very authors writing against Molière (see, for example, Montfleury's *La femme juge et partie* [1669]). While professional jealousy could certainly explain such bad faith, more significant distinctions were also at play.

The critical objections to Molière's play in the name of *bienséance* or *vraisemblance* can seem largely beside the point (how many readers or spectators would be inclined to question, as Boursault's characters do, the size of the rock that Agnès is required to throw at Horace?). However, underlying these objections is the extent to which these issues for the seventeenth-century public hinge on questions of genre and method of diffusion. What is tolerated in manuscript form may be reprehensible when printed; what passes without comment in a farce is unacceptable in a higher genre. Molière's enemies, in pointing out faults of *vraisemblance* and *bienséance*, certainly exaggerate their criticisms; nevertheless, their objections have as a backdrop the hierarchy of genres and Molière's own statements concerning the artistic respectability of comedy. Seeing in *L'École des femmes* a pretension to elevated literary status, Donneau de Visé and others respond by holding the play to the highest of standards in order to show its defects. That they did so with such vehemence suggests the very real threat that Molière's play presented as the new model for *la belle comédie*.

This also helps explain the selection of scenes or plot details that Molière's adversaries choose for commentary. The scene of the notary, the *équivoque* of the *le*, and Alain and Georgette's bumbling interactions with Arnolphe all constitute elements of farce. In addition to claiming that Molière has violated general standards of decency, Molière's critics are claiming that he has violated generic boundaries, including in his five-act, versified comedy vulgar (in every sense of the term) material that should have been excluded. For Molière to propose that comedy (and particularly his comedy) should deserve the same consideration as tragedy constituted an audacious and aggressive blurring of genres that his enemies were not willing to pardon.

Chapter Three

"L'on rit à les entendre, et l'on pleure à les lire": Print and Performance

Inherent in the accusation that *L'École des femmes* is a farce lies the more insidious accusation that Molière should not really be considered an author. Farce in the seventeenth century implied a performance-driven production devoid of literary merits or pretensions. As Donneau de Visé writes, "Les postures contribuent à la réussite de ces sortes de pièces, et elles doivent ordinairement tous leurs succès aux grimaces d'un acteur" (Molière [1971] 1:1111). Donneau de Visé explicitly links the passages of *L'École des femmes* identified by prior commentators as farcical in register with performance, emphasizing the nontextual character of these elements: "les grimaces d'Arnolphe, le visage d'Alain et la judicieuse scène du Notaire" (1:1111). Other writers will go further in elaborating a relationship between performance and laughter, a relationship that readily acknowledges the performed play's success in order to disparage the printed text. Robinet's Lidamon sarcastically asks Molière's defenders, "Toutes ces choses qui font miracle sur le théâtre ne paraissent-elles pas bien sur le papier?" (Molière [1971] 1:1078). Similarly, in Boursault's *Le Portrait du peintre*, the Comte, despite being a Molière partisan, is disappointed by his reading of *L'École des femmes*:

> Damis: Mais rit-on de l'endroit quand on rit d'y voir rire?
>   Pour juger d'un ouvrage, il faut lire …
> Le Comte: En effet,
>   Et voit-on, en lisant, les grimaces qu'on fait?
> Damis: Cette pièce …
> Le Comte: Ma foi, j'en ai fait deux lectures,
>   Mais je n'y puis trouver ces plaisantes postures.
>   *Eh! parlez! dépêchez! vite! promptement! tôt!*
>   On appelle cela réciter comme il faut.
>   Verra-t-on en lisant, fût-on grand philosophe,
>   Ce que veut dire un *ouf* qui fait la catastrophe?
>   (Molière [1971] 1:1053–54)

Molière's enemies are willing to acknowledge his talents as a comic actor and as a director.[31] Donneau de Visé in his *Nouvelles nouvelles* writes of the performance of *L'École des femmes*: "Jamais comédie ne fut si bien représentée, ni avec tant d'art, chaque acteur sait combien il y doit faire de pas, et toutes ses œillades sont comptées" (Molière [1971] 1:1021). He continues by praising Molière "pour avoir si bien joué son rôle, pour avoir si judicieusement distribué tous les autres, et pour avoir enfin pris le soin de faire si bien jouer ses compagnons, que l'on peut dire que tous les acteurs qui jouent dans sa pièce, sont des originaux que les plus habiles maîtres de ce bel art pourront difficilement imiter" (1:1022). Such remarks serve to establish an important dynamic between acting and authorship, and between success in the theater and in print. Recognizing Molière's acting talents in this sense becomes an oblique way of denigrating Molière the author and denying to *L'École des femmes* the literary status that its format suggested and that its author asserted. Praising Molière's acting also becomes a way to account for the success of *L'École des femmes* and to qualify it as superficial. Philippe de La Croix satirizes this position of Molière's enemies in the character of De La Rancune, who states: "Molière est bon comédien; mais il serait encore plus fort s'il ne se mêlait que de son métier; il veut trancher de l'auteur" (Molière [1971] 1:1140). When one of his interlocutors suggests that "il y a peut-être un peu de mérite" to justify Molière's success, De La Rancune exclaims: "Quel mérite, Monsieur? ... Ses pièces sont-elles si belles? C'est son jeu qui pipe et qui les fait paraître" (1:1141).

The *querelle*'s most sustained criticism of the performance versus the reading of *L'École des femmes* takes place in Montfleury's *Impromptu de l'Hôtel de Condé*, set at the Palais de Justice in front of the booksellers' stalls. The presence of a *marchande de livres* in the play allows for several reflections on print authorship and the success of Molière beyond the stage. Alis, the bookseller, asks the marquis: "Dites-moi donc, Monsieur, afin que je vous vende / De qui vous les voulez" (Molière [1971] 1:1117). The marquis, a ridiculous Molière admirer, exclaims: "De qui? Belle demande! / De Molière, morbleu!" (1:1117). Upon picking up a copy of *L'École des femmes*, the marquis is particularly interested by the engraving depicting Arnolphe seated and beginning his instruction to a standing Agnès. At the sight of the illustration, the marquis begins to laugh: "Ma foi, je ris encor quand je vois ce portrait" (1:1117). When the bookseller asks what the marquis finds amusing, he tellingly responds, "Je ris de souvenance" (1:1117)—it is the performance that is still generating the laughter.

The unusual attention paid to the printed edition of *L'École des femmes* is justified by the marquis's subsequent request of another

Chapter Three

Molière title from the bookseller: *L'Impromptu de Versailles*. Upon hearing that it has not been printed, the surprised marquis asserts the commercial success that a printed edition of the *Impromptu* would have: "Vous en vendrez beaucoup, et par toutes les places …" (1:1123). The marquis's friend Alcidon responds: "Il faudrait donc, Monsieur, vendre aussi ses grimaces, / Et de peur qu'en lisant on en vît pas l'effet, / Au bout de chaque vers il faudrait un portrait" (1:1123). The play's reliance on unprintable performance elements leads Alcidon to conclude: "Ma foi, je n'en veux point, pas un de nos libraires / N'en veut" (1:1123). When the marquis continues to protest, the bookseller insists:

> Mais, Monsieur, chacun sait ses affaires,
> Si quand il fait des vers il les dit plaisamment,
> Ces vers sur le papier perdent leur agrément;
> On est désabusé de sa façon d'écrire,
> L'on rit à les entendre, et l'on pleure à les lire,
> Et de ces mêmes vers tels qui seront charmés,
> Ne les connaissent plus quand ils sont imprimés;
> Sitôt que l'on les lit un chacun nous vient dire,
> Je voudrais bien savoir de quoi nous pouvions rire;
> Car de tout ce qu'il fait on ne reconnaît rien
> Que le titre, le nom des acteurs et le sien. (1:1123)

At this point, the purpose for the prior episode of the portrait becomes even clearer: Montfleury shows the Molière supporter amused, not by the printed text in front of him, but by the representation and the remembrance of the performance. As Alcidor and the bookseller emphasize, printing removes from *L'École des femmes* all that made it humorous and, by extension, successful. The effort to separate the actor from the author could not be more explicit, and Montfleury's tacit praise of the performance comes at the clear expense of the printed edition. Confronted with the prohibitive costs and technological limitations of selling "ses grimaces," Molière's play, reduced to mere text, is weighed solely on its literary merits by the characters of *L'Impromptu de l'Hôtel de Condé* and found wanting.

Robinet's *Panégyrique* picks up on the theme of performance versus print, and characteristically "defends" Molière with a withering *ad tu quoique* that as good as admits the accusation, while extending its scope. Responding to Lidamon, Crysolite states:

> Vous méprisez la scène d'Alain et de Georgette, l'équivoque du *le*, et les autres agréments que vous nommez de petits rebus, et vous dites que le succès que ces bagatelles ont sur le théâtre ne paraît point sur le papier. Je vous prie de me faire voir que les plus beaux vers aient le même effet sur le papier que sur la scène. Celui-ci:
> > *Je vis là Ptolomée, et n'y vis point de roi* ...
>
> ce vers, qui est des plus beaux du *Grand Pompée*, a-t-il le même brillant lorsqu'on le lit que lorsqu'il sort de la bouche de l'incomparable Montfleury? Cet hémistiche: *Hélas! tient-il à moi?* qui a produit un si bel effet sur le théâtre, dans *Le Faux Tyberinus*, sortant de la bouche de la merveilleuse des Œillets, a-t-il quelque chose qui en approche sur le papier? Ne sait-on pas que toutes ces beautés s'évanouissent hors du jeu qui leur donne la vie? (Molière [1971] 1:1080)

Crysolite responds to the accusation that Molière's play is weak on paper by leveling a general critique of all printed theater, irrespective of comedy or tragedy, and underscores his point by ironizing those, like Boursault, who, after disparaging Molière's printed text, proceed to print the text of their own polemical works: "[J]e leur demanderais volontiers si ce qu'ils ont fait sur ce sujet aura un grand relief sur le papier" (1:1080).

Crysolite's defense has the additional merit of corroborating statements made by Molière himself acknowledging the deficiencies of print.[32] No one was more aware of the differences between live performance and printed theater than the actor-author Moliere, and he certainly on occasion withheld works from print that depended too heavily upon "le jeu du Théâtre"—*L'Impromptu de Versailles* is a good case in point. However, to limit Molière to an "homme de théâtre" with an aversion to publication is as misleading as to make of him a consummate literary author: in his case, the activities of writing, performing, and publishing were necessarily linked. While critics like Bray have argued that Molière wrote with performance in mind (35, 171), this in no way excludes eventual publication, or even literary aspirations, as *L'École des femmes* and the subsequent quarrel clearly demonstrate. The subdivision of Molière into author and actor (and the privileging of the latter) was the war horse of Molière's adversaries; it certainly did not reflect his own thinking on the subject.[33]

That Molière thought of himself in terms of both writing and acting shows up most clearly in the professional targets of his

Chapter Three

satire: in *La Critique de L'École des femmes* and *L'Impromptu de Versailles*, Molière attacks both rival actors and authors, visibly signaling his dual ambitions. As Chevalier (another actor/author) wrote in *Les Amours de Calotin*:

> Ce qui plus me charma, c'est qu'en ces entretiens
> Il [Molière] berna les autheurs, et les comediens,
> Et je les voyois là faire fort bon visage,
> Quoyqu'au fond de leur ame ils fussent pleins de rage. (19)

If anything, Molière's fusion of acting and writing became more pronounced as his career progressed. Roger Duchêne has admirably shown through the records of La Grange that the repertoire of the Palais-Royal became increasingly dominated by Molière's own productions, with the final complete calendar year (1672) featuring a virtual monopoly: of the 153 performances, 151 were performances of Molière plays (647).[34] Molière, with the rarest of exceptions, only wrote for Molière; and increasingly, Molière only performed Molière. To try and separate out the terms of this solipsism is to lose the specificity that made Molière such a redoubtable foe for his rival authors and actors: it was his position as both actor and author, but neither exclusively, that allowed Molière to pursue Viala's *stratégie du succès* with such devastating effect. The anxieties of his opponents, and their eager efforts to drive a wedge between his two professions, prove the extent to which Molière posed a serious challenge to his contemporaries' ideas of authorship. La Croix's two Molière detractors, after having objected to calling Molière "author" ("Molière auteur! il n'y a que de la superficie et du jeu" [Molière [1971] 1:1140]), detail how he is eliminating the competition:

> De la Rancune: Il a rempli la place, Madame, on ne pourrait souffrir les autres quand ils feraient mieux que lui; on ne trouve rien bon que ce qui vient de Molière; on appelle cela un gâte-métier en bon français, encore roulait-on auparavant.
> Alcidor: Cela est damnable qu'un homme seul ruine tous les auteurs et les comédiens. (1:1140–41)

De La Rancune is elegantly vague as to whether he is referring to Molière's performances or publications; Alcidor, on the other hand, unambiguously cites both.

Even more importantly, the worlds of theater and literature are not as hermetically separate as Molière's critics would suggest. An offhand comment by Crysolite in Robinet's *Panégyrique de L'École des femmes* gives an interesting detail concerning the practices of those attending Molière's plays. After mentioning that for six months Molière's play has been avidly attended, Crysolite adds that many of the women go "en ayant même l'imprimé entre les mains pour le lire dans le temps qu'elles l'écoutent, sans doute afin de s'en rendre le plaisir plus sensible, et peut-être pour s'en mieux imprimer dans l'esprit les utiles leçons" (Molière [1971] 1:1083). The fact that certain spectators were following the stage action with their own purchased copy of the play suggests that the gap between *cabinet* and *spectacle* was at times almost nonexistent. Even those who saw the play prior to purchasing the text would still be able to bring to the text the memory of its performance, and Crysolite's discussion of Montfleury's or Des Œillets's delivery of certain lines underscores how powerful this memory could be. The printed text of the play could not fully render the performance, but neither was it completely free of crossover from the performance, and while Boursault's characters express confusion as to how the final *ouf* should be interpreted, it is apparent that none who saw the performance could fail to remember how Molière-Arnolphe had delivered it. Theater attendance far exceeded book sales; it is safe to assume that a large majority of those who purchased the Parisian edition of *L'École des femmes* had seen it in performance.[35] As with Molière's dual status as actor and author, reading and performance thus bleed into each other, and Boursault's admonition that a play's judgment should be based on reading alone becomes for the seventeenth-century theater public an impossible (or at least an artificial) task.

The Triumphant Author

The key themes of the attacks of Molière's adversaries were attempts at reduction and division: separation of Molière from his powerful proponents; distinction between Molière the actor and Molière the author; division of the text into comedy and farce, or into various bits of plagiarized sources. The fable of the jay, explicitly included in the polemical works, is omnipresent in spirit. This effort to partition the roles and the writings of Molière points to his unsettlingly powerful ability to unite otherwise heteroclite elements both in the construction of his own authorship and in the structure of his comedy.[36]

The modest reputation of the literary adversaries that rose to oppose Molière may at first suggest that the stakes of the *querelle de L'École des femmes* were limited to a small coterie of playwrights and critics. However, the aftereffects of the *querelle* demonstrate that Molière had gained the attention of powerful figures in the *champ littéraire*. In May or June 1663, shortly after the theatrical premiere of *La Critique de L'École des femmes*, Molière's authorship would be recognized through his inclusion on the list of writers to be granted royal pensions. The recommendation that he be named to this honor was made by Jean Chapelain, founding member of the Académie Française and author of the *Sentiments de l'Académie sur Le Cid*, who wrote of Molière: "Il a connu le caractère du comique et l'exécute naturellement. L'invention de ses meilleures pièces est inventée, mais judicieusement. Sa morale est bonne, et il n'a qu'à se garder de la scurrilité" (Molière, *Œuvres complètes* [1971] 1:629).

The lively *Remerciement* that Molière produced in response to this honor, his most important piece of nontheatrical writing, further confirmed his literary reputation. The characters in Robinet's *Panégyrique*, not disposed to speak favorably of Molière, extol at length the quality of his poem and the good opinion that it enjoys at court and among fellow authors. Palamède remarks, "J'ai vu ce *Remerciement*; en vérité, il est tout brillant d'esprit, et ç'a été le plus beau de tous ceux qui se sont faits, dont la plupart ne valent plus grand-chose" (Molière [1971] 1:1086). Considering the talent and standing of Molière's competition—Corneille, Benserade, Chapelain, and Racine were among the other recipients—the compliment carries significant weight. Lidamon recounts how much the court is taken with Molière's poem, and then hints that the *Remerciement* had even gained the approval of influential literary figures: "Mais vous savez que les plus éclairés des esprits, des gens qui sont les soleils du monde lettré, ont décidé que ce *Remerciement* était une très belle pièce, et c'est tout dire" (1:1087).

In addition, Molière gained powerful allies and admirers, either directly or indirectly, because of the *querelle*. Nicolas Boileau wrote his *Stances* in praise of Molière's embattled play and later developed a close friendship with the author. Even more importantly, the king himself would deliver the stroke that quieted the *querelle* in 1664 by becoming the *parrain* of Molière's firstborn son, thereby silencing the slanderous personal attacks into which the initial literary dispute had degenerated.[37] Confirming his support, Louis XIV would assume the patronage of Molière's troupe in 1665, granting them the title of "troupe du roi" and intensifying the long and productive cycle of Molière's involvement in royal court entertainments.[38]

Shortly after this event, Molière received an important confirmation of his literary status with the publication of his *Œuvres* in 1666.[39] Including Molière's published plays through *La Princesse d'Élide* (1664), the compilation in two volumes featured engraved frontispieces and opened with the author's *Remerciement au roi*, a striking way of reminding the reader of the royal favor that the author enjoyed, but also giving a literary tone to the collection.[40] Coming as early in Molière's career as it did, the 1666 *Œuvres* indicates the level of interest in Molière's work and the respectability that he had already attained, even prior to writing what were to be his greatest triumphs. The importance of *L'École des femmes* in the establishment of this reputation is evident from Chauveau's frontispiece for the second volume, featuring the comic muse crowning Arnolphe and Agnès. One could say, in light of the earlier discussion of writing in the play, that the frontispiece to the second volume of the 1666 *Œuvres* is a surprisingly apt celebration of Molière's theatrical vision: Agnès representing his views on authorship, and Arnolphe representing his own triumphant acting performance.

The 1666 *Œuvres* represented an important step in Molière's extraordinary ascension and consecration, and proved the efficacy of his authorial strategy. Beginning from a staunchly oppositional position with respect to his literary and theatrical peers, Molière by 1666 had legitimated himself and his genre through marks that could not be disputed: his double pension as both "bel esprit" and member of the king's official troupe; and the appearance of his collected works.[41]

The outcome of the *querelle de L'École des femmes* is not at all in doubt: the joint literary and theatrical successes that Molière enjoyed during this period indicate clearly that his victory, in particular from a literary perspective, was complete. Furthermore, the opinions and attacks of writers and actors did not cause him to

Chapter Three

alter in any significant way the artistic course that he had charted for himself. Just as Molière never disavowed his profession as actor, even on his deathbed, he never removed the heterodox elements of his theater, continuing to mix material from farce and high comedy, and to borrow material from both Ancients and Moderns for his own ends, until the end of his career. He likewise never abandoned his adversarial position with respect to other writers—plays incorporating a satire of authors or literature span his entire subsequent theatrical production: *Le Misanthrope* (1666), *Amphitryon* (1668), *La Comtesse d'Escarbagnas* (1671), and *Les Femmes savantes* (1672).

In this sense, then, the image of Molière the author, as forged in the *querelle*, has a future beyond the *démêlés* of *Tartuffe* and *Dom Juan*, and even beyond the rupture with Lully that will have serious consequences for Molière's career at court. Molière redefined the very nature of successful comedy on the dual fronts of performance and publication, establishing in the process a trademark style which (as the term suggests) was branded with his individuating ownership. The 1692 testimony of a successor, Charles Dufresny, echoes eloquently the protests of Molière's contemporaries: "Molière a bien gâté le théâtre. Si l'on donne dans son goût: Bon, dit aussitôt le critique, cela est pillé, c'est Molière tout pur. S'en écarte-t-on un peu: 'Oh! ce n'est pas là Molière!'"[42]

Chapter Four

"Je veux qu'on me distingue"

In the stormy first scene of *Le Misanthrope,* Alceste announces his intention to "rompre en visière à tout le Genre Humain" (1:651), a comically grandiose phrase that struck at least one contemporary: Jean Donneau de Visé cited it verbatim in the summary of the play that he wrote to a courtier (in Molière 1:637). The play must indeed lend itself to grand themes of rupture, since prominent critics have cited it as a crucial turning point in Molière's dramaturgy, the crossing of a comedic Rubicon. Jacques Guicharnaud famously made it the final play of a Molière trilogy (of which the first two parts were *Tartuffe* and *Dom Juan*) that, having explored the possibilities and limits of comedy, ended with an empty stage, a comedic *nec plus ultra* signifying the end of an aesthetic. Claiming that Molière's subsequent plays were largely either retreads of theatrical conventions or escapes from the theoretical problems that the trilogy had raised, Guicharnaud wrote, "Après *Le Misanthrope,* [Molière] aurait pu cesser d'écrire" (*Molière* 527). In *Molière, ou les Métamorphoses du comique,* Gérard Defaux similarly claimed that *Le Misanthrope* constituted a rupture, but for Defaux, it is because the play represented the moment when Molière's reputed comedic project of *castigat ridendo mores* turned back upon itself. If prior comedies had satirized the vices of the age, Defaux argues that *Le Misanthrope* satirizes the satirist, summarized in Philinte's "Et c'est une folie, à nulle autre, seconde, / De vouloir se mêler de corriger le Monde" (1:653). For Defaux, Alceste's farewell to the world is also Molière's authorial farewell to an erudite tradition of humanist (and moralist) satire. The future belongs to *folie*.[1]

If Guicharnaud and Defaux had paid attention to the publication history of Molière's theater, they might have added a further rupture to the list: in 1666, the year of *Le Misanthrope*'s premiere, Molière fell out with the initial group of *libraires* who

Chapter Four

had published his work since *Les Précieuses ridicules*. This split, brought to critical attention most prominently by Caldicott's *La Carrière de Molière*, was the first in a series of calculated editorial moves that show the playwright becoming increasingly involved in the publication of his work. Nor do these developments fail to leave their mark on the themes of the plays themselves, as *Le Misanthrope* amply demonstrates. While not an occasional piece on the order of *La Critique de L'École des femmes*, *Le Misanthrope* at its creation nevertheless plays out against the turbulent backdrop of Molière's struggles with the printing industry.

The Mid-Century State of the Publishing Industry and Molière's Early Publishers, 1660–66

The time period directly preceding *Le Misanthrope*'s theatrical debut saw the interruption of what had proved a fairly stable editorial process for Molière. Between *L'École des maris* in 1660 (which effectively ended the tumultuous clashes with Ribou, as discussed in Chapter 2) and 1666, Molière's plays were published by eight different Parisian *libraires*: Guillaume de Luyne, Charles de Sercy, Claude Barbin, Jean Guignard, Gabriel Quinet, Etienne Loyson, Louis Billaine, and Thomas Jolly.[2] This list includes some of the most prominent publishers of theater texts for the time period. Guillaume de Luyne, for example, published numerous Corneille editions, including the important in-octavo 1660 collected works that contained the *Discours de la tragédie* and the *examens* of each play (Picot 136). De Luyne also published, either by himself or in conjunction with other *libraires* (Jolly, Loyson, or Quinet), the first edition of thirteen of Quinault's sixteen plays (W. Brooks 23–38), while Barbin, Quinet, and Jolly published among them ten of Racine's eleven plays (Guibert, *Racine* 13–107).[3] While some of Molière's publishers also dealt in specialties other than theater (e.g., Guignard published legal works, and Sercy, books on gardening), all of them were involved in the printing and sale of *nouveautés*, a rather loose seventeenth-century term for what has come to be known (equally loosely) as literature: poetry, novels, short stories, and plays. Furthermore, in sheer number of new editions, four of Molière's publishers—Barbin, Guignard, Jolly, and Billaine—were among the twenty most prolific Parisian *libraires* for the last three decades of the century (Martin, *Livre* 2:708).

"Je veux qu'on me distingue"

Molière's eight publishers from 1660 to 1666 therefore represented mainstream *libraires* who would have been natural choices for a playwright coming into contact with the Parisian book industry for the first time.

Even for well-established publishers, though, the middle of the seventeenth century was a difficult time to be doing business. Louis XIV's government, continuing and extending policies enacted under Cardinal Richelieu, was seeking to police the book trade more closely by reducing the number of *libraires* and printers. In addition, higher paper prices and a general recession made for lower profit margins and a highly competitive market. As expensive luxury editions became less economically feasible, Parisian *libraires* relied increasingly on the volatile sales of *nouveautés*, whose quick printing and smaller formats translated to fewer production expenses for the publisher. However, the very factors that made *nouveautés* easy for Parisian *libraires* to produce made them tempting and convenient targets for provincial or Dutch counterfeiters, jeopardizing the profits that the capital's booksellers could realize (Martin, *Livre* 2:662–63).

In addition to the specific policy and business difficulties of the 1660s, more serious long-term shifts were fundamentally reshaping the economics of literary production and the relationship between author and *libraire*. A *mémoire* written in 1685 on behalf of the Parisian publishers casts a retrospective glance at the changes that had taken place in the printing industry from the sixteenth to the seventeenth century, insisting on the novelty of the *libraires*' newest business expense: paying the author.

> Autrefois, les auteurs donnaient de l'argent aux libraires pour contribuer aux frais d'impression de leurs ouvrages, et cet argent leur venait des pensions et des gratifications du Roi et de ses ministres qui les engageaient par ces bienfaits à travailler pour le public, et, si tous n'étaient en état de donner de l'argent, du moins n'en demandaient-ils pas. Aujourd'hui, l'usage est contraire, et soit qu'il doive son origine au besoin ou à l'avarice de quelques auteurs, soit que quelqu'autre l'y ait introduit, on s'y est tellement accoutumé que l'art de composer est pour ainsi dire devenu un métier pour gagner sa vie. (Martin, *Livre* 2:915)

Although the authors of this *mémoire* undoubtedly overstate the difficulties of the Parisian *libraires*, they are not entirely inaccurate in their portrayal of the changes that had taken place in the book trade over the previous century. An author in the sixteenth century typically received payment from publishers only if the author had personally paid the costs of obtaining the privilege for printing the book.[4] Instead of monetary payment, publishers often agreed to deliver to the author a certain number of copies of the finished book. These copies were not to be sold—only the *libraire* had the right to sell books—but instead allowed the author to present them as gifts to patrons, both actual and potential. In a 1540 contract for a translation of *Amadis de Gaule*, the publisher even agreed to the author's request to delay the book's sale to the public until the author had had time to bind and deliver his personal copies, increasing the value and symbolic exclusivity of the gift (Chartier, *L'Ordre* 56). Paying the author in gift books emphasizes the close relationship between writing and patronage in this era before, in Viala's phrase, the "naissance de l'écrivain," the appearance of the professional writer. The authors of the *mémoire* imply that the slow disappearance of the former patronage system, historically confirmed by the focusing and monopolizing of patronage by the crown and the dwindling numbers of dedicatory epistles throughout the seventeenth century, had led authors to seek other sources of income.[5] Even more importantly, the *mémoire* suggests that authors had come to realize the economic value of the commodity that they were generating and were demanding more equitable compensation in recognition of this fact from their publishers.

By contrasting the images of writing as unpaid vocation and writing as profession ("l'art de composer est pour ainsi dire devenu un métier pour gagner sa vie"), the *mémoire* also situates itself in the wider seventeenth-century debate about the function of writing and the social status of the author. Guéret and Boileau complain about the professionalization of the writer, lamenting that so few were writing simply for artistic glory and that the business aspect of writing "gâte tous les jours de bonnes plumes" (Guéret 77). On the other hand, the image of the writer who has to pay to have a text printed, or to have the public read it, also becomes an object of ridicule. Guéret recounts an anecdote about Ménage, who upon receiving a Dutch edition of his book, boasted of the universal diffusion of his work, only to hear the retort: "Oui ... parce que vous payez le port du passage et les frais de l'impression" (70). The poet Pinchesne, according to a story related by François Charpentier, was reading aloud the privilege he had just obtained to publish his poems when Santeuil stated that the clause prohibiting counterfeiting was not necessary. Pinchesne frostily replied that he was financing the edition himself, to which Santeuil added, "Bon pour cela ... mais il faut aussi faire afficher, que vous donnerez de l'argent à ceux qui voudront lire vostre livre" (Schapira 121). Evidently publishers' payments and book sales were rapidly becoming new benchmarks by which to evaluate an author's success.

The *mémoire* cited above, though, is unique in that it presents the changes in the nature of authorship from the publishers' point of view, people who now had to deal with an additional expense and with an author much more aggressively invested in the economics of the book trade. This new development must have seemed threatening indeed, and the *mémoire* equates authors with book pirates as the chief antagonists of the Parisian *libraires*: "Mais le risque le plus grand pour les libraires de Paris et qui les doit pleinement justifier de la cherté de leurs livres sont les récompenses excessives qu'ils sont obligés de donner aux auteurs et le peu de seureté qu'ils trouvent pour la seureté et l'exécution des privilèges" (Martin, *Livre* 2:919).

The *mémoire* estimates the going price for a manuscript at 300 to 500 *pistoles*, an over-generous figure considering the historical documents available. Viala notes that, other than "auteurs et œuvres à succès," publication rights generally brought authors from 300 to 1000 *livres*, a figure significantly lower than that quoted by the *libraires* (*Naissance* 108). It would appear that the going price for theater texts was actually much lower. Although reliable evidence is scant, Viala concludes from a study of the sales of several seventeenth-century plays that "les droits de publication étaient couramment de 200 à 300 livres," although he adds that "en cas de grand succès ils s'élevaient bien plus haut" (108).

The booksellers may well complain about having to satisfy "l'avarice de quelques auteurs," but at least one seventeenth-century commentator presents a very different picture of who was benefiting from the publication of theater texts. The Abbé Bordelon, discussing the sale of Molière's posthumous works, writes:

> Quelqu'autre vous a-t-il dit aussi bien que moi que le Sieur T. Libraire de la rue S. Jacques a donné quinze cens livres à la veuve de M ... pour les pièces qui n'avaient pas esté imprimées

Chapter Four

> du vivant de l'Autheur? Si cela est vray, il y a longtemps qu'il a retiré son argent, il y gagnera encore de quoy bastir un appartement des plus magnifiques dans le Ch. T. si l'envie luy en prend. (La Grange 151)

While Molière's plays would certainly have seemed a safer investment for a *libraire* than the works of his less popular contemporaries, they did not necessarily guarantee the fortune of all who bought the rights to print them, and even the most phenomenal theatrical success did not always translate into a profitable printing run. One of Gabriel Guéret's characters in the *Promenade de Saint-Cloud* mentions to the great surprise of his interlocutors that the publisher of *Tartuffe* (1669) had begun to regret the money that he had paid for it:

> —Comment! dit Cléante, est-il possible que le *Tartuffe*, qui a si fort enrichi Molière et sa troupe, n'enrichisse pas le libraire? Cette pièce, qui est devenuë un préservatif contre les surprises du bigotisme, n'est-elle pas d'une nécessité absoluë dans toutes les familles, et ne devroit-on pas même en faire des leçons publiques?
> —Ne vous y trompez pas, repartis-je; une pièce peut être bonne pour les comédiens, et ne valoir rien pour les libraires. Quand elle sort du théâtre pour aller au Palais, elle est déjà presque toute usée, et la curiosité n'y fait plus courir. (48–49)

In the particular case of *Tartuffe*, there may be several factors that contributed to its failure to generate a profit for its publisher, among them the high price paid to Molière for the manuscript and the presence of an earlier printed edition, as discussed in the following chapter. It is also clear that, despite Guéret's comments on a popular play being "toute usée," publishers would be far more disposed to take a risk on a successful play than to finance the printing of a theatrical failure. However, the disparity in the financial fortunes of these two printing runs emphasizes the unpredictable nature of publishing in the seventeenth century and the particular vagaries of theater texts.

These anecdotes also underscore how it was the *libraire*, not the author, who enjoyed the profits or suffered the losses associated with the economic fortunes of a printed book. As David Pottinger explains, the standard procedure of paying the author a single amount prior to the publication of the book divested the author from the book's subsequent fate:

> Even when the reading public grew large and business became self-conscious, the formalities of the transfer of a manuscript remained extremely simple. The author merely took his work to a publisher and sold it outright for a sum generally paid on the spot. ... Diderot gives us a statement of the procedure in many cases: "The author called upon the publisher and outlined his work; they agreed upon the price, the format, and other conditions. Conditions and price were stipulated in a document under private seal by which the author conveyed his work, in perpetuity and without return, to the publisher and his representatives." (44)

Such an arrangement was not necessarily to the disadvantage of the author. It merely implied that the *libraire* assumed all the risk in the business venture of printing, the potential for loss balancing out the possible profits. In the case of poor book sales, an author's initial payment could far exceed any royalties he would have earned under a different contractual agreement—Trissotin is alive and well, while it is his *libraire* who is "à l'Hôpital réduit" (Molière 2:591).

The costs and the risks involved in financing an edition were even greater for publishers and booksellers who did not have their own in-house printing facilities and had to contract out the typesetting and production of the manuscripts that they purchased. This was the case for far more *libraires* than one might think: even Claude Barbin, the undisputed chief publisher of literary *nouveautés*, did not possess a printing press and had his editions produced by the printing establishments of the Rue Saint-Jacques (Reed, *Barbin* 71). Among Molière's early publishers, Billaine, De Luyne, Quinet, Loyson, and Guignard similarly did not possess printing presses (Reed, *Barbin* 61). The printing costs that these publishers incurred could be substantial. Typical first printing runs for literary texts were between 1200 and 1800 copies (Martin, *French Book* 3); if the production costs given in the *mémoire* are accurate, expenses to produce a new edition would fall between 1800 and 3600 *livres*. Since the selling prices listed for an individual book are from 3 *livres*, 10 *sols* to 4 *livres*, the *libraire* would be obligated to sell roughly half of the first run just to meet printing costs.[6] The production of a new edition thus represented a considerable and uncertain capital investment, even without considering authors' fees, rampant counterfeiting in the provinces and abroad, and the fluctuating tastes of the *nouveautés* market.

This helps explain the widespread tendency for *libraires* to collaborate on new editions, finding associates and partners to help share the incurred costs and reduce the financial risk for each individual. Of Molière's first eight plays to be published, all but *Sganarelle* (Ribou's pirate edition discussed in Chapter 2) were collaborative efforts on the part of two or more *libraires*. Three publishers brought out the first edition of *Les Précieuses ridicules* (1660);[7] five published *L'École des maris* (1661) and *Les Fâcheux* (1662).[8] Two publishers printed *L'Étourdi* (1663) and *Le Dépit amoureux* (1663),[9] the privileges for which were actually obtained in 1660 (Guibert, *Molière* 1:97), and eight *libraires* joined together to print *L'École des femmes* (1663) and *La Critique de L'École des femmes* (1663).[10]

Apparent in this list is a general trend toward larger associations, and the growing number of publishers involved with these printing projects suggests both greater interest among *libraires* in Molière's work, due to his success in the theater, and the need for more capital to finance printing runs. Still, while the popularity and the controversy surrounding *L'École des femmes* could easily justify a large initial edition, to have eight publishers involved is unusual.[11] The first editions of Racine's plays, also extremely successful at the theater, were never published by groups of more than three *libraires*. Similarly, Corneille's works were typically published by associations of two or three *libraires* (De Luyne, Jolly, and Billaine in the 1660s).[12]

Caldicott has claimed that Molière's early publishers formed a powerful *nouveautés* monopoly or cartel centered around Claude Barbin (*Carrière* 123, 126). However, the existence of this "cartel des huit" is problematic: the bibliographies of Racine, Corneille, and Quinault show these same *libraires* working in fluid groups and with other publishers,[13] which indicates instead that Molière's case represents an exception, an arrangement of convenience among publishers who were competitors as well as colleagues. In the absence of additional information, attempts to explain the size and constitution of the group that printed *L'École des femmes* must remain conjectural, but it seems reasonable to infer that the popu-

"Je veux qu'on me distingue"

larity of the play and the fear of being excluded from its profits led most of the major publishers of *nouveautés* to seek to be involved with the edition.[14]

The language of Molière's royal privileges makes it clear that the author had little or no part in the formation of these professional collaborations among *libraires*, since he typically transferred his privilege to a single *libraire* who then shared it with his business associates. The privilege for *L'École des maris* (1661) states, for example, "Ledit Sieur de Moliers a cedé & tranporté son Privilege à Charles de Sercy, Marchand Libraire à Paris, pour en iouyr selon l'accord fait entr'eux," and then adds, "Et ledit de Sercy a associé audit Privilege Guillaume de Luyne, Iean Guignard, Claude Barbin & Gabriel Quinet, aussi Marchands Libraires, pour en jouyr ensemblement, suivant l'accord fait entr'eux."

There are limits as to how much the existing documentation can reveal about the exact relationship between Molière and his early publishers. The text of the privilege cited above designates with the phrase "l'accord fait entr'eux" the two critical private transactions that are not detailed in the official record: the sale of the manuscript from author to *libraire*, and the negotiations among *libraires* to arrange the manuscript's publication. The author is a participant in one but not the other, and the separation between these two events emphasizes the lack of control that the author had over the printing of a text once it was in the hands of a publisher. This in turn is indicative of a legal system that treated manuscripts as property sold from author to *libraire*, rather than as a collaborative project between the two parties involved.

The Crisis of the 1666 *Œuvres*

In 1666, Gabriel Quinet obtained a new privilege, valid for six years, authorizing the printing of a collected edition of nine of Molière's plays to date.[15] This privilege was then shared with the other seven publishers who had collaborated on *L'École des femmes* and *La Critique de L'École des femmes*. The participation of all eight publishers (as well as that of Robert Ballard, the publisher of *La Princesse d'Élide*) was a necessity for the 1666 collected works to be legal—most of the individual privileges for the plays included in the two-volume set had not yet expired and printing them without their owners' consent would have violated the monopoly clauses of their privileges. It would appear, though, that while all of Molière's previous publishers (with the understandable exception of Jean Ribou) participated in this project, the *libraires* did exclude someone else: the author. In the text of a 1671 privilege, Molière complains that Quinet obtained his 1666 royal permission to print the collected works "par surprise" and "sans en avoir son consentement" (Molière 2:418).

While it is clear from the text of the 1671 privilege that Molière was unhappy with the actions of the publishers involved with the 1666 collected works, it is difficult to determine precisely at what point he became dissatisfied. The fact that he waited five years before making an official protest seems to indicate that it was not as pressing an issue in 1666 as it was in 1671, and that only once Molière developed the idea for a magisterial edition of his complete works did he take action against his eight former publishers (see Chapter 5). If Molière could have made a convincing case to challenge the legitimacy of the 1666 edition, it would have been to his advantage to do so immediately upon its publication, allowing him to seize the edition and profit from it, as he had previously done in the case of *Sganarelle*, but there is no record that he did. On the other hand, it is more likely that while the edition may have been disadvantageous to the author, there was no case for challenging its legality—the publishers who had previously purchased the manuscripts had applied for and received a valid privilege. Molière's passivity in this case may not suggest apathy or tacit approval, but simply a lack of any legal recourse other than blocking the renewal of the publishers' privilege by obtaining his own shortly before the privilege's expiration.

That Molière was upset sooner rather than later by the events of 1666 is suggested by the fact that he did not sell any further manuscripts to his former publishers and immediately took his business elsewhere. But it is equally difficult to determine what grounds Molière could have had for breaking with his publishers. Caldicott sees in the 1666 edition an attempt on the part of Molière's publishers to renew their privileges and retain their rights to the published plays. If that is indeed the case, it is curious why this would have upset Molière, since he certainly would not have stood to profit from the lapsing of the privileges to his plays. Following the time period fixed by the *Chancellerie* during which a work could be exclusively published by the holder of the privilege, the work entered the public domain and could be printed by anyone without having to pay the author.

In examining the case of Molière's 1666 complete works, Bert and Grace Young wrote:

> En ce qui concerne le recueil de 1666 il reste la question des droits légaux qu'un auteur pouvait garder après qu'il avait cédé à un éditeur le privilège de son ouvrage. A l'expiration de la période pendant laquelle le privilège était valable, était-ce l'auteur ou l'éditeur qui avait le droit d'en demander le renouvellement? Ou bien, avant l'expiration du délai prévu, l'un d'eux pouvait-il demander une prolongation? (La Grange 144)

These questions are difficult to answer for several reasons. In the first place, it is doubtful whether the 1666 collected works would have been considered an extension (*continuation*) of the existing privileges in the standard sense. As the first edition of Molière's collected works with continuous pagination, the 1666 edition was evidently distinct enough to qualify for its own privilege.[16] The case of Racine's first collected works (1675) is similar: the playwright applied for and received a separate new privilege rather than extensions to the prior ones. Interestingly enough, in order to publish the edition Racine then had to reach an agreement with those *libraires* who still held valid privileges for his individual plays (Guibert, *Racine* 130). Gabriel Quinet's privilege to publish would likewise have been contingent upon the cooperation of the other *libraires* who still held rights to Molière's previously published works that had not yet expired.

If, though, Quinet's privilege had been considered a *continuation*, there were certain guidelines that had been established through legal precedents and decisions by the *Conseil du Roi*. Publishers desiring to maintain their exclusive rights to works beyond the expiration date of the original privilege had to meet the terms set by a 1665 royal decision that stated that all extensions had to be obtained a year before the privilege's expiration and, specifically in the case of the Classics, prohibited any new privilege or extension "à moins qu'il n'y ait augmentation ou correction considérable" (Martin, *Livre* 2:692–93).

It could be argued that the 1666 collected works represented a very significant augmentation of what had preceded it. However,

Chapter Four

even more to the publishers' advantage was the disjunction between the letter of the law ostensibly restricting the extension of privileges and the actual practice of the *Chancellerie*, who regularly extended the privileges of Parisian *libraires* in favor, in effect granting perpetual monopolies (Martin, *Livre* 2:763). Whether or not the 1666 edition did in fact constitute an extension of existing privileges, it would seem that Molière's publishers were benefiting from a quite normal prerogative in bringing out their edition of the collected works.[17]

There remains the question posed by the Youngs as to Molière's rights. However, any supposition that Molière had outstanding claims in this case, where he had previously sold the plays to his publishers, would imply the existence of an authorial copyright that survives publication, a notion that did not exist until the eighteenth century. Molière's case against Ribou, discussed in Chapter 2, demonstrates that a certain right did exist that allowed an author to choose the time and manner of publication (or at least the choice of publisher), but nothing suggests that an author retained any control over the text after the cession of his or her rights to a *libraire*. As Pottinger notes: "The author least of all had any 'rights.' He sold his manuscript to a publisher and thereafter had no financial interest in it. He could not print and sell his own books but was obliged to deal with a member of the guild. He might be given a small additional payment for a revised edition though not for new printings" (211).

Molière's reaction to the 1666 edition, and his subsequent break with his publishers, did not then stem from any legal misdeeds on the part of his *libraires*, but could be indicative of a slight to what he perceived as his moral rights as author. Perhaps he had in mind the 1660 edition of Corneille's works to which the author had contributed substantially by adding three theoretical *discours* and an *examen* of each play. Molière may also have resented the fact that his publishers gave him no opportunity to edit, correct, or alter his plays, but this is unlikely given that no Molière reprints (whether published by his earlier or later *libraires*) show evidence of significant authorial changes. It actually would be surprising if Molière's publishers had not asked him to participate in some way, since it would have significantly increased the interest in the edition and been to their financial advantage—since it was not reviewed, augmented, or corrected by the author, the new edition would have held no attraction for those who had already purchased separate editions of the plays doubtless still available. If in fact Molière was initially asked to participate in some manner, as Guibert suggests (*Molière* 2:564), then the disagreement may well have been over the author's remuneration in a case where the publishers already held the legal rights to the text.

If we posit a scenario in which Molière was somehow wronged by the publication of the 1666 collected works, there is an even more fundamental ambiguity to resolve: who broke the partnership first? While Molière's belated protests regarding the "surprised" privilege have oriented critics toward blaming the publishers, some inconvenient bibliographical facts complicate the narrative. Quinet received his privilege on 6 March 1666 (Guibert, *Molière* 2:567); it was registered with the *Communauté des libraires* on 24 March. However, on 30 December 1665, more than two months prior to Quinet's actions, Molière received a privilege for his latest work, *L'Amour médecin*, and presented it in person to the *syndic* of the *Communauté* for registration on 4 January 1666 (Guibert, *Molière* 1:157; Thuasne 22); he then transferred the privilege to Trabouillet, Girard, and Legras, three publishers with whom he had never worked before, sometime before 15 January 1666, the *achevé d'imprimer* for the edition. In other words, well before Quinet and his associates made any official move to print Molière's collected works, the playwright had already begun working with a different set of *libraires*.

The editors of the 2010 Pléiade edition postulate that this decision was due to the imminent project of the collected edition: "Au moment où les marchands-libraires qui avaient publié ses huit premières pièces s'apprêtaient à exploiter leur monopole en ajoutant *La Princesse d'Élide* à la première édition de ses *Œuvres* en 1666, Molière cessa toute collaboration avec eux pour s'entendre avec une autre association de marchands-libraires" (1:1427). But Molière's prior publishers had jointly printed *La Princesse d'Élide* with Robert Ballard in January 1665, a year before *L'Amour médecin*. We have no recorded document that shows any further preparation, any attempts somehow to appropriate Molière's plays, prior to Molière's own actions in December and January. Furthermore, if Molière knew about the proposed collection in December 1665, then the "surprised" privilege in March was really no surprise at all, emphasizing the notion that if Molière could have blocked it, or had wanted to in 1666, he had ample warning to do so.

In other words, the 1666 *Œuvres* (already something of a misnomer, since it did not include *L'Amour médecin*) is as likely the reaction to Molière's split with his former publishers as the cause. Seeing that Molière had found new business associates, Quinet and company could well have decided to solidify their hold on the plays that they had already purchased, and while it may run counter to our own sensibilities regarding authorship and ownership, there was nothing out of the ordinary or illegal about their actions. Molière had experience in getting illegitimate privileges annulled, as the crossed-out entry in the *Communauté*'s register of Ribou's 1660 privilege for *Les Précieuses ridicules* testifies (Thuasne 7). Quinet's privilege stayed on the books. And, as will be seen later, it proved useful to Molière that it did.

Whether or not Molière was "more sinn'd against than sinning" in this case, the publication of the 1666 *Œuvres* certainly exacerbated the rift between the two parties, and Molière did not ever work again with any of the *libraires* involved in its publication. Even more importantly, these events must have created deeper dissatisfactions with the legal and economic ordering of the Parisian book trade, dissatisfactions that would lead to surprising and more drastic ruptures with the *Communauté des Libraires* later in his career. At the very least, it presented to the playwright the curious image of a book (in two volumes with engraved frontispieces, no less) that listed him as its author, and yet which he had not authorized. Molière's fractious battles over his authorial image, his various constructions of an authorial identity or persona, during his early career and the quarrel over *L'École des femmes* had accustomed him to using his texts as vehicles for self-representation. With the edition published by Quinet and his associated *libraires*, Molière's plays took on an existence independent of their author, or to use Nehamas's distinction, their writer. The precision is useful, since the author was still very present: the 1666 *Œuvres*, much more so than the editions of the individual plays, relies on the author-principle for its internal logic and its external marketing. For the first time in a continuously paginated edition, the figure of Molière was used in order to group together certain texts. Furthermore, in addition to the playwright's prominent name on the title page, the facing-page frontispiece of the first volume contains no fewer than three Molières: Molière as Mascarille, Molière as Sganarelle, and an authorial bust crowned with laurels. In this case, the editors' over-compensation serves as the ironic sign of the author's practical absence. It will not be the last time that a Molière collected edition will exhibit this dissonance.

Regardless of who ended the association between Molière and his original publishers, the result in 1666 was a strange separation between author and book, an authorial consecration that the author himself disavowed. Quinet and his associates may not have been able to work any longer with Molière, but they demonstrated convincingly that they still had a share in "Molière," the authorial persona that was a product of the texts. However, to assert that Molière was powerless to do anything about this is misleading—while there appears to have been no immediate legal remedies, we might look for his response in a different, theatrical, venue: the universe of *Le Misanthrope*, in which these issues are reformulated in surprising ways, as individuals' reputations are made and broken through written representations that circulate largely outside of their control. Like the 1666 *Œuvres*, the play invites a consideration of the extent to which an author is synonymous with his work. In a setting where writing is a natural extension of social standing, the characters in *Le Misanthrope* engage with the same problems of reception and control that Molière was discovering were endemic to the enterprise of publication.

The Salon of Célimène, or A World of Letters

Writing about seventeenth-century literary culture, Jean-Paul Sartre observed, "Si [le lecteur] critique l'écrivain, c'est qu'il sait lui-même écrire. Le public de Corneille, de Pascal, de Descartes, c'est Madame de Sévigné, le chevalier de Méré, Madame de Grignan, Madame de Rambouillet, Saint-Évremond" (95). The reading public was also a writing public, or as Sartre states, "On lit parce qu'on sait écrire; avec un peu de chance, on aurait pu écrire ce qu'on lit" (95). Sartre's depiction of seventeenth-century society is one of authors among equals, where writers address those capable of responding and where a reader is always an "écrivain en puissance." The implications are that writing and (critical) reading become sides of the same coin, interchangeable activities

Chapter Four

that are undertaken in light of this potential alternation. For Sartre, reading and writing in the seventeenth century also carry socio-economic connotations: "[Le lecteur] fait partie d'une élite parasitaire pour qui l'art d'écrire est, sinon un métier, du moins la marque de sa supériorité" (95).

Sartre's depiction overly simplifies the contentious world of Viala's *écrivains*, but it corresponds well to the restricted world of *Le Misanthrope*—"élite parasitaire" is an apt description of certain denizens of Célimène's salon, and the corresponding link to writing and representation in this case holds true. There is, after all, nearly nothing else for this social class to do, as the two marquis Acaste and Clitandre make perfectly clear:

> Acaste: À moins de voir Madame en être importunée,
> Rien ne m'appelle, ailleurs, de toute la journée.
> Clitandre: Moi, pourvu que je puisse être au petit Couché,
> Je n'ai point d'autre Affaire, où je sois attaché. (1:680)

Letters, portraits, light verse: Célimène and her friends are involved in a dizzying circuit of literary production and consumption, and Donneau de Visé noted that those who criticized Molière's portrayal of this society only revealed their own ignorance and low social standing: "[L']on ne peut ne la [la pièce] pas trouver bonne, sans faire voir que l'on n'est pas de ce Monde, et que l'on ignore la manière de vivre de la Cour, et celle des plus illustres Personnes de la Ville" (1:644).

The second scene of *Le Misanthrope* will illustrate the importance of writing for "ce Monde," as well as Sartre's closed literary circuit that binds authors and readers (or more accurately, critics). Oronte has written a sonnet and asks Alceste's opinion of it—one amateur author soliciting the opinion of another author *en puissance* (a point to which I will return). The singularity (if there is any) of the sonnet is not in the fact that it is either good or bad: Donneau de Visé wrote that "le Sonnet n'est point méchant," though adding the stinging qualifier "selon la manière d'écrire d'aujourd'hui" (1:638); echoing him, Guicharnaud writes that the sonnet "n'est pas mauvais," and that it is at least as good as "certains passages ... écrits par Molière lui-même" (*Molière* 380) for the king's lavish (and relatively vapid) royal entertainments. Rather, the significance of the sonnet lies in its relationship to

"Je veux qu'on me distingue"

Oronte, which, *mutatis mutandis*, is much like Agnès and her letter: that is, Oronte's sonnet is a literary extension of himself, reflecting faithfully and without distortion the essential elements of Oronte's character. The sonnet is in the *style galant* common to salon culture, or as Oronte describes it, "Ce ne sont point de ces grands Vers pompeux, / Mais de petits Vers doux, tendres, et langoureux" (1:660). Oronte does not claim that the sonnet is original, striking, or significant from a literary standpoint. Rather, it is meant to showcase an urbane wit, and if it seeks to convey any true emotion, it does so beneath the façade of acceptable social banter. Like a sort of calling card, the poem is essentially a text that invites an equally dissimulating and socially coded response. As Philinte states to Alceste, Oronte presented the poem "afin d'être flatté" (1:666), and in this sense, the sonnet becomes a touchstone for the function of writing among the social elite, the first in a series of texts that the play's characters will create, debate, attribute, or even disavow.

Philinte's observation that the sonnet's true role is to solicit praise for its author illustrates the hypertrophied author-function that dominates the world of *Le Misanthrope*. Sonnets and letters (as well as books, as we will see) *must* be authored, and these texts' content is largely relevant only to the extent that it impacts the image of their implied authors. In his preliminary (and disingenuous) self-deprecations, Oronte may belittle the genre, style, and any effort made ("je n'ai demeuré qu'un quart d'heure à le faire" [1:660]), but the one thing that he will not disclaim is that he is the author. The sonnet is not anonymous; indeed, its entire *raison d'être* is to portray Oronte, an emphatic response to Foucault's epigraphical question regarding authorship, "Qu'importe qui parle?" (77). For Oronte, Alceste, Célimène, and their associates, nothing matters more.

Alceste's virulent critique of the sonnet demonstrates that while he and Oronte have deep-seated disagreements regarding style, tone, and ethos, they share the fundamental assumption that textual hermeneutics passes through the construction of an implied author. Alceste's comments move quickly from stylistics to a consideration of who is speaking:

> Ce style figuré, dont on fait vanité,
> Sort du bon Caractère, et de la Vérité;

> Ce n'est que jeu de Mots, qu'affectation pure,
> Et ce n'est point ainsi, que parle la Nature.
> Le méchant Goût du Siècle, en cela, me fait peur. (1:664)

For Alceste, the poem's artificiality and dissembling reflect back upon its author, and the poetic conversation between author and addressee consequently becomes a manifestation of the degraded nature of contemporary interpersonal relationships. The merit of the "vieille chanson" that Alceste proposes instead lies in the authorial ethos of the speaker. As he claims, "la Passion parle là toute pure," adding, "Voilà ce que peut dire un Cœur vraiment épris" (1:664). For Alceste, there is no distance between H.L. Hix's "creative author" and "created author," no room for a poetic "I" who differs from the agent who takes responsibility for the literary product. In this regard, Alceste is not so different from the society that he claims to scorn.

In his initial (and comically oblique) critique of the sonnet, Alceste moves rapidly from general remarks about writing to an attack on printing, asking his invented interlocutor (and in reality Oronte), "Et qui, diantre, vous pousse à vous faire Imprimer?" and counseling him:

> Et n'allez point quitter, de quoi que l'on vous somme,
> Le nom que, dans la Cour, vous avez d'honnête Homme,
> Pour prendre, de la main d'un avide Imprimeur,
> Celui de ridicule, et misérable Auteur. (1:663)

While Alceste's reaction is laughably exaggerated, his attacks on publishing seem particularly misplaced. Oronte suggests to Alceste that he is considering exposing the sonnet to the public, but it is unclear what Oronte intends. Oronte could be said to be "publishing" the sonnet in a general sense by sharing it with other members of a salon, as might befit a work couched as light, occasional poetry. Alceste's criticisms, though, are directed toward printing, assuming (perhaps with good reason) that Oronte's literary ambitions will not remain bounded by Célimène's salon.[18] The misanthrope's belittling of Oronte's writing itch, as he characterizes it, is cast in terms that Boileau's *Art poétique* will echo in 1674: printing is for desperate lower-class writers, and constitutes a derogation both of the noble art of writing and of the class superiority of the author.

"Je veux qu'on me distingue"

Of the three characters that constitute the play's central love triangle, it is striking that Alceste is the only non-author—both Célimène and Oronte are characterized by and through their literary productions. This is not to suggest that Alceste is free from all vestiges of authorship. Although he does not actually write anything (yet), Alceste—more so than the de facto authors in the play—incarnates the concepts that define authorship to the seventeenth-century mind: authority, authenticity, and originality (Randall 28). Refusing the social subterfuges in which all the other characters indulge themselves, Alceste alone claims (albeit unconvincingly) rigorous unity of character, a (semi-)consistent voice and tone. Against Oronte and Célimène, amateur writers, Alceste posits a view of traditional authorship that is loftily removed from the temporal vagaries of style and fashion, and certainly conceived entirely separately from the corrupt and degrading dealings of the publishing industry, that is, the actual production of printed books. True authorship, as opposed to the "jeu de mots" or "affectation pure" of fashionable scribbling, distinguishes itself by the direct expression in words of the author's original emotion.

If Alceste insists on authenticity, he also wishes to constitute himself as a source or creator of sorts. Responding to Célimène's claims that he does not love her as he should, Alceste replies:

> Oui, je voudrais qu'aucun ne vous trouvât aimable,
> Que vous fussiez réduite en un Sort misérable,
> Que le Ciel, en naissant, ne vous eût donné rien,
> Que vous n'eussiez ni Rang, ni Naissance, ni Bien,
> Afin que, de mon Cœur, l'éclatant Sacrifice,
> Vous pût, d'un pareil Sort, réparer l'Injustice:
> Et que j'eusse la joie, et la gloire, en ce jour,
> De vous voir tenir tout, des mains de mon Amour. (1:708)

Alceste, not unlike his predecessor Arnolphe in this respect, wishes to see the object of his love completely dependent on him, thus positioning him as sole benefactor. Imaginarily placing himself in this quasi-divine role, Alceste thus parallels the description of symbolic authorship given by Richelet, when he writes in his definition of *auteur*, "Dieu est l'auteur de notre félicité" (1:56). Alceste may not produce any literary works, but he aims at a higher form of authorship: he wishes to be the author of Célimène.

Chapter Four

And in one important sense he is: Alceste, so vocally opposed to writing and publication, was originally played by Molière himself, making connections between the character and authorship natural, or even inevitable. In the original *mise-en-scène*, Molière/Alceste's remarks to Oronte would have assumed strongly ironic overtones as he deprecates those who have to write for a living: "Si l'on peut pardonner l'essor d'un mauvais Livre, / Ce n'est qu'aux Malheureux, qui composent pour vivre" (1:663). Such a statement draws attention to the speaker's own literary career, even as it ostensibly derides it, recalling Molière's preface to *Les Précieuses ridicules*. This dramatic irony, in which Alceste is comically unaware of who he really is, amplifies the effect already introduced by Philinte in the previous scene when he compares Alceste and himself to Ariste and Sganarelle, "ces deux Frères que peint *L'École des Maris*" (1:651). Despite Alceste's dismissal of these "comparaisons fades" (1:651), the resemblance was striking indeed: Molière of course had played the earlier role. These opening passages, and the exchange with Oronte in particular, achieve their comic effect at least partly through reminding the audience that Molière is a successful playwright. The most fashionable author of 1666 cannot speak of the "Malheureux qui composent pour vivre" and expect to be taken seriously.

But Molière's row with his publishers means that complaints about "avides Imprimeurs" are less innocent in 1666 than they may at first appear. Given Molière's dissatisfaction with his former *libraires*, it is no coincidence that *Le Misanthrope* incorporates the most direct references to publication since *Les Précieuses ridicules*, nor is it surprising that the treatment of these themes has shifted. Indeed, the scene of Oronte's sonnet seems a calculated reworking of Mascarille's earlier impromptu, and juxtaposing the two scenes helps emphasize Molière's authorial evolution from 1660 to 1666. On the one hand, Mascarille is an imposter, an Oronte exaggerated to ridiculous proportions (but strikingly similar to the "authentic" marquis Acaste and Clitandre in *Le Misanthrope*). His impromptu is similarly exaggerated, a self-evidently comical deformation of salon style, confirmed by its fourfold repetition of "au voleur" in the final line. Oronte's sonnet, like Trissotin's two poems in *Les Femmes savantes*, is much closer to what actually would have passed as *style galant*. Donneau de Visé records that members of the audience at the premiere understood it in this sense: "J'en vis même, à la première Représentation de cette Pièce, qui se firent jouer pendant qu'on Représentait cette Scène; car ils crièrent que le Sonnet était bon, avant que le Misanthrope en fit la Critique, et demeurèrent ensuite tout confus" (1:638).

However, Donneau de Visé's description highlights a second important difference between the two scenes: the reception. While Philinte obligingly echoes Cathos and Magdelon's enthusiastic admiration ("Cathos: voilà qui est poussé dans le dernier galant" [1:18]; "Philinte: qu'en termes galants, ces choses-là sont mises!" [1:661]), Alceste provides a bracingly negative response entirely absent from the earlier scene. Nothing could more clearly indicate the thematic distance between the two plays than this critical bifurcation. A more serious Mascarille has found someone who will tell him his "vérités," and who is completely intractable. The best that even the *maréchaux* can accomplish through force is a grudging: "Monsieur, je suis fâché d'être si difficile ; / Et, pour l'amour de vous, je voudrais, de bon cœur, / Avoir trouvé, tantôt, votre Sonnet meilleur" (1:698). The irresistible force of authorial egoism, present in the earlier play, has encountered here the immovable object of critical reception.

We might counter that Alceste *wants* to dislike the sonnet. His "Esprit contrariant," as Célimène dubs it (1:678), leads him naturally to dislike what is receiving widespread praise. He resembles the description of Damis given by Célimène in her series of satirical portraits:

> Depuis que dans la tête, il s'est mis d'être habile,
> Rien ne touche son goût, tant il est difficile;
> Il veut voir des Défauts à tout ce qu'on écrit,
> Et pense que louer, n'est pas d'un bel Esprit.
> Que c'est être Savant, que trouver à redire;
> Qu'il n'appartient qu'aux Sots, d'admirer, et de rire;
> Et qu'en n'approuvant rien des Ouvrages du Temps,
> Il se met au-dessus de tous les autres Gens. (1:677)

The wordplay is telling, since Damis not only claims to find faults in everything, but subtly desires to do so. It is perhaps significant that this portrait causes Alceste, hitherto a silent observer, to break his silence and interrupt the social game. Célimène's critique of Damis comes too close to the mark, particularly in the way that it associates criticism and a desire for superiority. Let us not forget

Chapter Four

that Alceste's misanthropic "je veux qu'on me distingue" (1:649) contains paradoxically both a desire to be separate and the need for a crowd from which to be distinguished, or even to grant the distinction. Authorship parallels this, representing a triumphant self-contained subjectivity that must in turn be recognized by a community in order to be legitimate.[19] It is why authorship in general is threatening to Alceste—it represents the *distinction* of someone other than himself. For Alceste, the only good author is a dead one, or, even better, an anonymous one. The "vieille Chanson" (1:664) that he sets in opposition to Oronte's sonnet has one principal merit beyond its (arguable) expression of true passion: it has no author. The first-person pronouns of the song, like the positive authorial image that it creates, have no real antecedents. Praising it consequently does not equate to praising someone.

Oronte and Alceste may seem worlds apart, but for both of them there is no artificial division between literature and life. Alceste excuses his harsh critique of Oronte's sonnet by claiming that he does not possess "l'Art de feindre" (1:665), a phrase that describes Alceste's perspective on both contemporary mores and current literary style. This art of feigning in its twin manifestations creates engaging parallels with the play's opening scene: Alceste's violent over-reaction to Philinte's "complaisant" social behavior is matched by his blunt critique of Oronte's poem that degenerates into an actual dispute that has to be regulated by the *maréchaux*. The "haines vigoureuses" that, as Alceste explains, "doit donner le Vice aux Âmes vertueuses" (1:652) spill over into the literary domain, and it becomes a point of honor to hate current literary fashion as much as current social vices, both criticized under the notion of artificiality. Bad manners and bad writing become, for Alceste, capital crimes. As he states to Philinte in the opening scene: "Et si, par un malheur, j'en avais fait autant, / Je m'irais, de regret, pendre tout à l'instant" (1:648), a punishment echoed in his later continued condemnation of Oronte's verses: "Je soutiendrai, toujours, morbleu, qu'ils sont mauvais, / Et qu'un Homme est pendable, après les avoir faits" (1:683).

Of course, if Alceste considers Oronte "pendable," Oronte himself tries to implicate Alceste with writing that is, in a very real sense, incriminating. After losing his case to his unnamed adversary, Alceste exclaims at the opening of Act 5:

"Je veux qu'on me distingue"

> Et non content, encor, du Tort que l'on me fait,
> Il court, parmi le Monde, un Livre abominable,
> Et de qui la lecture est, même, condamnable!
> Un Livre à mériter la dernière Rigueur,
> Dont le Fourbe a le front de me faire l'Auteur!
> Et, là-dessus, on voit Oronte qui murmure,
> Et tâche, méchamment, d'appuyer l'Imposture! (1:713)

The scene recalls Foucault's claim that "[l]es textes, les livres, les discours ont commencé à avoir réellement des auteurs (autres que des personnages mythiques, autres que de grandes figures sacralisées et sacralisantes) dans la mesure où l'auteur pouvait être puni, c'est-à-dire dans la mesure où les discours pouvaient être transgressifs" (84). In the France of Louis XIV, certain authors were indeed "pendables," and Molière himself, during the aftermath of *Tartuffe*, had been labeled worthy of "un dernier supplice exemplaire et public, et le feu même, avant-coureur de celui de l'Enfer, pour expier un crime si grief de lèse-Majesté divine" (2:1166).

The episode of the "livre abominable" reinforces and nuances the authorial mechanism we saw at work with Oronte's poem. The sonnet achieved its function only to the extent that it was "authorized," that is, to the extent that it became Oronte's sonnet. The "bad book" demonstrates that such authorization does not necessarily imply the actual composition of the text in question, and Alceste's unnamed adversary, working with Oronte, exhibits a remarkably subtle, if perfidious, awareness of this slippage. Like Vernet's "nom sur le couverture d'un dossier" (21), "Alceste" becomes a mutable name that can be attached to a set of writings regardless of the person Alceste's actual relationship to a text. Alceste does not have to publish the text to be its author, nor even be the source—popular opinion (encouraged in this case by Oronte) can forge the link between the two. However, Alceste's name here is much more than a convenient label for grouping certain texts. In this era of the birth of the author as attributable and potentially culpable subject, Alceste runs the very real risk of incurring punishment if Oronte and his anonymous collaborator can indeed make the charges stick. This, however, appears unlikely, as Philinte points out to Alceste:

> Ce que votre Partie ose vous imputer,
> N'a point eu le crédit de vous faire arrêter;

> On voit son faux Rapport, lui-même, se détruire,
> Et c'est une Action qui pourraient bien lui nuire. (1:713)

What Philinte asserts in this passage is that authorship, similar in this respect to theatrical roles, is as much a question of *vraisemblance* as of *bienséance*. While it unquestionably would be inappropriate, and even criminal, for someone of Alceste's standing to have written the "livre abominable," the community of readers brings to the problem of attribution notions of likelihood, implying a measuring and estimation of character and text not unlike Nehamas's retroactive construction of the author as "a plausible historical variant of the writer" (109). Is Alceste the kind of person who could conceivably produce this sort of book? If the question of disputed authorship employs on the one hand an archaic sense of writing as a direct reflection of authorial character, it nevertheless also demonstrates a certain subtlety in the distance and ambiguity that it places between authors and books. While not allowing for egregious disjunctions between the author's social and literary personae, the ongoing inquiry and debate that Philinte describes certainly demonstrate an awareness of authorship as a negotiation. The blind spot in this argumentation, which *Le Misanthrope*'s conclusion brilliantly exploits, is the notion of the hypocritical author, the deliberate disjunction of Nehamas's writer (the actual individual who composes the text, with his or her actual opinions and biases) and author (the individual implied by the text).

Circulation and Publication (or Faithful Proofs of Authorial Infidelity)

Such a disjunction is at the heart of the most important examples of writing in *Le Misanthrope*: Célimène's letters. While the problem of Célimène's writing, along with the notions of attribution and authorship that it presents, only assumes its full significance in the final act, Donneau de Visé points out that Molière begins to develop this theme "dès le troisième Acte" (1:642). The witty orality of Célimène's salon (and chiefly of Célimène herself) had been a major component of Act 2, but as Donneau de Visé mentions, Act 3 increasingly revolves around literary objects, beginning with the agreement in the opening scene between Acaste and Clitandre that they will show each other the letters that they have received

"Je veux qu'on me distingue"

from Célimène. Célimène's correspondence is reemphasized in scene 4, when it furnishes her with an excuse to end the barbed repartees that she has been exchanging with Arsinoé, leaving the prude in the company of the newly arrived Alceste: "Alceste, il faut que j'aille écrire un mot de Lettre, / Que, sans me faire tort, je ne saurais remettre" (1:693). Célimène's announced writing project, however, takes on sinister overtones as Arsinoé, upon Célimène's departure, promises to furnish Alceste "une preuve fidèle" (1:697) of Célimène's unfaithfulness in the form of a love letter.

Alceste and Célimène's subsequent argument over the letter unquestionably serves to prepare the play's denouement, but it also helps to reinforce the modalities of authorship at work in the world of the play. The altercation revolves around two points. The first, and most certain, is that of the author. Alceste is convinced of the letter's authenticity because it is in Célimène's handwriting. As Alceste exclaims to Philinte:

> C'est de sa Trahison n'être que trop certain,
> Que l'avoir, dans ma poche, écrite de sa main.
> Oui, Madame, une Lettre écrite pour Oronte,
> A produit, à mes yeux, ma disgrâce, et sa honte. (1:701)

Recognizable in Alceste's cry of despair is an alleged connection between Célimène and her writing, rendered all the more apparent here by the dual sense of "main" as both body part and handwriting. Alceste knows that Célimène has written the letter because it bears her distinctive mark in the visual formulation of the letters. And, in a scene that recalls Agnès's letter to Horace but in a pseudo-tragic register (and the scene is borrowed from Molière's early serious play *Dom Garcie de Navarre*), Célimène's writing reveals the character of its author. Confronting Célimène with the proof of her "perfidie," Alceste trumpets, "Jetez ici les yeux, et connaissez vos Traits" (1:704), signaling again through the polysemous "traits" the link between writing and author—Célimène is ostensibly to recognize in the letter both her own handwriting and her own true self, her features, as the letter makes them clear. Just as Horace discerned Agnès's "naturel" in her missive accompanying the rock, and just as Oronte's gallant sonnet was an apt representation of his own social posturing, Alceste claims to see in Célimène's letter the key to understanding her true character.

For Alceste, the first issue—that of authorship, verifiable by the characteristic writing of Célimène's hand—leads to a second: that of the addressee. In this respect, though, Célimène initially strives to take advantage of the lone possibility afforded her to contradict Alceste's "témoin convaincant." The letter does not state its intended recipient, and Célimène accordingly suggests (while taking pains not to affirm it) that if the letter were written to a woman, then Alceste would have no grounds for complaint. When this fails, she pulls out her final trick. In a comic reversal not unlike Tartuffe's brilliant self-incrimination *cum* exculpation, Célimène acknowledges her authorship of the letter and its supposed addressee, creating an authorial and cognitive dissonance that Alceste finds unbearable. Capable of recognizing her handwriting and undoubtedly the recipient of his own stash of love letters (to whom has Célimène not sent them?), Alceste is unwilling or unable to jettison his beloved image of the author, asking instead for Célimène to present any sort of justification that would allow him to maintain a degree of consistency:

> Rendez-moi, s'il se peut, ce Billet innocent,
> À vous prêter les mains ma Tendresse consent ;
> Efforcez-vous, ici, de paraître fidèle,
> Et je m'efforcerai, moi, de vous croire telle. (1:707)

It will take Act 5's indisputable proof to convince all of the suitors together that the portraits of the author that they had individually forged are mutually exclusive.

Célimène's crimes are not so much of the heart as of the pen. Her principal mistake consists in choosing a poor genre for her literary talents. Her epistolary output is essentially a literary continuation of the oral satirical portraits that occupy much of Act 2. As Alceste points out, these portraits rely on their targets' absence:

> Allons, ferme, poussez, mes bons Amis de Cour,
> Vous n'en épargnez point, et chacun a son tour.
> Cependant, aucun d'eux, à vos yeux, ne se montre,
> Qu'on ne vous voie en hâte, aller à sa rencontre,
> Lui présenter la main, et d'un baiser flatteur
> Appuyer les Serments d'être son Serviteur. (1:677)

For Alceste, the courtiers' chief flaw lies in this behavioral duplicity between presence and absence, as Philinte demonstrated at the very beginning of the play. However, the acknowledgment of this duplicity also creates a complicity between Célimène and her audience: it is understood that in her series of portraits she drops polite social pretense, thus presumably lending to her words an aura of sincerity and truth, telling her true opinion of the individuals suggested by her entourage. Such an act of verbal sincerity assumes a tacit pact among the interlocutors that what is stated in Célimène's salon must stay in Célimène's salon. Célimène's own about-face behavior upon the entrance of Arsinoé in Act 3 shows how consistently the social game must be played even in the evident mutual loathing of the two interlocutors.

Célimène's literary genre of choice, though, creates a disjunction that ultimately leads to the author's downfall. Célimène's verbal portraits are dialogical, conceived and conveyed in a setting where speaker and listener are both physically present and where the satire leaves no physical trace: in the absence of the satirical target, the satire evaporates in the burst of laughter that it provokes. While gossip may circulate regarding the verbal criticism pronounced in the private salons—Arsinoé and Célimène both claim, albeit insincerely, to be providing each other a service by reporting directly to the person the statements and satires currently in circulation about them—the verbal nature of this communication causes it to remain removed and potentially untrustworthy. Célimène hears from Arsinoé that several people of exemplary virtue have criticized her; however, the source is not the alleged speakers themselves, but Arsinoé, whose sincerity is suspect. The inevitable refractions and distortions in this verbal relay allow the ego ample material for self-defense.

This is precisely why letters become problematic. Célimène's earlier dispute with Alceste had already revealed some of the genre's troubling characteristics. In the first place, a personal letter (unlike, significantly, a theater play) is more straight-forwardly univocal, with an identified (or identifiable) author and—generally—an identified addressee. Célimène could argue about the real recipient of the alleged letter to Oronte; she could not, however, dispute that she was the author. Nor could she hide behind the pretense of a narrator or a fictional persona ("C'est un scélérat qui parle"). As a genre closely tied to orality, letters present themselves as the written transcription of conversations that would or could have taken place in person if the individuals were present. As such,

Chapter Four

to the seventeenth-century imagination, letters become a vehicle for the author's presence, vouchsafed by her handwriting and conveying her thought transparently and without impediment, as Agnès's letter demonstrated in *L'École des femmes*.

And it is this authorial guarantee, the notion that writing conveys the author's author-ity, that dooms Célimène. As the reified record of personal conversations, Célimène's letters demonstrate an unacceptable duplicity. The personal, confessional voice that writes to Acaste and Clitandre turns out to be nothing more than a constructed fiction, adapting the content of the letter to fit the recipient, rather than remaining monolithically unified. The letters create a temporal disjunction as well. Where the rules of polite society demand that uncomfortable truths be silenced in the presence of the satirical target—as Célimène's reception of Arsinoé exemplifies—the letters preserve these satirical portraits. It is as if Célimène's evanescent critique of Arsinoé remained preserved in the air like Rabelaisian *paroles gelées*, still audible and resounding as Arsinoé enters the room.

In addition, the transformation of verbal portraits into written letters creates physical objects that can circulate in unpredictable, and uncontrollable, ways. Agnès had used this to her advantage in her letter to Horace, but *Le Misanthrope* emphasizes the dangers of the purloined letter. The transfer of letters from their privileged addressee, seen in the letters to the marquis as well as the letter allegedly to Oronte that Arsinoé has procured, corresponds reputedly to a parallel flightiness in Célimène's character. As Oronte reproaches her, "Et votre Cœur paré de beaux Semblants d'Amour, / À tout le Genre Humain se promet tour à tour!" (1:722). The intimate couple forged by the writing and reading of a letter here takes on the sense of a romantic relationship, and Célimène's various letters become so many amorous adventures. The "publishing" of Célimène's correspondence, in the more archaic sense of "making public," has as its aim the portrayal of Célimène as "publique," providing evidence for Arsinoé's earlier venomous assertions:

> Hélas! et croyez-vous que l'on se mette en peine
> De ce nombre d'Amants dont vous faites la vaine :
> Et qu'il ne nous soit pas fort aisé de juger,
> À quel prix, aujourd'hui, l'on peut les engager ? (1:692)

"Je veux qu'on me distingue"

The price, at least for a while, is merely the cost of paper and ink. But as Célimène's individual readers begin to compare notes, no amount of wit and style can assuage their anger and disappointment. Blaise Pascal described being "tout étonné et ravi" when, as a reader, he "s'attendait de voir un auteur" and found instead "un homme" (370; also Hammond 63). Célimène's readers thought that they had found a woman; they had really found an author.

Denouement

Given Molière's own dealings with the Parisian book industry in 1666, it is no surprise that *Le Misanthrope* stages the escape of written works from their creators' control. The passage from orality to literacy and the resultant implications for the author are as much at play on the stage as in the physical conditions surrounding *Le Misanthrope*'s printing. At the exact historical moment that Célimène must listen powerlessly as Acaste and Clitandre announce: "[N]ous allons l'un, et l'autre, en tous Lieux, / Montrer, de votre Cœur, le Portrait glorieux" (1:722), Molière was also watching his own authorial portrait circulate without his consent (and possibly as a result of his own flightiness in choosing *libraires*) in the frontispiece of the 1666 *Œuvres*. While certainly no "livre abominable," the edition was ample proof of the ability for works to take on a life of their own.

The publication history of his first three plays had introduced Molière to such vagaries (see Chapter 2), but *Le Misanthrope* adds a new layer to these now-familiar problems by highlighting the ways in which an author's persona is constituted (or invalidated) by the bringing together of disparate texts. The 1666 *Œuvres* creates a new composite picture of Molière just as Célimène's collected letters produce an authorial portrait that differs radically from that of the individual letters taken separately. Reputation, authenticity, and the dangers of reception are not merely concepts that Molière's characters must navigate in the heavily literary world of the play—they are issues with which Molière himself was wrestling in the wider arena of the Parisian *champ littéraire*.

A sonnet to be printed, a book in search of an author, and "published" private letters: in each of these three cases, *Le Misanthrope*

Chapter Four

explores the nuanced triangulations of writer, text, and audience. All three of these objects, however, are read or interpreted with one objective in mind: ascertaining the character of the author. With the assumption that writing conveys something of the writer's authentic self, every work becomes potentially another instantiation of Montaigne's *Essais*: "Icy, nous allons conformément et tout d'un trein, mon livre et moy. Ailleurs, on peut recommander et accuser l'ouvrage à part de l'ouvrier; icy, non: qui touche l'un, touche l'autre" (3:806). The book becomes essentially a metonym of its writer.

But such a concept is far removed from the Protean world of the stage. The allusion to *L'École des maris* in the opening scene of *Le Misanthrope* draws deliberate attention to this notion, playing off of the fact that despite the visual resemblances between Sganarelle and Alceste, Molière is now acting a different part. What is permissible in performance becomes transgression on paper, however, and readers (or at least recipients of *billets doux*) demand more consistency than spectators. Their demand is nothing less than Alceste's insistence for immutability, that an author remain as unalterable as the word on the page that she or he has written, as if fixed eternally in the readers' presence like an engraved frontispiece.

Theater's dual existence as performance and as printed text finds itself replicated in *Le Misanthrope*'s deliberate juxtaposition of orality and literacy. However, as Célimène moves across this boundary, her parallel declarations of affection (both oral and written) reveal a significant and idiosyncratic hierarchy: Célimène expects her spoken profession of love to carry more weight than a letter. When Alceste worries about the presence of so many other suitors and asks for proof that he is loved, Célimène responds, "Je pense qu'ayant pris le soin de vous le dire, / Un aveu de la sorte, a de quoi vous suffire" (1:669). The play's denouement proves such a rejoinder to be laughably inadequate. Célimène may have individually reversed usual communicative associations, making impermanent speech the vehicle for sincerity while fixing in writing nothing more than an assumed pose, but her interlocutors cannot accept this. In Célimène's salon, text has the last (and lasting) laugh.

Le Misanthrope's emphasis on text and reception marks a significant change for Molière. The quarrel surrounding *L'École des femmes* had seen the playwright fight actively to define his authorial image in a struggle with rival actors and authors. *Le Misanthrope* displaces this struggle, as if Molière realized that the missing term in this argument was perhaps the most important one: the publishers, or the owners of the very texts in which the debate was taking place. Just as Acaste and Clitandre now control the "portrait" of Célimène, Molière's own image is controlled to a significant extent by the owners of his prior plays. All evidence indicates that from the publication of *L'École des maris* onward, Molière had viewed the ownership and publication of his plays with relative disinterest, using *libraires* as a way of distributing his work and keeping it out of the hands of pirates, but without investing any greater degree of attention in the process. *Le Misanthrope* therefore marks the moment when Molière came to realize (and explore) the deeper implications of the split between authorship and ownership in seventeenth-century France.

The physical status of the first printed edition of *Le Misanthrope* reflects this growing awareness. Deliberately or not, the volume's composition foregrounds the themes that the play debates by opening with a sixteen-page letter by Donneau de Visé, the most extensive second-hand paratextual addition in any of Molière's original editions.[20] It is impossible to know whether Molière wanted the letter included or even approved of its contents—the *libraire* claims responsibility for its presence, although we might suspect that Molière at the very least did not mind, since the volume did not lead to a split between author and publisher like the 1666 *Œuvres*.[21] The presence of Donneau de Visé's letter orients the reader immediately toward the notions of textual reception, control, and interpretation: the reader is given the play in the context of the other documents that the owner chooses to present with it; furthermore, since Donneau de Visé's interpretation of the work precedes the play itself, *Le Misanthrope* is already mediated for the reader, a filter that further removes the possibility of a neutral reading. One of Molière's most richly ambiguous plays (if not *the* most) thus comes with the most extensive and reductive textual apparatus, a scene-by-scene synopsis in which Donneau de Visé's gloss stands in odd contradiction to what he himself notes about Molière's theatrical aesthetic: "Molière, par une Adresse qui lui est particulière, laisse, partout, deviner plus qu'il ne dit: et n'imite pas ceux qui parlent beaucoup, et ne disent rien" (1:644).

Chapter Four

Given the play's denouement, it is ironic that Donneau de Visé's commentary is couched as a letter to a nobleman. The author begins by specifying that the letter is private and intended for its recipient only: "[M]ais souvenez-vous de la sincère amitié que vous m'avez promise: et n'allez pas exposer à Fontainebleau, au jugement des Courtisans, des Remarques que je n'ai faites que pour vous obéir. Songez à ménager ma réputation; et pensez que les Gens de la Cour, de qui le Goût est si raffiné, n'auront pas, pour moi, la même indulgence que vous" (1:635). This initial delimitation of the audience is belied by the end of the letter, however, as Donneau de Visé concludes: "Ce long Discours ne devrait pas déplaire aux Courtisans, puisqu'ils ont assez fait voir, par leurs applaudissements, qu'ils trouvaient la Comédie belle. En tout cas, je n'ai écrit que pour vous; et j'espère que vous cacherez ceci, si vous jugez qu'il ne vaille pas la peine d'être montré" (1:644). The injunction at the letter's beginning proves to be highly conditional and, of course, the letter's inclusion in the published edition finishes this transformation of a private letter into a public document. In fact, the *libraire*'s note accompanying the letter states that it was "vue de la meilleure partie de la Cour" (1:635).

While Célimène's letters were not intended disingenuously to become public in this way, the similar transition that they undergo from private to public creates a strange thematic resonance with the paratext. As a result, the original edition of *Le Misanthrope*, text and paratext, seems a sustained exploration of Roger Chartier's axiom: "Les auteurs n'écrivent pas des Livres: non, ils écrivent des textes que d'autres transforment en objets imprimés" ("Le Monde comme représentation" 1513). These "autres," be they Quinet and company, or Acaste and Clitandre, that arise between an author and the now-objectified representation of the author's thought (whether printed or circulated in manuscript form), inevitably redirect the trajectory of the text. In addition, these others, by controlling the textual objects, also help to control the authorial image that these works create. Reversing the normal associations of authorial causality, books can create, or even threaten, their authors.

With an *achevé d'imprimer* of 24 December 1666, but listing 1667 on its title page, the original edition of *Le Misanthrope* occupies a liminal moment in Molière's career, a turning point that

"Je veux qu'on me distingue"

grapples with the implications of the 1666 *Œuvres* and anticipates new developments in Molière's approach to authorship and publication. New developments that can seem strikingly similar to events in the past—perhaps the edition's final irony is the identity of the *libraire* who published it: Jean Ribou, responsible for the thefts of Molière's first two published plays. If we accept the identification of Donneau de Visé with Neuf-Villenaine, as some critics have claimed, then Molière in 1666 found himself in the company of the same team responsible for the text and paratext of the pirated 1660 *Sganarelle*. The extensive *arguments* of the earlier play would therefore become the direct predecessor of *Le Misanthrope*'s letter, both scene-by-scene analyses presenting highly flattering descriptions of the plays that they introduce. One might be tempted to say that Molière, looking for new publishers, decided to go with those who *le distinguaient*, or perhaps that he preferred the editorial company of a Philinte to an Alceste. In any case, Ribou and his shadowy associates had certainly proved sensitive to issues of authorial image, as prior experience had shown, and the first edition of *Le Misanthrope*, with its engraved frontispiece and its lengthy laudatory letter, certainly strives to reassure the author that he is in good hands. It seems oddly appropriate that in his search for a *libraire* Molière would settle on someone who demonstrably was willing to go to great, and even illegal, lengths for the privilege of publishing his works.

It appears almost inevitable that *Le Misanthrope* itself should participate in the same authorial dynamics of identity and disjunction that it analyzes. A lone but notable example will have to suffice: in 1674, a year after Molière's death, Boileau will recommend in his *Art poétique* that writers of comedy imitate Molière in certain points, but avoid his farcical tendencies, adding: "Dans ce sac ridicule où Scapin s'enveloppe, / Je ne reconnais plus l'auteur du Misanthrope" (*Œuvres complètes* [1873]. ed. Fournier 164). Authorship and *Le Misanthrope* are here explicitly linked—for Boileau, the play, with its literary style and subject matter, is what makes Molière an author, employed here in its strictest and most lofty sense. But multiple plays, like Célimène's multiple letters, disrupt this unified authorial illusion. To employ Hix's terms, the singular proxy (the implied author of the lone work) cannot correlate to the synoptic proxy (the implied author of a body of works).

Chapter Four

The cognitive dissonance for Boileau created by disparate works of Molière causes his preferred authorial image of the playwright to disappear from view, eclipsed by the eminently theatrical Scapin, consummate actor and master of a thousand roles. Or, to place it in the terms of *Le Misanthrope*, Alceste's quixotic dream of exalted and authentic unity here cedes the stage to Célimène, author of countless letters and, consequently, of countless Célimènes. Boileau's public criticism of Molière's authorial "inconstancy" is in the end unnecessary—Molière had already staged it.

Chapter Five

The School for Publishers

Given Molière's experiences with the 1666 *Œuvres* and the subsequent examination of the perils of authorship in *Le Misanthrope*, it is tempting to agree with Abby Zanger's assessment that Molière viewed publication as a loss of control, a menacing circulation that can, and will, eventually turn against the author.[1] But an awareness of publication's dangers did not necessarily imply a fear or even a sustained avoidance of them. There was, after all, no good alternative, as Molière had learned from his first three published plays. But 1666 had added a new factor to the vexing problems of past pirate editions. With *L'École des maris* in 1661, Molière had decided that full participation in the official publication system would best protect his works from misappropriation. What he had not realized, and what the 1666 *Œuvres* made clear, was that the official system protected his works by taking them away from him.

By the standards of the time, Molière's previous *libraires* had done nothing wrong and they may not even have been the ones to initiate the rift with the playwright, as discussed in Chapter 4. However, the fact remained that they, and not Molière, were the (perpetual) owners of the plays that they had purchased, and the seventeenth-century legal and publishing systems were designed to preserve their rights. The reign of the author, when the legal tables would turn and confer rights upon authors that lasted beyond the initial publication of their works, was still more than a century away.

It would be anachronistic to see in Molière a modern writer, fully cognizant of his rights but trapped in an era that did not recognize them. Molière was certainly a product of his time, limited in his choice of subject positions and confined by contemporary power structures and ways of thinking. However, these power structures were in the process of shifting, not least of all in the ways that authorship and publication were construed. To perceptive individuals, and particularly to those who had a theatrical sense of the advantages that could come from adopting certain roles, new and advantageous possibilities were emerging. The extent to which Molière noticed these opportunities and exploited them demonstrates his own changing approach to authorship and publication. In fact, the actions of Molière from the publication of *Le Misanthrope* in 1666 to his death in 1673 show him addressing the vagaries of publication not by hesitating to publish, but instead by aggressively redefining the very terms of his interactions with the Parisian *champ littéraire*.

We do not necessarily have to attribute to Molière an overdeveloped authorial sensibility in order to explain his motivation for doing so. If such a consciousness manifests itself through an attention to revising and polishing texts or adding theoretical commentary *à la Corneille*, evidence would be difficult to find in Molière's case, given the lack of such features even in editions that Molière could have potentially overseen. However, as in the early case of *Sganarelle*, the playwright did seem instead possessed of a keen sense of ownership. Molière does not appear as troubled so much by the actual state of the printed text as by the circumstances of its publishing: who printed it; who subsequently owns it; who receives the payment for it.

From 1666 to 1673, Molière's approaches to these topics constitute creative (and even dubiously legal) solutions that create a trajectory unique for the time period. True to this individualistic path, his innovations do not change the system in which he operates, nor do they necessarily anticipate future developments like copyright. They constitute instead ingenious but *sui generis* experiments that show Molière, through the content and the format of his printed works, reformulating the issues raised in his early career in ways that provided him the greatest advantage, much to the chagrin of the *Communauté des libraires*.

Working with Jean Ribou, 1666–70

In his search for a new publisher, Molière settled on Jean Ribou fairly quickly. Either initiating or responding to problems with his prior *libraires*, Molière sold the rights to *L'Amour médecin* to Pierre Trabouillet, Nicolas Le Gras, and Théodore Girard in January 1666. These same publishers, now with the addition of Jean Ribou, brought out *Le Médecin malgré lui* in December 1666. Simultaneously, Ribou published *Le Misanthrope* by himself—the *achevé d'imprimer* is identical (24 December 1666). Ribou would then subsequently publish all of Molière's plays up to and including *Monsieur de Pourceaugnac* from 1667 to 1670. In addition to publishing the individual plays, Ribou also took advantage of the exclusive rights that the playwright had granted him by composing nonce editions (that is, volumes of individually printed plays bound together) that he sold as the third, fourth, and fifth volumes of the 1666 collected works brought out by his competitors.

Why Molière chose to work so closely with his former adversary remains a subject of speculation. H. Carrington Lancaster suggests that Ribou had become more established, and presumably more respectable, in the four years since his early altercations with Molière ("Molière" 33). He would thus have been a viable alternative to the author's previous publishers. For Caldicott, on the other hand, it was precisely Ribou's status on the margins that would have attracted Molière, angry with the conduct of the "legitimate" publishers who had excluded him from the 1666 edition ("Molière" 6).

It is difficult to determine how much of an "outsider" Ribou really was. By 1666 his shop was no longer on the Quai des Augustins, home to many less-fortunate booksellers and where Ribou had been located during his earlier run-ins with Molière, but was instead at the Palais de Justice, directly across from the Sainte-Chapelle (Lancaster, "Molière" 32). This was prime real estate for *libraires*, and it would have made him the neighbor of Claude Barbin, who also had his shop on the *perron* of the Sainte-Chapelle (Reed, *Barbin* 16), placing him at the very heart of the *nouveautés* market. Ribou's clientele also speaks to the centrality of the *libraire*: he was not only the exclusive publisher of nine of Molière's plays, but also printed a number of plays by Montfleury, Boursault, Donneau de Visé, and Thomas Corneille (Lancaster, "Molière" 34), and would later publish Racine's complete works in 1675, two years after Molière's death (Guibert, *Racine* 126, 130).

All this still would not explain, though, why Molière would agree to work with an individual who had printed the attacks of his adversaries and on two occasions tried to steal his work. Nor was Molière without other options; at least three other publishers—Trabouillet, Girard, and Le Gras—had shown themselves willing and capable. A final possible response to the question—simple yet compelling—is that Ribou may have been willing to pay more. Although records are scarce concerning the payment that Molière received from his publishers, contemporary sources indicate that Ribou gave Molière two hundred *pistoles* for *Tartuffe* (Martin, *Livre* 2:917).[2] Although the notoriety of *Tartuffe* prior to its publication made it something of an exception, Ribou's payment to Molière was ten times the going rate for a comedy, and his other payments, while perhaps not quite as elevated, could very well have been generous. In other words, in the aftermath of the 1666 edition and with Molière reluctant to work with many of the principal publishers of *nouveautés*, Ribou may simply have outbid the remaining competition.

However, Ribou's newfound respectability and prosperity did not mean that he had renounced his old ways. On the contrary, throughout his career Ribou continued to engage in illicit book sales and counterfeiting, and it was Ribou's legal trouble that eventually ended his collaboration with the playwright. Ribou and his relative Denis David were among the chief Parisian contacts for the Elzeviers and other Dutch printers (Martin, *Livre* 2:666) and they were arrested and thrown in the Bastille on 9 November 1669 "pour avoir fait venir de Hollande et avoir débité, par Paris, des libelles touchant les amours du Roi" (Lancaster, "Molière" 33). At their subsequent trial in May, the two *libraires* were condemned to be hanged, but a legal document from December 1670 indicates that this sentence was commuted first to a term in the prison galleys, and then commuted again (because Ribou and David were found "*invalides*") to flogging and banishment (Thuasne, appendix 4). A 1702 document published in the Bastille archives reveals that Ribou and David owed their lives as much to Molière's intervention as to their poor health: "[L]a peine des galères fut commuée en celle du fouet et bannis, attendu que David était affligé d'une descente, et Ribou ayant trouvé des amis, par le moyen de Molière, comédien pour lors en crédit, se tira d'affaire …" (Lancaster, "Molière" 34).

Ribou's legal troubles did not end with the commuting of his sentence, for a statement by the *Conseil d'État* on 10 December 1670 notes that, in defiance of the sentence banishing him from Paris and the book trade, Ribou was still in the city and had even registered a privilege in his name with the *Communauté des libraires* (Thuasne, appendix 4). The *Conseil d'État* ordered Ribou and David to close their shops immediately and asked the *syndic* and the *adjoints* of the *Communauté* to help in carrying this out. Ribou and David were officially served this order on 21 January 1671. Ribou did not stay banished for long: the king granted him entrance to Paris again on 27 April 1672. While the official letter permitting his return did not allow Ribou to resume practicing his profession, Ribou solved the problem by altering the text, "artificieusement et subrepticement" inserting "une clause de retablissement, en sa profession de libraire" (Thuasne, appendix 5). An order of 12 September 1672 signed by Colbert countermanded this forged approval and reiterated that Ribou was not allowed to sell or publish books (Thuasne, appendix 5). It appears that at some point Ribou was again permitted to ply his trade, but his steady commerce of "bad books" continued to cause him legal problems. In 1683, Nicolas de La Reynie, the *Lieutenant-Général de la Police*, had an illegal edition entitled *Le Médecin de soi-même* seized at Ribou's shop (Thuasne, appendix 6). In 1688, a warrant was issued for Ribou's arrest for printing *L'Almanach de Milan* and he was interrogated and banished yet again from Paris (Lancaster, "Molière" 34). In 1702, he was back in Paris and the Bastille archives record, "[I]l est très-sûr que Ribou, aussi bien que le fils de défunt David, qui a sa boutique aussi sur le quai des Augustins, et parent de Ribou, font le commerce de tous les livres dangereux" (Lancaster, "Molière" 34).

Caldicott sees in Ribou's 1669 arrest a conspiracy on the part of the "cartel" (the eight publishers responsible for the 1666 collected edition) and an effort to seize control of Molière's work by eliminating his favored publisher:

> En mettant ainsi l'imprimeur de Molière au ban de la corporation, et en exigeant la fermeture de son commerce, le syndic et ses adjoints portaient un coup très grave à la carrière de l'auteur, sans parler du malheureux imprimeur et de son épouse. C'était, bien entendu, un dénouement tout à fait heureux pour ceux du cartel (dont les deux adjoints du syndic) qui voulaient mettre fin à la carrière par trop indépandante d'un Molière auteur et éditeur qui, avec la collaboration dudit Ribou, avait réussi à faire imprimer neuf pièces entre 1666 et 1670. La coïncidence est trop commode pour ne pas éveiller des soupçons. En

> prenant sur eux l'application de la loi, les officiers de la Communauté des Libraires deviennent immédiatement suspects. N'avaient-ils pas dénoncé eux-mêmes l'imprimeur de Molière? (*Carrière* 133–34)

Caldicott suggests that Ribou's arrest was the result of professional jealousy and a struggle for control over Molière's plays, but this seems improbable for several reasons. In the first place, there is no direct evidence to show that any *libraire* denounced Ribou—the only existing documentation comes from the royal officers charged with policing the book trade. It also seems strange to impute such rapaciousness and malice to booksellers whose careers were, on the whole, reputable while excusing the conduct of Ribou, whose reputation for dealing in illicit material stretches for over forty years.

Furthermore, at least one of Molière's eight former publishers, Claude Barbin, showed no reluctance to deal with Ribou nor a desire to ruin him. Ribou had collaborated with Barbin, Loyson, and Quinet in the printing of *Les Diversités galantes* (1664), the volume that contained two contributions by Donneau de Visé to the *querelle de L'École des femmes* (*La Réponse à L'Impromptu de Versailles* and *Lettre sur les Affaires du Théâtre*). According to documents published by Gervais Reed, Barbin and Thierry purchased two-thirds of the rights to Molière's plays in 1673 from Anne David, Ribou's wife, leaving one-third in the possession of the Ribou family and making them a shadow partner in the collected editions that Barbin and Thierry would later produce (Reed, "Molière's privilege" 61).[3] Barbin also would collaborate actively with Ribou to issue collected editions of Racine's plays in 1675 and 1676 (Guibert, *Racine* 125, 130, 133).[4]

While it is possible, as Caldicott suggests, that Ribou was denounced by rival *libraires*, it is certain that he was caught engaging in questionable publishing practices at a time when it was increasingly dangerous to do so. If Ribou and David in 1669 were indeed circulating Dutch editions of "des libelles touchant les amours du Roi" (Lancaster, "Molière" 33), they were running enormous risks, and their arrest is not at all surprising. Henri-Jean Martin has demonstrated how Louis XIV and his government launched a major effort in the 1660s to crack down on counterfeiting and, even more importantly, on the import of foreign books that slandered those in power. The reduction in the number of printing establishments, the renewed enforcement of laws regulating book shipments, and the organization of a book police directed by La Reynie made it increasingly difficult to carry out such clandestine trade in Paris (Martin, *Livre* 2:695–98).

The officers of the *Communauté* were heavily involved in seeing that royal objectives were accomplished in these regards. Martin writes, "le syndic et les adjoints étaient désormais élus en présence de La Reynie, après avoir été soigneusement choisis parmi les plus inconditionnels soutiens du Pouvoir" (*Livre* 2:697). They were charged with inspecting "toute balle, caisse, ballot ou paquet de livres introduit dans la ville par des libraires forains ou parisiens" (2:697) and with making weekly visits to the *libraires* and printers to verify that everything was in order. The failure to fulfill these responsibilities could have serious consequences, especially during this period when the State was watching the Parisian book trade with ever-increasing vigilance. As the royal order concerning Ribou's arrest stated, the officers of the *Communauté* were to cooperate with La Reynie "à peine d'y respondre de leurs noms propres et privez" (Thuasne, appendix 4). Implying that the participation of the *syndic* and *adjoints* in the Ribou affair denotes a certain abuse of power for personal gain, Caldicott asks, "*Sed quis custodiet ipsos custodes?*" ("Molière" 8). The answer, apparently, is Colbert and La Reynie, who sought to turn the *Communauté des libraires* into an extension of royal power directly overseen by the officers of the *Chancellerie*.

The increased surveillance of *libraires* and the book trade undoubtedly provoked Ribou's fall and effectively ended his collaboration with Molière. Although Ribou would be back in Paris, and even back in business, periodically throughout the following decade, his continued troubles with the law would have posed significant obstacles to publishing high-profile works like Molière's plays.

Tartuffe

The most remarkable edition to come out of Molière's collaboration with Ribou was ironically the one in which the two maintained the greatest official distance. On 5 February 1669, Molière's troupe performed *Tartuffe*, the king's official permission having ended the five-year battle over the play. Unusually, the first edition of the play came out before the initial performance run was even over, although it should be noted that in *Tartuffe*'s case this period was exceptionally long: twenty-eight performances that lasted until 9 April, the beginning of the Easter break. Molière received his privilege, valid for ten years, on 15 March and registered it with the *Communauté des libraires* five days later. The printed edition was completed and ready for sale on 23 March at Ribou's stall at the Palais de Justice. But Ribou was only selling the books—he did not own the text or publish the edition. The title page of *Tartuffe* makes clear that the edition was "imprimé aux dépens de l'Auteur" (2:89), that is, that Molière had financed the edition himself. The abbreviated privilege included in the volume makes no mention of any transfer of Molière's rights to a *libraire*. By all measures, Molière was retaining the rights of the play for himself, contracting out the printing and sale through Jean Ribou but without ceding the rights and the ownership to the bookseller. The only plausible reason for this anomaly (the next printed play, *Monsieur de Pourceaugnac*, would contain neither of these features) is that *Tartuffe* was a book too dangerous for even Jean Ribou. Roger Chartier reminds us that while Foucault claimed that authorship was a function of finding an individual legally responsible for a book, the early modern period shows that often this responsibility (and by extension the possibility of punishment) was assigned to the publisher:

> Dans la répression, toutefois, la responsabilité de l'auteur d'un livre censuré ne semble pas considérée comme plus grande que celle de l'imprimeur qui l'a publié, du libraire ou du colporteur qui le vend, ou du lecteur qui le possède. Tous peuvent être conduits au bûcher s'ils sont convaincus d'avoir proféré ou diffusé des opinions hérétiques. (*L'Ordre* 65)

Ribou's own brushes with the law amply demonstrate a bookseller's legal liability.[5]

In the first edition of *Tartuffe*, Molière therefore assumes the role of both author and owner, investing him in the fate of his work to an unprecedented degree. Or perhaps we should say that it was Molière who invested in his work, since in this instance he outlaid the money for the edition's production. However, if Molière took on an additional degree of risk (a good part of which was financial) with *Tartuffe*'s publication, he also stood to receive an inordinate share of the benefits. Rather than the single payment that authors normally received when booksellers purchased the rights to their work, Molière would have received all profits from the edition's sale, once the overhead—in this instance, the printing and binding fees, as well as the amount that Ribou may have charged in order to sell the work at his stand—was deducted. Given the phenomenal theater receipts and the whiff of sulfur surrounding the previously banned play, sales must have been brisk, as attested by the prompt appearance of a second edition.

The real significance to Molière's publication experiment in the case of *Tartuffe* is not necessarily the amount of money that he potentially made. After all, a writer could earn just as much (or even more) money under the single-payment system, depending on how much a *libraire* was willing to pay for a new work. A popular play, where all the signs pointed to strong sales, would have undoubtedly encouraged bidding wars among potential publishers. The real interest surrounding Molière's particular publishing arrangements, however, stems from how this money was to be generated: presumably Molière received money from the purchase of each copy, meaning that the playwright's profits were in direct proportion to the book sales. The existing evidence points to only one potential precedent for this in Molière's career: the judgment regarding Ribou's illegal edition of *Sganarelle*, in which the judge awarded the author a sum based on a per-copy fee ("trente sols chacun exemplaire" [Jurgens and Maxfield-Miller 349]), essentially forcing the *libraire* to buy the books from the author. This still amounted to a set figure, though, and Molière's venture into self-publication should perhaps be viewed instead as the transposition of a theatrical model to the literary scene.

As Samuel Chappuzeau describes it in *Le Théâtre françois* (1674), theater troupes in the second half of the seventeenth century standardized the practice of paying the playwright based on the receipts from the initial performance run: "La plus ordinaire condition & la plus iuste de costé & d'autre est de faire entrer l'Autheur pour deux parts dans toutes les representations de sa piece iusques à un certain temps" (85–86). These shares, identical to those belonging to the actors, were calculated after subtracting the "f[r]ais ordinaires, comme les lumieres & les gages des Officiers" (87). In this way, the author's fees were tied directly to the critical fortunes of the work (Lough 46), or as Chappuzeau puts it, "Si la piece a un grand succez ... l'Autheur est riche, & les Comediens le sont aussi & si la piece a le malheur d'échouer ... on ne s'opiniâtre pas à la joüer davantage, & l'on se console de part & d'autre le mieux que l'on peut, comme il faut se consoler en ce monde de tous les evenemens fâcheux" (87).

When Chappuzeau mentions that this method of payment was "[l]a plus ordinaire," it is because another method existed as well, as he later describes: "Quelquefois les Comediens payent l'ouvrage contant, iusques à deux cens pistoles, & au-delà en le prenant des mains de l'Autheur, & au hazard du succez" (88). In other words, an approach parallel to the standard practice for selling manuscripts also existed in the realm of theater—the move from a set amount to a cut of the profits that takes place among actors and authors parallels the later move for publishers and authors toward a system of royalties. For Molière, well-versed in the theatrical model, a system of book royalties similar to the standard practice of theatrical payments might well have seemed "plus iuste."

At the very least, the theatrical system provided Molière with an alternative model that he could mobilize when Ribou proved reluctant to buy the rights to *Tartuffe*. Forced to be creative in order to bring his work to light, as he so often was during the struggle over the play, Molière decided to exploit a legal right written directly into the formulaic text of the privilege, but which authors seldom employed. Molière's privilege for *Amphitryon* (published with Ribou a year before *Tartuffe*), for example, contains the phrase, "Il est permis à I.B.P. DE MOLIERE, de faire imprimer par tel Libraire ou Imprimeur qu'il voudra choisir, une Piece de Theatre de sa composition, intitulée, L'AMPHITRYON," clearly authorizing the recipient, be he author or *libraire*, to contract out the printing of the edition. If the wording was standard, however, it was far from typical for an author to take personal responsibility for an edition's production and sale—as discussed previously, the aristocratic trappings surrounding writing discouraged even getting paid for one's texts, let alone becoming involved in the business details of a book's production.

Although the practice was rare, Molière was not the first author to do so, and Henri-Jean Martin mentions other earlier or contemporary seventeenth-century authors (Saint-Amant, Le Gall, and Gervais) who produced books at their own expense and even, in some cases (Nicolas de Blégny), sold the book at their own residence (*Livre* 2:920). Significantly, Martin also mentions the legal efforts undertaken by the Parisian *libraires* to reassert their rights as the only individuals permitted to sell books and for whom authors like Blégny would have represented a serious threat to their livelihood (*Livre* 2:920–21). Nor did the officials of the *Communauté des libraires* hesitate to remind authors of the legislation in force. When Philippe de La Croix registered his privilege for *La Guerre comique, ou La Defense de l'Escolle des femmes* (1664) with the *Communauté*, the *syndic* noted in the record a standard warning, "Registré à condition que les exemplaires dudit livre ne se pourront distribuer que par les libraires, et non autrement" (Thuasne 20).[6]

Molière's innovative solution, contracting out both the printing and the sale of his work, underlines some important developments. In the first place, it shows that Molière was growing ever more familiar with the Parisian publishing world, including the legal documents that governed it. He was obviously reading very carefully the rights that he was granted by the privilege system, and since the privilege system had been designed primarily for publishers, the playwright's active participation created some unusual possibilities. Molière was also now gaining exposure to the economic aspect of printing. Ribou, though reluctant to assume responsibility for the edition, undoubtedly must have helped Molière navigate these new waters. In addition, the first edition of *Tartuffe* emphasizes Molière's willingness to take risks in order to publish his works under favorable circumstances, or conditions that are advantageous to him. These developments will assume greater importance later in Molière's career. *Tartuffe* will not prove to be a failed experiment.

In the short term, Molière's edition must have convinced Ribou through its sales and its lack of legal recriminations that *Tartuffe* was an investment worth pursuing. The only source regarding the purchase comes from Gabriel Guéret, who claims that Molière sold the play to Ribou for two hundred *pistoles*, an extraordinary amount for the time period (Viala 108). If the amount is correct, and if Guéret's subsequent claim that Ribou did not make his money back on the second edition is also correct, then Molière made a deal worthy of his *bourgeois* upbringing: profiting off of the original edition in an unusually lucrative fashion, and then selling out for an extraordinary sum right before interest in the

Chapter Five

play waned. While the exact price may or may not be correct, it is certain that Molière eventually sold Ribou the rights to the play, indicating that the *Tartuffe* experiment was not intended to be a permanent arrangement—at least at this time. When Molière was not confronted with abnormal publishing circumstances, he was still content to operate within normal bounds. He must have retained positive associations from the experience, however, since the publication of his later plays, as discussed below, shows him eager to repeat it.

The typical seventeenth-century paratext is a joint creation of author and editor, particularly when the *libraire* is the one funding the work. In the case of *Tartuffe*, Molière played both roles for the first time, and we can therefore with more surety attribute certain distinctive features of the edition to him. The most prominent of these is *Tartuffe*'s lengthy preface, at eighteen pages easily the most extensive found in any of Molière's plays (Guibert, *Molière* 1:261). Duchêne notes the degree to which the preface constitutes an emphatic statement of Molière's triumph: "La préface mise en tête de sa pièce célèbre sa victoire sans modestie" (538). If Molière was indeed settling scores, he was paying for the privilege to do so.

The preface might have proved a selling point, and when Ribou bought the rights to the play, he retained the full preface and even expanded the polemical paratext by including Molière's three *placets* to the king. Ribou draws attention to these additions through his note "au lecteur," which states: "Comme les moindres choses qui partent de la plume de M. de Molière, ont des beautés que les plus délicats ne se peuvent laisser d'admirer, j'ai cru ne devoir pas négliger l'occasion de vous faire part de ces Placets, et qu'il était à propos de les joindre au *Tartuffe*, puisque partout il y est parlé de cette incomparable Pièce" (2:191). Whatever *beautés* the *placets* might contain, Ribou had other good reasons to include them—they distinguish his edition from the original one. Who would continue to buy the first when the second was available with brand-new content, especially when that content consisted of private correspondence with the king about the play's controversial ban?

Ribou's determination to own *Tartuffe*—apparently at any cost—demonstrates a further accomplishment of Molière's original edition. With the *libraire* originally concerned about printing such a controversial title, Molière's foray into self-publishing must have proved that the battle over *Tartuffe* was officially over. The printed excerpt of the royal privilege, issued by the king's legal counsel D'Alencé, precedes the text, forming a thematic bookend with Act Five's denouement, in which the king's officer arrests Tartuffe and restores Orgon and his family to their home and rights. The play's appearance in print is a dramatic statement of royal approval, amplified by the preface and later by the included *placets*. The king's support of Orgon in spite of accusations and incriminations (and even overlooking Orgon's missteps in the case of his suspect correspondence) takes concrete form in the paratext. The boilerplate statement that the edition is printed "avec privilège du roi" (2:89) in this case assumes increased significance, given the play's history, plot, and paratext.

In much the same way that knowledge of the denouement allows us to appreciate the foreshadowing in Dorine's early reference to the "troubles" of the Fronde and Orgon's loyalty to the king (2:106), Molière's later publishing career will make certain elements of *Tartuffe*'s first edition particularly significant. Chief among these is the pairing of self-publication and an appeal to the king's authority. In the play, Tartuffe's apparent triumph comes about because of the hypocrite's legal knowledge and his reliance on the letter of the law to enforce his cause. Orgon's Royalist stance affords him a sort of supra-legal status, since the absolute monarch can go beyond the normal legalities of the case in order to bring about true justice, based on moral sensibility, rather than on the strict facts of the case. For the performance and publication of the play itself, Molière could be said to rely on Louis XIV's authority in a similar way, and Molière's editorial independence in this case is a direct result of the rights granted to him through royal officers. The singular example of *Tartuffe* will prove to be ever more significant in light of Molière's subsequent publishing career.

Author, *Communauté*, and King

Ironically, it was a very different manifestation of royal power that precipitated the remarkable shift in Molière's publishing strategy: Ribou's 1669 arrest for selling books mocking Louis XIV's amorous exploits. After his release from the Bastille and before his trial in late 1670, Ribou had time to publish one more Molière play, *Monsieur de Pourceaugnac*. His subsequent banishment from Paris

Chapter Five

and the book trade meant that Ribou was unable to be involved directly with Molière's printed work up until the author's sudden death in 1673 (although as we might expect from him, Ribou was not entirely out of the picture, as discussed below). Ribou's legal troubles placed Molière in the same position that he had been in 1660 and 1666, an author without a regular publisher. Molière's reaction to the situation, though, demonstrates the extent to which he had evolved over the course of his career. Ten years before, Molière had been a new and reluctant author; in 1670, he was a seasoned professional with an inside knowledge of the publication industry and a solid connection to royal power. The experience of Molière's first decade in print allowed the playwright to rethink publication in ways that were innovative, or even potentially transgressive. A particularly precocious example of Bourdieu's *habitué*, Molière was capable of seeing not only how the game was being played in the literary *champ* of 1670s Paris, but also of anticipating how the game itself might be changed. Consequently, every work that the author published from 1671 to 1672 constituted a step forward in a remarkably individual and inventive approach to print.

The first of the volumes to indicate this shift was *Le Bourgeois gentilhomme*, published in 1671. Arguably the finest of Molière and Lully's *comédies-ballets*, the work has been seen as a landmark of sorts within Molière's corpus, or a touchstone for the playwright's evolving theatrical project. Gérard Defaux identified *Le Bourgeois gentilhomme* as the first mature expression of Molière's new aesthetic, abandoning the critique of social mores and embracing a carnivalesque celebration of pleasure and escape.[7] A key component to this is the work's composite genre, integrating theater, dance, and music. Comedy's impasses are resolved through the other arts, as Monsieur Jourdain is promoted to *mamamouchi* in the fanciful Turkish ceremony and tensions ultimately dissolve into the Ballet des Nations. Monsieur Jourdain is not cured of his delusions, nor is he exiled, the two options open to comedy's traditional blocking figure since Classical times. Instead, the reasonable members of the household join in Jourdain's *folie*, transforming themselves with him into theatrical participants, and eventually into spectators of the concluding ballet. Theater, dance, and music become the vehicles whereby the problems of real life are circumvented.

For Zanger, *Le Bourgeois gentilhomme* (and particularly the Ballet des Nations) confirms Molière's early hesitations regarding print and publication. Noting the way in which a printed *livret* is used in order to hierarchize and control the members of the audience during the ballet's performance, Zanger concludes that Molière was well aware of print's capacity to "paralyze" performance, connecting the *comédie-ballet* with Molière's declaration in the first edition of *L'Amour médecin* that plays are only meant to be played. Zanger's astute reading of a largely neglected episode in the ballet highlights how keenly Molière saw the functions and possibilities of publication.

Where we might usefully add to this conclusion is in pointing out that while Molière was certainly wary of such power at various points in his career, in 1671 he chose to use it for his own ends. Reviving the method behind *Tartuffe*'s initial publication, Molière chose to forego any editor and publish *Le Bourgeois gentilhomme* himself. As with the earlier play, Molière took out the privilege in his own name, but without any subsequent transfer of his rights to a *libraire*. Although the edition was sold by Pierre Le Monnier, the title page includes the phrase "et se vend pour l'Autheur," indicating that Molière once again had contracted out the printing and the sale of the edition. No documentation exists to specify the financial details, but there is significantly no mention of any *libraire* in the privilege, suggesting that Molière retained all legal rights to the play and would alone receive the profits (Guibert, *Molière* 1:337). If Molière's approach in this case recalls *Tartuffe*, however, there was one important difference. With *Tartuffe*, Molière took a financial risk in order to see his play published, and once its success was assured, he followed his usual pattern and transferred his rights to a *libraire*. With *Le Bourgeois gentilhomme*, there would be no subsequent transfer.

Perhaps Molière was merely waiting for Jean Ribou's legal troubles to clear, retaining the rights to the play until he could transfer them to his accustomed publisher. This may well be the case, particularly because, as the editors of the 2010 Pléiade edition note, Le Monnier was apparently running Ribou's shop in his absence—the title page indicates the edition is being sold at Le Monnier's usual *enseigne* (*au Feu divin*), as well as at Ribou's (*à l'image S. Louis*) (2:1452).[8] There nevertheless remains no record of a transfer or sale of the privilege. A heretofore contingency was turning into a standard publishing practice—the remainder of the plays printed in Molière's lifetime (*Les Fourberies de Scapin* [1671], *Psyché* [1671], and *Les Femmes savantes* [1672]) were also sold "pour l'Autheur."[9]

The publication of *Le Bourgeois gentilhomme* is significant for two other reasons. In the first place, it demonstrates that even in Ribou's absence Molière was unwilling to deal with his former publishers, the *libraires* with whom he had split in 1666. The second point (related to the first) is that Molière seems remarkably concerned with the ownership of his plays. By refusing to transfer his privilege, Molière bypassed the legal act that ended an author's control over the text and that had potentially led to Molière's dissatisfaction with his 1666 publishers. Once again, as was the case throughout his career, Molière's conception of authorship was closely tied to possession.

Le Bourgeois gentilhomme represents a step toward authorial independence—the first Molière play never to be owned by anyone other than the playwright himself. His next published play, however, would go significantly further, since it was not merely independence that Molière sought, but revenge. On 18 March 1671 Molière took out a privilege in his own name to publish his complete works—not just the works published since 1666, but *all* his plays. The 1671 privilege was extraordinary: it gave Molière the right to print his plays, regardless, in the case of works that had already been published, of who actually held the earlier privilege. Moreover, it went into effect immediately, even if existing privileges had not yet expired. Its duration was nine years (his previous privileges had typically lasted five to seven years)[10] and, although it made reference to a particular printing project, an illustrated edition of Molière's complete works, its scope was actually much wider, giving the author permission to print his plays individually or collectively as he saw fit.

The extraordinary nature of the privilege led to a refusal by Louis Sevestre, the *syndic* of the *Communauté des libraires et des Imprimeurs*, to register it.[11] This created a significant impediment to Molière's printing efforts, as registration with the *Communauté* was required in order to validate a privilege. Registration was typically a formality, and the *Communauté*'s uncharacteristic refusal to honor Molière's privilege has struck some modern critics as an infringement of the author's rights designed to rob him of the profits he could receive from his work's sale. Caldicott, labeling the *Communauté* "a corrupt, self-serving interest group" ("Molière" 8), writes: "The question naturally arises as to how the *Communauté des Libraires* could have been allowed to promote the interests of its own members in such a narrowly exclusive way" (7). While it is true that the *Communauté* in this situation did indeed defend the rights of its members, it seems somewhat disingenuous to expect it to act otherwise. Although Molière was asserting authorial rights that have now become firmly established, his former *libraires* could hardly be faulted at the time for claiming ownership of texts that they had duly purchased.[12]

A careful examination of Molière's 1671 privilege shows how thoroughly familiar the author had become with the laws governing publication. The text of the privilege takes pains to establish each of the necessary conditions for a *continuation* or extension—in other words, Molière was in reality requesting an extension of his publishers' 1666 privilege but substituting himself as the beneficiary.[13] The law stated that any request for an extension had to come a year before the expiration. The *achevé d'imprimer* for the prior collected edition is 23 March 1666 and the privilege was valid for six years; Molière's privilege is dated 18 March 1671. The law also stated that privileges for existing books should demonstrate considerable augmentation or correction of the original to qualify for continued protection. Stating that Molière "avoit cy-devant composé pour nostre divertissement plusieurs Pieces de Theatre," the privilege (written as if the king were speaking) specifies that only "partie desquelles il auroit fait imprimer par divers Imprimeurs ou Libraires," and then authorizes Molière to print "toutes les Pieces de Theatre par luy composées jusqu'à present," implying that the new edition will contain material not previously included in 1666. Furthermore, the privilege claims that in the 1666 edition, "il s'est fait quantité de fautes qui blessent la reputation de l'Autheur," who now desires to correct the mistakes in his work "pour les donner au public dans leur derniere perfection." The canny way in which Molière's stated arguments echo the royal jurisprudence regarding privilege *continuations* illustrates the extent to which the author was now prepared and able to manipulate the legal machinery surrounding the book trade to his own profit.

In his attempt to wrest legal control of his works away from his former publishers, Molière was playing his trump card. Many aspects of the privilege system had been established with Classical or religious texts in mind, works whose authors were no longer living and for which concepts like correction and augmentation implied scholarly research and the comparison of manuscripts. When applied to works by contemporary authors, though, these same concepts tilted any dispute over an edition's validity in favor of the author, able at will to add material or define the "correct" or "incorrect" state of any printed version of his or her work. The 1666 edition of Molière's collected works, by objective standards, is of good quality and relatively free of printing errors. Guibert states that its mistakes must not be too glaring, since they continue to show up in the 1674–75 and 1682 editions (*Molière* 2:565). Molière's pronouncement, though, that "il s'est fait quantité de fautes" is a strong argument, coming as it does from the only person able to declare if the printed text corresponds to the author's desired version.

Molière is certainly not the only author to use arguments of correction and augmentation to justify new editions of old works. Boileau, for example, publishing in 1666 the first edition of his *Satires* in order to combat an existing pirate version, states through his spokesperson and publisher Barbin, "Sa tendresse de père s'est réveillé à l'aspect de ses enfants ainsi défigurés et mis en pièces" (*Œuvres complètes* [1873], ed. Fournier 1), adding that Barbin is now publishing "les véritables originaux de ses pièces, augmentées encore de deux autres ..." (1). In 1701, Boileau returns to these same themes in the preface to his *Œuvres diverses*: "Parlons maintenant de mon édition nouvelle. C'est la plus correcte qui ait encore paru; et non seulement je l'ai revue avec beaucoup de soin, mais j'y ai retouché de nouveau plusieurs endroits de mes ouvrages ..." (in *Œuvres complètes* [1873], ed. Fournier 6). After informing the reader of the importance of continually correcting and improving a work, even after it has been published, Boileau states, "Il ne reste plus présentement qu'à lui dire quels sont les ouvrages dont j'ai augmenté ce volume" (6), adding a list of texts appearing in print for the first time.

In the case of Boileau, the corrections and additional works add incentives to buy the edition for those who already own the earlier versions. For Molière, however, the stakes are higher, since he is requesting that the previous publishers of his plays be divested of their property in his favor. By obtaining the 1666 privilege, Molière's former publishers confirmed their collective ownership of privileges that they already possessed individually. Molière's interest in applying for the 1671 privilege is not so much to end their monopoly on his works as it is to appropriate it for himself and extend it. His argument is not that the 1666 privilege should not have been granted—which would have caused great rejoicing among poorer publishers who relied on the texts in the public domain—but that it should have been granted to him. This may help explain why he acted in 1671 and not earlier: rather than dispute the privilege's legality (a difficult proposition at best, since the *libraires* seem well within their rights), he only protests the privilege once he is in a position to profit from it, waiting until the privilege can be renewed in order to obtain it for himself.

By speaking in terms of correction and augmentation, Molière establishes the needs of the new edition as ones that only he, as author, can supply. But he does not rely on aesthetic and artistic arguments alone. Molière opens his request for a royal privilege by reminding the king of the circumstances of his plays' composition: "Nostre cher & bien amé JEAN BAPTISTE POCQUELIN DE MOLIÈRE Nous a tres-humblement fait remontrer qu'il avoit cy-devant composé pour nostre divertissement plusieurs Pieces de Theatre. ..." Molière elides the fact that most of the disputed plays in the 1666 edition have little to do with his career at court and were certainly not penned with the king in mind, but his blanket assertion that his plays were written for the king makes clear that he intends to use his connection with royalty in order to invest the king personally in the fate of his theater. In doing so, Molière underscores, either consciously or not, the true foundations of the privilege system. As Mark Rose has pointed out in reference to similar institutions in seventeenth-century England, the existence of royal privileges belongs more to a system of patronage than to one of recognized common-law rights (16–17). After all, it was the granting of the royal privilege and permission to print that created both economic value (a text unable to be printed held no worth for a *libraire*) and concrete rights that could then be transferred. Even the very concept of term limits for privileges implies that the author possessed no inherent rights to intellectual property except as granted by the state and that the state had the power to set the time frame in which these rights were valid (Rose 45).

If Molière indeed possessed some property right to the plays contained in the 1666 collected works, this right would have long

Chapter Five

ago been sold, just as if he had sold his *libraires* a tract of land. If, on the other hand, all rights to the plays were contingent upon royal permission, the king could take away just as the king had given. By appealing to the king to restore his ownership of the plays, then, Molière paradoxically grounds the source of authorial rights in royal power, not in the act of authorship. Royal authority has granted the rights to his plays to his former publishers; only royal authority can restore them to him.

And royal power complies, granting Molière wide-ranging permissions and declaring "tres-expresses inhibitions & défenses à toutes personnes de quelque qualité & condition qu'elles soient, d'imprimer, vendre, ou distribuer aucune desdites pieces de Theatre, sans le consentement de l'Exposant, ou de ceux qui auront droit de luy." While this is a fairly standard clause granting the recipient the sales monopoly associated with the privilege, the violation of this provision, normally a fine, is in this case unusually harsh:

> Outre lesquelles Nous voulons que tous Libraires, Imprimeurs ou Relieurs, qui seront saisis d'aucuns exemplaires contrefaits desdites Pieces de Theatre, soient cassez & sequestrez du corps de la Librairie, sans pouvoir à l'avenir s'en mesler en aucune maniere.

Molière is certainly not pulling any punches, and his appeal to royal authority to countermand the 1666 privilege constitutes an aggressive and remarkable seizure of property, stripping his former publishers of rights they were supposedly guaranteed through 1672 and threatening them with the closure of their businesses if they continue to print or sell his plays. Asked to register this privilege, smacking of royal favoritism and so detrimental to the rights of several of the most prominent Parisian *libraires*, it is not surprising that Louis Sevestre and the *Communauté* refused.

Reed and Caldicott have suggested that the *Communauté*'s refusal to register Molière's 1671 privilege effectively prevented him from publishing his complete works. While this refusal did pose a significant obstacle, Molière's reaction and subsequent dealings with the print industry suggest that the author's sudden death in 1673 was the real cause of the project's ultimate failure, much more so than the *Communauté*'s resistance. Sevestre refused to register the privilege on 12 August 1671. Two days later, Molière had a bailiff dispatched to Sevestre, serving him an official *sommation* to register the privilege. The bailiff's order, later printed along with the text of the privilege in the 1674 edition of Molière's complete works, states that the *syndic* and the members of the *Communauté* "ayent presentement à faire l'Enregistrement dudit Privilege," adding that if Sevestre continues to refuse, "la presente signification vaudra Enregistrement, à ce que tant luy que ladite Communauté des Marchands Libraires n'en ignorent." In other words, the royal bailiff's *sommation* countermanded the *syndic*'s refusal and made the 1671 privilege legally valid.

Les Fourberies de Scapin

The continued refusal by the *syndic* neither prevented the validation of the privilege nor did it prevent Molière from publishing his plays. Four days after the *sommation*, Molière set out the legality and scope of the general privilege with the publication, appropriately enough, of *Les Fourberies de Scapin*. Perhaps no other Molière play gives such an ironic twist to the author's earlier statement that he does not recommend reading plays except to those "qui ont des yeux pour découvrir dans la lecture tout le jeu du Théâtre" (*Œuvres complètes* [2010] 1:603). While not obvious at first, the printed version of *Les Fourberies de Scapin* carries on the deceitful escapades of the farce and extends them to the plane of authorship itself.

In her study of farce, Bernadette Rey-Flaud has argued that the etymology of the verb *farcer* traces back to the twelfth century when it had essentially the same meaning as *tromper* (11). The most fundamental elements of farce, then, would be the ruses, the tricks, the frustrations of expectations, and the violation of rules of behavior or propriety. Just as the *fourbe* Scapin (originally played by Molière) dupes and robs the play's miserly old men, Molière the author used the publication of his farce to dupe and rob authors, critics, and even his former publishers. In other words, by reading carefully the original printed edition of *Les Fourberies de Scapin*, one can indeed discover "tout le jeu du théâtre," as the printed farce actually enacts the sort of tricks and ruses that are the hallmark of the genre.

Such a metatheatrical reading of the play is invited by Molière himself, who while ostensibly speaking in the role of Scapin might

Chapter Five

as well have been describing his own reputation as author and actor:

> À vous dire la vérité, il y a peu de choses qui me soient impossibles, quand je m'en veux mêler. J'ai sans doute reçu du Ciel un génie assez beau pour toutes les fabriques de ces gentillesses d'Esprit, de ces galanteries ingénieuses à qui le vulgaire ignorant donne le nom de Fourberies; et je puis dire, sans vanité, qu'on n'a guère vu d'Homme qui fût plus habile Ouvrier de ressorts et d'intrigues; qui ait acquis plus de gloire que moi dans ce noble Métier. (2:371; qtd. also in Venesoen 168)[14]

Publication might seem an unlikely avenue for Scapinesque escapades. Commenting on the energy of *Scapin*'s performance, Constant Venesoen has written, "[E]n effet, il faut reconnaître que sans jeu scénique … ce panaché des hauts moments de la farce traditionnelle risque de laisser à bon nombre de lecteurs un désagréable arrière-goût, voire l'impression de lire le scénario d'un spectacle de guignols" (159). To state this, however, is to overlook the ways in which Molière seems determined to make the written play itself a literary *fourberie*, transposing Scapin's disrespect for propriety and property into the very writing and printing of the work.

Some aspects of this have been extensively studied. Boileau's well-known objections in his *Art poétique* (1674) to the comedic amalgam that Molière had created from disparate theatrical traditions reflect Molière's deliberate frustration of literary expectations and genre.[15] In addition to the literary heresy of grafting a Classical comedy onto a farce, *Les Fourberies de Scapin* contains the most notorious example in Molière's corpus of literary theft or plagiarism, namely, the use of the *galère* scene from Cyrano de Bergerac's *Le Pédant joué* (1654). Such borrowings did not go unnoticed, as evidenced by the convoluted way in which Molière's early biographer Grimarest tried to defend the playwright's use of the scene, claiming that Cyrano had actually stolen the idea from Molière in the days when they were students together. By making Molière the original author of the *galère* scene, Grimarest authorized Molière's use of it in *Les Fourberies*, placing in Molière's mouth the now-infamous "Il m'est permis … de reprendre mon bien où je le trouve" (14). The phrase has had a long life in an altered version (significantly replacing "reprendre" with "prendre" *tout court*), which, if it violates the letter of Grimarest's phrase, perhaps more accurately captures the spirit of Molière's real compositional praxis. Donneau de Visé and others had accused Molière of plagiarism; as with the label of *farceur*, Molière here flaunts the very vices of which he is accused.[16]

Molière, perhaps more so than some of his colleagues, seems to have understood well how success could interface, and interfere, with notions of originality and ownership. The continued popularity of *Les Fourberies de Scapin*, particularly when contrasted with the relative obscurity of Cyrano's play, would argue that Molière successfully stole the *galère* scene away from Cyrano as ably as Scapin absconded with Géronte's five hundred *écus*. In both cases, the reader or spectator is free—and even encouraged—to admire the art of the ruse and the skill of the *fourbe*. It could even be argued that in both cases the goods are being put to better use. To admit this, however, is to condone farce's contamination of authorial ethics. Molière, in his *Critique de L'École des femmes*, has the character Dorante comment, "[C]'est une étrange enterprise que celle de faire rire les honnêtes gens" (1:505); it would seem, however, that laughter (and the implicit approval that it conveys) provides the key to succeeding in an equally delicate authorial enterprise: the appropriation of existing materials for one's own ends.

While Grimarest's justification of Molière's use of the *galère* scene is largely implausible, his portrait of Molière treating literary ideas in terms of goods is corroborated by the printed text of *Les Fourberies de Scapin*. As with Molière's literary borrowings, however, this commoditization of literature again leads to ambiguous distinctions between "taking" and "retaking," this time in the realm of legal ownership. The play's publication in fact constitutes a remarkable seizure of property on the part of the author-*cum-fourbe*. We might even say that the play's most spectacular double-cross is actually in the paratext, which included the 1671 privilege in its entirety. The book contained no additional privilege and convincingly proved that the *Communauté*'s refusal was at this point merely symbolic and carried no legal weight. In as ambiguous a sense as the *galère* scene, Molière had indeed taken back his "bien."

Like *Le Bourgeois gentilhomme*, Molière assumed direct financial responsibility for the edition, contracting Pierre Le Monnier to sell it, and thus reserving to himself all the rights to the play. Given that he was paying for the edition, it most likely was Molière who made the deliberate decision to include the full text of the general privilege, taking up four pages. Like *Tartuffe*'s preface, it was a proclamation of victory.

Molière certainly was not exaggerating when he wrote that, for those who have eyes to see, all the *jeu* of the theater can be seen in the printed edition, at least in the case of *Les Fourberies de Scapin*. It is a book that would make Scapin proud, from the phrase "et se vend pour l'auteur" on the title page, through Cyrano's *galère* scene, to the general privilege that ends the volume. One could say that the printed edition of *Les Fourberies* constitutes a compendium of sorts for all that Molière's contemporaries (both authors and publishers) found objectionable in the way that Molière played the role of author. Its publication shows that they were powerless to stop him. The creative subterfuge behind the printing of *Les Fourberies de Scapin* also shows that Molière had a remarkable familiarity with the parameters of the legal apparatus surrounding the Parisian book trade, and in particular the system's shortcomings or inconsistencies regarding royal privileges. Confirming the validity of Molière's privilege, the printed *Fourberies* invests Molière as the owner of his plays and completes a legal *coup de maître*, Molière's *école des libraires*. Molière's printing career began with a stolen manuscript printed against the author's will; with *Les Fourberies de Scapin*, Molière published a manuscript that stole, printed against his publishers' will.

Les Femmes savantes

Molière's next publication, *Psyché* (1672), followed many of the trends of its predecessors, but its important impact on Molière's theater merits a more extensive examination, conducted in the following chapter. In one sense, though, *Psyché* was one relay in a series that stretched from *Le Bourgeois gentilhomme* to *Les Femmes savantes*: all three plays were included in a single privilege that Molière received on 31 December 1670. *Le Bourgeois gentilhomme* had premiered in October at Chambord before the king; its first public performance run began in November at the Palais-Royal theater. *Psyché* would premiere on 17 January 1671—when Molière received his privilege, the *tragédie-ballet* was most likely about to begin rehearsals (Powell 14). *Les Femmes savantes*, incredibly, was more than a year away from its debut, which would come on 11 March 1672, and almost two years from its first publication on 10 December 1672. A project long in the planning, *Les Femmes savantes* completed the aesthetic program that Molière had laid out for himself at the end of 1670, a late trilogy bound together by a legal document and a distinctive approach to publication.

Like the other two titles mentioned in the same privilege, *Les Femmes savantes* was printed and sold "pour l'Auteur," and the very fact that the ownership of all three plays was bound up in the same privilege may perhaps explain Molière's insistence on retaining the rights. However, like all of Molière's editions after *Le Bourgeois gentilhomme*, the play represents a further, and in this case, final evolution in the way that Molière published his works. Whereas *Le Bourgeois gentilhomme*, *Les Fourberies de Scapin*, and *Psyché* were all sold by Pierre Le Monnier (whose connections with Ribou were noted previously), *Les Femmes savantes* was sold by Pierre Promé, whose shop was on the Quai des Grands-Augustins (the original location of Ribou's stall before his move to the Palais de Justice). While the title page mentions that the volume is also sold "au Palais," there is no mention of which *libraires* at the Palais de Justice carried the title. Alain Riffaud advances the plausible idea that Ribou had perhaps begun to resume his trade after his legal troubles, justifying the omission of Pierre Le Monnier, whose services would no longer be needed if this were indeed the case (Molière 2:1528). But although Ribou had been readmitted to Paris in April 1672, he had been re-banned from the book trade by Colbert in September (Thuasne, appendix 5). The mysteriously anonymous "au Palais" from the title page could either be the sign of Ribou's surreptitious participation or his complete absence. Given Ribou's recent offense and Colbert's firsthand awareness of the situation, the latter seems more likely, although far from certain.

But the inclusion of Pierre Promé makes Ribou's participation unnecessary. Both Guibert and Riffaud comment on the quality of the 1672 *Femmes savantes*: Riffaud notes that the play "a été imprimée avec beaucoup de vigilance" (Molière, *Œuvres complètes* [2010] 2:1528); Guibert even remarks that the edition "dépasse sensiblement en perfection les éditions de Jean Ribou" (*Molière* 1:352). Whoever was supervising the edition—whether Molière himself, Pierre Promé, or some proofreader in Claude Blageart's

Chapter Five

shop where the edition was printed—had outdone himself. Molière was not just getting by without an editor, but was actually improving the quality of his publications, changing personnel when needed. *Les Femmes savantes* constitutes the final play published in Molière's lifetime, but also a fine statement of Molière's achievement, underlining with a final flourish the independence and innovation that had come to characterize his dealings with the book trade.

Molière's authorial confidence and composure is reflected within the play as well. In fact, *Les Femmes savantes* constitutes the final part of an additional trilogy, this one spanning Molière's entire publishing career. Molière makes direct references to *libraires* or *imprimeurs* at only three points within his plays: Mascarille's lament in *Les Précieuses ridicules* that the *libraires* are pestering him to print his work; Alceste's reference to greedy printers in *Le Misanthrope*; and the quarrel between Trissotin and Vadius in *Les Femmes savantes*, in which we find mention of a publisher reduced to the poorhouse and the literary duel to take place at Claude Barbin's shop. These references punctuate Molière's career, appearing in his first printed play in 1660, his final one in 1672, and the chronological halfway point in 1666. They also coincide with significant moments in Molière's approach to publication: his foray into print, his break with his initial publishers, and his ultimate statement of emancipation. In addition, all three references occur in similar dramaturgical situations: the staging of a writer (more specifically a poet) and the reception of his work—Mascarille, Oronte, Trissotin, and Vadius form a literary continuum that revisits similar themes roughly every six years, a litmus test of sorts for Molière's thoughts on authorship, criticism, and publication.

Trissotin and Vadius represent the final stage of this evolution, combining the enthusiastic flattery of Mascarille and Jodelet with the humorous falling-out of Alceste and Oronte. But Trissotin and Vadius are professionals, defined by their status as authors. Their closest predecessor in this regard is therefore Lysidas from *La Critique de L'École des femmes* and *L'Impromptu de Versailles*—together they constitute the only three professional authors in Molière's theater. As in the earlier polemical plays, the presence of these two writers represents a distancing of Molière from the literary world that he is satirizing. The author of the preface to *Les Précieuses ridi-*

cules still has an uneasy relationship with his colleagues, "Messieurs les Auteurs."

Indeed, *Les Femmes savantes* stages this antagonism in a pronounced way. Trissotin and Vadius both discuss their treatment in Boileau's *Satires*, another good example of calculated literary antagonism, and Molière's use of recognizable models for the two authors (including the direct citation of Cotin's poetry) means that his literary attacks are more direct than at any point since the disparagement of Boursault in *L'Impromptu de Versailles*—and *L'Impromptu* was not published. The same holds true for *libraires*: Trissotin and Vadius will hold their *combat singulier* at Claude Barbin's shop, the only time in Molière's theater that a bookseller is mentioned by name. Barbin, of course, was one of Molière's original *libraires* and implicated in the 1666 *Œuvres*—Molière here makes his shop the staging ground for petty literary quarrels, perhaps even recalling his role in the earlier *querelle de L'École des femmes*.[17] In his final published play, Molière is calling out adversaries literally (and literarily) by name.

In a familiar trope, Molière establishes a strict unity between literary expression and character. As Clitandre remarks, he first met Trissotin through his writings:

> C'est par eux qu'à mes yeux il a d'abord paru,
> Et je le connaissais avant que l'avoir vu.
> Je vis dans le fatras des Écrits qu'il nous donne,
> Ce qu'étale en tous lieux sa pédante Personne. (2:546)

When Henriette remarks that Clitandre must have good eyes in order to see this through reading alone, Clitandre insists that Trissotin's writing allowed him to recognize the poet upon seeing him in person for the first time, confirming in every detail the image that he had already formed:

> Jusques à sa Figure encor la chose alla,
> Et je vis par les Vers qu'à la tête il nous jette,
> De quel air il fallait que fût fait le Poète;
> Et j'en avais si bien deviné tous les traits,
> Que rencontrant un Homme un jour dans le Palais,
> Je gageai que c'était Trissotin en personne,
> Et je vis qu'en effet la gageure était bonne. (2:546)

Chapter Five

As with Agnès in *L'École des femmes*, writing here reveals the "traits" of the author, fusing together Hix's creative author and created author. Or at least for clear-sighted readers—in a significant departure from Agnès's letter, Trissotin's poetry reveals to Clitandre the poet's pedantic and presumptuous character flaws, faults invisible to less sophisticated readers like Philaminte, Bélise, and Armande. Trissotin's texts thus differ in important ways from earlier and similar acts of reading in Molière's theater: they create a split among their readership, giving rise to antithetical implied authors. The onstage audience for Mascarille's *impromptu* was entirely enthusiastic (even if the audience is in on the joke); the split reception for Oronte's sonnet was not due to a split estimation of its literary value—Philinte deceitfully praises the poem because he sees that Oronte wants to be "flatté" (1:666); even the opinions of Célimène remain relatively unified, first in each character's certainty that she is sincere to him, and then in the universal denouncing of her authorial hypocrisy.[18] Trissotin's poetry presents instead the problem of a literary façade that only fools certain characters. For this latter group, who have taken the poet's authorial image at face value, the supposed unity between writer and author is ruptured when, upon receiving the (false) news of the family's disgrace, Trissotin abandons his proposed marriage to Henriette instead of enduring stoically. As Philaminte remarks: "Qu'il a bien découvert son âme mercenaire! / Et que peu philosophe est ce qu'il vient de faire!" (2:624).

Of course, Philaminte's view of true philosophy includes an almost entire abnegation of corporeal realities in favor of a refined life of the mind, constructing its own superiority on a repression of the physical world that is ultimately (and comically) impossible —underscored by the fact that Philaminte, mother of Armande and Henriette, was played by a man in the original performance.[19] In this sense, Philaminte's ideal of the intellectual life parallels a similar repression operative in the literary world, namely, the way in which early modern authors defined themselves as *honnêtes hommes* by their very opposition to intensive dealings with the book trade (Turnovsky 57). Trissotin's interest in money, evident by his refusal to marry an allegedly bankrupt and dowry-less Henriette, contradicts the disinterested public image that brought him a certain cultural capital in the literary circles in which he moved. It therefore functions as a literary equivalent to the insufficiently sublimated sexual appetites of Armande and Bélise apparent in their interactions with Clitandre, revealing that material realities are not as far from their minds as they would like it to appear.

This unnatural social performance of authorship and intellectuality is Molière's chief concern in *Les Femmes savantes*, and the central presence of professionals like Trissotin and Vadius allows the playwright to explore the conventions, rules (both spoken and unspoken), and rewards of the idiosyncratic "highly differentiated social world" of Parisian literary life. Trissotin and Vadius have reputations that precede them, but these reputations must be sustained through their continuously repeated rehearsal in the archipelago of salons and academies that they visit: authors are actors, just as actors are sometimes authors. In this case, the ridiculous nature of the performance and its underlying hypocrisy paint a strikingly negative picture of the literary profession, expressed most baldly by Clitandre, who belittles Trissotin and his literary colleagues by asking, "Que font-ils pour l'État vos habiles Héros?" (2:605), adding, "Il semble à trois Gredins, dans leur petit cerveau, / Que pour être imprimés, et reliés en Veau, / Les voilà dans l'État d'importantes Personnes" (2:605). Regarding authors like Trissotin, Clitandre concludes unambiguously with a scathing description of their qualities:

> Riches pour tout mérite, en babil importun,
> Inhabiles à tout, vides de sens commun,
> Et pleins d'un ridicule, et d'une impertinence
> A décrier partout l'Esprit et la Science. (2:606)

Clitandre comes dangerously close to implicating the art of comedy in his criticism, particularly since no other genre is as full of "babil importun," "ridicule," and "impertinence," or as devoid of any apparent useful application. However, it is important to note that what Clitandre is critiquing is specifically authorial presumption, the social status and broader cultural capital to which authors aspire and to which they feel entitled as a result of their preeminence within their own social sphere. What Molière is arguing for is proper perspective and a lack of pretense.

After all, to infer from Molière's criticism of authors that the playwright is opposed to writing and publication is to commit the same reductive error as the *femmes savantes*. The women's dream of a world entirely of the mind, or of loves that involve "la substance qui pense" but banish "la substance étendue" (2:621) is impossible. Likewise, Trissotin and Vadius do not exist merely on the printed page—their corporeal presence and their authorial identity are essentially linked. As with the literary objects in *Le Misanthrope*, texts in *Les Femmes savantes* cannot exist in anonymity, as the exchange regarding Trissotin's sonnet shows. Judging the sonnet (or Vadius's *ballade*) objectively becomes impossible, because the text is inexorably linked to an individual. The essential embodiment of authors dovetails with the major themes of the play, exposed (as is often the case in Molière) by the opening dialogue that contrasts Armande and Henriette, the one advocating a repression of the body in favor of the mind, and the other recommending, as Guicharnaud puts it, "la séparation des deux substances et leur coexistence sans conflit."[20]

Transposing Henriette's solution to the domain of page and stage may be the best way to summarize Molière's final thoughts on publication and performance. While the play may satirize authors and publishers, the printing of *Les Femmes savantes* had been foreseen for years. A peaceful coexistence was certainly possible in which the embodied performance and the abstracted letter were not mutually exclusive. Or perhaps to go further—the play could not sufficiently achieve its ends without both. When Philaminte haughtily dismisses the body as "cette guenille," Chrysale responds, "Guenille si l'on veut, ma guenille m'est chère" (2:564). The retort has useful implications, vindicating the corporeal performance as well as the printed edition. Physicality mattered to Molière, both in the form of the bodies on stage and the pages of the text. Molière actively participated in both, and while his commitment to acting is more easily visible—since in the end it kills him—he also invested himself significantly in the details of publication. While he may not have read proofs (although considering the polished state of this particular edition, perhaps *Les Femmes savantes* is the exception), the unusual publishing circumstances of *Les Femmes savantes* make clear that Moliere did not remove himself from the "sordid" world of printing, as did those authors who clung to an older and aristocratic authorial ethos. Like Chrysale (the role that the author played), Molière was attached to the physical support that permitted the life of the mind. Paper in the seventeenth century was, after all, made out of rags. Molière's word, like Chrysale's flesh, was made "guenille," but for the actor and playwright, such rags—whether acting bodies or printed pages—were valuable.

Conclusion

In the last years of Molière's life, his assertion of his authorial rights was doubly aggressive, attacking the normal prerogatives of *libraires* in his method of publication and sale, and through his exploitation of the legal structure governing the book trade. Whereas the system of royal privileges had been originally intended to guarantee the profit of the *libraires*, Molière used it to gain complete ownership of all his texts, even those he had previously sold, and then used royal power to force the validation of these rights from the *Communauté*, rendering previous privileges null and void. He furthermore proved no fewer than four times that he was capable of bypassing the *libraires* to a significant extent, contracting out the printing and sale of his later plays without ever having to cede his rights to another party. In a little over a decade, Molière had gone from being an author printed *malgré lui* to wresting almost complete control of his works from a system designed without an author's rights in mind.

Molière may have achieved a degree of control over his texts that in some ways resembles the *droit d'auteur* established more than a century later, but his methods look backward to an era of patronage and royal permission rather than forward to the regime of personal property. Molière is not a pioneering modern author, nor does he establish his legal rights to his plays in a way that anticipates future concepts like copyright. The affair of the 1671 privilege demonstrates the opposite: by refusing to recognize the validity of his former *libraires'* privileges, and by reversing his sale of the plays, Molière reacts against the notion that his plays are commodities that can be bought and sold. It is the commoditization of literature, though, that will in the following century give rise to the idea that intellectual property is property; that writing produces a sellable product; and that writers should have the right to control and profit from that product. If authors' control over their texts is not both codified and commoditized (specifically able to be sold or transferred), there is no reason for *libraires* to pay them, which is why Diderot will argue in 1764 for *libraires'* rights

Chapter Five

to perpetual copyright (Randall 90)—while it ostensibly benefits the booksellers, it also benefits authors by creating something of real value to sell.

Molière's victory over his *libraires*, then, was highly individual, a step forward for an author and two steps backward for authorship. There was no general legal precedent established, no new legal right recognized, in Molière's reconquest of his early plays. Writing about the legal oversight of the book trade, Pottinger comments, "The law ... did nothing to decrease the arbitrary nature of the privilege and of continuations; there was no attempt to establish regularity and uniformity" (223). Molière's goal was not to correct these ambiguities; on the contrary, the key to the author's success was his ability to perceive and exploit this inherent irregularity for his own personal gain.

In *Le Misanthrope*, Philinte advises Alceste that in order to win the lawsuit in which he finds himself involved he ought to follow the standard practice of personally soliciting the judges. When Alceste rejects this idea and states that he will rely instead on "la raison" and "l'équité," Philinte exclaims, "Aucun Juge, par vous, ne sera visité ?" Alceste responds with a firm "non" (1:654), refusing on principle to bring private influence to bear on the judicial process. Unlike his character Alceste, Molière could be said to have won his longstanding legal fight against the *libraires*, but it was by espousing the very tactics that Alceste eschewed: recognizing the personal relationships that underwrote all arbitration in a system where the State was synonymous with its sovereign.

Like Orgon, Molière might well have been moved initially to praise the king for the "bontés que son cœur nous déploie" (2:190), the royal privilege nullifying and overriding rival claims to Molière's theatrical possessions. But rights grounded in nothing but the king's favor were only as secure as that favor. As the following chapter shows, Molière, like his alter ego Sosie from *Amphitryon*, would experience firsthand the dangers of serving a master where "vingt ans d'assidu service" might not count as much as "le moindre petit caprice" (1:857).

Chapter Six

Collaboration's Pyrrhic Triumph

> At times a film set resembles a beehive or daily life in Louis XIV's court—every kind of society is witnessed in action, and it seems every trade is busy at work. But as far as the public is concerned, there is always just one Sun-King who is sweepingly credited with responsibility for story, style, design, dramatic tension, taste, and even weather in connection with the finished product.
>
> —Walter Murch
> quoted in *A Theory of Adaptation,* by Linda Hutcheon

In a happy coincidence, the comparison made by film editor Walter Murch (*Apocalypse Now, The English Patient*) between the auteurist tendency in film and the court of the Sun King recalls the observation made by Michel Foucault that certain kinds of literary texts began to "need" authors around the time period of Louis XIV's France.[1] However, if Murch depicts the process as a retroactive construction of an *auteur* (a Sun King crowned by the public), the case of Molière demonstrates that during the reign of Louis XIV, savvy individuals, aware of the new possibilities that the author-function provided, could fashion themselves as authors of works that needed to be "authorized." With the notable exception of *Tartuffe*, Molière's most concerted efforts to own and control a work were made on behalf of the piece to which he had perhaps the most dubious claim: the tragedy-ballet *Psyché*, first performed in 1671 and the result of the most extraordinary degree of collaboration in Molière's career, from both a compositional and a performance perspective.

The role that each of the collaborators played in putting the work together has been examined and documented (most notably

Chapter Six

by John Powell), but even more striking is the manner in which authorship of the collaborative work was pragmatically and even retroactively constructed through royal privilege, performance, and print. In particular, one collaborator, Molière, pursued such a successful campaign in establishing himself as the work's author and owner that the artistic triumph celebrated as a model of collaboration ended up shattering the working relationships of the chief individuals who had put it together. In a further irony, the methods that Molière used to assert his control over the work (and profit from it) became the very techniques used by his former partners—and now his new rivals—to attack the (literary) author's hegemony over the other arts.

Psyché represents an important challenge to the view of Molière as unconcerned about publication or suspicious of text and its reductionist—even absolutist—tendencies. In the first place, the printed edition contains both textual and paratextual evidence that runs counter to the notion of a playwright who celebrates the freedom of performance while eschewing the control exerted by text. Secondly, the play contains the greatest degree of collective authorship in Molière's corpus, and consequently resulted in the most notable attempts on Molière's part to establish his sole authorship and ownership. On a third and related note, *Psyché*'s inclusion of different media provided a contest for supremacy not only between rival artists, but by extension between rival art forms as well. The play thus poses directly the question of theater's generic split between the verbal and the visual, or between script and performance, and shows Molière arguing for an artistic hegemony in which literature is, to cite the personal motto of Louis XIV, *nec pluribus impar* ("not unequal to many")—or in other words, superior to all.

At first glance, *Psyché* might appear the least likely work to harbor such divisiveness. After all, its opening and closing themes are clear celebrations of harmony and reconciliation. The piece begins with Flore singing, "Ce n'est plus le temps de la Guerre" and a chorus responding, "Nous goûtons une Paix profonde" (2:424), in recognition of the 1668 treaty of Aix-la-Chapelle. The tragedy-ballet ends with Psyche's wedding to Cupid, marking the reconciliation of the two lovers and the appeasement of Venus's anger. A multitude of gods and goddesses take the stage, and as the spoken text gives way to song for the final interlude, Apollo and the accompanying muses metonymically express the union of the arts exhibited in the tragedy-ballet's composite aesthetic of dance, music, and text.

However, a current of jealousy and discord belies the seeming harmony, noticeable first of all from the changes that have been made to the traditional story. The myth of Psyche and Cupid is found originally in Apuleius's *The Golden Ass*, but a more immediate source may well have been Jean de La Fontaine, whose *Les Amours de Psyché et de Cupidon* had been published in January 1669. Relations between Molière and La Fontaine were friendly, so much so that Virginia Scott, for example, sees echoes of Molière in La Fontaine's character Gélaste (*Molière* 181). Gélaste seems the least interested of the four friends whose visit to Versailles constitutes the frame narrative for La Fontaine's retelling of Apuleius's tale, preferring comedy and laughter to the pathos of Psyche's suffering. Gélaste's possible real-world counterpart, regardless of his personal generic preferences, certainly knew how well the story could appeal to the tastes of his courtly audience. Gélaste may have been paying more attention than the narration would lead us to believe.

Molière's well-known and even recent sources for the story mean that the tragedy-ballet is an exercise in adaptation—indeed, it places the work in the company of *Amphitryon*, *L'Avare*, and *Les Fourberies de Scapin*, prominent examples of borrowing from (and reworking) Classical source material. The chronological proximity of these plays in Molière's theatrical production is notable, but Molière's motives in revisiting the literature of Greece and Rome remain difficult to discern. Modern adaptation theory has of course noted the almost infinite motivations that can underlie such intertextual gestures. Molière could potentially be seeking to add cultural cachet to his work by drawing on the prestige of Classical literature—or, even more preferably, by allegedly "surpassing" the illustrious first authors, as Saint-Évremond claims in a 1668 letter to the comte de Lionne: "Molière surpasse Plaute dans son Amphitrion," adding, "aussi-bien que Terence dans ses autres pieces" (1:147). Perrault, discussing works by Molière and Scarron, adds:

> Ces deux illustres Auteurs se sont contentez de prendre seulement les sujets de ces nouvelles & de ces comédies lesquels ils

> ont traités à leur manière qui est toute différente de celle de leurs premiers auteurs, laissant à juger à qui le voudra faire s'ils y ont bien ou mal réussi, ce qui est une émulation non seulement honnête & louable & qui n'offense personne, mais qui donne du plaisir & du contentement par la diversité de la narration & du style. ... (Yilmaz 174)

Unlike *Les Fourberies de Scapin*, whose heterodox composition offended "anciens" like Boileau, *Psyché* can be classified among Molière's honest "emulations," an adaptation that stays relatively faithful to the themes and tone of the original, while at the same time striving to alter and update the material for a new audience.

While Molière's *Psyché* does not appear to have an antagonistic relationship with its hypotexts (to employ Genette's phrase), it is interesting that Molière chooses in his adaptation to heighten the sense of competition and jealousy. The change is apparent from the very beginning when, after a chorus of divinities sings in celebration of peace, Venus descends and interrupts the festivities with a fiery opening speech that compares her resentment of the beautiful mortal Psyche to the episode of the golden apple of discord ("la fameuse Pomme" [2:430]) and the infamous beauty contest that launched the Trojan War. The brutal shift in tone also involves a change in medium—the chorus's singing gives way to Venus's spoken diatribe.

The myth's traditional plot revolves around Venus's jealousy of Psyche and the resentment of Psyche's sisters when they see her newfound happiness. While these plot elements, present in Apuleius's version of the tale and La Fontaine's more recent adaptation, certainly recur in the tragedy-ballet, Molière multiplies and accentuates these rivalries, particularly in the sections of the work that he personally wrote. This involved altering a major plot element: whereas the traditional tale (followed by La Fontaine) had Venus take vengeance on Psyche by making her beautiful but unloved, Molière surrounds her with suitors anxious to marry her, the "tout l'Univers" (2:433) decried by her sisters. Two characters new to the tale, Cléomène and Agénor, represent this intense competition for Psyche's hand. In another major change, Molière makes Psyche's sisters unmarried, turning them into jealous rivals of their sister. In a sense, then, Molière transforms Psyche into a new Helen, the perfect beauty courted by every eligible bachelor, complete with a similar agreement (as expressed by Cléomène and Agénor) that upon her choice all the others will peacefully withdraw. To the extent that Molière turns the first act into a contest between Psyche and her sisters (or possible doubles), it can be seen as a quasi-sublimation of the anxiety of influence, Molière's *Psyché* in competition with the other versions of itself, its older sister works. More significantly, the struggle for possession that Molière adds to the play by introducing the suitors will prove prescient to the tragedy-ballet's subsequent performance and print history. For, in the end, Molière's work will not only involve adaptation—it will also constitute an appropriation.

While the jealousy of Venus and Psyche's sisters continues to create conflict in the work, the honorable or "positive" jealousy of the male suitors is extended in the subsequent acts to include one of the play's major protagonists. Cupid proves himself to be an intensely possessive lover, even exceeding normal human parameters. When Cupid reproaches Psyche, "Vous ne me donnez pas, Psyché, toute votre âme" (2:469), the cause he alleges is Psyche's continued affection for her family. When she questions, "Des tendresses du sang peut-on être jaloux?" (2:469), Cupid responds:

> Je le suis, ma Psyché, de toute la Nature.
> Les rayons du Soleil vous baisent trop souvent,
> Vos cheveux souffrent trop les caresses du Vent,
> Dès qu'il les flatte, j'en murmure:
> L'air même que vous respirez
> Avec trop de plaisir passe par votre bouche,
> Votre habit de trop près vous touche,
> Et sitôt que vous soupirez,
> Je ne sais quoi qui m'effarouche
> Craint parmi vos soupirs des soupirs égarés. (2:469)[2]

Cupid's jealousy reaches its most violent in the moment when Zephyr spirits Psyche away from the mountain toward the enchanted palace. As Psyche's heroic suitors fall to their death in their attempts to save her, Cupid exclaims, "Allez mourir, Rivaux d'un Dieu jaloux, / Dont vous méritez le courroux, / Pour avoir eu le cœur sensible aux mêmes charmes" (2:459–60).

The presence of a jealous, but ostensibly admirable main character (whose nearest equivalent is *Amphitryon*'s Jupiter) has troubling repercussions, considering the status of jealousy in Molière's theatrical corpus. The defeat of such possessive *jaloux* as Arnolphe and Alceste is a recurrent theme in Molière's earlier plays, and as such it has led scholars to comment that Molière, through the demise of these characters, is largely critical of efforts at control and domination.[3] Yet at times Cupid's lines seem like odd echoes of *Le Misanthrope* or *L'École des femmes* and establish an unexpected parentage between the jealous god and some of Molière's earlier (and more ridiculous) protagonists. In the third act, Cupid will exhort Psyche:

> Ce tendre souvenir d'un Père et de deux Sœurs
> Me vole une part des douceurs
> Que je veux toutes pour ma flamme.
> N'ayez d'yeux que pour moi, qui n'en ai que pour vous,
> Ne songez qu'à m'aimer, ne songez qu'à me plaire…. (2:469)

In what sense could this be said to be fundamentally different from, for example, Alceste's objection to Célimène that "tout l'Univers est bien reçu de vous" and his request that she chase off the "cohue" that comes to visit her (1:668)? Or Arnolphe's fourth maxim to Agnès that instructs a future wife that "pour bien plaire à son Époux, / Elle ne doit plaire à personne" (1:436)? Alceste's jealousy of "tout l'univers" (the same phrase Psyche's sister used to describe the crowd of suitors) as well as Célimène's failure in Alceste's eyes to "trouver tout en moi, comme moi tout en vous" (1:725), leads to a scene remarkably similar to Cupid's rejection of Psyche, Cupid's "amour" changing to "courroux" just as Alceste tells Célimène, "Non, mon Cœur, à présent, vous déteste" (1:725). As the magic palace vanishes, Psyche finds herself "au milieu d'un Désert" (2:483)—Cupid's paradise turns out to share the same topography as Alceste's proposed retreat.[4] Arnolphe, Alceste, and Cupid all envision love as exclusive and exclusionary, including a rejection of otherwise normal social relationships. But if Alceste, Arnolphe, and many of Molière's other *jaloux* are mocked for their dictatorial attempts to control and possess, Cupid's jealousy is given a positive spin, even by Psyche's sisters. Psyche ends their visit by stating:

> Je viens vous dire Adieu, mon Amant vous renvoie,
> Et ne saurait plus endurer
> Que vous lui retranchiez un moment de la joie
> Qu'il prend de se voir seul à me considérer. (2:475)

Collaboration's Pyrrhic Triumph

Aglaure responds:

> La jalousie est assez fine,
> Et ces délicats sentiments
> Méritent bien qu'on s'imagine
> Que celui qui pour vous a ces empressements
> Passe le commun des Amants. (2:475)

Jealousy and the desire to possess, signs of character flaws in the major comedies, become in *Psyché* the signs of an elevated sensibility, the marks of true love. It therefore seems entirely appropriate that Cupid's last spoken line is "Je vous possède enfin, délices de mon âme!" (2:498). As Cupid and Psyche ascend in their theatrical *machine*, we might be tempted to view the final scene as the apotheosis of Arnolphe.

But can we infer from this celebration of absolutist love an authorial Molière who espouses the same values, who aspires to enjoy a relation with his work that parallels that of Cupid and Psyche (or of that wished for by Arnolphe)? *Psyché* could potentially be explained away as anomalous, its divergent values ascribed to the royal setting for which it was created, similar in this respect to *Amphitryon*.[5] However, a closer investigation of Molière's interactions with the work through publication and performance confirms some remarkable parallels between what H.L. Hix terms the created author (the author constructed by the text) and the creative author (the actual historical agent) (39), or even between what we might lightheartedly call the author-function and *Psyché*'s "husband-function." If Molière altered the legend of Psyche to turn it into a contest for possession, the alteration of the fiction presages his own real-world efforts to appropriate the play for himself.

This is due in part to the extraordinary number of potential authors for *Psyché*. While all of Molière's plays could be said to be written collaboratively to the degree that friends and actors helped shape their composition—as critics since Bray have pointed out (222–43)—*Psyché* is unique in that a majority of the text was not actually written by Molière. As the note from the "*libraire au lecteur*" states in the published text: "Molière a dressé le Plan de la Pièce," but the "Ordres pressants du Roi" meant that Molière had to "souffrir un peu de secours" (2:423). One might be tempted to dispute the choice of "peu," as the note explains that Molière only wrote "le Prologue, le Premier Acte, la première Scène du Second, et la première du Troisième." The note specifies that "M. Quinault a fait les Paroles qui s'y chantent en Musique, à la réserve de la Plainte Italienne" and that Pierre Corneille versified the remaining three and half acts of the five-act work (2:423).

In addition to the writers (Molière, Corneille, and Quinault), the work involved several of the era's most notable practitioners of the performance arts: Jean-Baptiste Lully for the music (and perhaps the lyrics to the *plainte italienne*); Pierre Beauchamp for the choreography; and the Vigarani family for the machines and scenic effects.[6] John S. Powell notes, "Never had a spectacle been mounted in France with such a collaboration of artistic talent" (4).[7] The creative efforts of these individuals were complemented by a small army of performers, including the actors in Molière's troupe, seventy dancers, and three hundred musicians. *Psyché* was lavish in scale even by Louis XIV's exaggerated standards.

Molière was certainly no stranger to this sort of artistic collaboration: working with Beauchamp, he had invented the comedy-ballet genre with *Les Fâcheux* in 1661, and he and Lully had worked together on ten comedy-ballets from 1664 to 1670. However, *Psyché* clearly involved a greater degree of collaboration than usual for Molière, who had already noted with some reservation at the creation of *Les Fâcheux* in 1661 that "tout cela ne fut pas réglé entièrement par une même tête" (1:150).

In the case of *Psyché*, some of this collaboration was born out of professional rivalry. According to the somewhat belated testimony of François-Joseph de La Grange-Chancel, the work's earliest beginnings allegedly stemmed from a competition between Molière, Racine, and Quinault, who each proposed a subject for the 1671 royal *fête* (Powell 3–4). How Quinault ended up working on Molière's project after his own was rejected remains a mystery, although some critics, given Quinault's later professional collaboration with Lully, suggest that the composer might have insisted on his participation.[8] Relations between Molière and Racine were strained at best—Racine had violated professional etiquette by transferring his 1665 play *Alexandre le Grand* from Molière's troupe to their rivals at the Hôtel de Bourgogne in the middle of the play's initial performance run. Two months before *Psyché* premiered at the royal festival, Molière's troupe performed Corneille's *Tite et Bérénice* in direct competition with Racine's *Bérénice*, staged by the Hôtel de Bourgogne. When Molière needed someone to help with versification, Corneille would have been a natural choice—they were already collaborating against Racine.

Despite the number of individuals involved, critics have argued for the work's artistic unity. Regarding the collaboration of Molière, Corneille, and Quinault for *Psyché*'s text, Georges Couton writes, for example, "Le plus extraordinaire est que cette triple collaboration, exceptionnelle dans l'histoire du théâtre du XVIIe siècle, ne gâta pas l'unité de ton de la pièce" (Molière, *Œuvres complètes* [1979] 4:144). Niderst speaks of the "heureux résultat" from this "travail d'une équipe," adding, "Il règne une harmonie générale dans la pièce" (283). Powell has similarly labeled *Psyché* the "seventeenth-century equivalent of the 'total art work'" (22).

The crucial distinction here between *Psyché* and a Wagnerian *Gesamtkunstwerk*, though, is the lack of a Wagner, the single dominant personality who dictates almost every possible facet of the work from beginning to end. One might even say, consequently, that *Psyché* lacks a clear author, in the more traditional sense of the word as it was employed in the seventeenth century: Furetière and Richelet both define an author as first cause, the original and originating agent who produces the work.[9]

It is by drawing on chronological and etiological arguments that Molière tries to establish himself rhetorically as *Psyché*'s author. The note to the reader in the first edition specifies that Molière had established the work's "plan," noticeably invoking the traditional rhetorical distinctions between *inventio*, *dispositio*, and *elocutio*. The note insists that Molière has performed the earlier and loftier (or more authentically authorial) work by coming up with the work's subject and elaborating the general outline of the plot, thus constituting him as the work's source. As Georges Couton writes:

> La pièce paraît sous le nom de Molière, figure dans ses œuvres. Les gens du XVIIe siècle n'auraient pas compris que nos éditions modernes la fissent paraître aussi dans un théâtre de Corneille. ... Le vrai père est l'auteur de l'invention, de la disposition. L'auteur ou les auteurs des vers viennent bien loin derrière lui. Ils sont des techniciens du vers, ils ont le mérite de traducteurs, sans plus; l'on n'attend pas d'eux des initiatives mais de l'obéissance. Osons dire qu'ils sont les ouvriers spécialisés de la mise en vers. ... (*Richelieu et le théâtre* 24)

Chapter Six

Couton traces a seventeenth-century hierarchy of authors: the author as intellectual source versus the author as physical worker or tradesman. We might be tempted to read the opening sentence of *Psyché*'s note differently in light of this distinction: "Cet Ouvrage n'est pas tout d'une *main*" (Molière, *Œuvres complètes* [2010] 2:423; emphasis added). But could it be said to be "tout d'un esprit"? The choice of "main" may serve subtly to differentiate between (and attribute value to) the kinds of authorial work being done by the various collaborators, particularly since such distinctions held widespread sway in the artistic discourse of seventeenth-century France. André Félibien, Colbert's appointed scribe in the *Académie royale de peinture et de sculpture*, makes a similar division in his preface to the published volume of the *Académie*'s first *conférences*, writing:

> Comme l'instruction & le plaisir qu'on reçoit des ouvrages des Peintres & des Sculpteurs ne vient pas seulement de la science du dessein, de la beauté des couleurs, ni du prix de la matiere, mais de la grandeur des pensées, & de la parfaite connoissance qu'ont les Peintres & les Sculpteurs des choses qu'ils représentent; il est donc vrai qu'il y a un Art tout particulier qui est détaché de la matiere & de la main de l'Artisan, par lequel il doit d'abord former ses Tableaux dans son esprit, & sans quoi un Peintre ne peut faire avec le pinceau seul un ouvrage parfait, n'étant pas de cet Art comme de ceux où l'industrie & l'adresse de la main suffisent pour donner de la beauté. (*9v–*10r)

Félibien maintains a crucial distinction between the mechanical work done by the hand and the intellectual work done by the mind, creating also a clear disparity between the two kinds of labor. And, in fact, the literary connection is made explicit a few lines later: "L'on fera donc voir que non seulement le Peintre est un Artisan incomparable, en ce qu'il imite les corps naturels & les actions des hommes, mais encore qu'il est un Auteur ingenieux & scavant en ce qu'il invente & produit des pensées qu'il n'emprunte de personne" (*10v). The hand of the artisan copies; the mind of the author invents.

But such distinctions, typical of older discourse surrounding authorship, will become increasingly tautological by the time of *Psyché*'s composition. The emergence of print as a new benchmark of authorship will even at times reverse the traditional causal relationship: if an author was initially seen as the original cause of his work, the later seventeenth century, by making the printed text the marker of literary authorship, will risk transforming the author into the product of the book. In this new era of the professional writer, as Alain Viala has labeled it (8), publication, circulation, and publicity are not only passive ways of disseminating an author's original thought; they (at times disingenuously) can construct the author as source and origin.

As the previous chapters in this study have shown, no one was more aware of this than Molière. From his difficult early encounters with the Parisian publishing industry, Molière had become increasingly aggressive in his print strategy, using the privilege system and publication in order to secure the rights to his plays. The case of *Psyché*, however, shows the playwright adding a new twist. Martial's epigram cited in Chapter 2, states, *mutare dominum non potest liber notus*, "a well-known book cannot change its master" (Randall 62). But does a book's master need to be the one who actually wrote it?

The literary coup began before *Psyché* even premiered: on 31 December 1670 Molière obtained a royal privilege for *Le Bourgeois gentilhomme, Psyché,* and *Les Femmes savantes*, securing for himself the printing rights (Mongrédien, *Recueil* 1:382). Molière thus made provisions for the tragedy-ballet's printing before rehearsals even started and, by Powell's estimation, well after it had become obvious that Pierre Corneille would be writing the majority of the text and that Quinault would be writing the lyrics (14). Molière's printing of the text was unusual for an additional reason, though—the title page of the first edition of *Psyché* maintains that the book "se vend pour l'Autheur." As he had done for *Le Bourgeois gentilhomme* and *Les Fourberies de Scapin*, rather than selling the text and the privilege to a bookseller (the normal practice for the period), Molière contracted out the printing and the book sales directly, reserving the rights and essentially creating a royalties system for himself.[10]

It could be countered that Molière might have in good faith seen himself as the work's intellectual "father," and therefore owner. The note from the *libraire* at the beginning of the volume does on the whole give credit where it is due—with the exception of the suspiciously omitted author of the *plainte italienne*. Molière had often been liberal in acknowledging contributors (although, in an interesting distinction, not sources), as witnessed by the preface

Chapter Six

to *Les Fâcheux,* which mentions Paul Pellisson's authorship of the prologue, a generous and even hazardous move to make, since Pellisson had been implicated in Nicolas Fouquet's fall from grace and was in the Bastille at the time. Molière had acknowledged "l'incomparable M. Lully" in his note *au lecteur* at the beginning of *L'Amour médecin* (1666), mentioning "les Airs, et les Symphonies" (1:603) regrettably lacking in the printed edition. And, on occasion, Molière's willingness to acknowledge contributors could even take on a fawning aspect, as when he attributed the scene of the hunter from *Les Fâcheux* to Louis XIV (1:147). *Psyché*'s subsequent fortunes in performance and print, however, demonstrate that Molière's acknowledgement of his fellow collaborators proved insufficient, particularly in the case of Lully.

The note *au lecteur* openly acknowledges the polyvocality of the work, but who is doing the acknowledging? While the seventeenth-century paratext is often the result of *libraires*' decisions, the unusual publishing arrangement of *Psyché* gives more grounds than usual to assume that Molière had a hand in the editorial choices. Since the rights to the play were still reserved by the author, the introductory note must not be the product of a publisher worried about the legal repercussions of selling a collaborative text only purchased from one of its many authors. By contracting out the printing and sale of the edition, Molière assumes the risk for the edition, including the possible legal consequences. But if (and the hypothetical nature of the argument should be kept in mind) Molière was behind the composition of the note, why would he label the speaker as the *libraire*, and not the author? We are here potentially confronted with a situation that strangely reenacts one of the play's central conceits—Cupid insisting on his possession of Psyche while at the same time insisting on his own anonymity. In any event, the note's inclusive gesture needs to be read in relation to the other documents surrounding the text: the title page, which unequivocally asserts that *Psyché* is "par I.B.P. Molière," and the royal privilege, which grants Molière the right to print and sell the work.[11]

Molière's construction of authorship in this case runs counter to Chartier's notion of the author's "primordial function of guaranteeing the unity and the coherence of the discourse" (Bennett 100), since Molière's claim to authorship nevertheless makes clear the fractures, specifying the exact textual moments where one writer cedes place to another. Rather, Molière's authorial gesture here seems to recall Vernet's reduction of the authorial signature: "Nous ... conviendrons que Molière n'est que ce nom sur la couverture d'un dossier, que le code qui permette, dans cette vaste mémoire qu'est la littérature, d'accéder à un ensemble de textes" (21). While acknowledging the contributions of other individuals, Molière is taking great pains to ensure that *Psyché* will be placed in his authorial "dossier," classified and categorized under his name, and Georges Couton has shown through one possible measure how successful this attempt proved: "De fait, si je ne m'abuse *Psyché* prend place dans le théâtre cornélien pour la première fois avec l'édition Marty-Laveaux, en 1862" (*Richelieu et le théâtre* 24). Prior to that point, for almost two hundred years the play had indeed remained under the authorial header "Molière."

And who would object? Pierre Corneille had versified the bulk of the text, but he owed much at the time of *Psyché*'s composition to Molière, since Molière's troupe was staging Corneille's *Tite et Bérénice* in opposition to their mutual foe Racine's *Bérénice* at the Hôtel de Bourgogne. Molière had paid the aging playwright extremely well—two thousand *livres*—for the play (Lough 36); *Psyché* could well have been a way to pay back this favor. And of course we know nothing of any additional private financial transactions that may have occurred between the two authors. Quinault's contribution to the text was minor by comparison, and the *plainte italienne* even more so. If Molière had merely appropriated the text of *Psyché*, there most likely would have been few repercussions.

Molière, though, claimed not only the rights to *Psyché*'s publication, but also to the performance. The key date in this regard is 18 March 1671. On this day, Molière and his troupe began renovations to the Palais-Royal theater that would allow them to perform *Psyché* for the Parisian public (Molière 2:1129–31). While the performance would not be as lavish as the royal version, it would still include the music, dances, and theatrical machines, and this necessitated substantial repairs and construction, as La Grange records in his register under the large heading "*Psyché*": "[I]l a été conclu de refaire tout le Théâtre particulièrement la charpente, et le rendre propre pour des machines" (in Molière 2:1129).

However, at the same time that Molière was equipping his theater to provide ever more spectacular theatrical performances, he was also embarking on a similarly ambitious project in the world of print. On the very same day that work began on the physical theatrical space of the Palais-Royal, Molière received his exceptional general privilege from the king that granted him the right to print all his plays (including the titles that he had previously sold to other booksellers). The temporal coincidence of these actions speaks in a powerful way to the subsequent critical debate over whether Molière was principally an author or a "man of the theater." Molière in this historical moment is obviously concerned with both, making provisions for future performances even as he seeks to preserve his plays in written form. Complementary processes, neither performance nor print can survive without the other, particularly in the French theatrical tradition with its significant textual grounding. Print and performance are symbiotic in this sense, dual forms of publication, since performance generates interest in the printed edition, and the increased fame of Molière the author brings spectators to the new productions.

The twin projects that Molière began on 18 March 1671 demonstrate that writing and performing are alternate, not alternative, activities. Molière obviously cannot do both at the same time, and so the closure of the theater here revealingly coincides with the beginning of the publication project—the stage theater ceding place to the "theater of the book" (as Julie Stone Peters termed it), an even more appropriate image if we bear in mind that the privilege specified that the plays would be accompanied by engravings, permitting a visual performance of sorts that would play on in perpetuity. Both acts are also bound up with the notion of appropriation and ownership, designed to secure Molière's control over his works, and for good reason—in only the two years between the public debut of *Psyché* in July 1671 and Molière's death in February 1673, it proved to be Molière's highest-grossing play, earning over 79,000 *livres*, easily besting *L'École des femmes* (65,642 *livres*) and *Tartuffe* (61,814 *livres*) (Clarke 33). The tragedy-ballet was a gold mine.

But the gold was flowing principally in only one direction. Of the collaborators who had worked with Molière on the play, only Beauchamp received any documented remuneration for his participation in the public performance run, and this was because he choreographed the dances and directed the musicians and dancers during the performance. As La Grange notes: "Dans le cours de la pièce, Mons. de Beauchamps a reçu de récompense pour avoir fait les ballets et conduit la musique onze cent [livres] ... non compris les 11 [livres] par jour que la Troupe lui a données tant p[ou]r battre la mesure à la musique que p[ou]r entretenir les ballets" (in Molière 2:1131). After the initial single payment to adapt the dances to the Palais-Royal performance space, Beauchamp was paid for his time like any other theater wage-laborer, albeit more generously. Transferring these composite works from their original royal setting to a public one had become a fairly standard practice, as seven of Molière and Lully's comedy-ballets had been performed at the Palais-Royal, apparently without any payment to Lully. If this had created no hard feelings before, though, things changed with *Psyché*, most likely because the scale had changed. Jérôme de La Gorce, in his biography of Lully, underscores the popularity of the Palais-Royal's staging of the work, noting: "De ce véritable succès, Lully ne tira aucun profit, alors qu'il était l'auteur de la partition. Dans ces conditions, il dut se sentir lésé et chercha à faire valoir ses droits quand l'occasion se présenta" (182–83; see also Caldicott, *Carrière* 114–15).[12]

Indeed, Moliere's lines from *Psyché*'s prologue in which Venus makes reference to the golden apple of discord ("la fameuse Pomme" [2:430]) seem particularly appropriate. *Psyché* the play could be said metaphorically to have rolled a golden apple into this mix of collaborators and art forms, and the sheer amount of money to be made can be seen as the principal point of contention between *Psyché*'s possible authors. Molière's appropriation of *Psyché* in both performance and print asserted not only the precedence of *inventio* and *dispositio* over *elocutio*, but also the superiority of literature over the other art forms: by virtue of his literary authorship, Molière claimed the right to perform and profit from the work, even with its accompanying music and dances. In protecting his own authorial rights, Lully would dispute this literary hegemony, and it was Molière himself who taught Lully in the months surrounding *Psyché*'s creation how convincingly a self-constructed author in the mid-seventeenth century could "faire valoir ses droits."

Following Molière's example, Lully launched a dual campaign focusing on performance and print in order to gain (or regain) control over his works and secure the profit from them. Molière had opened Lully's eyes to the utility, or profitability, of royal privileges, and Lully's opportunity came in March 1672, when he purchased the privilege for the founding of a Royal Academy of Music from the bankrupt Pierre Perrin. Announcing his intention to open a venue for the public performance of opera in Paris, Lully had the king grant him monopoly rights to all musical performances in excess of two singers and six musicians (Duchêne 632–35). This effectively would have shut down the Palais-Royal's performances of *Psyché*, but Molière managed to have the terms rendered less severe, permitting performances with up to six singers and twelve musicians—the amount that Molière needed for his staging (642). But beyond this small tactical victory for Molière, Lully had won a far more significant advantage—all the works that he would write necessitating a significant musical ensemble would be completely protected by the privilege.

In essence, Lully had obtained what theater authors had never succeeded in acquiring—a legal codification of permanent performance rights. A troupe's monopoly on performance only lasted until the play was printed, at which point any troupe conceivably could stage the work without paying the author. Pierre Corneille had requested from the king *lettres patentes* that would protect theatrical performance in 1643, and had been turned down (Corneille 1:1684–85).[13] Lully succeeded where Corneille failed at least partly because he merged individual rights with institutional ones—Lully's privilege conferred a blanket performance monopoly on the Royal Academy of Music. While at first the distinction between individual and institution was purely formal, since the Academy existed to perform Lully's works, the institution (later referred to as the Opera) would continue to enjoy these rights long after Lully's death.[14] The granting of a similar performance monopoly—for spoken theater in French—to the Comédie-Française in 1680 did not convey the same individual benefits. There were many playwrights; there was only one composer of *tragédies en musique*.

A short work appearing in 1688, discussed by Virginia Scott and other critics, suggests that Molière had an interest in obtaining the opera privilege in partnership with Lully. In this fictitious account set in the afterlife, Molière states, "Je dormois tranquillement sur la bonne foi de ce traité quand Lulli, plus éveillé que moi, partit de la main deux jours avant celui dont nous étions convenus; il alla au Roi demander le privilège pour lui seul" (qtd. in Nuitter and Thoinan 230). If this is indeed the case (and Scott

Collaboration's Pyrrhic Triumph

writes, "There is nothing inherently improbable in this anecdote" [*Molière* 236]), there is remarkable irony in how closely the account parallels Molière's general privilege, obtained (no doubt his publishers would have added "par surprise") a week before the possibility of renewing the 1666 privilege.[15] Lully was perhaps too apt a pupil, and if the legend has any truth to it, then the savvy *trompeur* in this instance was *trompé*.

While Lully's initial privilege addressed the issue of performance, an additional privilege obtained in September 1672 secured the printing rights to all the works that the composer would produce—it was, in effect, a general privilege much like the one that Molière had received the year before (Lully and T. Corneille 100–01). In addition, it gave Lully permission to publish all the words that accompanied his musical compositions. If Molière had claimed that authoring the words gave him the right to perform the music that accompanied them, Lully turned the tables by making the music the legal superior to the text.

Lully's decision to begin public opera performances in Paris led to a direct, if somewhat ironic, confrontation between the Palais-Royal and the Royal Academy of Music when it opened in November 1672. The Academy's first performance was *Les Fêtes de l'Amour et de Bacchus*, a composite work made up of selections from the prior comedy-ballets that Lully and Molière had written (La Gorce 187–88). The performance therefore included lyrics that Molière had written for Lully's music. On 11 November, the Palais-Royal theater began the third performance run of *Psyché*, using, of course, Lully's music (Molière 2:1139). At the exact same historical moment, Molière and Lully were staging their collaborative works in competition with each other, each appropriating for himself the elements created by the other.

Molière's death in February 1673 in a certain manner ended the direct feud between the two men, but it did not end the struggle over the works that they had created—*Psyché* in particular—or the wider issues of the performance and publication rights to composite works of theater, music, and dance. In the years that followed Molière's death, participants in the struggle continued to stake claims to *Psyché* through both performance and print, transforming the work into a bellwether for the fate of Molière's theater as a whole. In April 1673, the Parisian *libraires* Claude Barbin and Denis Thierry purchased the rights to Molière's plays, including his 1671 general privilege.[16] Even before the transaction was complete, Barbin issued a new edition of *Psyché* that listed the details of the forthcoming sale, using the play as a means to advertise his ownership of the entire Molière corpus. The printing of *Psyché* constituted, as we should come to expect in the tortured history of this work, a seizure of property and a betrayal of former associates, a vehicle for possession and appropriation.

Barbin and Thierry registered their privilege with the publishers' guild on 20 April 1673. At the very same moment, Lully moved to consolidate his performance monopoly on musical theater. On 28 April, Lully received permission to move the Royal Academy of Music to the Palais-Royal theater, evicting Molière's former troupe and giving Lully a venue already equipped—thanks to the renovations to accommodate *Psyché*—for the sort of lavish spectacles that he envisioned producing. Two days later (30 April), Lully restored his performance monopoly to its original conditions: performances with more than two singers and six musicians were prohibited (Nuitter and Thoinan 292). In 1678, pressed for time to provide an opera for the season (and with Philippe Quinault, his usual librettist, unable to help), Lully turned to *Psyché* as a proto-opera that could be adapted relatively quickly. Re-appropriating the music that he had composed—we might be tempted to recall here Molière's infamous and apocryphal maxim, "Il m'est permis de reprendre mon bien où je le trouve"—Lully left Quinault's lyrics unchanged, but enlisted the help of Thomas Corneille, Pierre's younger brother, to replace Molière and Pierre Corneille's spoken text, composing additional music to complete the project. The opera's libretto was printed in 1678 and, following Molière's model, Lully contracted out the printing while reserving all the rights to himself (Lully and T. Corneille 52).

Lully's adaptation of the original tragedy-ballet is interesting on a couple of fronts. In the first place, it is not, as has been claimed, a mere setting to music of the original text.[17] The critical edition of Lully's *Psyché* edited by Luke Arnason shows that a large portion of the text was substantially reworked. Not surprisingly, the majority of changes occur in the first act and in the opening scenes of the second and third acts. In other words, Lully very systematically eliminated Molière's authorial presence. Psyche's sisters, for example, are no longer jealous and vindictive in the work's beginning. Once the work reaches the areas composed by Pierre Corneille, the degree of adaptation lessens; Thomas Corneille tends to follow his brother's lead. However, Lully's *Psyché* is also unique because it runs counter to some of the conventional wisdom regarding adaptations. While it is generally the case that an adaptation makes its strongest claims regarding its independence from its hypotext through what is different or new in its use of the source material, Lully's opera may actually make its most significant statement through what remains the same: the original sections composed by Lully and Quinault remain unaltered (although some amplification takes place in some of the original musical interludes). By printing these sections, Lully is challenging the legal validity of Molière's privilege (or at least the legal rights of those who held the privilege at the time). While Lully's privilege advances the implicit claim that the work differs enough from the original to be considered distinct, the presence of these scenes in unaltered form suggests that Lully is countering Molière's assertion that the inventor of the plot owns the whole. Here, each author takes back what is his own, and Molière's contributions are rejected on the level of *elocutio*. It no longer matters that the general plot outline continues to follow the contours of the 1671 tragedy-ballet: the exclusion of Molière's words also excludes him from the work's ownership.

The inevitable response was, almost predictably, a publication and a performance. In 1682, a new edition of Molière's complete works was issued, allegedly overseen by La Grange, a member of Molière's troupe since 1659 and who had played the role of one of the rivals for Psyche's hand in the original production. *Psyché* appears in the sixth volume. *Psyché*'s performance revival came in 1684, when Molière's former troupe, reorganized as the Comédie-Française, again staged the tragedy-ballet. The troupe's records indicate that the performance involved the construction of stage machines and the hiring of an additional singer, demonstrating that Molière's theatrical heirs (perhaps even in violation of Lully's privilege) asserted the right to perform a work that their former colleague and director claimed as his own.

In Act 5, Apollo sings as he celebrates the appeasement of Venus's anger and the resultant union of Psyche and Cupid:

> Unissons-nous, Troupe immortelle;
> Le Dieu d'Amour devient heureux amant,

Chapter Six

> Et Vénus a repris sa douceur naturelle
> En faveur d'un Fils si charmant:
> Il va goûter en paix, après un long tourment,
> Une félicité qui doit être éternelle. (2:499)

The lines' banality is matched only by the god of poetry's unrelenting willingness to repeat them: Apollo will appear and state these unchanged lines in the 1671 performance of *Psyché*, the 1672 printed edition, Barbin's 1673 edition, Lully's 1678 opera, the opera's printed libretto, Molière's 1682 complete works, and the 1684 revival of the comedy-ballet by the Comédie-Française. Apollo's words in praise of peace and harmony will be staged by rival companies and printed as a means to backstab former collaborators and business partners. And, of course, these lines, trenchant with irony after fifteen years of struggle, were not even penned by Molière.

Nothing could ring more false, therefore, than *Psyché*'s harmonious final scene in which jealousies disappear and all dissolves into general rejoicing. This same scene, staged by rival troupes and printed by enemy authors, testifies instead to the pervading tension between the arts, and particularly between artistic collaborators. *Psyché*'s very success, coupled with Molière's attempts to construct himself as sole author and owner of the work, unleashed a struggle over the play that led eventually to the complete demise of this kind of composite work—the official performance landscape of Paris would progressively divide into spoken theater, domain of the Comédie-Française, and Lully's opera. As such, *Psyché* represents both a high point of collaboration among the art forms of seventeenth-century France and a central reason for their subsequent separation, not only demonstrating the period's changing notions of authors and owners, but precipitating or provoking some of those very changes. *Psyché*, more so than any of Molière's previous plays, shapes the aesthetic landscape in which the playwright lived his final year and provides the clearest glimpse into a possible future for Molière's theater (and for the French performing arts as a whole) that never was.

Considering the subsequent fate of *Psyché*, one could say that Molière's efforts to control the play were ultimately as doomed as Arnolphe's attempts to control Agnès. The polysemous nature of all literature (and theater in particular) makes this inevitable, as Riggs and Vernet would remind us. But what the case of *Psyché* illustrates is that if Molière's texts continued to escape him, it was not always for lack of trying. The struggle for *Psyché* suggests that Molière was well aware of the contingency and limits of authorship. He may well have agreed with Vernet that an author's name, fundamentally, is only a convenient label for grouping texts, but he used that knowledge in an attempt to ensure that *Psyché* would be placed in his authorial "dossier." Similar to Stephen Greenblatt's notion of Renaissance "improvisation"—the ability to perceive others' "preexisting political, religious, even psychic structures" and exploit them (227)—Molière's actions suggest an acute consciousness of the power of authorship for his contemporaries and the degree to which this notion was a fiction or construct, malleable and manipulable.

Living in this early modern period that Foucault sees as the birth of authorship, Molière sought actively to cast himself in the role of *Psyché*'s source and inspiration, providing a strange variation on Foucault's remark that the "author is the principle of thrift in the proliferation of meaning" ("What Is an Author?" 21).[18] Here it is not only meaning that is limited, but the proliferation of alternative authors. Recognizing the "thrifty" nature of the author-function, Molière took advantage of its tendency to conflate the multiple possible sources of a work into a single proper name. Considering the claim to hegemony, both individual and generic, that this constituted and the struggle that it provoked, it is perhaps appropriate that Molière's contribution to *Psyché* begins with the line, "Cessez, cessez pour moi tous vos chants d'allégresse" (2:428). The music and the chorus of other voices fall silent as the would-be author begins to speak, or—in its more possessive French formulation—*prendre la parole*.

Afterword

The Death of the Actor

> Saluons joyeusement la mort de Molière et puisque le Roi nous donne un ordre qui est l'ordre et accepte de poser la première pierre d'un bâtisse profonde, adoptons le vieux rite royal à notre usage, et crions tous ensemble: Molière est mort! Vive Molière!
>
> —Jean Cocteau
> 1947 speech at the Comédie-Française

The figure of Molière the author that emerges from this study is heteroclite and often paradoxical: author and actor; Terence and Tabarin; critic of the deficiencies of print while financing his own editions. If many of these tensions are a reflection of the century's competing notions of authorship—the contrast between Molière's stated reluctance to print and actual practice, for example—others demonstrate Molière's desire to explore and exploit the variety of possibilities opened up to writers through the social, economic, and legal changes taking place in the *champ littéraire*. The result is a highly individual trajectory, a "multiple alliance" (Viala's phrase) of great diversity. City, court, public, king, writers, actors, *libraires*—all of these elements play a part in the fashioning of Moliere's authorial persona.

Apparent also in the present study is the importance of print in shaping Molière's authorial ethos and in establishing his ownership of the plays. Publication (the rendering public through print) simultaneously creates both the book and the author, establishing the author as source and owner of the text in the eyes of the reading public. It was a lesson demonstrated throughout the playwright's career, from the publication of *L'École des maris* (1661) that asserted Molière's ownership of the individual play to the publication of *Les Fourberies de Scapin* (1671) that gave Molière ownership of his entire printed corpus.

Afterword

Furetière notes that the verb *imprimer* "se dit particulierement des livres, ou des feuilles de papier ou de parchemin qu'on applique sur une planche ou sur des caracteres rangez pour en tirer la figure" (Kk3r). Furetière's definition serves as an apt metaphor for printing's impact on authorship: the press creates a physical object (the book), but that physical object is a "figure," an indication of some other reality. Just as the pages bear the physical trace of the formes, they also suggest a "figure" of a different sort: the author, whose type or character is deduced from the physical object that bears his or her name.

In the case of Molière, print's capacity to create both the book and the author is most apparent in the 1682 edition of his complete works. Published nine years after his death, the *Œuvres de Monsieur de Molière* represents a remarkably complex effort by the playwright's contemporaries to reconcile the many competing aspects of Molière's authorship, and in so doing reveals to what extent the formation of Molière's posthumous authorial legacy was a collaborative effort. Fellow writers, actors, *libraires*, illustrators, and legal officials all participate in the 1682 edition—an edition nevertheless notable in the Molière corpus for its use of the lone author as an organizing principle. Such tensions make the 1682 complete works a valuable document for exploring how Molière's contemporaries dealt with his multifaceted artistic legacy. Conceived as a tribute to the playwright and actor, but with a strong commercial element present as well, the eight-volume collection is obliged to negotiate many of the issues surrounding authorship and ownership explored in the course of this study, complicated by the disappearance of the historical individual, Hix's creative author.

An Author's Book

The title page announces the 1682 edition as innovative and distinct from the collected editions that had preceded it.[1] Immediately beneath the title *Les Œuvres de Monsieur de Molière* appears the phrase "Reveuës, corrigées & augmentées," followed by the additional mention, "Enrichies de Figures en Taille-douce" (a1r). The primary purpose of the two phrases is publicity, an attempt to establish the quality and superiority of the edition. They do so, however, in ways that explicitly invoke the authority of the author. The first phrase, by stating that the text has been corrected, implies that the text for the edition has been established from a more authoritative model—in the *Avis au lecteur* that follows a few pages later, the editors specify that, at least in the case of *Le Malade imaginaire*, they have been working from the author's own manuscripts: "[*Le Malade imaginaire*] avoit esté si mal imprimée dans les Editions precedentes, qu'outre plusieurs Scenes, tout le troisieme Acte n'estoit point de Monsieur de Molière: On vous la donne icy corrigée sur l'Original de l'Autheur" (a10r).

Likewise, the mention of the engravings does more than simply advertise the visual appeal of the edition. As the text of the 1671 privilege indicates (included at the end of the sixth volume), Molière's project to "revoir & corriger tous ses Ouvrages pour les donner au Public dans leur derniere perfection" included "les Figures qu'il fait graver" (R2v). Echoing the language of Molière's 1671 privilege on the title page, the 1682 edition announces itself as the fulfillment of the author's undertaking. Purportedly authorized and authoritative, it claims to be "de Monsieur de Molière" in much more than just name, the edition that Molière would have produced had he lived to accomplish it.

Indeed, the 1682 editors compensate for Molière's death by organizing the edition emphatically around the figure of the author. The first volume begins with a biographical preface, a feature absent from earlier posthumous collected editions of Molière. Following the preface and the *avis au lecteur* are four poems celebrating the author, two in French (one of which is Boileau's *Stances* written during the *querelle de L'École des femmes*) and two in Latin.[2] With this unprecedented insistence on Molière's literary stature, the editors then depart in an additional significant way from the previous collected editions by arranging the plays and poems in chronological order.[3] This is rendered all the more explicit by the listing of performance or composition dates at the beginning of each piece. Such a change transforms the edition from a mere gathering of the plays to a history of the author, binding the plays to Molière's life and making the playwright's theater into a secondary biographical narrative. It also valorizes the author in new ways: whereas all the previous versions of Molière's collected works had begun with Molière's *Remerciement au roi* (1663), choosing to open with this reminder of the royal favor that Molière enjoyed, the *Remerciement* is placed in the 1682 edition between *La Critique de L'École des femmes* (1663) and *Les Plaisirs de l'Île enchantée* (1664). What Molière in 1682 might lose in royal prestige he gains in authorial self-sufficiency: the playwright's fame is no longer dependent upon royal recognition; the king merely acknowledges the talent apparent in the author's developing literary career, carefully traced for the reader through the *Œuvres*.

The editors of the 1682 edition, however, have a singular problem: while their texts are ostensibly "reveuës, corrigées & augmentées," the phrase "par l'auteur" is noticeably absent. The preface insists that this version of the *Œuvres* is "augmentée de sept Comedies & plus correcte que les precedentes," that it restores verses omitted or changed by "la negligence des Imprimeurs," and that it presents the plays "dans leur pureté" (a2r). What it cannot do is attribute these corrections and restorations directly to the author.

For this reason, the 1682 edition's central importance in the establishment of Molière's texts has recently come under serious scrutiny. While C.E.J. Caldicott noted in 1998 that it is "l'édition de base, source de toutes les édition modernes" (*Carrière* 189), in 2005 he argued that the 1682 edition raises a number of concerns, both biographical and bibliographical ("Molière's Duodecimos" 535). In addition to discussing the edition's "modernising and abbreviating" (536), Caldicott noted the uncertain identity and roles of the editors. While Jean Nicolas de Tralage in 1695 named Charles La Grange, an actor in Molière's troupe, and Jean Vivot, one of the playwright's friends, as responsible for the preface and the establishment of the text, this attribution (even if correct) gives few details regarding the editorial division of labor and the sources from which the editors worked. Caldicott commented particularly on the uncertain nature of La Grange's involvement, writing that "the part he played in the active role of proofing or verifying text rather than as a passive figurehead remains completely unknown" (534). Caldicott's conclusion is that the authenticity of the 1682 edition—understood in the sense of its fidelity to a Molière original—is "subject to caution" (537).[4]

The 2010 Pléiade edition of Molière's works (for which Caldicott served in an editorial capacity) extended this wariness of the 1682 collected works, while at the same time reconstructing with more accuracy and detail the involvement of Parisian *libraires* in the posthumous fortunes of Molière's plays and legal rights. As the editors note regarding the traditional reputed participation of La Grange and Vivot in the edition's preparation:

The Death of the Actor

> [O]n s'est persuadé que cette édition de 1682 offrait une exceptionnelle fiabilité due à la fidélité que ses amis auraient voulu témoigner à l'auteur et qu'elle correspondait au projet exprimé par lui dans son privilège de 1671. Malheureusement, rien, on va le voir, ne permet vraiment de justifier cette confiance, elle-même fondée sur la seule foi d'une note qui reste vague concernant la part dévolue à ces deux collaborateurs. (1:cxix)

As a result, the 2010 edition in general establishes its texts based on the original editions of the individual plays, arguing:

> L'une des différences majeures, sur le plan éditorial, entre Molière et ses deux confrères tragiques, Corneille et Racine, c'est qu'on ne peut généralement pas avoir d'hésitation, dans son cas, sur le choix des éditions fondant l'établissement du texte: il n'existe pas de "dernière édition revue par l'auteur," et les seules éditions publiées avec son aval (ou tolérées par lui) sont les originales. (1:cxi)

Some of the clearest proof for the unauthorized editorial tampering that casts doubt upon the "corrections" of the 1682 edition comes from *Le Malade imaginaire*. Most modern editions rely upon the version that appeared as part of the 1682 complete works, which specified that prior printed texts were corrupted pirate versions printed without authorization and without access to Molière's authentic text. The editors of the 2010 Pléaide choose instead to establish their text following a 1675 edition, included as part of an earlier collection of Molière's works. This text is, as the editors note, "à de menues variantes près" (2:1562), the same as purportedly unauthorized printings that had appeared shortly after Molière's death.[5] Forestier and Bourqui suspect that the troupe commissioned someone in 1682 to touch up the text in order to make it newer and more likely to attract buyers. They even go so far as to suggest a name: Donneau de Visé (2:1566).

We certainly cannot know with any degree of certitude whether or not the 1682 editors were working from a hitherto unpublished authorial manuscript. The alteration of certain lines to cast Molière in a more prescient and tragic light does raise suspicions, most notably when Béralde suggests that Argan (played originally by Molière) attend a Molière play. The 1675 text has Argan respond: "Ce sont de plaisants impertinents que vos Comédiens, avec leurs Comédies de Molière; c'est bien à faire à eux à se moquer de la Médecine. Ce sont de bons nigauds, et je les trouve bien ridicules

233

Afterword

de mettre sur leur Théâtre de vénérables Messieurs comme ces Messieurs-là" (2:696–97). In the greatly expanded dialogue between Béralde and Argan in the 1682 edition, Argan's attack has moved from the plural to the singular: "C'est un bon impertinent que votre Molière avec ses Comédies, et je le trouve bien plaisant d'aller jouer d'honnêtes gens comme les Médecins" (2:727). When Argan adds that, were he a doctor, he would not take care of Molière if he were sick (altered again from the original in which the threat is directed against the entire troupe), Béralde responds in a further addition: "Il a ses raisons pour n'en point vouloir, et il soutient que cela n'est permis qu'aux gens vigoureux et robustes, et qui ont des forces de reste pour porter les remèdes avec la maladie; mais que pour lui il n'a justement de la force, que pour porter son mal" (2:727–28). The 1682 version stresses the antagonism between Molière and the doctors, and furthermore paints Molière as already sick, heightening the pathos for an informed public who cannot help but think of Molière's coughing fit during the fourth performance of the play that led to his death. The irony is already present in the 1675 lines, but the Pléiade editors insist the script underwent posthumous alterations in order to add greater emphasis to Molière the individual, turning *Le Malade imaginaire* into a true *pièce-testament* for the troupe's now-legendary leader.

Artistic homage or not, the differences that the 1682 *Malade imaginaire* brings to the 1675 text are attributed ultimately by Forestier and Bourqui to an overriding financial motive: the need to sell a new edition of Molière's complete works:

> [P]our intéresser les acheteurs à un ultime volume d'œuvres posthumes de second plan (*Les Amants magnifiques, La Comtesse d'Escarbagnas*) ou déjà disponible (*Le Malade imaginaire*), il fallait jouer sur le fait que ce dernier texte était presque entièrement nouveau et qu'il présentait partout les qualités reconnues à la prose de Molière. En outre, un nouveau *Malade*, annoncé comme très différent des versions antérieures et couvert par un vrai privilège d'impression mentionnant de façon explicite le titre de la pièce ... ne pourrait plus subir la concurrence des éditions présentées comme le résultat d'une captation scénique. (2:1565)

The desire for a new text is thus driven by the desire to own the text, and Molière's personal authority is invoked in order to repudiate the prior version and justify the changes. James Marino, in his study of Elizabethan published drama, has similarly commented on the "two fundamentally opposite demands" that govern each new edition of Shakespeare: "It must be demonstrably new, and demonstrably the editor's own, but persuasively authentic and archaic, imagined as entirely Shakespeare's" (6). Marino notes that the establishment of the text contains implicitly "the obligation to provide a text which can legally be published and enjoy protection under the laws of copyright, an original edition sufficiently distinct from all those that have gone before it" (3). In the case of Molière, Forestier and Bourqui argue in effect that this principle is already well at work in 1682.[6]

The Fractured Author

To their credit, however, the 1682 editors, in their desire to guarantee the authenticity of their edition by invoking the author's ethos, do not elide the difficulties of Molière's authorship discussed in this study, and the resultant edition, in seeking to render the author transparently to the reader, bears the marks of these paradoxes. The preface states that the farces were not printed and were suppressed because they did not fit with Molière's later high moral objective for his theater. However, this attitude sits uneasily alongside a rival editorial sensibility, that of reverence for everything produced by the author. The *Avis au lecteur* states:

> Tous les vers qui sont marquez avec deux virgules renversées qu'on nomme ordinairement Guillemets, sont des vers que les Comediens ne recitent point dans leurs representations, parce que les Scenes sont trop longues, & que d'ailleurs n'estant pas necessaires, ils refroidissent l'action du Theatre. Monsieur de Molière a suivy ces observations aussi bien que les autres Acteurs. Cependant comme ces vers sont tous de luy, & que tout ce qu'il a fait doit estre estimé, on s'est contenté de les marquer, sans vouloir en rien retrancher, afin de vous donner tous ses Ouvrages dans leur entiere perfection. (a10r–a10v)

The 1682 edition contains striking examples of this stated desire to preserve all of Molière's writings: in addition to the seven plays printed in the 1682 collection for the first time,[7] the edition also includes Molière's "Bouts-Rimez commandez sur le bel Air" (8:120), a short piece of occasional poetry.[8]

The statement from the *Avis au lecteur* cited above also highlights another of the tensions in Molière's authorship, namely, that of his dual profession as actor and author. If La Grange did indeed

235

Afterword

share some responsibility for the edition, this sensitivity to the theatrical text is understandable, but it remains unusual—none of Molière's previous play editions, whether collective or individual, had pointed out the discrepancy between the play text and the printed text. Faced with literary texts and a performance tradition, the 1682 editors reach an interesting compromise, printing the text while allowing the reader to reconstruct the theatrical version. The figure of Molière lends authority to both: Molière the author penned the lines in question; Molière the director suppressed them. If the solution favors the literary version, it nevertheless calls into question the fixed nature of the text, underlining theater's fluid nature. At the same time, such an editorial stance compromises the edition's opening premise, namely, that the plays are here presented in their corrected or "pure" form. The editorial honesty that allows the reader to see the variant states of the plays raises serious questions concurrently about the very possibility of a single correct (or corrected) version.

The same ambiguity applies with respect to the author's attitude regarding print. If the 1682 edition casts itself as the fulfillment of Molière's projected complete works, the inclusion of plays that Molière had chosen in his lifetime not to print seems a betrayal of authorial intent. In this sense, respect for the author may even undermine the authorial prestige that he was seeking to cultivate. Did Molière want these plays published? Since print implied making certain literary claims, Molière may well have wanted to keep unpolished work or plays prejudicial to his literary reputation (e.g., *Dom Garcie de Navarre*) from making the leap from the "théâtre" to "la galerie du Palais" that he famously described in the preface to *Les Précieuses ridicules*.

The editorial respect for everything written by the author, if at times possibly running counter to Molière's own wishes, overall serves him well in presenting a composite portrait of Molière's life and work. Thus, even though the 1682 edition invests more than any prior collected edition in crafting the image of Molière the literary author, this image sits alongside the evidence of a Molière *farceur* and man of the theater. The preface may present Molière as abjuring the early farces, but the immediate context is the triumph of the farcical performance before the king in 1658. The chronological ordering of the plays prevents any hierarchy: *Le Misanthrope* (1666) sits alongside *Le Médecin malgré lui* (1666). All are honored with an engraved frontispiece, whether it represents the graceful lovers of *Mélicerte* or the grotesque apothecaries of *Monsieur de Pourceaugnac*. Molière the philosopher-*farceur*, who had disturbed his contemporaries with his combination of theatrical genres and registers, thus finds himself admirably represented and preserved in the 1682 collected works.

The Legacy of Molière's 1671 Privilege and the Legality of the 1682 *Œuvres*

The 1682 edition's unique tension between the proposed surface unity of the great author and the underlying and evident ambiguities is equally present in the issue of the edition's legality. The edition is reputedly the culmination of Molière's own authorial project to publish his illustrated complete works outlined in the 1671 general privilege. In reality, the 1682 collected works contains no fewer than four privileges, and its publication is fraught with ethical and legal issues.

As discussed in earlier chapters, Molière's relations with the Parisian *libraires* were difficult and led to the atypical approach to publication that Molière eventually adopted. In particular, Molière's 1671 general privilege, opposed by the *Communauté des libraires* yet registered by the bailiff's order, had created an unusual situation, and the author's death in 1673 added the question of inheritance to the legal uncertainties of privileges and their extensions. If an author could reclaim legal vagaries of a text, as Molière had done, to whom did that ownership pass upon the author's death? While the 1671 privilege had been used in the publication of *Les Fourberies de Scapin*, Molière had never used the privilege for the project that it described. Taking advantage of the uncertainty surrounding the ownership of the plays, Molière's eight former publishers responsible for the 1666 *Œuvres* reissued in 1673 their collected edition of the nine plays that they had previously published,[9] in effect arguing that Molière's ownership of the plays had ended upon the author's death. The two volumes included Quinet's 1666 privilege, even though it was only valid for six years and would have expired in 1672.

However, in a rival example of publication as literary claim-staking, Armande Béjart issued an edition of *Le Médecin malgré lui* a little more than a month after the death of her husband. The book was published by Henri Loyson, but sold "pour la Veuve de l'Autheur," and in addition it included the 1671 general privilege and the text of the *sommation*. By retaining the rights for herself, contracting the printing, and using the general privilege to establish the legality of the edition, Armande continued in the course that her husband had established and also sent a clear message to the *Communauté des Libraires* as to who owned the rights to the intellectual property of the deceased author.

It is reasonable to infer that this shot across the bow of the Parisian *libraires* was what convinced Claude Barbin that in order to continue to profit from Molière's works he would need to acquire the 1671 general privilege, which he and Denis Thierry accordingly did on 15 April 1673. The purchase, documented in Barbin's privilege for his 1673 edition of *Psyché* and also in notary records brought to light by Gervais Reed, was from Anne David, the wife of Jean Ribou. Reed notes that Thierry and Barbin purchased two-thirds of the rights—this allowed the Ribou family to receive a third of the profits resulting from future editions (Reed, "Molière's Privilege" 61). Ribou, of course, was at the moment banned from the book trade, meaning that his name had to be conveniently left off of all title pages and printed legal documentation. Given Ribou's continued legal troubles, it is understandable that all negotiations had to take place in the name of his wife.

However, there is no indication of how the Ribou family became the proprietors of the 1671 privilege in the first place, since no document traces the privilege's transfer to either Ribou or his wife, and it is unsure whether this transfer occurred before or after the death of Molière. An ambiguous business transaction did occur between Molière and the Ribou family in November 1672, the evidence for which survives in the inventory taken of Molière's property following his death:

> *Item*, un autre escript soubz seing privé en datte du seize novembre mil six cens soixante-douze, signé Jean Ribou et Anne David, sa femme, par lequel les soubzsignez ont recogneu debvoir audict deffunct sieur de Molliere la somme de sept cens livres valleur de luy receue qu'ilz auroient promis sollidairement luy payer en quatre payemens esgaux de trois en trois mois ainsy qu'il est porté audict escript. ... (Jurgens and Maxfield-Miller 580)

The editors of the 2010 Pléiade edition have claimed that this represents Molière's sale of the 1671 general privilege to Ribou and his wife. If so, the price is rather low—roughly the price of two or three plays (Viala 108). Ribou had paid nearly three times as much in 1669 just for *Tartuffe*. It could be argued, *Tartuffe* being *Tartuffe*, that the seven hundred *livres* represented instead the price for the nine older plays included in the 1666 *Œuvres*, plus *Les Fourberies de Scapin*, the only play published using the 1671 privilege. However, when the Ribou family sold only two-thirds of the rights to these plays in 1673, it was for the sum of 1650 *livres* (Reed 61). It is possible that Molière received additional money from Ribou, and that the written note in 1672 only indicates the remaining balance to be paid, spread over multiple payments. These essentially are all arguments from silence, however—the 1672 transaction could as easily be a loan from Molière to the couple. Forestier and Bourqui argue that such a loan would have constituted a *rente* (1:cxv) with a specified interest rate; this would only be the case, though, if Molière was charging interest. As economic historians have noted, as long as no interest was charged, private loans were perfectly valid (Hoffman et al. 296), and given the Ribou family's legal troubles, this is a likely possibility.[10] In any event, whether the sale of the privilege ever took place or whether the Ribou family had defaulted on payments, Armande Béjart will clearly argue in her new edition of *Le Médecin malgré lui* that the 1671 privilege belonged to her. Whatever the financial arrangements that subsequently occurred, they must have also involved to some extent Molière's widow and her claim to the plays.[11]

Following the April 1673 transaction with Anne David, Barbin moved quickly to solidify the legal claim to Molière's legacy. Between 1673 and 1675, he not only reprinted the nine plays contained in the 1666 collected edition but also issued new editions of ten plays previously published by Ribou and others. For certain of these, such as his 1674 version of *Amphitryon*, Barbin used the privilege that Molière had taken out, substituting his own name for Ribou's as the publisher to whom the author was transferring the rights. In other editions like his 1675 *L'Avare*, Barbin obtained a new privilege in his own name, basing his legal claim, no doubt, on his purchase of the general privilege. Using his own editions as well as the stock obtained from Anne David, Barbin issued nonce

Afterword

volumes that could serve to complete either the 1666 or 1673 editions of Molière's complete works, much as Ribou had done previously. While Molière's unexpected death most likely created a resurgence of interest in these plays, Barbin's editions were not merely calculated to take advantage of this momentary spike. After all, if Barbin and Thierry's intention was to profit from the immediate publicity surrounding Molière's work in the aftermath of his death, they should have issued all of the plays (or at least as many as possible) in 1673; the fact that works such as *Le Misanthrope* or *L'Avare* were reissued as late as 1675 suggests instead that Barbin and Thierry were taking possession of the Molière corpus in a methodical and steady manner in view of the long-term profits to be made.

Denis Thierry, Barbin's partner in the purchase of the privilege from Anne David, was serving as the guild's *syndic* at the time, and his position in the *Communauté* made the registration of the 1671 privilege relatively simple. Thierry's language, however, was careful—the extraordinary rights granted to Molière, and now transferred to Barbin and Thierry, still made the privilege suspect in the eyes of the *Communauté*. This led to the unusual qualifications that Thierry added to the text:

> Registré sur le Livre de la Communauté des Marchands Libraires & Imprimeurs de Paris, pour servir d'Enregistrement du 14. jour d'Aoust 1671. suivant la signification à la Requeste dudit Sieur Jean Baptiste Poquelin de Moliere, faite au Sieur Loüis Sevestre lors Syndic de ladite Communauté; sans neantmoins que le present Enregistrement puisse nuire ou préjudicier à ceux auxquels ledit Sieur de Moliere avoit cede aucuns Privileges desdites Pieces de Theatre par luy composees, ou leur empescher l'impression de celles dont les Privileges n'estoient écheus avant l'obtention de la presente continuation de Privilege; & ce conformement à l'Arrest du Parlement de Paris du 8. Avril 1653. & à celuy du Conseil Privé du Roy du 27. Fevrier 1665. Fait à Paris ce 20. Avril 1673. D. THIERRY, Syndic. (1682 edition, 6:R4r–v)

Noticeable is the fact that Thierry did not mention directly that he would be enjoying the use of the privilege. Instead, he writes that the privilege has been transferred to Claude Barbin and "sa compagnie," choosing to remain anonymous. Thierry's reluctance to name himself as part of the purchase has led to the erroneous notion that Barbin acquired the 1671 privilege in the name of the publishers of the 1666 *Œuvres*, with Thierry only becoming involved at a later date.[12] Reed's research disproves this theory, showing that Thierry was a full partner with Barbin at the initial purchase in 1673. Thierry's association with Barbin is not at all unusual: the two publishers' collaboration and friendship predated the purchase from Ribou and would continue for several more decades, as Reed notes in his monograph study of Barbin: "[Thierry] et sa mère servirent de témoins au mariage de Barbin en 1669; Thierry réclama en 1680 de la part de Barbin le remboursement des déficits de la Confrérie de Saint Jean l'Evangéliste; et ce fut Thierry qui, lors de la famine monétaire de 1695, prêta à Barbin la somme de 5.000 livres" (71). Thierry's close association with Barbin explains why the deliberately vague "compagnie" is employed—it serves to hide the fact that a remarkable coup has just been orchestrated, and one that involves a striking conflict of interest. For Thierry to "register" the privilege in 1673 is itself somewhat absurd, since the bailiff's order had already done so in 1671. And while Thierry's careful provisions might express why the privilege's registration would have been opposed in the first place, they are also fairly meaningless: the 1666 privilege had expired in 1672, a year earlier. By registering this privilege, Thierry grants Molière's first *libraires* a meaningless right—the ability to use their privilege until its (already past) expiration date—in exchange for preventing the plays from falling into the public domain. And, of course, he also nicely elides his own interest in the negotiations.

In 1674 and 1675, Barbin and Thierry jointly issued a new edition of the complete works in six volumes, including for the first time all the plays printed from 1666 to 1672. To this they later added a nonce volume containing *Le Malade imaginaire* (1673) and *L'Ombre de Molière* (1674), a short play by Brécourt celebrating Molière's memory and featuring several of his best-known characters. In every volume except the last, Thierry and Barbin included the complete seven-page 1671 privilege, preferring to print the entire text, the *sommation*, and the registration, rather than the customary abridged version. While supposedly covered by the 1671 general privilege, the 1674–75 edition does not match the project described in the privilege's text, as it lacks the illustrations. Since the length and scope of the privilege was justified at least in part because of the projected costs of the engravings ("comme il luy faut faire une grande dépense, tant pour l'impression que pour les Figures qu'il fait graver" [1682 edition, 6:Rv2]), the legal status of the 1674–75 edition is not above suspicion (without even mentioning Ribou, Barbin and Thierry's illegal shadow partner).[13]

Equally questionable was the omission of an *achevé d'imprimer* date for the 1674–75 edition. Privileges began to lapse from the completion of printing, and omitting the date made it difficult to determine the moment that the privilege would expire. Molière's 1671 privilege had a stated length of nine years, and accordingly in 1680 Thierry and Barbin faced challenges from those claiming that their privilege had lapsed. Arguing that the privilege had only been used once, for the 1674–75 edition, Thierry presented a request to the officers of the *Chancellerie* for an extension in order to discourage those who might bring out rival editions of Molière's plays. Thierry was granted a liberal extension of six years beyond the lapse of the 1671 privilege, determined to be 1684 (nine years from the printing of the edition's final volume in 1675), thus guaranteeing his rights to Molière's plays through 1690.

The approval of Thierry's request is an admirable illustration of the *Chancellerie*'s tendency to extend the privileges of those who already held them and to deal generously with *libraires* in political favor. As the text of the extension reminded, Thierry was not only a "Marchand Libraire Imprimeur," but was also an "Ancien Consul de nostre bonne ville de Paris" (1682 edition, 1:N9r). However, Thierry's claim that the privilege's nine-year duration should begin in 1675 willfully ignores the fact that the 1671 privilege had been used on at least two prior occasions by Molière and his wife. *Les Fourberies de Scapin*, for example, should have legitimately entered the public domain in 1680. Although it may be an overstatement to suggest that Thierry obtained his extension under false pretenses, his description of the situation borders on misrepresentation.

These legal ambiguities help explain why the 1682 edition is covered not so much by a single privilege as by a patchwork of privileges in different permutations. At the end of the first volume, the extension of the 1671 privilege granted to Denis Thierry is printed in full, accompanied by a note indicating when it was registered with the *Communauté* and the *achevé d'imprimer*. This is also printed at the end of the next three volumes. The fifth volume contains an abridged version of the extension, while the sixth volume, the last to contain previously printed material, presents the entire 1671 privilege with the text of the *sommation* and without an *achevé d'imprimer*, exactly as it appears in the 1674–75 collected works. The final two volumes contain the complete text of a new privilege granted to Thierry in 1682 for the publication of Molière's posthumous works. *L'Ombre de Molière*, Brécourt's play that concludes the eighth volume, is preceded by its own privilege, granted in 1674 for a period of five years.

As evidenced by the sheer amount of paper used to print these privileges, Thierry and Barbin take great pains to convince the reader of their edition's legitimacy. The *libraires*, however, protest too much. The tortuous history of the 1671 privilege, the questionable extension, and the blatantly lapsed privilege to Brécourt's play mean that of the four privileges covering the 1682 edition, only one is absolutely above reproach: Thierry's privilege to the posthumous works, obtained after duly purchasing the plays from Armande Béjart.

As shown in prior chapters, the Parisian book trade was rife with shady business practices and ambiguous legal questions. However, the responsibility for the 1682 edition's legal complications is not Thierry's and Barbin's alone. Molière's own dubious printing practices—and in particular, his 1671 general privilege—are at least partly the cause for the legal confusion apparent in the paratext of the 1682 collected works. While those looking to see evidence of Molière's participation in the publication of his works may not find it in carefully established texts or consistent punctuation, the legal disarray of *Les Œuvres de Monsieur de Molière*, apparent despite the *libraires*' best efforts, presents in actuality one of the clearest indications of the author's tempestuous and involved printing career.

The Paradoxical Tribute

The legal and editorial issues discussed above highlight the 1682 edition's dual nature: while establishing Molière the author as its focus and organizing principle, this edition of the collected works simultaneously demonstrates the extent to which authorship is constructed by a variety of individuals and institutions. The participation of editors (traditionally identified as La Grange and Vivot), *libraires* (Thierry, Barbin, Trabouillet), authors

Afterword

(Boileau, Mézeray, Brécourt, Marcel), illustrators (Brissart, Sauvé, Chauveau), and family members (in particular, Armande Béjart, who furnished the manuscripts of the posthumous works) is readily apparent. This is not restricted to the edition's innovations, such as the biographical preface—the 1682 edition also reprinted elements from earlier editions of the individual plays that did not necessarily need to be included. Donneau de Visé's *Lettre écrite sur la comédie du Misanthrope*, and the *libraire*'s note at the beginning of *Psyché*, for example, are both present. By including these texts, the editors and *libraires* show a remarkable sensitivity or respect for the physical aspect of each play's first edition, a respect that could be characterized as historicizing.[14] If they purportedly revise and correct the text, they preserve the paratext, choosing, for example, to reproduce, rather than replace, François Chauveau's famous engraving of Arnolphe and Agnès from the first edition of *L'École des femmes* (1663).

Such an editorial approach means that Molière's own efforts at authorial self-fashioning are on full display. The edition faithfully reproduces all of Molière's prefaces and dedicatory epistles, allowing the reader to follow the ways in which Molière played the role of author throughout his career. Nor is Molière's role restricted to these well-defined rhetorical moments—by including the full text of the 1671 general privilege, Molière's interest and efforts in creating a theater of the book are also apparent. In other words, the same edition that includes Molière's stated reluctance to print also presents the primary evidence for the author's increasing involvement in publication.

While the landmark 1682 *Œuvres* has always been of central importance in Molière scholarship, its interest is not limited to its claim to produce the definitive versions of the plays, those corresponding most closely to the author's vanished copies, or the information regarding Molière's life presented in the preface. Concentrating on these elements veils one of the edition's truly remarkable accomplishments. While obviously dedicated to the image of Molière the *grand auteur*, single and original cause, guarantor of the text's authenticity and authority, the 1682 edition does not conceal the fissures in this construct: the fluid theater text, the uneven literary registers, the plural and collaborative nature of authorship. If the editors' establishment of the play texts has recently been questioned, they are nevertheless to be praised for crafting an edition that does not reduce Molière's complexity or that of theatrical authorship in general.

One of the clearest signs of this is the edition's inclusion of Brécourt's *L'Ombre de Molière*, originally published in 1674. Separate printings of the play had been previously bound and sold with *Le Malade imaginaire* as part of an *ad hoc* seventh volume for Barbin and Thierry's earlier collected edition, but in 1682 for the first time the play is continuously paginated with the rest of Molière's theater, and concludes the eighth and final volume. Staging the arrival of Molière's shade in a Classical afterlife, the play revisits some of Molière's most famous comic creations, as the author is confronted by accusatory doctors, cuckolds, and *précieuses* before Pluto's final adjudication places Molière in the illustrious comedic company of Terence and Plautus. While Brécourt's encomiastic play is obviously intended as a bookend for the laudatory biographical preface at the beginning of the first volume, it nevertheless makes explicit the fictionalization of the author—in crossing from life to death, Molière also becomes a literary character. If the 1682 edition begins with biography (or even hagiography), it ends with the author-as-actor in dialogue with his own fabrications, *primus inter pares*. In this sense, *L'Ombre de Molière* serves both a demystifying and a mythologizing purpose: in its staging of the character Molière, it elevates the author to legendary status, but subtly reminds us that the authorial persona is and always has been a theatrical role.

Furthermore, by including a play by one of Molière's former actors in an edition of the playwright's collected works, the 1682 editors—wittingly or not—draw attention once more to the messy nature of theatrical authorship. While "Molière" increasingly became a marker of single authorship and ownership, Molière of all people knew full well how ultimately *invraisemblable* that particular persona really was. He consciously used this collective fiction to his advantage, as the previous chapters have shown, but he certainly could not have objected to this transmigration of character, which merely extended a process that he had already begun. That his fellow theatrical practitioners adapted this character and turned it into the patron saint of the newly combined royal troupe merely continued the playwright's own use of "Molière" as a sort

Afterword

of theatrical synecdoche, a unifying and appropriating shorthand (or even substitute) for the complex realities of composition and performance.

To the credit of the 1682 edition, it does not attempt to distill a "pure" authorial Molière out of his theater, mirroring and incorporating instead the very problems of authorship and ownership that it confronts. The case of Molière's "pièce-testament" is perhaps the best example. If, as Forestier and Bourqui have claimed, *Le Malade imaginaire* in 1682 bears the traces of textual alteration, of theatrical adaptation or evolution, the play is simply undergoing a transformation that had always been cloaked by the convenient mask of "Molière," the name that had served to represent the troupe's activities for years. At what point can we ever access what Molière truly wrote, free from any suggestions, polishing, or editing from his partners in what ultimately constituted a joint theatrical venture? We might usefully consider what Marino has written regarding editorial decisions in the realm of English drama: "The quest to rid Shakespeare of theatrical interference is fundamentally quixotic" (11). If textual changes took place during rehearsals and performance, why should we reject the result of that same process when it is at work in 1682? If Molière's friends helped him revise scenes and tighten up language (as they claimed to have done), why reject out of hand any possible (and speculative) additions of a Donneau de Visé? Do we really think that the plays published before Molière's death were free from this same "interference?" Decades after Barthes and Foucault, do we truly believe in a pseudo-Romantic notion of the lone genius, the dominating consciousness who is the sole source and guarantor of the work that he produces, the longed-for "seul texte dont on ne peut contester qu'il soit de Molière" (2:1566)?

At the same time that the 1682 editors sought to forge the image of Molière, the *grand auteur*, they left the telltale signs of their own fictionalizing, grounding their own authority in ultimately an imagined Molière of their creation—just as the author himself had done. The result is that the 1682 edition serves as a remarkable *summa*, concretely staging the tensions and paradoxes in Molière's authorship and seventeenth-century authorship in general. The contrasts between print and manuscript, the performed text and the theater of the book, the rhetoric of authorship and the practice of publishing, are all manifest and incorporated into the edition's format. The 1682 collected works advertises itself as the author's book, restoring Molière's text and corresponding to his publishing intentions. If it in fact accomplishes this goal, it does so on a much deeper level, reproducing the tensions and challenges that Molière's authorship posed. Metonymically preserving and presenting Molière's astonishing variety, the edition represents a remarkable tribute to the man of the theater and the man of letters; poet and pirate; *farceur* and philosopher. If, as the edition's prefatory material claims, Molière is his age's prince of comedy (to paraphrase Marcel's poetic epitaph), the *Œuvres de Monsieur de Molière* also bears eloquent witness to the seventeenth-century comedy of print, publication's ability to stage that most captivating of characters: the author.

Notes

Introduction
The Death of the Author

1. Suzanne Dulait conducted a comprehensive study of these signatures, including an evaluation of their authenticity, in her *Inventaire raisonné des autographes de Molière* (1967).

2. Unless otherwise indicated, all quotations from Molière in this study are taken from the 2010 Bibliothèque de la Pléiade edition edited by Georges Forestier and Claude Bourqui.

3. See Guibert, *Molière* 1:157 for the description of the original edition. Molière's role in obtaining the privilege is confirmed by the records of the *Communauté des libraires et des imprimeurs* (Thuasne 22–26).

4. Duchêne notes that in 1669, the troupe only staged two plays not written by Molière, adding, "C'est l'aboutissement d'une évolution quasi constante" (550). Similarly, for 1672, Duchêne writes, "Sur 153 pièces mises à l'affiche, comportant 17 des 29 titres qu'il a déjà produits, seul *Le Fin Lourdaud*, donné deux fois, n'est peut-être pas de lui" (647).

5. Grimarest's admittedly suspect account of Molière's final day records that upon seeing Molière's declining health, Armande and Baron "le conjurèrent, les larmes aux yeux, de ne point jouer ce jour-là" (30). Citing his need to support the members of the troupe, Molière rejects their supplications, and the effort required by the performance leads to his death.

6. For an excellent analysis of this theoretical transformation, see Larry Norman's chapter "Molière Author!" in *The Public Mirror: Molière and the Social Commerce of Depiction*. In his discussion of Molière's literary fortunes, Norman writes that Bray "in no way denies the playwright's legal or practical authorship of the plays," but that instead "Bray deprives Molière of what he, as well as an entire critical tradition, considers to be the essential points of the author's status" (26).

7. As Riggs writes, "Study of Molière's tyrannical solipsists shows that trying to judge and control others from a detached, transcendent point of view makes the desire of the solipsist into an absolute. Method, which is always a set of abstract rules applied to what are in reality very different situations and relationships, elevates solipsism to the level of metaphysical truth and quasi-sacred duty. Precisely by being playful, comedy *performs* a cultural process that undermines the 'new seriousness' (Cascardi 87) of modernity's postulation of universal law, regularity, and rule" (*Molière and Modernity* 206).

8. Discussing Berman's idea of postmodernism's acceptance of "necessary epistemological incompleteness," Riggs notes in his preface to *Molière and Modernity* that Molière consistently criticizes his *ridicules'* illusions of "epistemological adequacy, or of intellectual self-sufficiency" (viii). By extension, the author himself then embraces the polysemous nature of theater.

9. Riggs in particular notes how often Molière's domineering characters rely on texts as means to effectuating their will to power (see *Molière and Modernity* 12, 29, 114–15).

10. Maya Slater comments, "As [Molière] wanted his plays to be seen, not read, he saw publication as more or less irrelevant" (162). Riggs adds, "It is important to remember that Molière was never happy about his plays' *becoming texts* at all" (*Molière and Modernity* iv). Zanger specifies, "Molière is not wary of writing. ... Rather, Molière is wary of what occurs when something is written down and disseminated, he is wary of literature as an act of precision, as a phenomenon that is linked to publishing information in a collectable form" (184).

11. A few exceptions can be named: Mademoiselle Desjardins's *Récit en prose et en vers de la Farce des précieuses* (1660) contains interesting variants when compared to Molière's edition of *Les Précieuses ridicules*, possibly indicating an earlier form of the play in performance; *Le Mariage forcé* was issued as a *livret* in 1664, differing from the later printed version in 1668; *Dom Juan*, due to its controversial subject matter, exists in a number of different forms, discussed in the 2010 Pléiade edition's notes for the play (2:1646–48); *Le Malade imaginaire*, first printed in 1674, underwent substantial expansion in its 1682 printing.

12. In addition, the notion that a writer would necessarily want to be free from connections to noble patrons is a modern interpretive projection, as Geoffrey Turnovsky has shown (18). Most early modern writers actively sought such client relations, or pursued them while at the same time participating in what we might consider more modern commercial ventures.

13. For discussions of the early modern stigma of print, see G. Brown (48), Rose (21), and Chartier (*Publishing Drama in Early Modern Europe* 51). Peters writes about this dilemma: "[E]ven if dramatists could dissociate from the workaday playhouse, with its treatment of its playwrights as hired help, even if their plays appeared in dignified and ennobling editions, a contradiction remained: genteel poets were not to sell their labour, but genuine poets were monumentalized in printed books, and books were for sale. The image of the dramatist had run up against the commercial world of print" (204).

14. In a pamphlet to Corneille, Mairet accuses the playwright of printing *Le Cid* early expressly to punish the actors of the Marais, who allegedly did not pay him enough: "[C]e ne fut pas tant la demangeaison de vous voir relié en velin ... comme le dessein de nuire à Messieurs les Comediens, qui d'abord ne reconnurent pas assez largement le bien-heureux succez de vostre piece" (Gasté 290).

15. The exception to this is the errata, which could be established later, after an author had had the opportunity to read the printed pages. Note that this would only on very rare occasions lead to a reprinting of individual sheets; it would merely alert the reader to the presence of errors, which the reader was asked to correct in his or her individual copy. La Fontaine, for example, comments in an edition of *Les Fables*: "Il s'est glissé quelques fautes dans l'impression; j'en ai fait faire un Errata; mais ce sont de légers remèdes pour un défaut considérable. Si on veut avoir quelque plaisir de la lecture de cet Ouvrage, il faut que chacun fasse corriger ces fautes à la main dans son Exemplaire, ainsi qu'elles sont marquées par chaque Errata, aussi bien pour les deux premières Parties, que pour les dernières" (202).

16. "The emphasis on finding an earlier originary moment might presuppose that the desire to 'live by the pen' and to write 'autonomously' in the sense of writing without any need for aristocratic protection is a universal ahistorical one, which only required writers sufficiently lucid and self-aware to give expression to it" (Turnovsky 18). As Turnovsky's study indicates, early modern writers often defined their modernity in ways antithetical to our own notions of authorship.

17. This claim may in fact be the central drawback to Caldicott's study—Caldicott's wish to see in Molière a modern authorial sensibility leads him to commit two interpretative errors. In the first place, retrospectively applying later notions of intellectual property, Caldicott justifies conduct on the part of Molière that, taken in its historical context, would have been highly unorthodox, as discussed in Chapters 4 and 5. Secondly, Caldicott's modernizing approach ignores or passes over aspects of Molière's career that are anything but progressive: particularly in his dealings with his publishers, Molière exhibits an authorial attitude that hearkens back to a prior era of personal privilege, in effect rejecting the embryonic notions of intellectual property that were beginning to surface toward the end of the seventeenth century.

18. Of course, any attempt to reconstruct the life of the writer inevitably leads to a similar kind of participatory creation, as Virginia Scott admirably describes in her biography of Molière: "What that means is that I order what I know or believe I know so as to create characters—whom I choose to call Molière and Madeleine—who could have made with some degree of probability the choices I believe the real Molière and the real Madeleine to have made. I am not in pursuit of 'truth,' so much as what Elizabeth Hardwick calls a 'consistent fiction'" (*Molière* 4).

19. In the connection that he draws between author and text, Molière recalls Nehamas's distinction between writers and authors: "Writers own their texts as one owns one's property. Though legally their own (*eigen*), texts can be taken away from their writers and still leave them who they are. Authors, by contrast, own their works as one owns one's actions. Their works are authentically their own (*eigentlich*). They cannot be taken away (that is, reinterpreted) without changing their authors, without making the characters manifested in them different or even unrecognizable. Authors cannot be taken apart from their works" (113).

20. As La Bruyère wrote, "La condition des comédiens était infâme chez les Romains et honorable chez les Grecs: qu'est-elle chez nous? On pense d'eux comme les Romains, on vit avec eux comme les Grecs" (352).

21. Randall's admirable discussion of the historical constants associated with the notion of authorship is developed in her book *Pragmatic Plagiarism* (see in particular p. 28).

22. Michaut, *Les Luttes de Molière* (1925): "C'est un fait que tout ce qui nous a été rapporté de l'inconduite d'Armande et de la jalousie de son mari a été, ou bien déduit arbitrairement des comédies de Molière, ou transmis, soit par des pamphlétaires indignes de confiance, soit par ce biographe sans autorité qu'est Grimarest" (32).

23. In *La Critique de L'École des femmes*, for example, when Climène exclaims, "[J]e suis dans une colère épouvantable, de voir que cet auteur impertinent nous appelle *des animaux*," Uranie responds, "Ne voyez-vous pas que c'est un ridicule qu'il fait parler?" (1:503). On a similar note, see Molière's famous "C'est un Scélérat qui parle," interposed in the printed text of *Tartuffe* during Tartuffe's seduction scene with Elmire (2:168).

24. "Pour moi, je ne ferais point difficulté d'envoyer ma femme à un pareil sermon, et de lui mettre entre les mains pour s'instruire; et je ne voudrais pas lui choisir rien de meilleur pour sa direction, étant assuré que, pourvu qu'elle s'imprimât bien dans l'esprit ces maximes, elle vivrait en honnête femme et non en coquette" (Mongrédien, *La Querelle* 1:215).

25. Larry Norman has drawn attention to the utility for Molière the satirist in creating this sort of ambiguity—it allows the author to disavow what he has written, if the occasion demands (131–32). Molière would therefore in this sense be at times complicit in the misunderstanding of his work.

26. Molière 1:651, 2:831–82, 2:696–97 or 2:727 (note that the 2010 Pléiade edition casts some doubt on the authenticity of the 1682 text [2:1561–66]).

27. As Gérard Genette notes regarding proper names, "De toute évidence, le pseudonyme est déjà une activité poétique, et quelque chose comme une œuvre. Si vous savez changer de nom, vous savez écrire" (53).

28. An excellent example is the royal privilege system, which combined a primitive recognition of authors' intellectual property rights with traditional notions of patronage, as discussed in Chapter 2.

Chapter One:
Molière's Writers

1. If authorship is taken in its broadest (and even metaphorical) sense, a metadramatic reading like that demonstrated by Judd Hubert in his article "Molière: The Playwright as Protagonist" could include every play. Understood more narrowly, the plays in the corpus with the fewest actual writers are *Sganarelle* (although it includes a discussion of good and bad reading materials), *Dom Juan*, the *Pastorale comique*, *Psyché* (with the assumption that the oracle dictating Psyché's fate is spoken), *Le Médecin malgré lui* (in which Sganarelle nevertheless makes reference to numerous medical authorities), *Amphitryon* (nothing beyond Mercure's initial remarks concerning poets), *L'Amour médecin* (only the notary's contract), and perhaps *Mélicerte* (Myrtil's poem, recited orally, is an ambiguous case).

2. See Molière 2:23–25, 654–56, and 205.

3. Zanger makes an important distinction, however, between writing and print, noting that "Molière is not wary of writing," and adding, "Molière is wary of what occurs when something is written down and disseminated, he is wary of literature as an act of precision, as a phenomenon that is linked to publishing information in a collectable form" (184).

4. A few examples include Sganarelle comically citing Hippocrates on hats in *Le Médecin malgré lui* (1:746), Valère's quotation in *L'Avare* of "le dire d'un Ancien, *il faut manger pour vivre, et non pas vivre pour manger*" (2:38), or of course Thomas Diafoirus, who "s'attache aveuglément aux Opinions de nos Anciens" (2:676).

5. As Anaxarque explains to his son, "Tous deux ont recherché mon assistance, et je leur promets à tous deux la faveur de mon art; mais les présents du Prince Iphicrate, et les promesses qu'il m'a faites, l'emportent de beaucoup sur tout ce qu'a pu faire l'autre. Ainsi ce sera lui qui recevra les effets favorables de tous les ressorts que je fais jouer; et comme son ambition me devra toute chose, voilà mon fils notre fortune faite" (2:985).

6. For texts that are actually presented within the plays, Molière's theater includes some sixteen letters, a *placet*, Arnolphe's *maximes*, three examples of business records or transactions (Harpagon's loan articles, Monsieur Jourdain's *mémoire* of Dorante's debts, Monsieur Purgon's bills), and part of a Latin theme (written by the Comtesse d'Escarbagnas's son), in addition to the poems mentioned by Magne. There are also eight songs whose lyrics are specifically attributed to characters in the plays.

7. Molière 2: 283–84, 1:721–22, and 2:1029–30. Vadius's letter in *Les Femmes savantes* detailing Trissotin's plagiarisms is another useful example (2:606–07).

8. Molière 1:369–70.

9. Molière 1:113, 443–44.

10. Although not all of these false letters flatter the shrewdness of their writers—Lélie's attempt in *L'Étourdi* predictably succeeds only too well, blocking what would have been a triumphant *fourberie* on his behalf by Mascarille (1:238).

11. Molière 1:565–66, 573–74, 2:269, 271–73.

12. Harpagon's loan contract could also possibly be added to this list, since although the terms are sufficiently clear, the reason for the elevated interest rate is undoubtedly deceitful (2:23). Note that I am limiting this statement to those texts that actually appear in the plays. There are other examples of duplicitous writers and texts referenced in Molière's theater, some of which will be discussed below.

13. Truchet's *Thématique de Molière* contains a useful inventory of these moments (232–34). See also Hénin 32.

14. See in particular Bourdieu's prologue "Flaubert, analyste de Flaubert" in *Les Règles de l'art* (18–71), which serves to establish the basic terms that Bourdieu will use in his analysis of the construction of the nineteenth-century *champ littéraire*.

15. Tellingly, even as Boileau will strive to impose (or re-impose) order on the *champ littéraire* in his *Art poétique* (1674), he will use the terms *auteur* and *écrivain* indiscriminately, or even reverse their earlier distinction (see excerpt below).

16. We might also include characters who parody this type, such as Sganarelle from *Le Médecin malgré lui*.

17. We should add Jodelet from *Les Précieuses ridicules* as well, since he states that he is "un peu incommodé de la veine Poétique, pour la quantité des saignées que j'y ai faites ces jours passés" (1:25–26).

18. However, Faret warns against attempting to write poetry, since there are "tant de malheureux faiseurs de vers, qui profanent la Poësie, & entre les mains desquels elle perd tout son prix & toute sa gloire" (53).

19. In this sense, they hearken back to older models of aristocratic artistic creation, like that demonstrated by Cardinal Richelieu and the *cinq auteurs*—the cardinal would devise the play's plot, giving out the individual acts to be versified by the professionals. See Georges Couton's discussion in *Richelieu et le théâtre* (25–34).

20. Curiously, this scene presents an idea that Molière's adversaries will use against him, namely, that Molière receives his material from others and then merely stitches it together into *rhapsodies*. Norman discusses the implications of this in *The Public Mirror: Molière and the Social Commerce of Depiction* (28–34).

21. The attitude extends beyond literature to art as well: in *Le Sicilien*, the painter will write concerning his friend, the "Gentilhomme Français" Adraste: "Gardez-vous bien, surtout, de lui parler d'aucune récompense: car c'est un Homme qui s'en offenserait, et qui ne fait les choses que pour la gloire, et pour la réputation" (1:819).

22. Molière's own mockery of such authorial affectations needs to be considered when reading his own purported reluctance to print. A good case in point is *Les Précieuses ridicules*, in which Molière's language in the preface echoes that of Mascarille, creating deliberately ironic overtones (see the Introduction for a further discussion of the early modern "stigma of print").

23. Molière himself will be accused of pursuing a similar strategy by Baudeau de Somaize (see Chapter 2). While *Les Précieuses ridicules* pokes fun at the practice, it is certain that Molière participated in the same kind of private readings and performances that Mascarille describes, as shown by the numerous private visits that La Grange records.

24. See, for example, Boileau's *Stances à M. Molière, sur la comédie de L'École des femmes que plusieurs gens frondaient* (1662), which will subsequently be included in the posthumous 1682 *Œuvres de Monsieur de Molière*. Boileau will also address his second satire to the playwright.

25. For examples, see the preface to *Les Précieuses ridicules*, Uranie's observation in *La Critique de L'École des femmes*, La Nuit's statement in *Amphitryon*, and Julie's remarks in *La Comtesse d'Escarbagnas* (1:4, 507, 852, 2:1022).

26. Montfleury, *L'Impromptu de L'Hôtel de Condé* (in Mongrédien, *La Querelle de L'École des femmes* 2:349).

27. For Georges Forestier, it is particularly the fact that a certain part of the work is explicitly fictional that allows the rest to assume an appearance of reality: "[T]oute inclusion d'un espace désigné comme fictionnel dans une action dramatique dégage par contre-coup une zone non-fictionnelle que les spectateurs perçoivent comme réelle: la répétition à laquelle se livrent les comédiens à partir de la scène 3 de *L'Impromptu* confère à tout le reste les apparences du vrai" (*Le Théâtre dans le théâtre* 269).

28. Similarly, the sharp exchange between Molière and his wife owes more to a comedic tradition of quarreling husbands and wives, and to the illusion

Notes to Pages 53–57

of truth (the *effet de réel*) that the argument creates than to any attempt at a realistic depiction of the couple's domestic relations.

29. Forestier notes, "Car, ne l'oublions pas, tout personnage est un masque. Dans *L'Impromptu*, Molière met le masque de Molière et présente une certaine image de lui, celle qu'il veut que le public retienne" (*Le Théâtre dans le théâtre* 269).

30. It also challenges the view that Molière fell out of favor with the king because of his insistence on pursuing his authorial rights. See, for example, Caldicott, who writes, "Si seulement il [Molière] avait accepté de ne pas faire valoir son statut d'auteur, manifestement incompatible avec son comportement antérieur de fidélité exclusive, il aurait pu garder la faveur du Roi" (*Carrière* 118). I would argue that it was actually Lully's increasing authorial consciousness that pushed Molière out of the king's favor instead—see Chapter 6.

31. As Molière states of his opponents, "Et lorsqu'ils ont délibéré s'ils joueraient *Le Portrait du Peintre*, sur la crainte d'une riposte, quelques-uns d'entre eux n'ont-ils pas répondu *qu'il nous rende toutes les injures qu'il voudra, pourvu que nous gagnions de l'argent?*" (2:840).

32. Speaking of Boursault and the *querelle*, Molière states, "C'est un homme qui n'a rien à perdre, et les Comédiens ne me l'ont déchaîné, que pour m'engager à une sotte guerre, et me détourner par cet artifice des autres ouvrages que j'ai à faire" (2:841).

33. Turnovsky writes that "the numbers always seem both highly illuminating and utterly impenetrable. ... For one thing, viewed from this side of three centuries of currency changes and inflation, they strike us as alien and inconvertible. ... Some studies offer conversion systems, but with confusing, improbable, and arbitrary ratios they only seem to make matters worse, raising more questions than they answer" (26).

34. Martin, *Livre* 2:917.

35. As discussed in Chapter 5, Molière's arrangement with his *libraires* changes after 1670. He may well have earned substantially more from the book sales of his final four plays.

36. La Grange occasionally mentions times when pensions or gratifications paid to the troupe included a share for the author (2:1117, 1121, 1142).

37. Pléiade 1:1035, 1036, 1039, 1041, 1042, 1045, 1051–52. Strangely enough, there is no record of a payment for *L'École des maris*.

38. Chappuzeau might very well be reporting the practice of Molière's troupe, who performed his *Riche impertinent* in 1661.

39. La Thorillière also records that the troupe paid an *orfèvre* twenty-four *livres* on Racine's behalf, presumably meaning that Racine's total payment for *La Thébaïde* was 372 *livres* (Schwartz 1066).

40. Many of these extra shares could be created on a given night in order to pay exceptional expenses, as Chevalley notes (178). However, the lack of details means that the explanation for the number of shares on a given night remains enigmatic, as Chevalley expresses: "Le nombre de parts des comédiens étant en principe invariable—12 parts pour 13 comédiens—, ce multiplicateur pose des problèmes que je constate sans pouvoir les résoudre" (178).

41. To take an example where Chevalley has been able to recover the precise number of parts, for three days (17, 20, and 22 January) of the troupe's 1673 revival of *Psyché*, the troupe only had an excess of 1 l. 5 s., 7 l. 10 s., and 2 l. 10 s., respectively, after the division of the receipts.

42. See 1:1045. Duchêne notes that Molière's take as author constituted in this case a quarter of all the theatrical receipts for the seven performances (271).

43. Further evidence for this is provided by La Grange's note that the 1674 performances of *Le Malade imaginaire* included "parts d'auteur pour Mlle de Molière" (Molière 2:1562). It would be reasonable to conclude that the troupe's arrangement here with respect to Armande Béjart remained that enjoyed by her husband.

44. See Bray's chapter on "Le Poète et ses interprètes" (222–43). Noting the possible contributions of the various actors to the parts that they play, Bray concludes, "Molière a conçu ses comédies en fonction de leur interprétation" (242). Possible variant states of a few plays also point to their evolution over the course of the performance run—examples include Mademoiselle Desjardins's published description of *Les Précieuses ridicules*, and the earliest printed versions of *Le Malade imaginaire*, substantially different from the 1682 edition.

45. For example, at the beginning of the rehearsal, Molière corrects La Grange's delivery: "Ce n'est point là le ton d'un Marquis, il faut le prendre un peu plus haut" (2:831). He will address similar corrective remarks to Brécourt (2:832).

46. Studies that mention the interactions (professional or even stylistic) between Molière and the Italians include Bourqui's *La Commedia dell'arte: Introduction au théâtre professionnel italien entre XVIe et le XVIIIe siècles* (in particular 136–43), Scott's *The Commedia dell'Arte in Paris*, and Andrews's *Scripts and Scenarios: The Performance of Comedy in Renaissance Italy* (245–47).

47. Molière describes the beginning of *Les Fâcheux* in the following manner: "D'abord que la toile fut levée, un des Acteurs, comme vous pourriez dire moi, parut sur le Théâtre en habit de Ville, et s'adressant au Roi avec le visage d'un homme surpris, fit des excuses en désordre sur ce qu'il se trouvait là seul, et manquait de temps, et d'Acteurs pour donner à Sa Majesté le divertissement qu'elle semblait attendre" (1:150). This apology was the cue for a number of surprising theatrical effects that revealed the sham behind Molière's supposed lack of preparation: twenty water fountains, a large shell revealing a Naiad, and dryads, fauns, and satyrs emerging from the surrounding statues and trees. The effect must have been charming enough that Molière decided to revisit the idea for the *Impromptu*, the next of his plays to have a royal premiere.

Chapter Two
The Early Plays and the Pirates Who Loved Them

1. For a good summary of what is known about Ribou and these authors, see Couton's comments (Molière, *Œuvres complètes* [1971] 1: 257, 292). Further information on Baudeau de Somaize can be found in Georges Mongrédien's *Comédies et pamphlets sur Molière*. In addition, C.E.J. Caldicott in his *Carrière de Molière* includes information on Ribou's background and professional activities (141).

2. I borrow my use of these terms from Georges Couton (Molière, *Œuvres complètes* [1971] 1:293) and from Marilyn Randall in *Pragmatic Plagiarism* (76–77), although Randall's definition of plagiarism differs in some respects from the way the term will be used here, as discussed below.

3. Such editions frequently included the words "sur l'imprimé" on the title page to indicate that they were modeled on a previous, presumably authorized, edition. Far from being a disincentive, such an open acknowledgment would have served as an advertisement for the provincial or foreign clientele for whom such editions were produced: buyers in these markets would have been unable or unwilling to pay the full price of a Parisian edition, and thus would have eagerly sought a faithful derivative sold at a reduced price.

4. Examples include La Rochefoucauld's politically charged *Mémoires* (1662) concerning the Fronde and Bussy-Rabutin's *L'Histoire amoureuse des Gaules* (1665) chronicling the love affairs of several prominent members of the nobility. The latter publication earned the author thirteen months in the Bastille followed by banishment from Paris. See Hubert Carrier's article, "La Propriété littéraire en France au XVIIe siècle."

5. Cynthia Brown discusses in particular the 1504 case involving the author Jean de la Vigne and the *libraire* Michel Le Noir, concluded in favor of de la Vigne. It is also important to note that courts consistently ruled in Molière's favor in his later legal actions against publishers, suggesting that he was acting within his rights. The enforceability of these rights, however, posed a greater problem (see below). Viala lists later cases (1586, 1606) that similarly confirmed an author's control over his or her text (87–90, 97–98).

6. Excellent recent book-length studies of plagiarism include Hélène Maurel-Indart's *Du Plagiat* (1999) and Marilyn Randall's *Pragmatic Plagiarism: Authorship, Profit, and Power* (2001). It should be noted also that while Randall's definition of plagiarism includes the notion that the literary borrowing is not meant to be perceived, I adopt here a much looser definition, including in the term *plagiarism* efforts by Baudeau de Somaize and F. Doneau that openly identify their source. In a sign of the changing definition of the term, both Somaize and Doneau were accused of plagiarism by their contemporaries, despite their own acknowledgement of their borrowing.

7. Molière was not only frequently subjected to such accusations, but also provided one of the most notable—Richelet in his dictionary cites Trissotin's "impudent plagiaire" as an example of usage (2:171).

8. For a further discussion of the distinctions made between borrowing from past and present authors (or native versus foreign authors), see Randall 192–93.

9. La Bruyère describes in his *Caractères* what could be called the inertial law of authorial reputation. Once over the initial difficulty of "making a name," reputation alone is sufficient to guarantee the success of a new publication: "Il n'est pas si aisé de se faire un nom par un ouvrage parfait, que d'en faire valoir un médiocre par le nom qu'on s'est déjà acquis" (68).

10. *Le Songe du resveur* (see below) attributes the theft of *Les Précieuses ridicules* to Baudeau de Somaize: "Cet autre [Somaize] ... Luy deroba ses Precieuses; / Puis à l'imprimeur les livra, / Pour cent francs qu'il en retira" (17).

11. Georges de Scudéry, for example, had attributed the success of Corneille's *Le Cid* to the performance and costumes of the actors (Gasté 71).

12. Zanger has argued that Molière's hesitation was at least in part related to this lack of control over future performances (170, 178). On a cautionary note, the place of Molière's own productions in the troupe repertoire should not be exaggerated: in 1659, Molière's troupe performed his two plays twenty-two times; in the same period they performed plays by other authors ninety-seven times (Duchêne 739–43).

13. See, for example, Gabriel Guéret's satire of "Panégyriques à la Montoron" in *La Promenade de Saint-Cloud* (98).

14. My reading on this point diverges significantly from Zanger's: whereas Zanger states that Molière "cannot become part of the association or confrérie of authors because his work is marked by neither authorial preparation nor control" (179), I argue that, as a deliberate stance, Molière's refusal of the conventions of authorship is itself an authorial strategy. It is precisely in the oppositional stance that Molière takes with respect to "Messieurs les Auteurs" that he comes closest to espousing what Viala has labeled a "stratégie du succès," that is, an authorial strategy based on difference, novelty, and popular appeal (see Chapter 1).

15. Scott's similar conclusion is that "[t]he accusation that Molière had stolen all or part of the play from an earlier work by the abbé de Pure is perfect fantasy" (*Molière* 103).

16. Chappuzeau in *L'Académie des femmes* (1661) satirized venal rogue printers such as Ribou, including the risk of incarceration that they ran:

> Hortense: Tu sçais [que] nous nous voyons dedans une saison,
> Où d'écrire chacun [a] la demangeaison,
> Qu'il ne manque non plus pour produire un ouvrage
> D'Imprimeurs affamez, qui sans craindre la cage
> Mettent tout sous la presse, et soûs l'espoir du gain
> Le debitent bien-tost hautement. (Peters 211, 411)

17. There is some ambiguity as to whether Molière had his privilege registered with the *Communauté*: it does not appear in Thuasne's record, but Molière will claim in the subsequent trial that he had it registered on 14 June 1660 (Jurgens and Maxfield-Miller 347).

18. Huguette Gilbert suggested that, based on a note she discovered in a register concerning the privilege, Doneau is in fact Jean Donneau de Visé, adding that it is the "plus vraisemblable solution" to the mystery of the author's identity (203–05). Gilbert also mentions that Donneau de Visé had a sister named Henriette, who could serve as the likely addressee of the dedication. I am inclined to agree with Gilbert's attribution, although I cautiously here employ the *nom de plume* that the author gave himself. I am more ambivalent concerning Forestier and Bourqui's suggestion that the sieur de Neuf-Villenaine is also Donneau de Visé—the evidence in this case (Donneau de Visé's enthusiasm for *Sganarelle* and the accompanying *arguments* in the *Nouvelles nouvelles*) is less convincing. While I agree that the strategies employed by F. Doneau and Neuf-Villenaine are very similar, I have chosen here the part of critical caution and refer to them by their separate pseudonyms. In doing so, I follow *Le Songe du resveur*, which suggests that the two authors are different people: an "archigredin" steals *Sganarelle*, while "un sot" writes *La Cocue imaginaire* (16).

19. Roger Chartier and Julie Stone Peters both list numerous examples of play texts stolen through memorial reconstruction, but this typically involves a team of professionals working together, not an amateur memorizing the play "by accident" (Chartier, *Publishing Drama* 28–46; Peters 78–79).

20. Neuf-Villenaine's comments here refer to the practice that allowed a play to be performed by any troupe following its publication. By publishing *Sganarelle*, Neuf-Villenaine is voiding the performance monopoly that Molière's troupe currently enjoys. Neuf-Villenaine justifies this by pointing out that the play is at the end of its initial (and very successful) performance run, the normal moment for printing. What Neuf-Villenaine fails to justify is why he, rather than Molière, should receive the *libraire*'s payment for the play's publication.

21. Furetière and Richelet insist on this point in their definitions of *auteur* (see Chapter 1).

22. Randall and Rose have both discussed the ways that early modern authorship allowed for such splits between author and owners of a text (see in particular Randall 268). In a sense, the privilege system itself obligated an eventual division of these roles, since only *libraires* were allowed by law to sell books.

23. The same information is also given by Thuasne (49–52).

24. A similar example is the publication of the *Récit en prose et en vers de la Farce des précieuses* (1660) by Mlle. Desjardins. The edition was produced by Claude Barbin, one of the original holders of the privilege to *Les Précieuses ridicules*.

25. In the case of Neuf-Villenaine, of course, Molière does miss out on the payment that he would have received from a publisher had *Sganarelle* been published through the normal legal process.

26. It should be noted that it was a literary commonplace among authors to complain about the poor quality of both pirate and legitimate editions of their work. See, for example, Sorel's preface to his *Francion* (1623), where he labels his printers "bestes" (48), or Corneille's dedicatory epistle to *L'Illusion comique* (1636) where he loudly apologizes to the reader for the printer's errors (1:613–14). In the case of pirate editions, writers like Boileau used arguments that could be called authorial (e.g., fear of a careless printing job) to pursue aims that were at least in part proprietary or economic (bringing out "authorized" versions of their work), as in Boileau's preface to his 1666 *Satires*.

27. Guibert has suggested the first of these two possibilities: "[C]'est que le sujet de ses autres comédies avait déjà été traité plus ou moins directement, soit dans le théâtre italien comme l'Etourdi, le Dépit Amoureux et Sganarelle, soit dans la Prétieuse ou le Mystère des Ruelles de l'Abbé de Pure et les Précieuses du même auteur pour ses Précieuses Ridicules" (*Molière* 1:60). While this interpretation has some interesting ramifications, as discussed below, the latter possibility seems more likely, given the troubled printing history of Molière's earlier plays.

28. It should be noted that this assertion also omits all the individuals connected with the book trade—*libraires*, printers, type-setters—who make the actual publication possible, and who, incidentally, were responsible for the legal troubles of the earlier plays.

29. Peter Jaszi, discussing modern copyright law, describes this successful appropriation of public intellectual property by private individuals in terms of homesteading (41); articles by Rosemary Coombe and David Sanjek in the same volume similarly present the ironic examples of Michael Jackson and Madonna, "practiced *bricoleurs*" (Woodmansee and Jaszi 12), suing over alleged copyright infringements.

30. "A well-known book cannot change its author" (Randall 62, W. Ker's translation; Randall astutely points out that a better rendering would read "master" instead of "author," which lends further support to the idea of authorship as constructed).

31. The principal exponent of this view is C.E.J. Caldicott, who, in discussing the often stormy relations between Molière and his publishers, has written, "Animant cette combativité de l'auteur, et bien plus profondément ressentie que les prises de position idéologiques parfois attribuées à Molière, est la conscience de ses droits, et par delà sa conscience d'auteur" (*Carrière* 138).

32. The recurrent metaphor for these writers in the *Songe* is that of the *fripier*, defined by Richelet as "celui qui vend & achette de vieux habits, & qui en fait aussi de neufs" (1:354). The plagiarist is here associated both with indigence and a particular method of literary composition: patching together texts out of used (previously written) scraps that he has accumulated. The image is particularly striking considering that paper in the seventeenth century was produced from a pulp made from rags.

33. Alexander Pope's fictional English plagiarist in the *Dunciad* has made ample use of Molière: "Next, o'er his Books his eyes began to roll, / In pleasing memory of all he stole / ... Here lay poor Fletcher's half-eat scenes, and here / The Frippery of crucify'd Molière ..." (Peters 232).

Chapter Three
Comedic Authorship and Its Discontents

1. In one particular case, there is a possible connection between the two groups: Donneau de Visé, quite possibly the F. Doneau of *La Cocue imaginaire* (Gilbert 203–05), was also one of Molière's principal antagonists in the *querelle de L'École des femmes*, a strange turn of events given the laudatory preface of Doneau's play. As Bourqui and Forestier note in the 2010 Pléiade edition, perhaps Donneau de Visé was embittered by the pro-Molière *Songe du Rêveur* that had criticized *La Cocue imaginaire* in harsh terms and labeled its author a "sot" and an "infâme" (1:1230).

2. See Chapter 1.

3. For both *L'École des femmes* and the 1666 *Œuvres*, Guibert accurately describes the editions but misattributes the role of Agnès to Armande Béjart, Molière's wife. Mademoiselle de Brie created the role of Agnès and continued to play it for another thirty years. The engraving for the second volume of the *Œuvres* is consequently not an "hommage à Molière et à sa femme" (Guibert, *Molière* 2:565), but instead is a tribute to the marvelous comedic pairing of the characters Arnolphe and Agnès.

4. Other prominent examples are Philinte's reference in *Le Misanthrope* to *L'École des maris*, angrily dismissed by Alceste-Molière (1:651), and Béralde's offer to take Argan to a Molière comedy in *Le Malade imaginaire*, which provokes Argan-Molière's virulent censure of Molière's medical satires (2:696–97).

5. As mentioned in Chapter 1, both Furetière and Richelet define the phrase *nommer son auteur*, meaning "to cite an authority as proof or guarantor of what has been stated."

6. Larry Riggs notes as well how print gains authority through the way that it divests writing of corporeality: "Until the advent of mechanical printing, however, writing remained similar to speech in that it carried the ineradicable evidence of the particular body which produced it. Mechanically produced print eliminates the traces of a physical, personal producer, and therefore of the energies and motives which drove him to produce it" (*Molière and Plurality* 37).

7. Christopher Braider notes Arnolphe's attempts to distance himself from society, and by extension, to then impose his will on it: "Arnolphe is the transcendental spectator who ... is empowered by his remoteness from the spectacle on which he acts to supervise and, by supervising, change a world to which he would otherwise be in thrall. And the ultimate fruit of the change is a radical act of self-fashioning, shaping the world so as to impose on it the stamp of the identity inscribed in his new (and 'proper') name" (227).

8.
Et je vis par les Vers qu'à la tête il nous jette,
De quel air il fallait que fût fait le Poète;
Et j'en avais si bien deviné tous les traits,
Que, rencontrant un Homme un jour dans le Palais,
Je gageai que c'était Trissotin en personne,
Et je vis qu'en effet la gageure était bonne. (2:546)

9. La Fontaine had already signaled this in his letter to Maucroix regarding the premiere of *Les Fâcheux* at Vaux, in which he writes: "Nous avons changé de méthode: / Jodelet n'est plus à la mode, / Et maintenant il ne faut pas / Quitter la nature d'un pas" (*Œuvres* 526).

10. In *The Reinvention of Obscenity: Sex, Lies, and Tabloids in Early Modern France* (2002), Joan DeJean argues that Molière was even one of the primary instigators of the quarrel and was complicit in its continuation. She writes, "The scandal of *L'École des femmes* is a clear sign that a new definition of literary value was becoming accepted: a work was good if people went to see it or if it sold copies. An author's primary objective was, therefore, to do whatever was necessary to attract wide public attention" (101). She adds that "the controversy continued just as long as authors and newsmen and publishers could keep it going" (101). This view has also been advocated by Georges Forestier and Claude Bourqui in their article "Comment Molière inventa la querelle de *L'École des femmes* ..." (*Littératures classiques* 81 [2013]: 185–97).

11. The complete list of texts and their authors is as follows, in chronological order: Molière, *L'École des femmes* (December 1662); Donneau de Visé, *Nouvelles nouvelles* (February 1663); Molière, *La Critique de L'École des femmes* (June 1663); Donneau de Visé, *Zélinde* (August 1663), Boursault, *Le Portrait du peintre* (September or October 1663); Molière, *L'Impromptu de Versailles* (October 1663); Robinet, *Panégyrique de L'École des femmes* (November 1663); Donneau de Visé, *Réponse à l'Impromptu de Versailles ou la Vengeance des marquis* (November or December 1663); Donneau de Visé, *Lettre sur les affaires du théâtre* (December 1663); Montfleury, *L'Impromptu de L'Hôtel de Condé* (December 1663); Chevalier, *Les Amours de Calotin* (February 1664); La Croix, *La Guerre comique ou la Défense de L'École des femmes* (March 1664).

12. For ease of consultation, texts from Molière's opponents in the *querelle* (with the lone exception of Chevalier's *Les Amours de Calotin*) are cited from Georges Couton's 1971 Pléiade edition of Molière's complete works, which includes most of the relevant pieces in an appendix to Volume 1. Quotations from Molière's works are from Forestier and Bourqui's 2010 Pléiade edition.

13. See Chapter 2.

14. It is certain that *Dom Garcie de Navarre*, with its five acts, serious subject matter, and noble characters, was an attempt by the playwright to gain success in a more respectable genre. Its rejection by the public, however, must have discouraged Molière from further work in this direction.

15. Molière himself heavy-handedly defended the tastes and judgment of the court in his *Critique*: "Sachez, s'il vous plaît, Monsieur Lysidas, que les

Courtisans ont d'aussi bons yeux que d'autres; qu'on peut être habile avec un point de Venise, et des plumes, aussi bien qu'avec une perruque courte, et un petit rabat uni: que la grande épreuve de toutes vos Comédies, c'est le jugement de la Cour; que c'est son goût qu'il faut étudier pour trouver l'art de réussir; qu'il n'y a point de lieu où les décisions soient si justes; et sans mettre en ligne de compte tous les gens savants qui y sont, que du simple bon sens naturel et du commerce de tout le beau monde, on s'y fait une manière d'esprit, qui, sans comparaison, juge plus finement des choses, que tout le savoir enrouillé des Pédants" (1:505–06).

16. Bray's claims have certainly not gone unchallenged. Gérard Defaux's *Molière, ou les métamorphoses du comique*, to name one important critical response, describes Molière's changing aesthetic as a movement from the humanist tradition of *castigat ridendo mores* (which does in fact oppose the playwright to his audience in a certain sense) to a euphoric "Fête ... dont le personnage central, symbole, par la grâce même de sa folie, de notre condition risible et imparfaite, est devenu le Roi, l'Ordonnateur et le Poète inspiré" (30). For Defaux, this change is the result of a long dialectic between Molière and his audience, but not at all the sign of conformism. As Defaux states succinctly, "Molière est un artiste qui pense" (27).

17. Duchêne's figures show that private performances and royal gifts account for only 22.5% of the troupe's income (750).

18. "[L]a question de l'utilisation des sources dans le théâtre du XVIIe siècle, en particulier dans le genre comique, reste mal explorée; elle a pourtant toute son importance si on considère que la grande majorité des comédies de l'époque est traduite ou adaptée d'œuvres de langue étrangère" (Bourqui, *Sources* 10).

19. In his dedication to *L'Amant de sa femme* (1660), Dorimon describes the play as "une chose nouvelle" and adds that "cet ouvrage ne doit rien aux sujets estrangers, sa création n'est deuë qu'à son Autheur, ne tient rien de l'Espagnol, ny de l'Italien" (151). Hauteroche states about his comedy *Le Deuil* (1673), "On saura que j'ai tiré le sujet de cette Comédie des Contes d'Eutrapel; mais, quand on prendra la peine de les lire, on verra que je n'en ai pris que fort peu de chose, & qu'il y a beaucoup de mon invention. Je veux pourtant bien qu'on sache que ce Livre m'en a fourni les premieres idées; & que je me ferois un scrupule de n'en pas avertir le Lecteur" (2:3). The phrase most often attributed to Molière to describe his treatment of sources, "Je prends mon bien où je le trouve," is doubly problematic: it is a deformation in both phrasing and meaning of Grimarest's "Il m'est permis ... de *reprendre* mon bien où je le trouve" (14; emphasis added), in which Grimarest has Molière defend his own invention of a passage allegedly stolen from Cyrano de Bergerac. Grimarest's account is, of course, highly dubious. Roland de Chaudenay, while inadvisedly excusing Molière based on Grimarest's anecdote, nevertheless adds, "Molière a suffisamment pillé pour que nous n'alourdissions pas son dossier" (69).

20. The attribution of sources is also a way to highlight the lowly generic origins of Molière's comedy. Donneau de Visé's list, in particular, emphasizes that Molière's play is taken from *contes* and *nouvelles*. See below for a further discussion of genre in the *querelle*.

21. Corneille's *Cinna* (1642) can serve as an example: the preface contains the Latin selection from Seneca where Corneille found the story, as well as Montaigne's translation and commentary on the passage. The unconcealed erudition of this preface plays an important role in establishing the lofty tone of the tragedy and in constructing the image of the author. Far from concealing the sources of his art, Corneille provides a detailed bibliography for the reader, and, with the addition of the play's *examen* in 1660, walks the reader carefully through the process of how he transformed the historical account into a tragedy, including the identification of which parts he borrowed and which he invented. Such an approach allows for (and encourages) the kind of *génétique* study that Georges Forestier has undertaken (see Forestier's *Essai de génétique théâtrale: Corneille à l'œuvre*).

22. In their prologues to the *Menaechmi* and the *Eunuchus*, Plautus and Terence respectively identify the conventions and stock characters of Roman comedy (Goldberg 91). As Terence concludes, "In fact nothing is said that has not been said before. So you should recognize facts and pardon new playwrights if they present what their predecessors presented before them" (1:239)

23. La Fontaine will adapt the fable in 1668, again with a reference to plagiarists: "Il est assez de geais à deux pieds comme lui, / Qui se parent souvent des dépouilles d'autrui, / Et que l'on nomme plagiaires" (*Fables* 147–48). Hélène Maurel-Indart has underscored the irony in La Fontaine (and Horace before him) "borrowing" accusations against plagiarists: "Horace, aussi bien que La Fontaine, devait sourire de son emprunt à Ésope en écrivant ces lignes sur les méprisables plagiaires!" (13).

24. As mentioned in Chapter 2, Randall has pointed out that plagiarism is and has always been in the eye of the beholder (or in this case the reader), and making a charge of plagiarism "stick" involves much more than internal evidence: the status of the authors and the judgment of the public play a preponderant role, particularly in an era where no formal law prevented plagiarism (Randall 4–5).

25. The example of *Dom Juan* (1665) provides an interesting example of how cultural capital interfaces with literary property and attribution. In 1674, Dutch booksellers issued a *Dom Juan* that they ascribed on the title page to Molière; the text was in fact Dorimond's *Le Festin de Pierre* (1659). Instead of stealing from Molière (as Ribou had done), unscrupulous publishers were actually attributing to him works that he had not written in order to profit from his reputation and the public's confusion. In this particular instance, Molière actually acquired the property of another author without even intending to do so.

26. An interesting point of comparison is La Bruyère, who in *Les Caractères* begins the section "Des ouvrages de l'esprit" with the previously cited literary complaint: "Tout est dit, et l'on vient trop tard depuis plus de sept mille ans qu'il y a des hommes et qui pensent" (67). La Bruyère ends the section,

though, by asserting his ability to make his own the thoughts that may have been expressed by others: "Horace ou Despréaux l'a dit avant vous. —Je le crois sur votre parole; mais je l'ai dit comme mien. Ne puis-je pas penser après eux une chose vraie, et que d'autres encore penseront après moi?" (95).

27. Alcidor has previously announced that he has composed a new five-act play based on an episode of Roman history. He worries about the possible reception, though, since his play is "toute sérieuse." Alcipe counsels him, "Hé, le sérieux plaît encore quand il est bien manié; mais, ma foi, le comique accommode mieux les gens. Ne feignez point d'y en mettre" (1:1137).

28. Nor would Corneille and Molière always be typed as contrasting models. Years later, Boileau, writing to Racine during the fight over *Phèdre*, includes both Molière and Corneille as examples of embattled playwrights whose works eventually triumphed despite their detractors (see Boileau's *Epître VII*). This suggestive parallel indicates the extent to which Boileau sees retrospectively in the *querelle de L'École des femmes* the echo of Corneille's earlier struggles, with similar aesthetic stakes and a similar triumph of successful literary innovation over the petty rivalries of lesser authors.

29. These statements suggest a certain ambiguity in Molière's literary ambitions—while claiming that plays need only please, he nevertheless declares that his play follows the theatrical rules. His subsequent silence on the issue (since Dorante does not proceed to demonstrate the play's regularity) is difficult to interpret: is it due to the possible weakness of his position or to insouciance regarding such demonstrations? It is similar in this respect to his vague promise in the preface of *Les Fâcheux* that "[l]e temps viendra de faire imprimer mes remarques sur les Pièces que j'aurai faites," mentioning his intention to grapple with Aristotle and Horace, but noting that this study "peut-être ne viendra point" (1:149–50).

30. See DeJean's discussion of this scene and its subsequent reappearance in the literature of the *querelle*, including the wider context of censorship and obscenity (102–03).

31. The distinction must be made between Molière the comic actor and the tragedian: the latter is subject to frequent satire during the *querelle*, the most famous being the description given by Montfleury of Molière in the role of César:

> Il est fait tout de même; il vient le nez au vent,
> Les pieds en paranthèse, et l'épaule en avant,
> Sa perruque qui suit le côté qu'il avance,
> Plus pleine de laurier qu'un jambon de Mayence,
> Les mains sur les côtés d'un air peu négligé,
> La tête sur le dos comme un mulet chargé,
> Les yeux fort égarés, puis, débitant ses rôles
> D'un hoquet éternel sépare ses paroles. ... (Molière 1:1119)

32. See in particular the preface to *L'Amour médecin*, discussed in the Introduction.

33. Detailing the moral opprobrium that surrounded acting in the seventeenth century, Braider writes, "Given then both [Molière's] genre and his profession, the claim to authority constitutes a scandalous breach of decorum: it was simply not *bienséant* to nourish the pretensions he did. This seems indeed to have been one of the motives behind the *querelle* provoked by *L'École des femmes*, reflected in the personal animus feeding the attacks he underwent: to punish him for usurping a station to which he was not entitled" (228–29).

34. The other two performances were of *Le Fin Lourdaud*, whose author is unknown—it quite possibly could be one of Molière's lost farces.

35. Typical print runs for new publications were only between 1200 and 1800 copies (Martin, *The French Book* 3). While the *parterre* price to attend a play was 15 *sols*, a book cost several *livres*.

36. Gaines and Braider point out the similarities in this respect between Molière and some of his most famous characters. Gaines writes, "[W]hat goes on to typify Molière's characters is that they are not only aware of the paradoxical situations in which they find themselves, but that they try to appropriate for themselves the wisdom and power associated with paradox itself" (45). Braider draws a parallel between Molière and Arnolphe, noting that "the project of self-fashioning linked to the hero's name mirrors an exactly similar project on the author's part" (227).

37. The most infamous examples are the obscene *chanson de la coquille* (sung at the end of the Hôtel de Bourgogne's performance of *Le Portrait du peintre*) and Montfleury's *placet* accusing Molière "d'avoir épousé la fille, et d'avoir autrefois couché avec la mère."

38. Caldicott suggests that Molière's popularity almost obligated the king to enlist him—the most glorious king had to have the most popular and glorious of entertainers. See in particular Caldicott's tracing of Molière's interactions with Louis XIV in *La Carrière de Molière* (63–90).

38. The irony of the 1666 *Œuvres* is that Molière may well have objected to its publication. For a more in-depth discussion of the edition, see Chapter 4.

40. La Grange attaches particular importance to the inclusion of Molière's *Remerciement* in the *Œuvres*, including a marginal note in his *Registre* to this effect (Guibert, *Molière* 2:752).

41. Viala nevertheless notes that Molière never obtained a "consécration effective dans l'espace académique" (233). Whether Molière was actively excluded from the Académie Française, or whether his early death prevented his entry, remains a subject of speculation. Gaines writes that the Académie Française "took great pains not to include playwrights, and comic playwrights in particular," adding, "A few dramatists, such as Boisrobert, owed their academic robes directly to political toadying, but none among the early generations to the stage alone" (9).

42. *Le Négligent*, Prologue, scene 3; qtd. in Robert Garapon's edition of La Bruyère's *Les Caractères* (67).

Chapter Four
"Je veux qu'on me distingue"

1. Critical responses to this claim have varied. For example, Caldicott argues that if Molière's aesthetic changes, it is more realistically because of his closer association with the king and because of his struggles with *libraires* (see below): "[O]n constate que le changement de direction le plus décisif de la carrière de Molière fut l'adoption de sa troupe par Louis XIV lors de la fête de l'Assomption 1665, suivie par sa décision de rompre avec le cartel des libraires en 1666" (*Carrière* 23). Norman has noted a certain continuity in Molière's approach to social satire (186–87), while Riggs has stressed a common resistance to the kind of modernity emerging in the seventeenth century that is apparent in Molière's plays from the beginning of his career to the end (*Molière and Modernity*, for example, moves from *L'École des femmes* to *Les Femmes savantes*).

2. We could add to this list the name of Robert Ballard, the royal printer who issued *Les Plaisirs de L'Île enchantée*, containing the text of *La Princesse d'Élide*, in 1665, but Molière was not involved with the edition.

3. *La Thébaïde* (1664), *Andromaque* (1667), *Les Plaideurs* (1669), *Britannicus* (1670), *Bérénice* (1671), *Mithridate* (1673), *Iphigénie* (1675), *Phèdre* (1677), *Esther* (1689), *Athalie* (1691).

4. An exception was the case of translations, where a translator was occasionally paid a fee by the *libraire* (Chartier, *L'Ordre* 55).

5. Lough writes that after the beginning of Louis XIV's personal reign, "it became less common to dedicate plays to patrons" (43).

6. Pottinger points out for *libraires* "the necessity for getting back all or nearly all of their investment by the sale of the first edition" (44), the extensive pirating of popular titles making subsequent print runs less profitable.

7. De Luyne, Sercy, and Barbin.

8. De Luyne, Sercy, Barbin, Quinet, and Guignard.

9. Barbin and Quinet.

10. De Luyne, Sercy, Barbin, Quinet, Guignard, Loyson, Billaine, and Jolly. Note that while Guibert was unable to find an edition of *La Critique* published by Sercy, his name is mentioned on the privilege (Guibert, *Molière* 1:144–45).

11. Chevalier's *Les Amours de Calotin* (1664), one of the texts in the *querelle de L'École des femmes*, was also published by eight *libraires*—De Luyne, Sercy, Quinet, Guignard, Loyson, Jolly, Pierre Bienfait, and Pierre Trabouillet.

12. On at least two occasions a Corneille *privilège* was shared four ways: a 1655 collected works and a 1665 edition of *L'Imitation de Jésus-Christ* produced by Robert Ballard, Jolly, De Luyne, and Billaine (Picot 133, 170).

13. Racine's *Andromaque*, for example, was published by Barbin, Jolly, and Théodore Girard in 1667. While Molière at this point was no longer working with the first two, Girard helped publish *Le Médecin malgré lui* the same year. See also the example of Chevalier's *Les Amours de Calotin*, n11, where

the eight publishers include six of Caldicott's eight, but with the exclusion of Billaine and Barbin, and the addition of Bienfait and Trabouillet.

14. The size of the group may be linked to a need to produce the edition extremely quickly. A 1640s document mentions large associations of printers that would form in order to release a book sooner than the competition or, presumably, counterfeiters (Martin, *Livre* 2:557–58).

15. *Les Précieuses ridicules, Sganarelle, L'École des maris, Les Fâcheux, L'Étourdi, Le Dépit amoureux, L'École des femmes, La Critique de L'École des femmes, La Princesse d'Élide*.

16. Earlier editions of Molière's collected works exist, but they are editions constructed by binding together previously printed copies of the individual plays (nonce editions).

17. Pottinger notes that the Council's 20 December 1649 *arrêt* "gave preference to original owners in case of renewal" (221). He also notes, however, that this clause was not ratified by the Parisian *parlement*. As he observes elsewhere, the debate over the renewal and continuation of privileges "was never really settled in the *ancien régime*" (215). In part, this was because it opposed the monarchy (in favor of tighter control over printing and therefore of granting privileges and extensions to a select group of Parisian booksellers) to the provincial *parlements* (who opposed privileges and extensions in order to grant local booksellers access to the works printed in Paris). Pottinger writes that by 1665 "on the whole a fair compromise had been worked out: the provincial publishers were given access to the important body of classical texts, and the privileged publishers were encouraged to look forward to long possession of their monopolies of modern authors" (223).

18. Hammond, in his analysis of how authorship and authority are linked in the play, comments, "It is precisely this dimension of authorship—trying to circulate creative writing—that provokes Alceste's wrath" (61). Hammond also notes that Alceste very explicitly equates "the term 'auteur' with the idea of 'se faire imprimer'" (61).

19. Discussing Bourdieu's theory of symbolic capital in the similar instance of a court setting, William Earle points out the need for group recognition of such "consecrations," noting, "Prestige, in court society is no more arbitrary, in the sense of creatable *ad libitum* or *ex nihilo*, than authority or credibility within a particular scientific field" (184).

20. The nearest equivalent is Neuf-Villenaine's series of *arguments* in the original edition of *Sganarelle* (see Chapter 2). If Forestier and Bourqui are correct and Neuf-Villenaine and Donneau de Visé are in fact the same person, the connection becomes particularly telling, as discussed below (p. 173).

21. Grimarest claims that Molière "en fut irrité" and burned all the copies containing Donneau de Visé's letter, but that after the playwright's death the letter was reinstated (24). The anecdote seems unlikely, given the bibliographical evidence. The 2010 Pléiade edition states, "Il n'y a pas lieu de douter que ce texte de Donneau de Visé ait été imprimé avec la bénédiction—si ce n'est la collaboration—de Molière" (1:1435).

Chapter Five
The School for Publishers

1. Zanger illustrates Molière's wariness of "publishing information in a collectable form" by citing the end of *Le Misanthrope*: "this is the case of Célimène, who loses all her seductive power when the letters she writes her lovers are discovered and passed around" (184).

2. By comparison, Racine allegedly received only 200 *livres* from Girard, Jolly, and Barbin for *Andromaque*, while Denis Thierry paid Armande Béjart 1500 *livres* for Molière's seven posthumous plays, including *Le Malade imaginaire* (Reed, *Barbin* 67–68).

3. See the Afterword for a more complete discussion of this sale and its ramifications for Molière's printed corpus.

4. As early as 1673, Barbin and Ribou issued nonce editions of Racine's works by binding together copies of the individual plays (Guibert, *Racine* 125).

5. For a further example, see DeJean's discussion of *L'École des filles* whose publisher, like Ribou, was banished from Paris for a period of time (*Reinvention* 64).

6. The distinction that Molière's books are sold "pour l'auteur" and not "par l'auteur" is important—Pottinger writes, "[U]nless an author were a printer member of the guild, he was not allowed to print or sell his own works. The law of 16 June 1618 was emphatic on this matter, forbidding authors even to advertise their own books; and numerous later laws and judgments confirmed the prohibition" (44). He notes, "[T]hough an author could not legally sell his own books, he might pay for having his work manufactured by a printer and then hire a dealer to take care of the distribution" but describes such arrangements as "unusual and of course only vestigial remnants of the times when books were published not for profit but for the esteem and other indirect benefits accruing from them" (97). Molière, however, is taking advantage of the possibility of such arrangements to change the economic conditions of his theater's printing and sale.

7. As Defaux writes, Molière's "comédie seconde manière" reaches its "plénitude" first with *Le Bourgeois gentilhomme*, and then with *Le Malade imaginaire* (30).

8. Le Monnier was a particularly apt colleague to be running Ribou's shop. He too had numerous encounters with the law, including a stint in the Bastille in 1664 for selling Jansenist literature. Like Ribou, he was condemned to row in the galleys, but the penalty was commuted (Renouard 276).

9. Furthermore, Molière's example of contracting out the book's printing and sale will be followed by Racine (*Bajazet*, 1672), Molière's wife (a 1673 edition of *Le Médecin malgré lui*—see the Afterword), and, most significantly, Lully (see Chapter 6).

10. Later in Molière's career, and most likely as a function of his increasing interest in the rights to his plays, there is a noticeable increase in his privileges' durations: the privilege for *Tartuffe* was for ten years, as was the three-play privilege for *Le Bourgeois gentilhomme*.

11. The official record book of the *Communauté* actually shows that Sevestre began to record the privilege before crossing it out (Thuasne 40), a marvelous illustration of the moment when the full extent of Molière's privilege became apparent to the *syndic*.

12. My views here are corroborated by the editors of the 2010 Pléiade version, who write: "Cependant la Communauté avait parfaitement le droit de refuser l'enregistrement de ce privilège si elle estimait qu'il contrevenait à des privilèges encore en vigueur; c'était effectivement le cas puisque les précédents privilèges des pièces de Molière n'étaient pas tous échus au mois d'août 1671. La Communauté jouait là son rôle de vigilance corporative vis-à-vis du respect de la réglementation, même si en l'occurrence elle le faisait au détriment de l'auteur, et sans doute avec une certaine mauvaise foi" (2:1477).

13. Further evidence for this comes from the privilege's subsequent registration in 1673 by Denis Thierry (see Afterword), in which Thierry refers to Molière's 1671 text as a "continuation de privilege" (Thuasne 43)

14. Rey-Flaud notes that Baudeau de Somaize had labeled Molière "le premier farceur de France" (201). While the intention was pejorative, Molière here seems to take ironic pride in the title.

15.
> C'est par là que Molière, illustrant ses écrits,
> Peut-être de son art eût remporté le prix,
> Si, moins ami du peuple, en ses doctes peintures,
> Il n'eût point fait souvent grimacer ses figures,
> Quitté, pour le bouffon, l'agréable et le fin,
> Et sans honte à Térence allié Tabarin.
> Dans ce sac ridicule où Scapin s'enveloppe,
> Je ne reconnois plus l'auteur du Misanthrope.
> (Boileau, *Œuvres* [1961] 181)

16. See, for example, Donneau de Visé's *Zélinde* (1663), discussed in Chapter 3: "C'est pourquoi vous devez, pour ajouter quelque chose de beau à ce que je vous viens de dire, lire comme [Molière] tous les livres satiriques, prendre dans l'Espagnol, prendre dans l'Italien, et lire tous les vieux bouquins" (in Molière 1:1038).

17. During the quarrel, Barbin had printed *Zélinde*, and a volume containing *La Réponse à l'Impromptu de Versailles* and the *Lettre sur les affaires du Théâtre*. Barbin's role in the quarrel, however, should not be overemphasized, particularly since Ribou also was involved in printing the attacks of Molière's enemies.

18. The closest equivalent is perhaps Monsieur Tibaudier's "strophes" in *La Comtesse d'Escarbagnas*: the vicomte obviously perceives their poor literary quality, while the comtesse herself states, "[P]our des Vers faits dans la Province, ces Vers-là sont fort beaux" (2:1031).

19. For a discussion of Philaminte's cross-casting (and for a more general discussion of cross-casting in seventeenth-century performance), see Julia

Prest's landmark study *Theatre under Louis XIV: Cross-Casting and the Performance of Gender in Drama, Ballet and Opera*. As Prest reminds us, Philaminte "is a woman who wears the metaphorical trousers and at the same time a man who is wearing a real dress" (39).

20. My reference here is to p. 2 of Guicharnaud's unpublished manuscript concerning Molière's late plays contained in the Beinecke Rare Book and Manuscript Library at Yale University (Jacques Guicharnaud Papers, Uncat. MSS 826, box 2).

Chapter Six
Collaboration's Pyrrhic Triumph

1. Foucault writes, "Dans notre civilisation, ce ne sont pas toujours les mêmes textes qui ont demandé à recevoir une attribution" ("Qu'est-ce qu'un auteur?" 84). Noting that early literary texts "étaient reçus, mis en circulation, valorisés sans que soit posée la question de leur auteur," Foucault suggests that this changed in the seventeenth or eighteenth century, when "les discours 'littéraires' ne peuvent plus être reçus que dotés de la fonction auteur" (84–85).

2. As discussed below, these lines are attributed by the prefatory note of the published edition to Pierre Corneille (in echo of Théophile de Viau's *Pyrame et Thisbé*). However, I am holding the note to its word: it states that the *versification* is Pierre Corneille's, and my critical assumption here is that Molière employed a similar compositional strategy to the process that Louis Racine ascribes to his father, writing out a preliminary version of each act in prose (Racine 35). I would add that this is also the stance of the 2010 Pléiade edition: "À la fin du mois de décembre, Molière avait établi le plan de *Psyché* et rédigé un canevas en prose contenant le découpage en scènes et la structure des répliques" (2:1491). Consequently, while the strict poetic wording of this passage may be Corneille's, the general sense of the dialogue is Molière's. Cupid's jealousy, a fundamental character trait and a motor of the plot, would undoubtedly have been present in Molière's original *plan*. I wish to thank Stephen Fleck for pointing out to me this important distinction.

3. Riggs's reading of *L'École des femmes* and *Le Misanthrope* argues for a Molière who teaches that "transcendent subjectivity is impossible" (*Molière and Modernity* 114) through the failings of figures like Alceste and Arnolphe. Max Vernet, in his *Molière: Côté jardin côté cour*, also uses *L'École des femmes* as a means to examine Molière's critique of efforts (including those of literary critics) at total control (21).

4. At the conclusion of *Le Misanthrope*, Alceste announces his intention to "fuir tous les Humains," retiring to "mon Désert, où j'ai fait vœu de vivre" (1:724).

5. Genre might also play a major role in the shift, although it should be noted that Molière's other "serious" play, *Dom Garcie de Navarre* (1661), represented a criticism of jealousy that matches that of the comedies—so much so that sections of it were fit *verbatim* into *Le Misanthrope*.

6. Herbert Schneider, in the 2009 edition of Lully's *Psyché*, attributes the *plainte* to Francesco Buti, but provides no explanation or justification for this choice (1). The editors of the 2010 Pléiade edition note that the *plainte* was attributed to Lully beginning in the eighteenth century (2:1492).

7. John Powell's article "*Psyché*: The Stakes of a Collaboration" contains an excellent scholarly reconstruction of the contributions that each of these individuals made toward the final product (11–20).

8. Powell, for example, writes, "We might speculate that Quinault's participation was a *fait accompli*—that Lully simply chose to work with Quinault rather than Molière—and that Quinault's appearance may foreshadow the rift that may have already been developing between 'les deux grands Baptistes'" (16).

9. See Furetière V2v and Richelet 1:28. See also the discussion of early modern authorship in Chapter 1.

10. See Chapter 5 for a further discussion of this development in Molière's printing career.

11. Zanger writes, "The dissidence between the publisher's note and the title page echoes Molière's ambivalence over the new authority and control of authorship (in publication), an authority he repeatedly undermines" (183). I would argue that the note rhetorically establishes Molière's superiority over the other authors and that, while fully cognizant of the ambiguities surrounding authorship, Molière exploits this to establish his control over the text. He is, after all, the one who obtains the privilege and prints the work at his own expense.

12. The relative financial inequality of the two men (and their cordial relationship at the time) can be inferred from the fact that on 14 December 1670 Lully borrowed 11,000 *livres* from Molière in order to construct his new house (Jurgens and Maxfield-Miller 578).

13. Corneille's request reads almost exactly the same as a print privilege, listing the works to be protected (*Cinna*, *Polyeucte*, and *La Mort de Pompée*), and asking for a specific time period in which he would enjoy a performance monopoly "à compter du jour qu'elles auront été représentées la première fois," with penalties stipulated for violators (1:1684–85).

14. Victoria Johnson's excellent book *Backstage at the Revolution* traces the continuation of the Opera's performance monopoly during and after Lully's death (see in particular pages 6–7).

15. See Chapter 5.

16. See the Afterword for a more complete discussion of the fate of Molière's printed theater after the playwright's death.

17. Couton writes in the 1971 Pléiade edition of Molière's works: "Il est caractéristique au reste que Lulli ait pu reprendre le sujet en 1678, fait transformer les alexandrins en vers irréguliers par Thomas Corneille, composé en quinze jours pour eux une musique récitative, réutilisé les intermèdes de 1671 et redonné *Psyché* sous le nom d'opéra" (2:793).

18. The phrase does not occur in the original French edition of Foucault's article, but comes from a subsequent revised version given at SUNY–Buffalo, translated by Josué V. Harari ("What Is an Author?" 9).

Afterword
The Death of the Actor

1. In addition to the 1666 edition, discussed at length in Chapter 4, the 1682 edition was preceded by collected editions issued in 1673, 1674–75, and, arguably, 1681 (Lacroix considers the 1681 edition a pirate copy; Guibert claims that it is in fact a legitimate new edition [Guibert, *Molière* 2:594–98]).

2. Marcel is the author of a madrigal in French and a Latin epitaph. The remaining poem is a Latin epitaph written by the historiographer Mézeray. Ironically, the same volume also reproduces Molière's preface to *Les Précieuses ridicules* with the reference to authorial "précautions:" "I'aurois parlé aussi à mes amis, qui pour la recommandation de ma Piece, ne m'auroient pas refusé, ou des Vers François, ou des Vers Latins" (K3v–K4r).

3. With respect to Georges Couton's 1971 edition, the 1682 edition differs in the locations of *Le Remerciement au roi* (1663) and *Tartuffe* (1664), and reverses the order of *Le Mariage forcé* (1664) and *Les Plaisirs de l'Île enchantée* (1664), *George Dandin* (1668) and *L'Avare* (1668), and *Les Fourberies de Scapin* (1671) and *Psyché* (1671). Some of these decisions are due to a different ordering system—the 1682 edition privileges the opening performance date at the Palais-Royal theater over the royal premiere. The 1682 edition is even at times more consistent in its editorial choices than Couton. Couton places the *Remerciement* in order with the plays while placing *La Gloire de Val-de-Grâce* (1669) in the back; the 1682 edition integrates both chronologically with the plays. Forestier and Bourqui's 2010 edition opts for an organization according to publication date. We could tentatively argue, therefore, that the three editions each take a different aspect of Molière as their point of departure, with the 2010 edition privileging Molière as author, Couton viewing Molière as court entertainer, and the 1682 edition emphasizing Molière's role in the public theater (commensurate with the edition's efforts to tie Molière to the newly formed Comédie-Française).

4. Caldicott's 2005 analysis is somewhat skewed by the particular historical narrative that he constructs regarding Molière's relations with his early publishers. Maintaining that Barbin and Molière's first *libraires* constituted a "cartel" of sorts, Caldicott assumes that it was this group that acquired the rights to Molière's plays after his death, due to Barbin's use of the word *compagnie* in the registration of the privilege (see Chapters 4 and 5, and also the discussion of the 1671 privilege's sale below). Caldicott's suspicion of the 1682 edition is consequently due at least partly to the notion that it fell "under the influence of the cartel" ("Molière's Duodecimos" 537).

5. In other words, what the 2010 editors have done is the Molière equivalent of basing their text on a Shakespearean "bad quarto"—in fact, the case of *King Lear* in Shakespeare editions (D. Brooks 7–8) foreshadowed the bibliographical method leading to the privileging of the 1675 *Malade imaginaire*. The claims from Molière's 1682 editors and from Heminge and Condell, responsible for the 1623 Shakespeare first folio, are strikingly similar: disavowing as corrupt the previous texts that had already appeared, the editors claim in both cases to possess authorized manuscripts (in Shakespeare's case, the "true originals"), which they are now delivering to the public. These versions, while appearing later, are presumed to restore the text to its earlier, and more authorial, state (D. Brooks 11–12).

6. Of course, the gentle irony here is that the editors of the 2010 Pléiade edition also show these principles at work in 2010. Forestier, Bourqui, and the other members of the editorial team are ultimately under the same constraints as their 1682 forebears, charged with producing a new and marketable version of an old text that is arguably Molière's and also their own. To reproduce Georges Couton's 1971 text would be unacceptable and the only way to market and sell the edition is if the text becomes not just "Molière," but "Forestier and Bourqui's Molière." Ironically, the editors justify their changes to what has come to be the accepted text in the same manner as the 1682 editors, appealing to an author principle: "[N]ous avons choisi de reproduire le seul texte dont on ne peut contester qu'il soit de Molière" (2:1566), rejecting any changes that may have accrued due to Molière's theatrical partners in order to bill the text as authentically and authorially Molière's. And, like the 1682 edition, the editors seek to advertise the newness of their own version of Molière by presenting "un nouveau *Malade*, annoncé comme très différent des versions antérieures" (2:1565).

7. *Dom Garcie de Navarre* (1661), *L'Impromptu de Versailles* (1663), *Dom Juan* (1665), *Mélicerte* (1666), *Les Amants magnifiques* (1670), *La Comtesse d'Escarbagnas* (1672), and the altered version of *Le Malade imaginaire* (1673), with both prologues.

8. On perhaps two signal occasions, however, the edition is unwilling or unable to adhere faithfully to this stated goal. The first is well-documented: the 1682 *Dom Juan* was censored by La Reynie, the modern text surviving in a Dutch edition (Wetstein, 1683; see Guibert, *Molière* 1:414). The second is anecdotal: Tralage stated that Thierry refused to publish Molière's translation of Lucretius's *De Rerum Natura* due to its unorthodox statements regarding the nature of the soul (Guibert, *Molière* 2:611).

9. *Les Précieuses ridicules* (1660), *Sganarelle* (1660), *L'Étourdi* (1663), *Le Dépit amoureux* (1663), *Les Fâcheux* (1662), *L'École des maris* (1661), *L'École des femmes* (1663), *La Critique de L'École des femmes* (1663), and *Les Plaisirs de l'Île enchantée* (*La Princesse d'Élide*, 1664).

10. In a footnote to their transcription of the financial document, Jurgens and Maxfield-Miller note that Ribou had just been released from the Bastille when the transaction took place, indicating that they may have been more likely in the position of needing a loan than investing significant capital in a new printing project (580).

11. Guibert goes so far as to suggest that it was Armande who sold the privilege to Anne David, either not wanting to deal directly with Barbin and Thierry, or in order to help the impoverished couple (1:339, 2:569, 578). Of course, we could just as easily surmise, given Ribou's history, that the wily *libraire* realized the value of the privilege and somehow managed to purchase it before any of his competitors. However, if it was really Armande Béjart who sold the rights to the Ribou family, then Barbin subsequently misrepresents the transaction: in his 1673 edition of *Psyché*, Barbin will claim that it was Molière who sold the rights to Anne David (although Barbin is no stranger to such tactics, as discussed below). The 1674–75 collected edition, which published the full text of the 1671 privilege, should have resolved the issue, but remains purposefully vague regarding the privilege's sale and transfer: "Le Privilege cy-dessus a esté cedé à CLAUDE BARBIN & à sa Compagnie, Marchands Libraires à Paris, suivant les actes passez pardevant les Notaires du Châtelet de Paris." The double ambiguity (who transferred the privilege to whom?) created by the passive voice and the catchall "compagnie" does indeed suggest the sale was somewhat *sub rosa* (not particularly surprising, given Ribou's involvement).

12. The reference to Barbin's company is at least partly what leads Caldicott to speak of the "cartel des huit" (*Carrière* 131–32). As shown by Reed, however, Barbin's "compagnie" is certainly not the 1666 group of publishers. In fact, Barbin was most likely double-crossing the other 1666 publishers, negotiating with Thierry and the Ribou family to acquire the exclusive rights to Molière's theater. In other words, Caldicott's suspicions were fully justified—his initial study merely accused the wrong set of *libraires*. Far from oppressing Ribou in order to acquire the rights to Molière's plays, the leaders of the guild were collaborating with him to outmaneuver Barbin's earlier business partners. If anything, I would argue that Molière's first *libraires* were in fact doubly victimized: first by Molière's own questionable dealings, and secondly by Barbin and Thierry

13. While the 1674–75 edition lists as publishers Claude Barbin and Denis Thierry, new title pages printed in 1676 add a third publisher, Pierre Trabouillet (Guibert, *Molière* 2:593). As noted in the 2010 Pléiade edition, Trabouillet purchased the remaining third of the rights to Molière's plays from Ribou in 1676, thus bringing to a close Ribou's long and eventful involvement with Molière's theater (1:cxv).

14. The exception is *Sganarelle*, presented without the Sieur de Neuf-Villenaine's letters and *arguments*. This could possibly be evidence against either Donneau de Visé's identification with Neuf-Villenaine, or his involvement with the edition, both of which are suggested by Forestier and Bourqui (1:1230; 2:1566).

Bibliography

Andrews, Richard. *Scripts and Scenarios: The Performance of Comedy in Renaissance Italy.* Cambridge: Cambridge UP, 1993.

Armstrong, Elizabeth. *Before Copyright: The French Book-Privilege System, 1498–1526.* Cambridge: Cambridge UP, 1990.

Aubignac, François Hédelin, Abbé d'. *La Pratique du théâtre.* 1657. Genève: Slatkine Reprints, 1971.

Barthes, Roland. "La Mort de l'auteur." *Œuvres complètes.* Ed. Eric Marty. Paris: Seuil, 1994. 491–95.

Bennett, Andrew. *The Author.* London: Routledge, 2005.

Boileau, Nicolas. *Œuvres.* Paris: Garnier, 1961.

———. *Œuvres complètes.* Ed. François Escal. Bibliothèque de la Pléiade. Paris: Gallimard, 1966.

———. *Œuvres complètes de N. Boileau.* Ed. Edouard Fournier. Paris: Laplace, Sanchez, 1873.

Bourdieu, Pierre. *Raisons pratiques: Sur la théorie de l'action.* Paris: Seuil, 1994.

———. *Les Règles de l'art: Genèse et structure du champ littéraire.* Paris: Seuil, 1992.

Bourqui, Claude. *La Commedia dell'arte: Introduction au théâtre professionnel italien entre XVIe et le XVIIIe siècles.* Paris: Sedes, 1999.

———. *Les Sources de Molière: Répertoire critique des sources littéraires et dramatiques.* Paris: Sedes, 1999

Braider, Christopher. *Indiscernible Counterparts: The Invention of the Text in French Classical Drama.* Chapel Hill: U of North Carolina Dept. of Romance Languages, 2002.

Bray, René. *Molière, homme de théâtre.* Paris: Mercure de France, 1954.

Brooks, Douglas. *From Playhouse to Printing House: Drama and Authorship in Early Modern England.* Cambridge: Cambridge UP, 2000.

Brooks, William. *Bibliographie critique du théâtre de Quinault.* Biblio 17. Paris, Seattle, Tübingen: Papers on French Seventeenth Century Literature, 1988.

Brown, Cynthia J. *Poets, Patrons, and Printers: Crisis of Authority in Late Medieval France.* Ithaca: Cornell UP, 1995.

Brown, Gregory S. *A Field of Honor: Writers, Court Culture and Public Theater in French Literary Life from Racine to the Revolution.* New York: Columbia UP, 2005.

Bibliography

Calder, Andrew. *Molière: The Theory and Practice of Comedy.* London: Athlone Press, 1993.

Caldicott, C.E.J. *La Carrière de Molière entre protecteurs et éditeurs.* Amsterdam: Rodopi, 1998.

———. "Molière and His Seventeenth-Century Publishers." *Nottingham French Studies* 33.1 (Spring 1994): 4–11.

———. "Molière's Duodecimos: Phases of Publication and the Status of the 1682 Edition." *Papers on French Seventeenth-Century Literature* 32.63 (2005): 519–37.

Callières, François de. *Histoire poétique de la guerre nouvellement declarée entre les Anciens et les Modernes.* 1688. Genève: Slatkine Reprints, 1971.

Carrier, Hubert. "La Propriété littéraire en France au XVIIe siècle." *Les Cahiers de Propriété Intellectuelle* 13.2 (Jan. 2001): 311–32.

Chappuzeau, Samuel. *Le Théâtre françois.* Lyon: Michel Mayer, 1674.

Chartier, Roger. "Le Monde comme représentation." *Annales* 44.6 (Nov.–Dec. 1989): 1505–20.

———. *L'Ordre des livres: Lecteurs, auteurs, bibliothèques en Europe entre XIVe et XVIIIe siècle.* Aix-en-Provence: Alinea, 1992.

———. *Publishing Drama in Early Modern Europe.* London: British Library, 1999.

Chaudenay, Roland de. *Les Plagiaires: Le Nouveau Dictionnaire.* Paris: Perrin, 2001.

Chevalier, [Jean]. *Les Amours de Calotin.* 1664. Turin: J. Gay et fils, 1870.

Chevalley, Sylvie. "Le 'Registre d'Hubert': Étude critique." *Revue d'Histoire du Théâtre* 25 (1973): 147–95.

Civardi, Jean-Marc. *La Querelle du Cid (1637–1638).* Paris: Champion, 2004.

Clarke, Jan. "The Material Conditions of Molière's Stage." *The Cambridge Companion to Molière.* Ed. David Bradby and Andrew Calder. Cambridge: Cambridge UP, 2006. 15–36.

Corneille, Pierre. *Œuvres complètes.* Ed. Georges Couton. Bibliothèque de la Pléiade. 3 vols. Paris: Gallimard, 1980.

Couton, Georges. *Richelieu et le théâtre.* Lyon: Presses universitaires de Lyon, 1986.

Defaux, Gérard. *Molière, ou les métamorphoses du comique: De la Comédie morale au triomphe de la folie.* Lexington, KY: French Forum, 1980.

DeJean, Joan. *The Reinvention of Obscenity: Sex, Lies, and Tabloids in Early Modern France.* Chicago: U of Chicago P, 2002.

Delègue, Yves. *Le Royaume d'exil: Le Sujet de la littérature en quête d'auteur*. Paris: Obsidiane, 1991.

Dobranski, Stephen B. *Milton, Authorship, and the Book Trade*. Cambridge: Cambridge UP, 1999.

Doneau, F. *La Cocue imaginaire*. 1662. Ed. Paul Lacroix. Turin: J. Gay et fils, 1870.

Donneau de Visé, Jean. *Conversation dans une ruelle de Paris sur Molière défunt*. 1673. *Molière jugé par ses contemporains*. Ed. A.-P. Malassis. Paris: Isidore Liseux, 1877. 2–29.

Dorimon. *The Theatre of Nicolas Drouin, dit Dorimon, a Contemporary of Molière*. Ed. Alice Thor Pianfetti. New York: Philosophical Library, 1977.

Duchêne, Roger. *Molière*. Paris: Fayard, 1998.

Dulait, Suzanne. *Inventaire raisonnée des autographes de Molière*. Genève: Droz, 1967.

Earle, William. "Bourdieu Nouveau." *Bourdieu: A Critical Reader*. Ed. Richard Shusterman. Oxford: Blackwell, 1999. 175–91.

Faret, Nicolas. *L'Honeste Homme ou L'Art de plaire à la cour*. Paris: Pierre David, 1640.

Félibien, André. *Conférences de l'Académie royale de peinture et de sculpture*. London: David Mortier, 1725.

Forestier, Georges. *Essai de génétique théâtrale: Corneille à l'œuvre*. Genève: Droz, 2004.

———. *Molière en toutes lettres*. Paris: Bordas, 1990.

———. *Le Théâtre dans le théâtre*. Genève: Droz, 1996.

Forestier, Georges, and Claude Bourqui. "Comment Molière inventa la querelle de *L'École des femmes*…" *Littératures Classiques* 81 (2013): 185–97.

Foucault, Michel. "Qu'est-ce qu'un auteur?" *Bulletin de la Société Française de Philosophie* 64 (July–Sept. 1969): 73–104.

———. "What Is an Author?" Trans. Josué V. Harari. *The Death and the Resurrection of the Author?* Ed. William Irwin. Westport, CT: Greenwood, 2002. 9–22.

Furetière, Antoine. *Dictionnaire universel*. 3 vols. La Haye: Arnout et Reinier Leers, 1690.

Gaines, James F. *Molière and Paradox: Skepticism and Theater in the Early Modern Age*. Tübingen: Narr, 2010.

Gasté, Armand. *La Querelle du Cid*. 1898. Genève: Slatkine Reprints, 1970.

Bibliography

Genette, Gérard. *Seuils*. Paris: Seuil, 1987.

Gilbert, Huguette. "L'Auteur de *La Cocue imaginaire*." *XVIIe Siècle* Apr.–June 1981: 203–05.

Goldberg, Sander M. *Understanding Terence*. Princeton: Princeton UP, 1986.

Greenblatt, Stephen. *Renaissance Self-Fashioning*. Chicago: U of Chicago P, 2005.

Grimarest, Jean-Léonor Gallois de. *Vie de M. de Molière*. 1705. Molière, *Œuvres complètes*. Paris: Seuil, 1962. 13–32.

Guéret, Gabriel. *La Promenade de Saint-Cloud*. 1669. Genève: Slatkine Reprints, 1968.

Guibert, A.-J. *Bibliographie des œuvres de Jean Racine publiées au XVIIe siècle et œuvres posthumes*. Paris: CNRS, 1968.

———. *Bibliographie des œuvres de Molière publiées au XVIIe siècle*. 2 vols. Paris: CNRS, 1961.

Guicharnaud, Jacques. Jacques Guicharnaud Papers. Beinecke Rare Book and Manuscript Library, Yale U.

———. *Molière, une aventure théâtrale*. Paris: Gallimard, 1963.

Hammond, Nicholas. "Authorship and Authority in Molière's *Le Misanthrope*." *Essays on French Comic Drama from the 1640s to the 1780s*. Ed. Derek Connon and George Evans. Oxford: P. Lang, 2000. 55–70.

Harned, Arthur R. "Molière and Lully." *Molière and the Commonwealth of Letters: Patrimony and Posterity*. Ed. Roger Johnson Jr., Editha S. Neumann, and Guy T. Trail. Jackson: UP of Mississippi, 1975. 31–48.

Hauteroche, Noël Breton, sieur de. *Théâtre*. 2 vols. Paris: Compagnie des Libraires, 1772.

Hénin, Emmanuelle. "Du portrait à la fresque ou du *Sicilien* au *Val-de-Grâce*: Molière et la peinture." *Œuvres et critiques* 29.1 (2004): 30–56.

Hix, H.L. *Morte d'Author: An Autopsy*. Philadelphia: Temple UP, 1990.

Hoffman, Philip T., Gilles Postel-Vinay, and Jean-Laurent Rosenthal. "Private Credit Markets in Paris, 1690–1840." *Journal of Economic History* 52.2 (June 1992): 293–306.

Hubert, J.D. *Molière and the Comedy of Intellect*. Berkeley: U of California P, 1962.

———. "Molière: The Playwright as Protagonist." *Theatre Journal* 34.3 (Oct. 1982): 360–71.

Hutcheon, Linda. *A Theory of Adaptation*. New York: Routledge, 2006.

Jaszi, Peter. "On the Author Effect: Contemporary Copyright and Collective Creativity." *The Construction of Authorship: Textual Appropriation* in *Law and Literature*. Ed. Martha E. Woodmansee and Peter Jaszi. Durham, NC: Duke UP, 1994.

Johnson, Victoria. *Backstage at the Revolution: How the Royal Opera Survived the End of the Old Regime*. Chicago: U of Chicago P, 2008.

Jurgens, Madeleine, and Elizabeth Maxfield-Miller. *Cent Ans de recherches sur Molière, sur sa famille et sur les comédiens de sa troupe*. Paris: Imprimerie Nationale, 1963.

La Bruyère, Jean de. *Les Caractères de Théophraste traduits du grec: avec Les Caractères, ou les Mœurs de ce siècle*. Ed. Robert Garapon. Paris: Garnier, 1962.

La Caille, Jean de. *Histoire de l'Imprimerie et de la Librairie*. Paris: Jean de la Caille, 1689.

La Fontaine, Jean de. *Fables*. Paris: Flammarion, 1995.

———. *Œuvres diverses*. Paris: Gallimard, 1958.

La Gorce, Jérôme de. *Jean-Baptiste Lully*. Paris: Fayard, 2002.

La Grange, Charles Varlet. *Le Registre de La Grange, 1659–1685*. Ed. Bert Edward Young and Grace Philputt Young. Paris: Droz, 1947.

Lancaster, Henry Carrington. *A History of French Dramatic Literature in the Seventeenth Century*. 9 vols. Baltimore: Johns Hopkins UP, 1929–42.

———. "Molière and Jean Ribou." *Romanic Review* 28 (1937): 32–35.

Lanson, Gustave. "Molière et la farce." *Revue de Paris* (May 1901): 129–53.

Levin, Harry. "From Terence to Tabarin: A Note on *Les Fourberies de Scapin*." *Yale French Studies* 38 (1967): 128–37.

Lévy-Lelouch, Claire. "Quand le privilège de librairie publie le roi." *De la publication: Entre Renaissance et Lumières*. Ed. Christian Jouhaud and Alain Viala. Paris: Fayard, 2002. 139–59.

L'Hermite, Tristan. *Le Page disgracié*. 1643. Paris: Gallimard, 1994.

Loewenstein, Joseph. *The Author's Due: Printing and the Prehistory of Copyright*. Chicago: U of Chicago P, 2002.

Loiselet, Jean-Louis. *De quoi vivait Molière?* Paris: Deux-Rives, 1950.

Lough, John. *Seventeenth-Century French Drama: The Background*. Oxford: Clarendon, 1979.

Louis XIV. *Mémoires, suivis de Manière de visiter les jardins de Versaillles*. Ed. Joël Cornette. Paris: Tallandier, 2007.

Lully, Jean-Baptiste, and Thomas Corneille. *Psyché*. 1678. Ed. Luke Arnason. Mémoire de maîtrise. Paris: Université de Paris IV-Sorbonne, 2005.

Magne, Bernard. "Fonction métalinguistique, métalangage, métapoèmes dans le théâtre de Molière." *Cahiers de Littérature du XVIIe Siècle* 1 (1979): 99–129.

Maître, Myriam. "Les Escortes mondaines de la publication." *De la publication: Entre Renaissance et Lumières.* Ed. Christian Jouhaud and Alain Viala. Paris: Fayard, 2002. 249–65.

Marino, James. *Owning William Shakespeare: The King's Men and Their Intellectual Property.* Philadelphia: U of Pennsylvania P, 2011.

Martin, Henri-Jean. *The French Book: Religion, Absolutism, and Readership (1585–1715).* Baltimore: Johns Hopkins UP, 1996.

———. *Livre, pouvoirs et société à Paris au XVIIe siècle (1598–1701).* 2 vols. Genève: Droz, 1969.

Maurel-Indart, Hélène. *Du Plagiat.* Paris: Presses Universitaires de France, 1999.

Maurevert, Georges. *Le Livre des Plagiats.* Paris: Arthème Fayard, 1944.

Merlin, Hélène. *Public et littérature en France au XVIIe siècle.* Paris: Les Belles Lettres, 1994.

Michaut, G. *Les Débuts de Molière à Paris.* Paris: Hachette, 1923.

———. *Les Luttes de Molière.* Paris: Hachette, 1925.

Molière, Jean-Baptiste Poquelin. *Amphitryon.* Paris: Ribou, 1668.

———. *L'Escole des maris.* Paris: Barbin, 1661.

———. *Œuvres complètes.* Ed. Georges Couton. Bibliothèque de la Pléiade. 2 vols. Paris: Gallimard, 1971.

———. *Œuvres complètes.* Ed. Georges Couton. 4 vols. Paris: Garnier-Flammarion, 1979.

———. *Œuvres complètes.* Ed. Georges Forestier and Claude Bourqui. Bibliothèque de la Pléiade. 2 vols. Paris: Gallimard, 2010.

———. *Œuvres de Molière.* Ed. Eugène Despois and Paul Mesnard. 13 vols. Paris: Hachette, 1873–1927.

———. *Les Œuvres de Monsieur Molière.* 2 vols. Paris: Louis Billaine, 1666.

———. *Les Œuvres de Monsieur de Molière.* 8 vols. Paris: Thierry, Barbin et Trabouillet, 1682.

———. *Sganarelle ou Le Cocu imaginaire.* Paris: Ribou, 1660.

Mongrédien, Georges. *Comédies et pamphlets sur Molière.* Paris: A.-G. Nizet, 1986.

———. *La Querelle de L'École des Femmes.* 2 vols. Paris: Marcel Didier, 1971.

———. *Recueil des textes et des documents du XVIIe siècle relatifs à Molière.* 2 vols. Paris: CNRS, 1965.

Montaigne, Michel de. *Les Essais.* Ed. Pierre Villey. 3 vols. Paris: Presses Universitaires de France, 1999.

Monval, Georges. *Recueil sur la mort de Molière.* Paris: Bibliophiles, 1885.

Moore, W.G. *Molière: A New Criticism*. Oxford: Oxford UP, 1964.

Nehamas, Alexander. "Writer, Text, Work, Author." *The Death and Resurrection of the Author?* Ed. William Irwin. Westport, CT: Greenwood, 2002. 95–115.

Niderst, Alain. *Molière*. Paris: Perrin, 2004.

Norman, Larry F. *The Public Mirror: Molière and the Social Commerce of Depiction*. Chicago: U of Chicago P, 1999.

Nuitter, Charles, and Ernest Thoinan. *Les Origines de l'opéra français*. 1886. Genève: Minkoff, 1972.

Ong, Walter. *Orality and Literacy: The Technologizing of the Word*. New York: Routledge, 2002.

Pascal, Blaise. *Pensées*. Ed. Michel Le Guern. Paris: Gallimard, 1977.

Peters, Julie Stone. *The Theatre of the Book, 1480–1880: Print, Text, and Performance in Europe*. Oxford: Oxford UP, 2000.

Picot, Émile. *Bibliographie Cornélienne*. Paris: Auguste Fontaine, 1876.

Pottinger, David T. *The French Book Trade in the Ancien Régime, 1500–1791*. Cambridge: Harvard UP, 1958.

Powell, John S. "*Psyché*: The Stakes of a Collaboration." *Reverberations: Staging Relations in French since 1500*. Dublin: U College Dublin P, 2008. 3–32.

Prest, Julia. *Theatre under Louis XIV: Cross-Casting and the Performance of Gender in Drama, Ballet and Opera*. New York: Palgrave Macmillan, 2006.

Racine, Jean. *Œuvres complètes*. Paris: Seuil, 1962.

Randall, Marilyn. *Pragmatic Plagiarism: Authorship, Profit, and Power*. Toronto: U of Toronto P, 2001.

Reed, Gervais E. *Claude Barbin*. Genève: Droz, 1974.

———. "Molière's Privilege of 18 March 1671." *The Library* 5th ser. 20 (1965): 57–63.

Renouard, Philippe. *Répertoire des imprimeurs parisiens, libraires et fondeurs de caractères en exercice à Paris au XVIIe siècle*. Nogent-le-Roi: Laget, 1995.

Rey-Flaud, Bernadette. *Molière et la farce*. Genève: Droz, 1996.

Richelet, Pierre. *Dictionnaire françois*. 2 vols. Genève: Jean Herman Widerhold, 1680.

Riggs, Larry. *Molière and Modernity: Absent Mothers and Masculine Births*. Charlottesville, VA: Rookwood, 2005.

———. *Molière and Plurality: Decomposition of the Classicist Self*. New York: P. Lang, 1989.

Rose, Mark. *Authors and Owners: The Invention of Copyright.* Cambridge: Harvard UP, 1993.

Saint-Évremond, Charles Saint-Denis de. *Lettres.* Ed. René Ternois. 2 vols. Paris: Marcel Didier, 1967.

Sartre, Jean-Paul. *Qu'est-ce que la littérature?* Paris: Gallimard, 1948.

Schapira, Nicolas. "Quand le privilège de librairie publie l'auteur." *De la publication: Entre Renaissance et Lumières.* Ed. Christian Jouhaud and Alain Viala. Paris: Fayard, 2002. 121–37.

Schneider, Herbert. Preface. *Psyché.* By Jean-Baptiste Lully and Molière. Ed. John S. Powell and Herbert Schneider. Hildesheim: Georg Olms, 2009.

Schwartz, William Leonard. "Light on Molière in 1664 from *Le Second Registre de la Thorillière.*" *PMLA* 53.4 (Dec. 1938): 1054–75.

Scott, Virginia. *The Commedia dell'arte in Paris, 1644–1697.* Charlottesville: UP of Virginia, 1990.

———. *Molière: A Theatrical Life.* Cambridge: Cambridge UP, 2000.

Shaw, David. "Molière and the Art of Recycling." *Seventeenth-Century French Studies* 15 (1993): 165–80.

Slater, Maya. "Molière and His Readers." *Reading Plays: Interpretation and Reception.* Ed. Hanna Scolnicov and Peter Holland. Cambridge: Cambridge UP, 1991. 161–74.

Songe du resveur, Le. 1660. Ed. Paul Lacroix. Genève: J. Gay et fils, 1867.

Sorel, Charles. *La Bibliothèque françoise.* 2nd ed. Paris: La Compagnie des Libraires du Palais, 1667.

———. *Histoire comique de Francion.* Ed. Yves Giraud. Paris: Flammarion, 1979.

Terence. *Terence.* Trans. John Sargeaunt. Loeb Classical Library. 2 vols. Cambridge: Harvard UP, 1974.

Thuasne, Louis. *Les Privilèges des éditions originales de Molière.* Paris: Henri Leclerc, 1924.

Truchet, Jacques. *Thématique de Molière.* Paris: Sedes, 1985.

Turnovsky, Geoffrey. *The Literary Market: Authorship and Modernity in the Old Regime.* Philadelphia: U of Pennsylvania P, 2010.

Van Vree, Th.-J. *Les Pamphlets et Libelles Littéraires contre Molière.* Paris: Imprimerie Jos. Vermaut, 1932.

Venesoen, Constant. *Quand Jean-Baptiste joue du Molière.* Biblio 17. Paris, Seattle, Tübingen: Papers on French Seventeenth Century Literature, 1996.

Vernet, Max. *Molière: Côté jardin, côté cour.* Paris: A.-G. Nizet, 1991.

Bibliography

Viala, Alain. *Naissance de l'écrivain*. Paris: Minuit, 1985.

Woodmansee, Martha, and Peter Jaszi. *The Construction of Authorship: Textual Appropriation in Law and Literature*. Durham, NC: Duke UP, 1994.

Yilmaz, Levent. *Le Temps moderne: Variations sur les Anciens et les contemporains*. Paris: Gallimard, 2004.

Zanger, Abby. "Paralyzing Performance: Sacrificing Theater on the Altar of Publication." *Stanford French Review* 12.2–3 (Fall–Winter 1988): 169–85.

Index

actor (medieval term), 20–21, 23, 62
Arnason, Luke, 224
auctor, 20–21, 23, 62, 64, 76
auteur, 38–40, 253n15
authorship, 9, 13, 17, 29, 54, 59–60, 76–77, 84–85, 91–92, 94, 98–110, 114–15, 133, 136, 138–39, 145, 154, 157, 159–60, 162, 164–66, 171, 173, 175–76, 182, 190, 194–95, 200, 203, 206, 208, 216–18, 221, 227, 229–30, 235, 243–46. *See also* writers; writing
author's rights, 22, 66–70, 94–95, 149–52, 175–76, 185, 189, 193–94, 197, 205–06, 217, 221, 224–25, 238, 257n5
early modern characteristics of, 10–12, 22–24, 36, 38–40, 103–04, 110, 115, 175–76, 216–17, 227, 229, 244–47, 250n12, 251n16, 269n6
as performance, 15–16, 21, 27, 53, 64, 203, 245
reputation and print, 4, 12, 67, 72, 75–77, 162, 169, 258n9
rhetorical distinctions of, 42–43, 59–60, 122, 208, 215–16, 221, 225, 254n19
strategies of, 48–51, 115–17, 119

Barbin, Claude, 47, 85–86, 93, 142, 147, 177, 180, 200–01, 223–24, 226, 238–43
Barthes, Roland, 7–8, 14, 246
Beauchamp, Pierre, 214, 220–21
Boileau, Nicolas, 11, 17, 45, 51, 54, 111, 138, 144, 158, 173–74, 192, 196, 201, 210, 231, 265n28

booksellers. *See* publishers
Bourdieu, Pierre, 15–16, 23, 36–37, 188, 268n19
Bourqui, Claude, 14, 121, 153, 232–35, 239, 246
Boursault, Edme, 115, 131, 177
  Le Portrait du peintre, 123, 132
Braider, Christopher, 261n7, 265–66n33, 266n36
Bray, René, 6–7, 10, 119–20, 213, 256n44
Brécourt, Guillaume Marcoureau de, 123, 244
  L'Ombre de Molière, 241, 243, 245
Brown, Gregory, 22

Caldicott, C.E.J., 12–14, 142, 148, 177, 179–81, 191, 194, 232, 251n17, 255n30, 260n31, 266n38, 267n1, 273n4, 275n12
champ littéraire, 10, 15–16, 36, 48–50, 52, 103, 138, 176, 229
Chapelain, Jean, 5, 56, 114, 138
Chappuzeau, Samuel, 56–57, 61–62, 183–84
Chartier, Roger, 12, 39, 172, 182, 218
Chevalier, Jean, *Les Amours de Calotin*, 51, 127–28, 136
Chevalley, Sylvie, 57
collaboration, 42–43, 59, 122, 124, 207–08, 213–16, 221, 244–46
comédie-ballet, 3–4, 32, 188–89, 214, 221, 226
Communauté des libraires, 5, 24–25, 68, 72–73, 93, 153–54, 176, 179–82, 185, 190–91, 194–95, 197, 205, 237–38, 240

Index

contracts and legal documents in Molière's plays, 28–29
Corneille, Pierre, 11–12, 17–18, 49–50, 56, 71, 78–79, 113–15, 122, 127–29, 138, 148, 176, 214–15, 217, 219, 222, 224, 233, 265n28
Corneille, Thomas, 177, 224–26
Couton, Georges, 15, 42–43, 81, 114, 215–16, 219

Defaux, Gérard, 141, 188, 263n16
DeJean, Joan, 262n10
Delègue, Yves, 20
Doneau, F., 66, 71, 86, 89–94, 101–02, 259n18
Donneau de Visé, Jean, 115, 131, 173, 177, 180, 246, 259n18, 261n1
  Conversation dans une ruelle de Paris sur Molière défunt, 1, 6
  Lettre écrite sur la comédie du Misanthrope, 18–19, 33, 156, 160–61, 164, 171–72, 244
  Lettre sur les affaires du théâtre, 118, 128–30, 132
  Nouvelles nouvelles, 112–14, 116, 120–22, 132–33
  La Vengeance des marquis, 116
  Zélinde, 116, 118–20, 124
Duchêne, Roger, 5, 92, 119, 136, 186

Earle, William, 36, 268n19
écrivain, 38–40, 45, 155, 253n15. *See also* writers

farce, 75–77, 80, 82–84, 113, 126–32, 140, 195, 235–37
Faret, Nicolas, 42
Félibien, André, 216
Forestier, Georges, 14, 70, 153, 232–35, 239, 246, 254n27, 255n29, 259n18

Foucault, Michel, 7, 121, 157, 163, 207, 227, 246
Furetière, Antoine, 12, 39–40, 230

Gaines, James, 266n36, 266n41
genre, 4, 21, 75–77, 103, 112–14, 119, 122–23, 126–29, 131, 139, 167, 188, 195–96, 214, 237
Greenblatt, Stephen, 16–17, 227
Grimarest, Jean-Léonor Gallois de, 196–97, 249n5
Guéret, Gabriel, 144, 146, 185
Guibert, A.-J., 192, 199
Guicharnaud, Jacques, 141, 156, 204

Hôtel de Bourgogne theatrical troupe, 51, 103, 111, 115, 214–15, 219
Hix, H.L., 14, 173–74, 213, 230

imitation, 70–71, 120–26, 209–10

La Bruyère, Jean de, 11, 264–65n26
Lacroix, Paul, 92
La Croix, Philippe de, 131
  La Guerre comique, 65–66, 117, 123, 127, 130, 133, 136, 185
La Fontaine, Jean de, 209–10, 250n15, 262n9, 264n23
La Gorce, Jérôme de, 221
La Grange, Charles Varlet, 55, 57–58, 136, 219, 225, 232–33, 235–36, 243
La Mothe Le Vayer, François de, 70
Lancaster, H. Carrington, 177
La Reynie, Nicolas de, 179, 181
L'Hermite, Tristan, 38
libraires. *See* publishers
Loiselet, Jean-Louis, 55, 58
Louis XIV, 53, 63, 118, 138–39, 163, 180–81, 186–87,

193–94, 206–07, 218, 222, 232, 236
Lully, Jean-Baptiste, 2, 140, 188, 214, 218, 221–26, 272n6

Magne, Bernard, 33, 41
Marino, James, 234–35, 246
Maurevert, Georges, 69
Michaut, Gustave, 19
Molière (Jean-Baptiste Poquelin)
  acting career, 5–7, 17, 21, 59, 124–25, 132–37, 140, 160, 170, 219–20, 235–36, 265n31, 265–66n33
  attitude toward print, 1–6, 10, 12–15, 23–25, 29, 74–77, 100–02, 135–36, 170–71, 175–76, 184–86, 188–98, 200, 203–06, 208, 219–20, 226–27, 229, 236, 243
  authorial image, 74–80, 83–84, 86–88, 94, 97, 100, 102, 114, 137–40, 154–55, 173–74, 195–96, 198, 217–18, 229, 244–47
  income from writing, 53–59
  privilege of 1671, 190–95, 197–98, 205, 220, 223, 226, 231, 237–44
  self-marginalization from mainstream literary community, 50–52, 77–79, 113–16, 119, 140, 200–01, 258n14
  Works:
  Les Amants magnifiques, 4, 31–32, 43, 63
  Amphitryon, 8–9, 140, 184, 206, 209, 211, 213, 239
  L'Amour médecin, 2–3, 6, 24–25, 28, 40, 153–54, 189, 195, 218
  L'Avare, 28–29, 110, 209, 239–40

Le Bourgeois gentilhomme, 28, 30–31, 34, 40, 43, 110, 188–90, 197–99, 217
La Comtesse d'Escarbagnas, 4, 33, 42, 45–46, 110, 140, 270n18
La Critique de L'École des femmes, 27, 34–36, 43, 47–53, 99, 111–12, 115–16, 117, 121, 123, 129–30, 136, 142, 148–49, 197, 200
Le Dépit amoureux, 28, 33–34, 40, 77, 148
Dom Garcie de Navarre, 4, 15, 34, 56, 58, 113, 129, 165, 236
Dom Juan, 4, 29–30, 140, 264n25, 274n8
L'École des femmes, 8, 19–20, 28, 34, 97, 103–14, 117, 120–22, 125, 130–33, 137, 139, 148–49, 165, 202, 211–13, 226, 244
L'École des maris, 28, 34, 95–102, 110, 113, 120, 122, 148, 160, 175, 229
L'Étourdi ou Les Contretemps, 35, 77, 113, 120, 148, 253n10
Les Fâcheux, 4, 34, 40, 42, 56, 58, 63, 113, 120, 122, 148, 214, 218, 256n47
Les Femmes savantes, 27–28, 30, 33–36, 43, 46–48, 110, 140, 160, 190, 198–205, 217
Les Fourberies de Scapin, 75, 173–74, 190, 195–99, 209–10, 217, 229, 239, 242
George Dandin, 27–28, 42
L'Impromptu de Versailles, 4, 27, 34–35, 43–44, 51–54, 57, 59–64, 111–12, 114–15, 117–18, 123, 127, 134–36, 200–01

Molière *(Continued)*
  La Jalousie du Barbouillé, 41, 76
  Le Malade imaginaire, 4, 6, 29, 34, 40–41, 231, 233–34, 241, 245–46
  Le Mariage forcé, 35, 40–41
  Le Médecin malgré lui, 30, 32, 236–38
  Le Médecin volant, 76
  Mélicerte, 4, 237
  Le Misanthrope, 4, 18–19, 27, 33, 35, 37, 42, 44–45, 110, 140–42, 155–75, 200, 202, 204, 206, 212, 236, 240
  Monsieur de Pourceaugnac, 28–29, 182, 187, 237
  Œuvres complètes (Bibliothèque de la Pléiade, 2010), 14, 153, 232–35, 239, 246
  Œuvres de Monsieur de Molière (1682), 75, 225, 230–37, 242–47
  Les Œuvres de Monsieur Molière (1666), 105, 139, 149–55, 160, 169–73, 175, 177, 201, 237, 239–40
  Pastorale comique, 4
  Les Précieuses ridicules, 4, 14–15, 27, 33, 35, 42, 44, 46, 49, 56, 72–80, 83–84, 88–89, 93, 95, 97, 104, 112–13, 115, 120, 142, 148, 160–61, 200–02, 236, 273n2
  La Princesse d'Élide (in *Les Plaisirs de l'Île enchantée*), 3, 34, 42, 149, 153, 232
  Psyché, 5, 190, 198–99, 207–27, 238, 244
  Remerciement au roi, 138–39, 231–32
  Sganarelle ou Le Cocu imaginaire, 56, 86–95, 113, 120, 122, 148, 173, 176, 183, 275n14
  Le Sicilien, ou L'Amour peintre, 34–35

Tartuffe, 21, 27, 55, 140, 146, 166, 178, 181–87, 189, 198, 206–07, 239
Montaigne, Michel de, 170, 264n21
Montfleury, Antoine Jacob, 115, 131, 177
  L'Impromptu de L'Hôtel de Condé, 127, 133–34
Moore, W.G., 6

Nehamas, Alexander, 164, 251n19
Neuf-Villenaine, sieur de, 66, 86–89, 101–02, 173, 259n18
Niderst, Alain, 215
Norman, Larry, 1–2, 121–22, 249n6, 252n25, 254n20, 267n1

Ong, Walter, 29, 31, 106
originality, 81, 120–26
ownership, 5, 12–13, 69, 85–86, 92–94, 98–100, 149–50, 152–53, 176, 182–83, 190–95, 197, 205–07, 217–18, 220, 223–27, 229, 237–43, 260n29

Pascal, Blaise, 155, 169
performance, 2–4, 6–7, 9–10, 18, 21, 24, 29, 59, 64, 74–76, 83, 89, 98, 114, 132–37, 139–40, 170, 187, 189, 196, 204–05, 207–08, 219–26, 231, 235–36, 245–47
Perrault, Pierre, 70–71, 209–10
Peters, Julie Stone, 110, 124–25, 220
piracy, 66–69, 71–74, 86, 102, 143, 267n6
plagiarism, 66–67, 69–72, 80–82, 84, 86, 90–91, 102, 117, 120–26, 257n6
Plautus, 70, 123, 245
Pottinger, David, 146–47, 206, 267n6, 268n17, 269n6

Powell, John, 208, 215, 217
Prest, Julia, 270–71n19
print, 1–6, 9–12, 14, 22, 24, 29–32, 39, 45, 47, 74, 76, 98, 114, 132–35, 187–89, 200, 208, 216–21, 223, 229, 236, 246–47. *See also* stigma of print
printing, 2–3, 5, 11–14, 21–22, 40, 44–46, 67–69, 72–74, 77, 88–89, 94–95, 100, 107, 134, 142–49, 158, 180–86, 189–90, 196, 198, 204–05, 217–18, 223–25, 236, 238, 242–43, 258n12, 259n20. *See also* publication
privilege system, 2–3, 67–69, 85–86, 95–96, 142–54, 182, 184–87, 190–95, 198, 217, 221–24, 237–43, 268n17
publication, 1, 3–5, 9–14, 40, 44–47, 55–56, 67, 69, 72–78, 87–88, 91, 95–96, 98–103, 124, 135–36, 140–42, 145–55, 160, 169–73, 175–76, 183, 186–91, 195–200, 203–05, 208, 213, 217, 220, 223, 225, 229, 237, 243–44, 247
publishers (or booksellers and *libraires*), 66–68, 72–74, 85–86, 93–94, 141–55, 158, 160, 171–73, 175–201, 204–06, 237–43, 260n28

querelle de L'École des femmes, 37, 51–52, 65–66, 76, 102–03, 111–40, 180, 201, 231
Quinault, Philippe, 101, 142, 148, 214–15, 217, 219, 224–25

Racine, Jean, 57, 122, 148, 177, 180, 214–15, 219, 233, 269n2
Randall, Marilyn, 17, 71, 76, 99, 264n24

Reed, Gervais, 180, 194, 238, 241
Rey-Flaud, Bernadette, 195
Ribou, Jean, 66, 72–75, 86–89, 92–96, 101–02, 173, 176–90, 199, 238–42
Richelet, Pierre, 39–40, 159
Riffaud, Alain, 199
Riggs, Larry, 7–8, 29–30, 226, 249nn7–9, 250n10, 261n6, 267n1, 271n3
Robinet, Charles, 115, 131
  Panégyrique de L'École des femmes, 19–20, 125–28, 132, 134–35, 137–38
Rose, Mark, 193
rules, seventeenth-century French theatrical, 49, 117–18, 130–31, 265n29

Saint-Évremond, Charles Saint-Denis de, 209
Sartre, Jean-Paul, 155–56
Scott, Virginia, 51, 209, 222–23, 251n18
Shakespeare, William, 235, 246, 273–74n5
Somaize, Baudeau de, 66, 79–86, 89, 91, 101–02, 112, 120, 123
Songe du resveur, Le, 92, 100–01
stigma of print, 10–11, 44–47, 53–55, 74–75, 143–45, 158, 202, 204, 250n13
stratégie de la réussite, 48–49
stratégie du succès, 49–51, 115–17, 119, 124, 136, 258n14

Terence, 36, 70, 98, 123, 209, 229, 245, 264n22
Thierry, Denis, 223–24, 238–43
Turnovsky, Geoffroy, 37, 43–45, 55, 251n16

Venesoen, Constant, 196
Vernet, Max, 8–9, 13, 21, 97, 163, 219, 226–27, 271n3

291

Viala, Alain, 10, 48–50, 55–56, 116, 119, 136, 144–45, 229, 266n41

writers, 6, 10, 14, 24, 33, 35, 38, 40, 44–45, 51, 64, 109, 116, 144, 154, 164, 170, 175, 183, 200, 202, 217. *See also* authorship; *écrivain*
amateur, 41–44
payment to, 10–11, 55–56, 67, 72, 143–48, 178, 182–86, 219, 269n2
professional, 43–51, 200, 203
relation to public, 15–17, 38, 49–51, 112, 115–20, 122, 124–25
writing, 7, 14, 17, 21, 24, 27–35, 38–43, 45, 56, 63–64, 76, 98, 104–11, 125, 129–31, 135–39, 144, 155–58, 160, 162–66, 168, 170, 184, 196, 203, 205, 220, 235. *See also* authorship
and authority, 29–34, 64, 76, 104–08
as expression of character, 35, 109–11, 156–58, 164–70, 201–02

Young, Bert Edward, and Grace Philputt Young, 151

Zanger, Abby, 9, 29, 32, 59, 189, 250n10, 252n3, 269n1, 272n11

About the Book

The Would-Be Author: Molière and the Comedy of Print
Michael Call
PSRL 63

Michael Call's *The Would-Be Author* is the first full-length study to examine Molière's evolving—and at times contradictory—authorial strategies as evidenced both by his portrayal of authors and publication within the plays and by his own interactions with the seventeenth-century Parisian publishing industry. Historians of the book have described the time period that coincides with Molière's theatrical activity as centrally important to the development of authors' rights and to the professionalization of the literary field. A seventeenth-century author, however, was not so much born as negotiated through often-acrimonious relations in a world of new and dizzying possibilities.

The learning curve was at times steep and unpleasant, as Molière discovered when his first Parisian play was stolen by a rogue publisher. Nevertheless, the dramatist proved to be a quick learner: from his first published play in 1660 until his death in 1673, Molière changed from a reluctant and victimized author to an innovator (or, according to his enemies, even a swindler) who aggressively secured the rights to his plays—stealing them back when necessary—and acquired for himself publication privileges and conditions relatively unknown in an era before copyright.

As Molière himself wrote, making people laugh was "une étrange entreprise" (*La Critique de L'École des femmes*, 1663). To an even greater degree, comedic authorship for the playwright was a constant work in progress, and in this sense, "Molière"—the stage name that became a pen name—represents the most carefully elaborated of Jean-Baptiste Poquelin's invented characters.

About the Author

Michael Call received his PhD in French from Yale University and joined the faculty of Brigham Young University in 2006. His research focuses on the theater of seventeenth-century France.

"This study is carefully and perceptively written, well researched, and extremely up-to-date in its bibliographical apparatus. It presents diverse points of view fairly and offers extremely sensitive readings of some scholars who have been a bit overlooked."
—James Gaines, University of Mary Washington

www.ingramcontent.com/pod-product-compliance
Lightning Source LLC
Chambersburg PA
CBHW061432300426
44114CB00014B/1652